Manga and Anime Go to Hollywood

Manga and Anime Go to Hollywood

Northrop Davis

Bloomsbury Academic
An imprint of Bloomsbury Publishing Inc

B L O O M S B U R Y

NEW YORK · LONDON · OXFORD · NEW DELHI · SYDNEY

Bloomsbury Academic

An imprint of Bloomsbury Publishing Inc

1385 Broadway	50 Bedford Square
New York	London
NY 10018	WC1B 3DP
USA	UK

www.bloomsbury.com

BLOOMSBURY and the Diana logo are trademarks of Bloomsbury Publishing Plc

First published 2016

© Northrop Davis, 2016

Library of Congress Cataloging-in-Publication Data
Davis, Northrop.
Manga and Anime Go to Hollywood / Northrop Davis.
pages cm
Summary: "The first ever look at how major Hollywood movies were adapted from Japanese manga and anime"– Provided by publisher.
Includes bibliographical references and index.
ISBN 978-1-62356-248-9 (hardback)– ISBN 978-1-62356-144-4 (paperback) 1. Animated films–United States–History and criticism. 2. Animated films–Japan–History and criticism. 3. Film adaptations–United States–History and criticism. 4. Television adaptations–United States–History and criticism. 5. Comic books, strips, etc.–Japan–Adaptations. 6. Motion pictures and comic books–United States. 7. Motion pictures and comic books–Japan. I. Title.
NC1766.U5D37 2015
791.43'3409520973–dc23
2015018667

ISBN:	HB:	978-1-6235-6248-9
	PB:	978-1-6235-6144-4
	ePub:	978-1-6235-6038-6
	ePDF:	978-1-6235-6663-0

Typeset by Fakenham Prepress Solutions, Fakenham, Norfolk NR21 8NN
Printed and bound in the India

Contents

Acknowledgments

I am very grateful for the generosity of all who helped with this book. First, I would like to acknowledge my debt of gratitude to my research assistant Austa Joye for her professional and untiring work on this project. She was an indispensable "Jill of all trades" with her deep knowledge of publication resolution characteristics for the book's images and brilliant skills as a young person aspiring to become a mangaka (professional manga creator); and without her untiring professionalism I would have been in deep trouble. Second, thanks to Ashley Poston for the very large job of transcribing most of the interviews I conducted and for additional critical image work. A special thank you is due to Clint Eastwood for his generosity in allowing the use of photographs of himself in the book and to his attorney Bruce Ramer for facilitating that. And a very special thanks must also be extended to our University of South Carolina's wonderful and most supportive Vice President of Research Dr. Prakash Nagarkatti and Mary Anne Fitzpatrick, without whose very generous grants this extremely ambitious book would simply not have been possible.

I am very fortunate to have such strong and consistent support for my scholarship and creative production from other key persons in Carolina's administration as well, including Mary Alexander, Michael Amiridis, Anne Bezuidenhaut, Helen Doerpinghaus, Lacy Ford, Dawn Hiller, Sarah Livingston, Steven Lynn, Allen Miller, President Harris Pastides, Yoshitaka Sakakibara, and Tan Ye—they have all been wonderful supporters in this cross-cultural journey I have been on. I would also like to thank mangaka Hirohiko Araki for approving the inclusion of his likeness and manga character's image, as well as to Kazuo Koike and Takao Saito for permission to publish photographs of them. And I am also especially fortunate and honored to have the opportunity given to me by all the absolutely brilliant star Japanese mangaka, who allowed me to reprint their wonderful work. And a heartfelt thanks to all my wonderful colleagues in Hollywood and the manga/anime industries at the pinnacle of these fields who assisted me in this endeavor. These include but are not limited to the amazing Michael Arias, Geof Darrow, Grant Hill, Roy Lee, Nobuo Masuda, and Robert Napton, both for their terrific interviews and also because they were key persons connecting me to others (as did Mikhail Koulikov and Matt Biliski). I would also like to thank the book's other stellar interviewees for their candor and generosity, including Peter Chung, John Gaeta, Jason Hoffs, Joyce Jun, Yukito Kishiro, Joshua Long, Leiji Matsumoto, Syd Mead, Salil Mehra, Hikaru Sasahara, Eugene Son, Ken Tsumura, Shinichirō Watanabe, and Christine Yoo. Masuda, Gaeta, and Arias were particularly helpful and generous in providing valuable additional information requested by me after their interviews. And Frenchy Lunning provided key guidance. I was also very lucky to have master manga/anime scholars Helen McCarthy and Fred Schodt as indispensable mentors who patiently gave tireless answers and wise advice in response to my endless questions.

I was also fortunate to learn the practices of academic publishing from Professor Evan Smith and Drs. Andrew Graciano and Vivian Sobchack—as well as Ian Condry, who helped me get off to a great start with enthusiastic encouragement after reading my book proposal and sample chapters.

I am deeply indebted to all who facilitated images for this book, which are among the top manga/anime and American animation/comics characters in history. Elizabeth Ellis of VIZ Media was absolutely standout in this regard, as equally was Yoshimi Suzuki of Tezuka Productions, and I would also like to give special thanks to the extreme generosity of Japanese companies Bandai Visual Co., Ltd, Hakusensha, Kodansha (Yae Sahashi, Yuko Ogawa, and Ben Applegate), Shueisha, *Spur* magazine, Sunrise, Inc., Tatsunoko Production, Tezuka Productions, Toei Animation, Toho Co., Ltd., VIZ Media, and Voyager Holdings (Keisei Miayata). Equally, special thanks is due to American publishers Dark Horse (Carl Horn and Mike Gambos), DC, Funimation (Josh Kokurek), Last Gasp (Colin Turner and Ron Turner), and Vertical (Ed Chavez). I owe an equally big thank you to American networks and studios including Cartoon Network (Patricia Cottington and Barbara DeBuys), Disney Enterprises, Inc. (Maxine Hof and Margaret Adamic), Dreamworks Animation (Kam Naderi), Nickelodeon (Jessica Furer), and Photoshot/Collection Christophel (Katy Galli). Photos outside of my own are thanks to Deb Aoki, Amherst College, Stephen Fisher, Yoko Hayashi, James Henderson, Louisa Kwan, Bert Le, Mead Art Museum, Professor Samuel Morse, the Richard Templeton Photography Fund, Mary Robinson, Aldo Sarellano, Fred Schodt, Kaori Suzuki, Sayuri Suzuki, Shinichi Suzuki, Tokyobling, Tomohiro Kageyama, Ricardo G. Willems, and Ofer Wolberger. I am so grateful to Christopher Macdonald and Mitsuru Uehira, who were absolutely critical and extremely patient and professional in the image approval process—and Chris went way beyond that into extreme generosity to this project.

I want to give a very thankful acknowledgment to Yoko Hayashi as my partner on several adventures described in this book and for kindly providing excerpts (and translations) of her interviews with several manga and anime legends. Robert Myman and Dan Stevens provided generous and important mentorly advice. My other research assistants, Amber Brown-Rodgers and Kat Feelings, made key contributions, as did the talented Jennifer Blevins, Courtney Diles, Gregory Goetz, Adam Griffey, Steven Greenbank, Nobuaki Hosoda, Manami Iiboshi, Mariko Koizumi, Shunko Muroya, and Matt Thorne. A special thank you to Mrs. Nakazawa and the memory of Keiji Nakazawa and for his great work and all that he stood for.

A giant thanks must be extended to my terrific editor Katie Gallof and the excellent Mary Al-Sayed at Bloomsbury Academic. This was a huge, developing project, and they have stayed enthusiastic and flexible throughout. I also want to thank Tristan Defew (typesetter), Kim Storry (project manager) and Ronnie Hanna (copy editor) for their excellent work on this large project. Adam Berkowitz, Rob Kenneally, Jon Levin, and Scott Rosenbaum have generously granted me access into high levels of the American television and film industries. I would also like to acknowledge my terrific chairs at the University of South Carolina School of Visual Art and Design (SVAD), Peter Chametzky, Cynthia Colbert, Brad Collins, and Thorne Compton, and additionally mentors Walter Hanclosky and Bob Lyon for their outstanding encouragement and support. I also gratefully appreciate Daniel Baugh, Jeremy Bickford, Bryan Fetner, Austin Grebenc, Jarad Greene, Marlowe Leverette, Skyler Smith, Graham Stowe, Yoshiki Yamamoto and colleagues Rebecca Boyd, Lydia Brandt, Abby Callahan, Lauren Chapman, Susan Felleman, Minuette Floyd, Kim Gore, James Henderson, Susan Hogue, Chris Horn, Anna House, Dawn Hunter, Olga Ivashkevich, Evan Meaney, Stephanie Nace, Faye Riley, Kathleen Robbins, June/Chris/Mary Robinson, Sara Schneckloth, Lauren Steimer, Erica Tobolsky, Marius Valdes, David and Pam Voros, Amanda Wright and Qiana Whitted. The very dedicated staff at our outstanding Thomas Cooper Library have been amazing and tireless throughout my research, including Gary Geer, Joshua Smith, Bill Suddith, Amy Trepal, and Mark Volmer.

I especially wish to thank my students both at the University of South Carolina and previously at the University of California, Irvine, who have given me such joy and satisfaction through their hard work, intelligence, and artistically adventurous courageous/unique artistic spirits. I am so proud of them! If I was not limited in book length, I would have liked to publish hundreds of pages more of their wonderful manga in this book.

Finally, I would like to thank both my priceless daughter Lisa for encouraging her Dad's creative endeavors and being who she is, and my mother Nancy for having blessed me with her extremely positive creative energy mixed with a love of life and her children and shrewd wisdom. If there is anyone who I have left off this list, please understand it is an unintentional omission and do know that I recognize you and thank you for your contribution to this book.

This page (upper right) from *Pastel White*, a manga by my student and research assistant Austa Joye, sums up my feelings upon finishing this book. I hope that you enjoy it and learn some things too.

© Photographer Kaori Suzuki © SPUR/SHUEISHA Inc.

Figure F.1 Mangaka Hirohiko Araki (whose *JoJo's Bizarre Adventure* has sold over 90 million copies with 111 volumes so far) meets his idol Clint Eastwood. Image courtesy of Clint Eastwood, Hirohiko Araki, *Spur* magazine/Shueisha and Kaori Suzuki. Images are from Shueisha *Spur's* mook, *JOJO menon*.

© Photographer Kaori Suzuki © SPUR/SHUEISHA Inc.

Figure F.2 Clint Eastwood playfully poses alongside a main character from *JoJo's Bizarre Adventure*. Images courtesy of Clint Eastwood, Hirohiko Araki, *Spur Magazine*/Shueisha, Inc., and Kaori Suzuki. Images are from Shueisha *Spur's* mook, *JOJO menon*.

Figure F.3 According to manga artist Takeshi Obata of the mega hit manga *Death Note* (now a Hollywood adaptation project), the antagonist/anti-hero Ryuk (above) was inspired by *Edward Scissorhands.*
DEATH NOTE anime: ©Tsugumi Ohba, Takeshi Obata/Shueisha
© DNDP, VAP, Shueisha, Madhouse

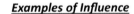

Examples of Influence

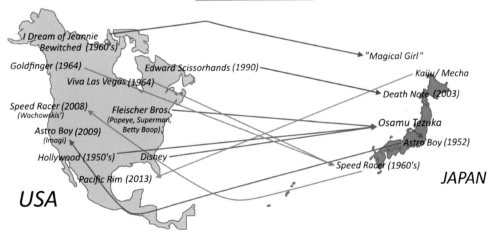

Figure F.4 A few examples of manga/anime/Hollywood cross-influences.[a]

[a] Map by Austa Joye.

Figure F.5 Modern manga and anime's founding creator Osamu Tezuka at Paramount Pictures in Hollywood, CA, in the 1980s on location for the TV show *World Now—The Real Face of Hollywood*.[b] © Tezuka Productions

---

[b]TV show title translated by Frederik L. Schodt. This book will, where possible, use English language titles of works.

Preface

Manga is the name for Japanese comics; and anime is Japanese limited-animation, which is often based on manga sources. Both have a unique style and form the underpinning of the Japanese visual narrative media entertainment industry that has swept the world. Manga/anime and Hollywood live-action feature films, television, and animation share a relationship that goes back to modern manga's origins immediately after World War II. Manga and anime earn tens of billions of dollars each year, illustrating that they, along with Hollywood films and television, are the dominant forms of visual storytelling entertainment worldwide.

Despite the staggering success of manga/anime and their interconnectedness with Hollywood, no book has been written about this influential relationship, which has existed since the invention of the modern manga form.

Part of the argument of this book is that …

Hybridization is the past, present, and the future of scripted mass media entertainment

Manga and anime were never a pure form to begin with, with their Japanese cultural, pictorial, and literary ancestry mixing in with Hollywood influences and even Russian novels, which were favored partially for their long-form story structure facilitating richly developed characters. And as this book will make clear, many future movies, animation, and television shows will consist of creators picking the best attributes of various forms suitable to their storytelling requirements.

This book focuses on the biggest part of this global hybridity: manga/anime's relationship with Hollywood. It is a fascinating and important story that has never been told in full before now.

A note to those new to manga and anime, who perhaps picked up this book out of curiosity

Even if you know very little about manga and anime, you will learn the important facts about these amazing forms here, including how they got started, their success, and their traits/characteristics—because these are the tools you need to then go on and learn about their relationship with Hollywood's forms. And you'll be led further into the subject through the history of Hollywood and Japanese manga/anime, including well-known icons like *Superman, Mighty Mouse, Pinocchio, Betty Boop,* and *Bambi* that inspired the manga (and, by extension, the anime) form. The impact of American television on manga creators was similar to that of Hollywood movies—for example, *I Dream of Jeannie* and *Bewitched* had an influence upon the "Magical Girl" genre of manga/anime (including Osamu Tezuka's[a] *Marvelous Melmo* and Naoko Takaeuchi's popular *Sailor Moon*).[1]

My central point:

The media industries in the United States and Japan, specifically the manga/anime industry and Hollywood film and TV industries, are similar in much the way some animals on Earth share similar DNA. According to genetic theory, creatures that evolved from the same origins can appear to be very different from one another but still possess many identical genomes in their DNA. But while, say, a horse and a kangaroo may be in many ways similar on a genetic level, they are also very different. Similarly, manga/anime and Hollywood filmmaking/television share a common bond and origins but developed separately; and throughout they continued to influence each other, growing into their present, intense interaction.

Studying the strengths and weaknesses of each form is valuable for a variety of reasons, including to governments, educational institutions, and entertainment industries worldwide seeking to compete with the highly successful Hollywood and Japanese models. Today, Hollywood creators are doing much more to involve manga/anime style and tropes in their own work, and we'll also discover some of what Japanese creators have done and are currently doing to incorporate Hollywood style into their own manga and anime. And, whether one is a fan, artist, writer, businessperson, educator, or generalist, to be involved with this global media confluence requires understanding the similarities and differences between manga/anime and Hollywood productions. Additionally beneficial to the reader is a peek into the future of global hybridity, which will likely meld not only the Japanese

---

[a] Tezuka (1928–89) was the legendary "father-creator" of modern manga and anime television series as well as a producer, newspaper columnist, and licensed medical doctor. He and his work are widely considered to be Japanese national treasures. As many have noted, his work is as vital today as it ever was.

and Hollywood tropes and styles but also combine with styles from other countries. Part of my argument is that this hybridity will form a large part of the future of worldwide media visual storytelling—specifically comics, movies, television, and even video games!

A different way of stating what I mean by "hybridity" is:

Creators taking the elements of each form and combining them—one work building off the other, and then the next generation builds off that work, ping-ponging back and forth across the Pacific Ocean. Practically unknown to the public are the many ways that these interactions are occurring, and have been occurring, since modern manga came into being around the time of World War II.

Deeper understanding of the nuts and bolts, business, artistic hows and whys of the Hollywood and manga/anime production systems

This book is also valuable for those who desire to look behind the curtain into the inner workings of these two industries. The manga/anime and Hollywood production worlds are generally difficult to penetrate on any meaningful level (where important facts are learned about their operation/artistic practices) unless one is an insider. This book also examines the complex issue of adaptation, such as how Hollywood screenwriters adapting manga/anime are paid, the nature of their contracts inducing them to make extensive changes, and the process of acquiring manga remake rights. The mass media also fails to delve deep into the business or creative inner workings of American and Japanese television, which are an integral part of the story and a focus of this book.

The way these American media art forms and industries work impacts the maintenance of the integrity of adapted Japanese works—and even the Japanese experts cannot agree whether these adaptations are a good idea at all. This book covers the debate regarding how closely the adaptions should hew to their original, with surprising revelations by creators, executives, writers, directors, artists, visual effects designers, and producers. For another example, on the subject of Hollywood screenwriters adapting manga/anime to live-action projects, this book examines such complex issues as what attracted Hollywood producers, writers, and directors to those works, what characteristics cross over successfully and which do not, and how Japanese creators are inspired by American films and television.

Suggested background reading

Some excellent books have been written about manga—such as Frederik L. Schodt's landmark masterpieces *Manga! Manga! The World of Japanese Comics*, *Dreamland Japan*, and *The Astro Boy Essays*. However, this book, *Manga and Anime Go to Hollywood*, is the first devoted entirely to this subject of manga and anime's interaction with Hollywood.

Frederik L. Schodt is the most acclaimed writer in the manga and anime studies field: he was awarded the Japanese government's prestigious Order of the Rising Sun, Gold Rays with Rosette, for his manga/anime scholarship. Schodt translated *Astro Boy* (for Dark Horse) as well as many other important Japanese works.

Schodt also has great credibility in the field because he was friends with Osamu Tezuka, legendary inventor of both the modern manga and anime forms. Tezuka wrote the foreword to *Manga! Manga!* Without Schodt's

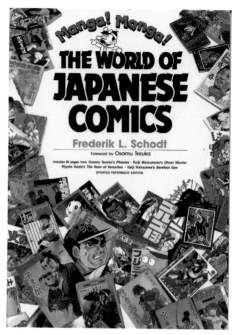

Figure P.1 *Manga! Manga! The World of Japanese Comics* by Frederik L. Schodt, published by Kodansha International © 1983 (reprint Kodansha USA, 2013)

Figure P.2 Frederik L. Schodt is seen here with Tezuka and Ward Kimbal (1914–2002), one of Walt Disney's famous original animators, at Kimbal's home.[2] Kimbal, who created Pinocchio's sidekick and conscience Jiminy Cricket, was considered a genius by Disney.[3] A train fan, seen here with his model train set, Kimbal owned a full-sized locomotive, as also, allegedly, did Walt Disney at his own home.[4] Photo courtesy of Shinichi Suzuki.

Figure P.3 Paul Gravett's *Manga: Sixty Years of Japanese Comics,* published by
Lawrence King © 2004
Astro Boy © Tezuka Productions

pioneering scholarship,[b] there probably would not be a basis for manga/anime studies as
we know it.

Also of value to manga/anime scholars are Patrick Drazen's *Anime Explosion! The
What? Why? & Wow! Of Japanese Animation* and Paul Gravett's *Manga: Sixty Years of
Japanese Comics.*

Additionally, several images from this book first appeared in Helen McCarthy's
masterful book *The Art of Osamu Tezuka, God of Manga,* as well as her observations
on Tezuka's specific modeling of characters on golden age Hollywood stars, and she
graciously allowed me to extensively quote her observations which I have augmented by
using specific screen grabs of these stars to visually illustrate her associations.

This book builds on their shining accomplishments, and each author has generously
answered my questions whenever I wanted clarification or background information on
anything they had written. A wonderful resource on the subject of anime's arrival in
the US is also Fred Ladd's (written with Harvey Deneroff) terrific *Astro Boy and Anime
Come to the Americas, An Insider's View of a Pop Culture Phenomenon.* Also, *Samurai
from Outer Space* by Antonia Levi is an illuminating addition to these books, focusing on
Japanese culture as it impacts manga/anime (which Fred Schodt's and Patrick Drazen's
books also emphasize). Jonathan Clements and Helen McCarthy's wonderful *The Anime
Encyclopedia: A Guide to Japanese Animation Since 1917* and *The Dorama Encyclopedia:
A Guide to Japanese TV Drama Since 1953* (by Clements and Motoko Tamamuro) are
terrific guides to the works (and their plots) that were produced during those periods.

---

[b] Schodt's fluency in Japanese as a high level professional translator and interpreter, and having lived there, enables him
to access publications and manga that are published only in Japanese.

I recommend all of these books for a great background on this subject, and several others throughout this narrative.[c]

There are other major benefits to reading this book that go well beyond an interest in manga/anime and their relationship with Hollywood and the other advantages I have described.

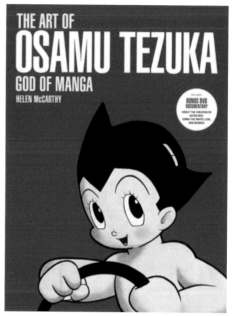

Figure P.4 Helen McCarthy's excellent *The Art of Osamu Tezuka, God of Manga*, published by Abrams/Comic Arts (UK publishers, Ilex) © 2009 (latest revision)
Astro Boy © Tezuka Productions

Why else should this book interest you?

For one thing, since manga, anime, and Hollywood films represent the most popular forms of entertainment worldwide, they bear studying in detail, in part because each form has advantages and disadvantages as a story-telling form and character development/relationship methods and **tropes,**[d] so studying these, no matter what side of the Pacific you reside on, is a big advantage in freshening your work as a creative storyteller.

History

This book is also valuable for those seeking to understand history, particularly Japan's World War II and post-war relationship with Hollywood and America, the development of the Japanese and American publishing and entertainment industries, and the ways that these industries had an effect on each other as they developed.

The more I worked on this book, the more the DNA analogy (i.e. the fact that manga/anime and Hollywood productions and American comics may be 95% similar but that the 5% difference ultimately determines their identities) seemed accurate—and this was confirmed when I "tried it out" on a few of the artists/creators that I interviewed involved in these productions. The three students that I briefly quoted were hand-picked for their insights out of the approximately 1,000 students I have taught at the University of South Carolina since I arrived here over six years ago from Hollywood. Their insights are also valuable because, although there are many screen and TV writing classes in universities, there is, as of yet, only one manga production class at a United States university, which is mine at the University of South Carolina School of Visual Art and Design (a class which I started at the University of California, Irvine). So my students are on the front line of this hybridity. (Many of my students' manga can also be found at wemakemanga.com.)

---

[c] Manga, anime scholarship is rapidly growing, and there are other excellent books and papers on the subject, which are unfortunately too numerous to list all here.

[d] We will learn more about "tropes" in Chapter 7, but for now, they are defined as conventions, expectations and devices.

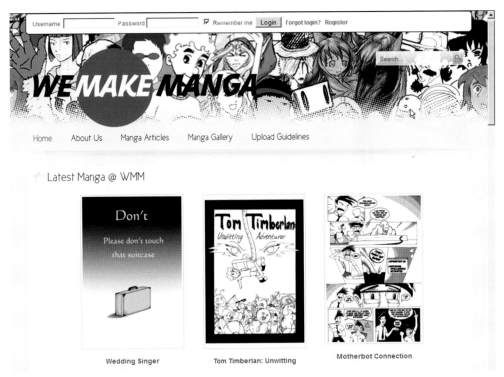

Figure P.5 The wemakemanga.com website where student manga is displayed from my manga classes. There are perhaps thousands of screen and TV writing classes at United States' universities, but there is, as yet, only one manga production class at a United States university, which is mine at the University of South Carolina School of Visual Art and Design (a class which I started at the University of California, Irvine).

Figure P.6 My student Lauren Elizabeth's *Domo Nation*.

Figure P.7 *Wedding Singer* by my student Louise Wang, who, after taking the manga class, was hired by one of Taiwan's top animation studios, Next Animation, by Ken Tsumura, a producer of the *Astro Boy* Hollywood adaptation.[e]

---

[e] Happily, through my introduction.

Figure P.8 An example of hybridity is *Doughnut Cop*, by my student Akeem Roberts. Certain manga aesthetics, such as characters' limbs spilling over frames, and oversized eyes and sound effects, combine with his colored approach, the latter not being characteristic of "classic" manga.[f]

[f] It should be noted that each semester these mostly undergraduates usually take four other courses, including in the sciences and math, while enrolled in the manga class and yet still create this remarkable work.

My students have also created a hybrid form of manga and American comics/graphic novels in the same way that shows on USA's Cartoon Network, Adult Swim, and other American animation networks have been taking cues from manga/anime. These American TV shows significantly impacted my students when they were growing up and continued to impact these young artistic pioneers as they blazed new paths in highly creative manga forms in my classes—particularly in their use of color, which is used sparingly in traditional manga. And as we will learn, much Japanese black and white inking of manga is exceptional and reflects various traits based in Japanese history and culture.

Most of the interviewees in this book are high-end participants in this hybridity between manga/anime and Hollywood

The majority of the interviews derive from relationships in the American movie, TV, and Japanese manga/anime industries that I developed in my career before becoming a professor.

Why else am I qualified to write this book?

I am a screenwriter who graduated from California Institute of the Arts. CalArts was funded by Walt Disney, who left it one quarter of his estate. I was enrolled in the live-action department.

Desiring to broaden my education beyond the CalArts live-action department, I was lucky enough to be mentored by the animation department's chair at that time, Robert Winquist, who took in a few of us who were not officially part of that elite department. I was drawn by the intensely creative, collaborative, and energetic atmosphere and the emphasis in storytelling on the development of characters "first and foremost" that the animators emanated.

By his example, Bob also instilled a distinct attitude in me to be the most excellent and inspiring practitioner/teacher that I could be, hiring me and a couple of others (including fellow student Ash Brannon, who later was an animator on *Toy Story* and co-directed *Toy Story 2* and *Surf's Up* and tried to get my 20th Century Fox-owned screenplay *Alien Safari* made so he could direct it) to teach classes at CalArts. I taught a class about film genres, storytelling, and mythology. These experiences were valuable when I became a professor.

Based on my short live-action films created while at CalArts, I was signed upon graduation by a top talent agency, ICM, where I was immediately hired to write a feature screenplay by Columbia/Sony and producer Robert Stigwood (his credits include *Saturday Night Fever*, *Gallipoli*, *Grease*, *Tommy*, *Jesus Christ Superstar*, and *Evita*), and I joined the Writers Guild of America, West. But after graduating from CalArts I still had little knowledge of what manga/anime were, beyond having seen the anime television show

Astro Boy as a toddler in NYC, and being struck by its strange style and later, like so many others of my generation, watching such anime as the original *Speed Racer* TV show. As we will see, the Japanese origins of such works were purposefully kept hidden from the American public, so I was largely ignorant of manga and anime, including while enrolled at CalArts. Instead, I was focusing on making a career in Hollywood in live-action screenwriting. I went on from the Stigwood project (unproduced, as most [even purchased] screenplays are in Hollywood) to sell my own spec. screenplay to Warner Brothers. I also directed some commercials for KCRW, LA's flagship public radio station that aired in local theaters and on television. It was then that I really fell in love with manga and anime after traveling to Japan.

The trip to Japan led me to discover an amazing manga series by Yukito Kishiro (who was interviewed for this book), *Battle Angel Alita* (known as *Gunnm* in Japan). Manga images from it appear in Chapter 6. *Battle Angel Alita* is a story with characters that have dark and light sides mixed together (duality)—an amazingly immersive, philosophical, emotional, and detailed world anchored with a wonderful father–daughter dynamic.

I felt that *Battle Angel Alita* had all the hallmarks of what director James Cameron would be attracted to, and after I pitched it to his executive at 20th Century Fox Film Corporation, that studio acquired the movie rights to it for Mr. Cameron.[g] Then leading manga publisher Shueisha allowed me to pitch my own manga project to the editor of *Ultra jump* magazine, which is the manga magazine that published *Battle Angel Alita*. This was an incredible opportunity for anyone, especially a non-Japanese person. And although I was unsuccessful in setting up my manga story as a serialized manga at Shueisha (an experience that I describe in Chapter 5), the experience continued the education I was receiving about that art/industry as I pursued writing my screenplays, beginning with *Alien Safari*, which I sold to 20th Century Fox as a pitch and then wrote. Emboldened, I pursued other manga series that I was passionate about for adaptation into Hollywood films. I was involved in an unsuccessful negotiation for the live-action rights by a Hollywood studio of the manga/anime classic *Berserk* along with my then business partner, Yoko Hayashi. Yoko had come on board to negotiate shopping agreements[h] to Japanese rights holders in coordination with our terrific entertainment lawyers in Hollywood, Bob Myman and Darin Frank. We were also involved in an attempt to secure rights for an American television adaptation of an extremely successful television/movie/manga/anime series (*Densha Otaku*, English title: *Train Man*)—which gave me a great education about the Japanese entertainment business.

---

[g] I am not a screenwriter on, or otherwise currently involved with, *Battle Angel Alita*.
[h] Where the rights holder agrees to let the producer/writer/director "shop" the adaptation rights. It may take the form of an option agreement, which is described in Chapter 10.

Figure P.9 Test image from the artists originally working on my own manga. Illustration by Kriss Sison and Brian Vileza, star field and additional alien jellyfish coloring by Ashley Poston. Character limbs and bodies crossing irregular-sized panel frames, sound effects, emphasis on physical environment for setting the scene and the protagonist's over-sized eyes are a few manga characteristics depicted here.

My own creativity is enormously influenced by manga/anime

I recently received a grant from my university to pay a mangaka (which in brief means a seasoned professional artist or writer/artist of manga) to create a manga that I am adapting from one of my own screenplay stories, for which I have received a publishing deal.

At the School of Visual Art and Design, I have continued to develop and teach the manga course that I began at UC Irvine. My students are creating increasingly excellent manga, and the class already has had several successful grads.

Figure P.10 My manga class at the University of South Carolina. Back row, right to left are Professor Nobuaki Hosoda of Osaka Arts University's Character Creative Arts Department, and Nobuo Masuda, consultant and point man for Sunrise's (the large anime studio that produces *Gundam* and *Cowboy Beebop*) Hollywood movie deals, who both visited here, observing my manga class in 2013. Successful mangaka teach at OAU (Kazuo Koike, the writer of the famous manga *Lone Wolf and Cub* and several other classics, lectured about manga story on the day I visited OAU) and major manga publishers' editors have visited there.[i] My students loved the opportunity for feedback. Left back row, my lead research assistant Austa Joye, a talented aspiring mangaka lauded by Professor Hosoda for her storytelling transitions (tempo)—see her hybrid Cartoon Network style manga, *Pastel White,* below. Photo: James Henderson.

---

[i] I was fortunate to be invited to visit and learn from OAU's faculty at the same time as a similar invite, which also included presenting my research, issued to me by the prestigious manga program at Kyoto Seika University in 2015. At Kyoto Seika University, students are also taught by seasoned professionals.

Figure P.11 *Pastel White* by my student Austa Joye exhibits hybrid American 1980's/1990's Cartoon Network style mixed with anime characteristics.

Figure P.12 One of the panels I organized to discuss the topic of this book at Anime Expo with Nobuo Masuda and Ken Tsumura, a producer of the *Astro Boy* adaptation (Director: David Bowers), who, along with many other front-line participants, will candidly discuss successes and failures in this book. Photo: Burt Le.

Figure P.13 Presenting my research for this book at the annual four-day Anime and Manga Studies Symposium at Anime Expo, held at the Staples Center in Los Angeles, CA, July 4, 2014. Over 80,000 people attended Anime Expo out of 220,000 total turnstile visitors, which was a 30% increase from the year before.[5] Attendance increased again when I spoke there in 2015, to 260,700 turnstile and a new record of 90,500 attendees for the peak day, as well as bidding wars that erupted over USA anime distribution rights, all indicating a sustained upswing in manga/anime popularity in the United States. Photo: Aldo Sarellano.

So my artistic practice, my research interest, and my business acumen have coalesced into the study and creation of manga/anime. For all of these reasons, I decided that I would share this fascinating journey with others in this book. I also want to provide an accessible, "easy way in" to manga and anime for people who don't really know what manga is, but have heard about it and want to learn more. But even if you feel that you already know the basics of manga and anime from other readings, I would not suggest skipping earlier chapters, as there is a great deal of useful information for anyone, no matter how well schooled in the subject you may be.

The fact that my career background and passion lie in that intersection between manga/anime and Hollywood makes me unusual, as extremely few careers cross both areas. Also my experience as a teacher at my one-of-a-kind (outside of Japan) university manga production class (as well as covering manga's history and cultural and artistic roots), makes me uniquely qualified to tell this story.[j]

Now that I have told you the advantages to reading this book and given you my background and motivations for writing it, let us begin this fascinating journey. …

Figure P.14 The author with Kazuo Koike, the famous writer of the classic wandering-samurai *Lone Wolf and Cub* manga, at Osaka Arts University in 2015.

---

[j] This, of course, does not make me infallible. I hope readers will forgive any errors or omissions, any of which would be unintentional. I made a concerted effort to research and confirm all of the facts in this book, including through the extremely generous help that I have received from many experts. I have also tried to fairly present the viewpoints of both sides when data or opinions were contradictory; if I have made any mistakes, please feel free to contact me through the publisher or through my email address, quoting your source, so that they can be corrected in future editions.

1

Introduction: Wind from the East—The Worldwide Success of Manga and Anime and an Overview of their Impact on Hollywood

- Manga[a] and anime's success—why they are so attracted to Hollywood, beginning with a description of their enormous popularity.
- And an introduction as to how they have influenced American entertainment.

Manga is Japanese comics and anime is Japanese limited-animation, which is a form of animation that utilizes fewer frames than the classic Disney animation and a variety of other cost-saving techniques. In the English language, manga is defined as Japanese comics, which are highly stylized.[b] It is widely acknowledged that these forms are eye-catching and stylistically influential; their impact extends into fashion, advertising, art direction, video gaming, and fine art. But perhaps their biggest effect outside of Japan is on comics/graphic novels, live-action movies, TV, and animation. This book is about the interrelationship between manga/anime and Hollywood films, television, and animation—a relationship that began during the World War II era.

---

[a] A note for readers: traditional style manga in Japan is read right to left. Although more recently as the form began being created outside of Japan, non-Japanese creators have chosen which direction to flow the action on the page according to their own country's comic publishing norms. For example, American aspiring mangaka, including my students, often choose left to right flow, which is the American comic industry's standard. Therefore, please read each manga in this book in the appropriate manner.
[b] In English, *manga* means comics created in Japan, or by Japanese creators. In the Japanese language, however, the term simply means "comics." Characterization and storytelling are extremely important elements of manga and anime. As many artists have shown, non-Japanese comic creators can make manga too, and a very few non-Japanese have also become mangaka (see a more in-depth definition of "mangaka" in the next page's footnote and in the glossary).

But for those of you who are just dipping your toes into the manga/anime world with this book, I need to quickly cover these forms' backgrounds and traits before explaining their fascinating relationship with Hollywood-produced movies, TV, and animation. So, to begin with, you will receive a quick education about the Japanese forms. The opening chapters will provide the tools to understand the later parts of the book.[c] Readers who are more familiar with manga and anime, and even hardcore fans (in Japan, the most dedicated are called "otaku") may be tempted to skip forward. But, I caution against this. The book updates information that, in the case of Frederik L. Schodt's masterpiece of manga studies, *Manga! Manga! The World of Japanese Comics*, is over 30 years old. And three of the other leading books about manga and anime were first published over ten years ago. Furthermore, manga series created more recently also shed great light on the subject, including *Bakuman* (by *Death Note*'s superstar writer/artist team of Tsugumi Ohba and Takeshi Obata) which, through its storyline about two young mangaka (professional manga creators[d]) with a hit series at leading manga publisher Shueisha, exposes the detailed inner workings of the industry.

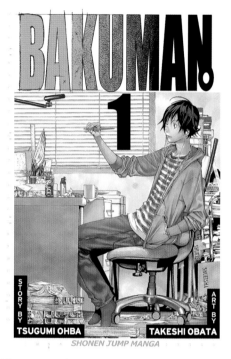

Figure 1.1 A mangaka protagonist works in his office in the youth-obtaining-their-dreams *Bakuman*. BAKUMAN. © 2008 by Tsugumi Ohba, Takeshi Obata/SHUEISHA Inc.

And with the advent of the internet, much more information—including mangaka and insider interviews—has recently come to light. And since those books were published, more Westerners have become mangaka and mangaka's assistants, and one even became a notable anime director in Japan: Michael Arias (*Tekkonkinkreet*, Studio 4°C, 2006), who is interviewed for this book. This book includes fascinating new information in the opening chapters for even

---

[c] And for unfamiliar terms that are not footnoted, please consult the glossary at the back of the book. I have tried to make it as comprehensive as I could, without it becoming too unweildy.
[d] To accurately be called a mangaka, a writer/artist needs to have a professional reputation as having produced manga under the intense serialization schedule that creators of manga face when published in that system.

the most expert in the field, partially because I conducted several interviews for the first chapters of the book. To achieve the maximum benefit, I recommend that you read the entire book.

Commercial success

Sales: Manga's huge success compared to US comics

In Japan, manga are first published in phonebook-sized magazines where several, usually serialized[e] stories run concurrently. The successful ones are then turned into individual graphic novels (called tankōbon) and possibly anime, live-action television shows, animated and live-action movies, drama CDs, video games, musicals, merchandising (like card games, toys), and even Hollywood films. The three biggest manga publishers are Shueisha, Kodansha, and Shogakukan, and they each have multiple manga magazines.[f]

Manga, due to its various traits, is extremely successful and dwarfs American comics in sales. First, let's look at statistics as to how successful manga is and then we'll compare it to statistics regarding the success of American comics. Here are a few excerpts from news stories attesting to manga's success:

From Comipress.com (which is a news site for comics):

> Launched in 1968 by Shueisha, *Weekly Shonen*[g] *Jump* competed with the already successful *Weekly Shonen Magazine* (Kodansha) and *Weekly Shonen Sunday* (Shogakukan). *Shonen Jump* soon became one of the top-selling shōnen (weekly) magazines in the market. At the height of its popularity, thanks in part to popular series like *Dragon Ball* and *Slam Dunk*, the New Year's issue of *Shonen Jump* (issue 3–4) in 1995 sold over 6.53 million copies.[1]

But those with some knowledge about manga's explosive growth beginning right after World War II through the mid 1990s and the drop off in circulation in *Shonen Jump* to the sub three million a week level more recently might think that manga's heyday is past, and thus hits are no longer on such titanic sales levels.[2] This is an incorrect assumption.

Here is a list of a few manga that have appeared in *Weekly Shonen* [means "boys"] *Jump*—notable also because this is just one magazine.

---

[e] In this case, serialized means stories that develop over an "arc"—a multi-episode period.
[f] *Kodakawa* is also a major publisher.
[g] Means, in this case, "boys."

All-Time Best Selling *Jump* Series (Only series over 70 million in sales listed)

Title	Vol. & Status	Circulation
One Piece	BEST SELLING MANGA SERIES IN HISTORY	SEE ARTICLE EXCERPTED BELOW
Dragon Ball	42 complete	230,000,000
Naruto	72 ongoing	205,000,000
Kochikame	192 ongoing + related books	156,500,000
Slam Dunk	31 complete	120,000,000
Fist of the North Star	27 complete	100,000,000
JoJo's Bizarre Adventure	111 ongoing	90,000,000
Captain Tsubasa	91 ongoing	82,000,000
Bleach	65 ongoing	82,000,000
Rurouni Kenshin	30 complete	70,000,000[3]

From Anime News Network (the foremost anime news/ journalism site), November 21, 2013:

VIZ Media [the American publishing arm of several major manga publishers] revealed on Thursday that Eiichiro Oda's *One Piece* pirate manga has 345 million copies in print worldwide. Shueisha had announced last month that as of the manga's 72nd volume, which shipped in Japan in November. *One Piece* has been published in more than 25 countries worldwide.[4]

In June 2015, *One Piece* was recognized by the Guinness World Records committee as the comic book series with the most copies published by a single author.

The only competitor to *One Piece* sales is *Harry Potter*

The only fiction book series to my knowledge that has outsold *One Piece* is *Harry Potter*, at 450 million copies[5] (estimated, 2013). However, given its escalating sales rate, by the time you read this book, *One Piece* may have topped *Harry Potter*. And the anime sales of *One Piece* are also enormous.

Figure 1.2 *ONE PIECE*
© 1997 by Eiichiro Oda/SHUEISHA Inc.

How do American comics stack up in sales against manga?

Comparing single-issue sales is also helpful. For example, the top-selling American comic in the last decade, according to the 2011 article "The 10 Bestselling Comic Book Issues of the Past Decade" on the American comics website Newsarama.com, is *Amazing Spider-Man #583* by Zeb Wells and Todd Nauck, which features Barack Obama on its cover and which benefitted from media attention when it was released just two months after the Obama presidential election (and the week before his inauguration). It sold 530,500 copies. However, according to the article, "a high volume of [the issue's] mainstream media coverage attracted attention (and sales) beyond the traditional comic book crowd."[6] That phrase "traditional comic book crowd" is revealing, as comic book readers in America are a tiny subset as compared to manga readers in Japan and worldwide.

Taking the media attention factor out of it, the second highest-selling American comic of the past decade, according to The HollywoodReporter.com, was DC's *Justice League #1* at 361,138 unit sales, as of 2011.[7] Therefore, *One Piece*'s volume 69, released in March of 2013, which sold 3,147,224 copies,[8] sold approximately 8.7 times as many copies as DC's *Justice League #1*. This difference between American and Japanese comic sales is magnified because, as we will see again and again, manga often run to many more volumes than American comics, further enabling manga sales to tower over those of American comics. (Note that DC is owned by Warner Brothers. Several manga/anime live-action adaptation projects are in development at Warners, which has already produced *Speed Racer*. Clearly, as we will see throughout this book, the Hollywood studios recognize manga/anime as a potential source for projects.)

Profit of *One Piece* manga (merchandise and anime sales not included)

From Anime News Network, October 23, 2012:

> As of February of 2012, the volumes of *One Piece*, a family comedy/adventure pirate tale had brought in at least 112,126,800,000 yen (US $1,404,220,000) in revenue.[9]

Figure 1.3 ONE PIECE © 1997 by Eiichiro Oda/SHUEISHA Inc.

This figure does not even include *One Piece*'s huge anime sales, which go beyond the animated movies and are box-office smashes in Japan, nor the series' enormous merchandising. For example, over 700 half-hour anime episodes have been produced and aired for the *One Piece* anime show for television.[10]

Manga longevity—series sometimes run for years and decades

Several of the top manga series have had jaw-dropping longevity

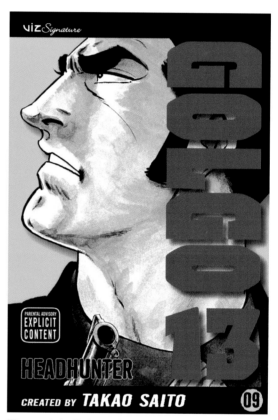

Golgo 13, about an amoral hit man with a soul so dark that he was named after the hill, Golgotha, on which Jesus was crucified, has been running for decades and has sold over 200 million copies.[11]

From *Asahi Shimbun* (a respected daily newspaper in Japan): "Manga *Golgo 13* celebrates 45 years of continuous publication":

> More than 300 industry professionals and other bigwigs turned out at the Imperial Hotel in Tokyo to celebrate Japan's oldest manga still in publication ... Takao Saito's *Golgo 13* graphic novel series about an eponymous professional assassin for hire marked its 45th anniversary on Nov. 13. Even Deputy Prime Minister Taro Aso joined the party in the Yurakucho district ... *Golgo 13* began in Shogakukan's *Big Comic* magazine in 1968. "I have been working at my desk single-mindedly," Saito said. "So even if someone tells me it has been 45 years, it doesn't ring a bell to me, and I feel like, 'it's been that long?'"[12]

Figure 1.4 *Golgo 13*'s creator Takao Saito is a "gekiga" (Japanese for "dramatic-pictures") artist. The drawing style is more realistic as opposed to the art in regular manga. In one episode, *Golgo 13* takes a huge payment from two separate enemies, each requiring him to kill the other, and then kills both. In another episode, he puts a bullet in the forehead of his target by bouncing the bullet off the arched roof of a mosque at a 110-degree angle.
© 1982, 2001 Takao SAITO/LEED PUBLISHING CO., LTD.
© SAITO PRODUCTION 2007
© 2000 Shogakukan

Another article notes that, "When the *Golgo 13*'s creator Saito was asked about the manga at its 45th anniversary celebration, he replied, 'I always had nightmares about my manga getting cut, and I thought it would get ended right away, so I had an ending prepared.' However, when asked about when the manga will end, he said, 'It's not something that can be decided on ... The manga has continued so long that it is no longer the property of the author; it belongs to readers.'"

The 77-year-old manga creator added, "'The ending and even its panel layout are all inside my head. And that's fine, but I'm going to do my best until the 200th volume.' He added with a laugh that the details of the ending are a 'trade secret.'"[13]

Figure 1.5 Takao Saito, creator of *GOLGO 13*.

Figure 1.6 Golgo 13 on the job. Gekiga style abandoned the window-pane-sized eyes, making characters often appear more Asian.
© 1982, 2001 Takao SAITO/LEED PUBLISHING CO., LTD.
© SAITO PRODUCTION 2007
© 2000 Shogakukan

Here are the Japanese manga titles (across all publishers) that have sold over 100 million copies:[h]

Manga series	Author(s)	Publisher	Demographic	No. of collected volumes	Serialized	Approximate sales
One Piece	Eiichiro Oda	Shueisha	Shōnen	76	1997–present	345 million
Dragon Ball	Akira Toriyama	Shueisha	Shōnen	42	1984–95	230 million
Naruto	Masashi Kishimoto	Shueisha	Shōnen	72	1999–2014	205 million
Golgo 13	Takao Saito	Shogakukan	Seinen	174	1969–present	200 million
Black Jack	Osamu Tezuka	Akita Shoten	Shōnen	17	1973–83	176 million
Kochira Katsushika-ku Kameari Kōen-mae Hashutsujo	Osamu Akimoto	Shueisha	Shōnen	192	1976–present	156.5 million
Case Closed	Gosho Aoyama	Shogakukan	Shōnen	85	1994–present	140 million
Oishinbo	Tetsu Kariya and Akira Hanasaki	Shogakukan	Seinen	110	1983–present	130 million
Slam Dunk	Takehiko Inoue	Shueisha	Shōnen	31	1990–6	120 million
Astro Boy	Osamu Tezuka	Kobunsha/Kodansha	Shōnen	23	1952–68	100 million
Doraemon	Fujiko Fujio	Shogakukan	Shōnen	45	1969–96	100 million
Fist of the North Star	Buronson and Tetsuo Hara	Shueisha	Shōnen	27	1983–8	100 million
Touch	Mitsuru Adachi	Shogakukan	Shōnen	26	1981–6	100 million

[h]These numbers are even more astounding due to the widespread Japanese practice of one manga being passed onto several other people, including at "manga cafés."

Between 50 million and 100 million copies

Manga series	Author(s)	Publisher	Demographic	No. of collected volumes	Serialized	Approximate sales
Hajime no Ippo	George Morikawa	Kodansha	Shōnen	108	1989–present	94 million
JoJo's Bizarre Adventure	Hirohiko Araki	Shueisha	Shōnen/Seinen	111	1986–present	90 million
Kindaichi Case Files	Yōzaburō Kanari, Seimaru Amagi, and Fumiya Satō	Kodansha	Shōnen	68	1992–present	90 million
Sazae-san	Machiko Hasegawa	Kodansha	Josei	45	1946–74	86 million
Bleach	Tite Kubo	Shueisha	Shōnen	65	2001–present	82 million
Captain Tsubasa	Yōichi Takahashi	Shueisha	Shōnen	91	1981–present	82 million
Vagabond	Takehiko Inoue	Kodansha	Seinen	37	1998–present	82 million
Rurouni Kenshin	Nobuhiro Watsuki	Shueisha	Shōnen	28	1994–9	70 million
Sangokushi	Mitsuteru Yokoyama	Ushio Shuppansha	Shōnen	60	1971–86	70 million
Kinnikuman	Yudetamago	Shueisha	Shōnen	48	1979–present	66 million
Hunter × Hunter	Yoshihiro Togashi	Shueisha	Shōnen	32	1998–present	65 million
Fullmetal Alchemist	Hiromu Arakawa	Enix/Square Enix	Shōnen	27	2001–10	64 million
Boys Over Flowers	Yoko Kamio	Shueisha	Shōjo	37	1992–2003	60 million
Rokudenashi Blues	Masanori Morita	Shueisha	Shōnen	42	1988–97	60 million
Shoot!	Tsukasa Ooshima	Kodansha	Shōnen	33	1990–2003	60 million
Bad Boys	Hiroshi Tanaka	Shōnen Gahōsha	Shōnen	22	1988–96	55 million

Manga series	Author(s)	Publisher	Demographic	No. of collected volumes	Serialized	Approximate sales
H2	Mitsuru Adachi	Shogakukan	Shōnen	34	1992–9	55 million
Major	Takuya Mitsuda	Shogakukan	Shōnen	78	1994–2010	53 million
Minami no Teiō	Dai Tennōji and Rikiya Gō	Nihon Bungeisha	Shōnen	128	1992–present	53 million
Ranma ½	Rumiko Takahashi	Shogakukan	Shōnen	38	1987–96	53 million
The Prince of Tennis	Takeshi Konomi	Shueisha	Shōnen	42	1999–2008	51 million
Dragon Quest: Dai no Daibōken	Riku Sanjo, Yuji Horii, and Koji Inada	Shueisha	Shōnen	37	1989–96	50 million
Glass Mask	Suzue Miuchi	Hakusensha	Shōjo	49	1976–present	50 million
Baki the Grappler	Keisuke Itagaki	Akita Shoten	Shōnen	110	1991–present	50 million
Great Teacher Onizuka	Tooru Fujisawa	Kodansha	Seinen	25	1997–2002	50 million
Rookies	Masanori Morita	Shueisha	Shōnen	24	1998–2003	50 million
YuYu Hakusho	Yoshihiro Togashi	Shueisha	Shōnen	19	1990–4	50 million[14]

Anime has had the same enormous success as manga

Japanese "anime" is the term used for the form of "Japanese limited-animation" that the father-creator of modern manga, Osamu Tezuka, also invented (specifically, he invented the Japanese limited-animation TV show, his prototype of which, *Astro Boy*—or in Japanese, *Tetsuan Atom*—American TV network NBC aired in America in 1963). Thus Americans', and most non-Japanese people's, first experience with the Japanese forms is often through anime.

The merchandizing for successful manga and anime can be very large as well

Gundam, featuring giant flying "mobile suits," is another hugely selling anime series

Gundam refers to the mobile suits often piloted by the main characters. And in the *Turn A Gundam* series (pictured next page), all eight of the mobile suits were designed by Hollywood designer/visual-futurist Syd Mead, who also designed Rick Deckard's (played by actor Harrison Ford) "spinner car" in the classic film *Blade Runner* (director: Ridley Scott, Warner Brothers, 1982) and the marines' spaceship in *Aliens* (director: James Cameron, 20th Century Fox, 1986). Mead also designed the revised version of the main space ship in *Star Blazers 2520* (in Japan, titled *Yamato 2520*), making him notable for designing centerpieces (including the main mechas)[i] of two of the most famous anime.[15]

Nobuo Masuda, as US liaison/consultant for Sunrise, the giant Japanese anime production company (with big hits *Gundam*, *Cowboy Bebop*, and *Outlaw Star*, to name a few), has long experience in various aspects of animation business and production. Previously, he was director of production at Bandai Entertainment, and his IMDb, which lists his credits, has a large number of the very top anime shows. He also is the point man for Hollywood studios, directors, and producers attempting to get rights to Sunrise-produced anime for Hollywood adaptations. He pointed me to Bandai Group's annual statements as evidence of *Gundam*'s huge sales:

Gundam's giant sales

Like *One Piece*, *Gundam*'s net sales revenue shows an upward trajectory from 2013 to 2014, moving from $560 million to about $688 million.[j][16] Since *Gundam* began as a series in 1979, with *Mobile Suit Gundam*, this figure is especially impressive.[17]

Merchandising is also a big component

Included in this calculation is significant merchandising revenue.

> According to Bandai Namco's financial statements for the fiscal year ending on March 31, 2012, sales of *Gundam* toys and hobby kits in particular grew from 13.4 billion yen (about US $168 million) to 15.6 billion yen (about US $196 million) as well.[18]

---

[i] Mecha can mean robots or humanoid-shaped machines, including those controlled by people.
[j] Calculated at the dollar–yen exchange rate on November 17, 2014.

Figure 1.7 *Gundam*'s mobile suits do not have their own intelligence, but rather are piloted. TURN A GUNDAM © SOTSU, SUNRISE

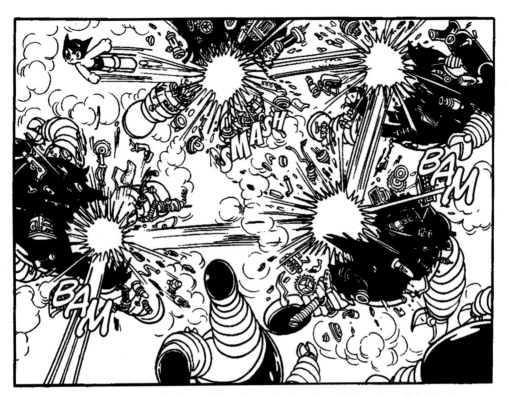

Figure 1.8 Tezuka's robots in *Astro Boy*. *Astro Boy*'s anime's American TV debut in 1963 and in other countries triggered the manga/anime tidal wave that swept the world. © Tezuka Productions

These Tezuka robots (pictured above) are the ancestors of *Gundam, Gigantor,* and *Ambassador Magma* that then influenced the Hollywood movie *Pacific Rim* (director: Guillermo Del Toro, Warner Brothers Pictures/Legendary Pictures, 2013)—see image next page. Furthermore, *Ambassador Magma* was originally a Tezuka manga before it became a Japanese live-action television show called *Space Giants* when it was localized[k] in America and Mexico. *Ambassador Magma* also, according to Del Toro, was a staple of his childhood in Mexico.[l] The Japanese giant-robot aesthetic, as we will see, also indirectly influenced the *Transformers* movies (director: Michael Bay, Dreamworks, various dates).

Pacific Rim is the first big Hollywood movie that links manga/anime aesthetic together with Kaiju ("strange beast") style. There will be more later about Del Toro's inspirations as a boy growing up in Mexico, where he was exposed to several series that never made it to America and that probably formed his *Pacific Rim* influences.

Pacific Rim tells the story of giant robots manned by two pilots who share a "neural link" battling Kaiju—the term for Japanese monsters which, beginning with *Godzilla* (director: Ishiro Hondo, Toho Films, 1954), have been widely regarded as metaphors for

---

[k] Meaning to dub and re-edit the program or movie to be understood and hopefully successful in the local culture where it is being broadcast/exhibited.
[l] See Del Toro interview quotes in Chapters 6 and 10.

Figure 1.9 Japanese actress Rinko Kikuchi manipulates a giant robot's "neural link" controls to fight Kaiju in *Pacific Rim*, director: Guillermo Del Toro, Warner Brothers Pictures/Legendary Pictures, 2013.

nuclear weapon radiation. It is commonly thought that Godzilla's skin was designed to look like the keloid scars of Hiroshima's survivors as he was born from nuclear radiation.[m]

The atomic weapons theme is also seen in the manga and anime *Akira* (director: Katsuhiro Otomo, Tokyo Movie Shinsha, 1988), to which actor Leonardo DiCaprio's Appian Way productions acquired the Hollywood remake rights.

In *Akira* a nuclear explosion levels Tokyo—understandable given that Japan is the only country ever to experience nuclear attacks with the bombing of Hiroshima and Nagasaki. The genre has come a long way since Godzilla suit-wearing actor Haruo Nakajima stomped across large model sets, squashing buildings and fleeing people alike. Soon people in the Kaiju movie and television show industry began coining the term "suitmation" to describe this phenomena.

Back then, that movie's biggest expense was the cost of destroying the sets, which thus necessitated carefully choreographed movements of Godzilla and his fellow monsters.[19] Nakajima later joked that his Godzilla's staggering gait was due to another cost-saving method—that of the crew spray-painting the monster suits while he was still inside, to save time and money (which was spent at a breathtaking rate to pay film production crews), and to allow one monster suit to quickly convert to another—implying that the fumes made him dizzy.[n][20]

---

[m] The American Kaiju expert, August Ragone, who wrote the biography *Eiji Tsuburaya: Master of Monsters*, alleges, however, that the skin was designed to resemble that of an alligator (August Ragone, *Eiji Tsuburaya: Master of Monsters: Defending the Earth with Ultraman, Godzilla, and Friends in the Golden Age of Japanese Science Fiction Film* (San Francisco: Chronicle Books, 2007), 46).

[n] Ragone attributed Godzilla's suit-man's dizziness from the fumes to rags soaked in kerosene being burned on the set to create smoke and the illusion of the city on fire (Ragone, *Eiji Tsuburaya*, 46).

"The suit weighed 220 pounds," Nakajima said in a conversation with CBS news in 2014. "And I was [surrounded] by [hot] lights. I stuck a thermometer inside the suit; 140 degrees!"[21]

This was another example of Japanese entertainment's endemically low budgets accidentally leading to an advantageous visual style that revolutionized Japanese cinema and made it a distinctive player on the world stage. Chapter 6 explains why such low production budgets also created anime's distinctive characteristics that accidentally helped make it attractive to Hollywood and popular with non-Japanese audiences.[o]

Anime series longevity

Series can run for decades. Longevity is another hallmark of several of the top anime series. Even longer running than *Gundam* and *Golgo 13* is *Sazae-san*, a domestic comedy about a housewife and her family that began being published as a comic in the *Asashi Shinbun* newspaper in 1946; the manga ran almost 30 years until 1974, selling 86 million copies, and also holds the world record for number of years in production and airing as an animated TV show. Receiving the *Guinness World Record* certification in 2013, *Sazae-san* has aired for over 45 years—since 1969—exceeding USA's champion of animated TV series longevity record holder *The Simpsons'* record run by many years. With a jaw-dropping 2,250 episodes, as of this book's publication[p] *Sazae-san* was still running as a top-rated anime television series in Japan and has far outlived its female pioneer creator Machiko Hasegawa (1920–92).[22]

The series is so long-running that voice actors and others associated with the show die of old age, the latest being the voice actor for Sazae's father Namihei, Ichirô Nagai (who passed at the age of 82 in 2014).[23] MIT Associate Professor Ian Condry—a cultural anthropologist and author who specializes in media and popular culture, including the Japanese anime industry—worked for a year in the anime industry researching his book *The Soul of Anime: Collaborative Creativity and Japan's Media Success Story* (Duke Press), and mentions a martial arts fighter friend who watches the show yet professes that he dislikes it. Asked why he still watches it, the man described it as "comfort food."[24]

Giant robots and housewives like *Sazae-san*—this gets down to a core reason for manga/anime's popularity: genre diversity ("genre maturity" as American comics scholar Scott McCloud calls it).[25] We'll explore the breadth of genres as well as many other reasons for manga/anime's success that make manga/anime so attractive to Hollywood.

---

[o] Famous Japanese animation director Hayao Miyazaki blames Tezuka for these tiny budgets that persist today—we will learn why this practice started in Chapter 6.
[p] *The Simpsons* total episode count was approaching 600 at the time of the finishing of this book. Anime/manga franchise *Naruto* (over 200 million manga sold, 72 volumes) also surpasses *The Simpsons* total number of episodes, with 641 anime episodes (220 of the original series and 421 of *Naruto Shippuden*) ongoing as of August 2015.

A worldwide phenomenon

Despite having been created solely for a domestic (Japanese) readership and audiences, manga and anime have gone mainstream worldwide, a phenomenon that was initially as surprising to Japanese mangaka and anime directors as anyone else. Tezuka remarked about the improbability that a show created on *Astro Boy*'s small, limited-animation budget would become an American hit.[26] Even up until 15 years ago only a limited number of Americans knew what anime and manga were. Now these two forms have exploded in popularity, at one point being the fastest growing segment of the US fiction market, filling bookstores and influencing almost every area of the commercial arts. For years, people have crowded into the manga sections of American bookstores. The 2008 recession impacted publishing in general in the US, and worldwide, and manga/anime were not immune. But recently manga and anime US sales have bounced back.

From Anime News Network, November 11, 2013:

> Manga sales in the United States grew for 2013 through the first half of the fourth fiscal quarter. According to the ICv2 White Paper released at the ICv2 Conference, overall graphic novel sales are up 6 %, with manga growing faster than graphic novels overall.[27]

"KAIJU"—strange beast

Manga and anime are also extremely popular in Latin America. For example, Del Toro grew up in Mexico on manga and anime and several series that were never published or distributed widely the way *Astro Boy* was. These series included one based upon Tezuka's manga *Ambassador Magma* (the live-action version was called *Space Giants* in America) and the live-action *Ultra Man* (titled *Captain Ultra* in Mexico), as well as *Ultra Q*, which was similar to the classic US shows *The Outer Limits* and *The Twilight Zone* and originally had a monster-of-the-week type format.

Masuda notes that "*Captain Ultra* is another live-action TV series (produced by Toei),[q] and somewhat resembles a *Captain Future* take-off [sci-fi pulp fiction written by Edmond Hamilton]. In this series, a space patrol team like the one in *Captain Future* battles against Kaijus, instead of a superhero like *Ultra Man*."[28] As with *Godzilla*, due to the lower budgets of Japanese television versus Hollywood shows, *Ultra Man*'s cast and crew often had to make do with less than ideal circumstances. *Godzilla*'s suit-man Nakajima also played many of the star monsters in *Ultra Man*. The monsters often sport low-rent costumes of the type that possibly caused spray-paint damage to Nakajima's lungs, many times cobbled together from other monster suits.[29] Nakajima—fortunately—was an outdoor

---

[q] Toei is basically a movie studio/distributor in Japan, like Warner Brothers and 20th Century Fox in America. They produce anime, live-action movies, and TV series. The extremely successful *Power Ranger* series, which was imported to American TV, is also based on Toei TV shows.

sports and martial arts enthusiast, physical conditioning which came in handy as he staggered under the heavy weight, through heat and cold. On one occasion a platform collapsed covering the performer in ice.

Sometimes the director framed the action to cut off Nakajima's legs, which were often exposed to support the unwieldy costumes. No matter how bizarre or aggressive the creature, the creators often tried to give it a relatable motivation, even if it did need to be stopped. This trait of providing a relatable motivation for the creature shows up with monster antagonists in many manga/anime such as *Battle Angel Alita* (movie rights controlled by James Cameron) and reflects the duality theme so prevalent in Japanese storytelling. This theme of "duality" means that there is a dark and light side to many characters' personalities, which gives believable complexity to characters and adds more drama by having characters wrestle with their "darker impulses," and can create more

Figure 1.10 Kaiju on the warpath, a poster for the 1954 original *Godzilla* movie.
© 1954 Toho Co., Ltd. All Rights Reserved.

empathy for antagonists as they often have relatable justifications for their actions.

The Kaiju giant monster genre (which *Pacific Rim* mixed together with the giant robot genre so well) was spawned after Eiji Tsuburaya, the legendary "Master of Monsters," gave birth to his brainchild *Godzilla* in 1954. Tsuburaya, along with director Hondo, was inspired by *King Kong* (directors: Merian C. Cooper and Ernest B. Schoedsack, RKO Pictures, 1933) to create *Godzilla*.

King Kong: Father of Godzilla (but who was Kong's father?...)

Regarding *King Kong*, *Godzilla*'s main inspiration, few zoos in the Western world had ape exhibits in the early twentieth century, stoking the public's fascination with the mystery of the jungles of Africa, the so-called "Dark Continent." *King Kong* itself may have been funded due to the runaway success of a Blaxploitation movie, a fake documentary set in Africa (*Ingagi*, RKO, 1930) that immediately drew fire from censors due to its storyline's inference that black women were mating with apes. The women, who turned out to have been white actresses in blackface, were depicted as sacrificing one of their own to an ape at the conclusion of the film (the rest was largely stock animal documentary footage) with sexual overtones. So audiences were most interested in the ending, intensified by the women being depicted as being naked (though they were blocked from view by strategically placed shrubbery). RKO, which was also *King Kong*'s eventual studio, enjoyed the massive returns (reportedly over $5 million, a princely sum in those days) of the movie before it was yanked from distribution and came to the conclusion that a pretty woman plus a giant ape meant enormous profit. The point here is that without that film we probably would have never gotten *Godzilla*.[30] So *King Kong* begets *Godzilla* begets *Pacific Rim*, with other Kaiju cousins mixing in too, like Daiei Film Co.'s *Gamera* (resembling a giant flying turtle with fiery sparks coming off it, spinning like a circular saw to cut its monster opponents) and other Kaiju success stories. The back and forth inspiration between manga/anime and Hollywood productions depicted throughout this book is partially mirrored by the Kaiju movies and other Japanese live-action films after the world saw the huge success of Godzilla and his family of monsters. For example, some Kaiju movie producers became partners with American studios that helped fund them and inserted American actors like Raymond Burr who appeared in the American version of *Godzilla* (1954). Ragone notes that the American localization of this original *Godzilla* worked well and, "manages a gritty, moody feel that lends this adaptation a life all its own. In fact, Toho was well aware of, and involved in, all the steps in making the U.S. version, including inspection and approval."[31] But later Kaiju films distributed in America often contained bizarre rewrites of the dubbed American actors' dialogue and re-edits of the picture as American producers attempted to slant the film toward the American actors or redo the music score with the goal of achieving wider acceptance by American audiences. August Ragone recounts the "butchering" of Toho's *Godzilla Raids Again* (1955): "Stock footage runs rampant throughout the Americanization— shots of Japanese commerce, crowd scenes, praying masses, and even clips from U.S. wartime propaganda films, quite badly disguised. One shot, used to describe the military's mobilization, is an animated graph of the imperial Japanese government's wave of conquest."[32] The circle came back around when the inspiration source for Godzilla battled him in *King Kong vs. Godzilla* (1962), produced after Universal Pictures producer John Beck, rebuffed in Hollywood when he proposed a movie featuring King Kong battling Frankenstein, pitched it to Toho as co-starring Godzilla instead.[33] Toho produced it, and Eiji Tsuburaya was happy to work on it due to having been swayed to get into special effects when he watched *King Kong* in 1933.[34] But the project was heavily edited in its US version, leading to its negative reputation.[rst35]

---

[r] Willis O'Brien, *King Kong*'s special effects master, had first pitched the project in Hollywood, but failing in that, brought it to producer Beck.

[s] The plot of this adventure classic is that a Japanese expedition team capture King Kong from his home on Faro Island to bring him back to Tokyo, but he escapes. Meanwhile, Godzilla is menacing Japan having been awoken from being frozen in an iceberg. According to August Ragone, Beck may not have understood that the film was meant to be satirical, and cut scenes of American reporters commenting upon the action into the American version of the film and eliminated "wonderful sequences of the Japanese cast." Ragone also alleges that the excellent score by master film composer Akira Ifukube was "replaced by stock music from such films as *Creature from the Black Lagoon* supposedly because it sounded 'less Oriental'" (Ragone, *Eiji Tsuburaya*, 70)

[t] This author found the Japanese sections of the co-production version very entertaining and fast moving with excellent atmospheric scenes, such as the stalking giant octopus seeking Kong's home island's narcotic "berry juice"—and it was

Eiji Tsuburaya's later-formed Tsuburaya Productions's TV shows *Ultra Q*, *Ultra 7*, and *Ultra Man* benefitted from his good relationship with *Godzilla*'s production studio Toho Films. So he was given use of Godzilla's and other monsters' costumes to modify into other creatures for those shows.

Tezuka's *Ambassador Magma* manga was turned into a live-action television show (it aired from July 4, 1966, to September 25, 1967, with a total of 52 episodes) and was the first color *tokusatsu* show. Tokusatsu are live-action films or television shows that employ extensive special effects (*tokusatsu* literally translates as "special filming") and are often typified by the science fiction or horror genres. They are known for their use of "suitmation."[36] Tokusatsu has origins in early Japanese theater, specifically Kabuki (with its action- and fight-scenes) and Bunraku (traditional Japanese puppetry which originated in Osaka in 1684).[37]

Figure 1.11 Chest-firing missles—Tezuka's *Ambassador Magma* manga was later spun into the live-action *Space Giants* TV show, which was aired in America, following the pattern of *Astro Boy*'s earlier adaptation into its own live-action TV show. © Tezuka Productions

After Del Toro migrated to Hollywood, he created *Pacific Rim*, which as noted, reflected these Kaiju and Japanese manga/anime giant robot aesthetics as strong influences. Above and below: similarities in chest armament in Tezuka's *Ambassador Magma* (top image) and *Pacific Rim*.

---

clearly meant to be fun, often comedic and light. At times the suitmation actors playing Godzilla and King Kong deploy pro-wrestling moves, and the humans firing the "berry juice" inside a rocket shell at King Kong near the climax to drug him and then lifting him by large balloons to float towards Godzilla, who is meanwhile loping around on Mount Fuji so they can battle and hopefully destroy each other, seems like satire. But the city-stomping, crowd-scattering and smoky-night-city scenes are epic in scale—with great actor chemistry, rudely interrupted by the low-budget banal "talking head" scenes of American actors who comment upon the action from cheap sets. American producer Beck's apparent misestimation of the movie's tone aside, it is understandable that, with an investment to protect and aiming for a broader commercial market, he did not believe that American audiences of that era could accept an all Asian cast, no matter how entertaining and well made it was. Kong wins the final fight although Godzilla is still alive to return another day, and the big ape swims home to his island (with Godzilla reportedly screeching in the background in the Japanese version, as if to say "I'll be back!"). The film starred two Japanese "Bond girls" who had roles along with British agent 007 (played by Sean Connery) in *You Only Live Twice*, which was set partially in Japan. *King Kong vs. Godzilla* was the biggest commercial hit of all Japanese *Godzilla* films. In fall 2015, Hollywood trade publications announced that Warner Brothers and Legendary Pictures would produce a new *King Kong vs. Godzilla* movie in addition to a sequel to their 2014 hit *Godzilla*.

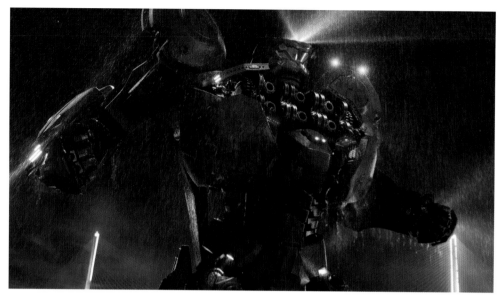

Figure 1.12 A "jaeger" sports similar armament (to *Ambassador Magma*) in *Pacific Rim*, directed by Guillermo Del Toro, Warner Brothers Pictures/Legendary Pictures, 2013. Del Toro specifically cites *Ambassador Magma/Space Giants* as an influence: "And then we loved another series that was called *Space Giants,* and the fights with the Kaijus were just fantastic." See interview excerpt at the end of Chapter 6.

Hierarchy/genealogy of these shows

According to Masuda, the *Ambassador Magma* and *Ultra Man* TV series "were aired almost at the same time, and I believe *Ultra Man* was developed quite independently, just trying to build up on the success of *Ultra Q*. On the other hand, I think the TV series of *Ambassador Magma* was born out of their efforts to make some Kaiju TV series like *Ultra Q*. Tezuka's original manga version [of *Ambassador Magma*] is a bit more serious sci-fi story (there weren't so many Kaijus in there), and the TV producers adapted it into 'a monster of the week type format a bit forcefully.'" Masuda continues, "My general impression is that most Japanese fans think *Ultra Man,* and following [that] *Ultra Seven* [yet another "Ultra" show] had more worth and historical significance than the TV series of *Ambassador Magma*, not to mention that the 'Ultra' franchise has been far more popular through these decades. But this is just my impression." Masuda adds that *Captain Ultra* replaced *Ultra Man* in the same time slot after *Ultra Man* was cancelled, despite the fact that *Captain Ultra* was produced by Toei and not Tsuburaya Productions.[38]

Figure 1.13 Major Motoko Kusanagi in a scene from the *Ghost in the Shell: Stand Alone Complex*, based on the manga written and illustrated by Masamune Shirow (publisher: Kodansha; studio: Production I.G.). In 2015, Hollywood actress Scarlett Johansson (*The Avengers, Lost in Translation*) became attached to play the role of Kusanagi in a Hollywood adaptation of *Ghost in the Shell* for the Dreamworks movie studio, and the movie was assigned a premiere date of April 14, 2017.
© 2002–2005 Shirow Masamune-Production I.G/KODANSHA

For manga and anime fans Andy and Lana Wachowski, *The Matrix* was their first conscious attempt to bring anime/manga styling to Hollywood live-action. The film was felt by many to have been inspired in part by *Ghost in the Shell*, a multi-media franchise based upon the "seinen" manga of the same title.[u,v]

The Wachowskis' cubist/pop-art-inspired *Speed Racer* (2009)[39] is a direct adaptation of the classic manga/anime of the same name. The latter was itself partially created in 1967 by combining elements from the style of Elvis Presley's (and Anne Margaret's) movie *Viva Las Vegas* (director: George Sidney, MGM, 1964) and the James Bond classic *Goldfinger* (director: Guy Hamilton, United Artists, 1964). These films were red hot in Japan at the time—especially Elvis's racing car garb (neckerchief and pompadour hair style) and Bond's gadget-packed Aston Martin car that allegedly inspired *Speed's* famous Mach Five racing car.[40]

---

[u] Seinin means a "young man" of 17 into his 40s. The female version of seinen manga is josei manga.
[v] *The Matrix* trilogy as well as *Speed Racer*'s (the Wachowskis' adaptation of the classic anime/manga) principal producer Joel Silver said in the documentary about the making of *The Animatrix, Scrolls to Screens: A Brief History of Anime* (director: Josh Oreck) that "the Wachowski Brothers showed me *Ghost in the Shell* and they showed me what they wanted to do with that type of action and photography and make it with real people, with real actors, and create a hybrid."

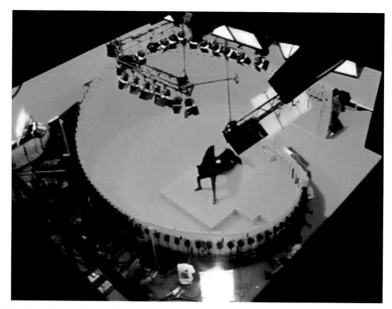

Figure 1.14 *The Matrix*'s multi-viewpoint camera rig was invented to film still images in a computer-dictated sequence and results in the manga/anime convention of viewing a scene from many angles—but in this case achieved in live-action form.[w] Viewing fight scenes from many angles is often found in manga/anime due to their trait of "deliberate time decompression," which will be covered in more detail in Chapter 2.[x]

Figure 1.15 The racing cars in *Viva Las Vegas*, similar to *Speed Racer* anime's Mach Five, as Elvis's co-star Anne Margaret walks in the foreground. Trixie, Speed's girlfriend, is more the capable and pretty girl-next-door type than Ann Margaret's radiant character, who might have had more charisma (Ann Margaret arguably outshone Elvis, thus worrying his manager Colonel Tom Parker and allegedly resulting in the casting of lesser actresses in Elvis's future films, leading to a decline in their quality).[41] *Viva Las Vegas* (director: George Sidney, MGM, 1964).

---

[w] The rig's developer, John Gaeta, will discuss this in his interview in Chapter 2 and 8.
[x] From the making of the *Matrix* documentary.

Figure 1.16 Elvis in a racing car similar to *Speed Racer*'s Mach Five race car in *Viva Las Vegas* (director: George Sidney, MGM, 1964).

The Wachowskis' *Speed Racer* has continued to build its reputation on DVD and Blu-ray and, I will argue, so far is the most accurate (in spirit and style) Hollywood adaptation of a manga/anime.

Below: Comparing car images from *Viva Las Vegas*, the original *Speed Racer* anime and the Mach 5 in the Wachowskis' live-action/hybrid/CG version. Note the similarities in all the cars.

Figure 1.17 The *Speed Racer* anime, a wildly successful show worldwide.
MACH GO GO GO (SPEED RACER) © Tatsunoko Production

Figure 1.18 *Speed Racer*, the Hollywood version, successfully captures the spirit of the original, directors Lana and Andy Wachowski, Warner Brothers, 2008.[y]

Dragonball Evolution (director: James Wong, 20th Century Fox, 2009) was a less faithful and more controversial live-action movie adapted from the Japanese manga/anime series. Director/producer George Miller (*Babe, Mad Max, Happy Feet*) cites *Akira* as a key influence and once considered doing an anime version of his *The Road Warrior* sequel *Mad Max: Fury Road* (Warner Brothers, 2015).[42] And echoing the two-way street that will be described in this book, *Battle Angel Alita*'s mangaka Yukito Kishiro cites *The Road Warrior* as personally having even a more important impact than *Blade Runner*.

Figure 1.19 *The Road Warrior*'s Lord Humungus, tyrant ruler of the post-apocalyptic Australian desert wasteland (here his double-chinned lieutenant announces his arrival). Lord Humungus's makeshift vehicle army resembles that of the character Den's in *Battle Angel Alita* (Figure 1.20). Director: George Miller, Warner Brothers, 1981.

---

[y] See interviews in Chapter 8 with producer Grant Hill (who produced the movie with Joel Silver), brilliant lead visual effects designer John Gaeta, and visionary graphic novel artist Geof Darrow, a man with a wild imagination who designed the look of key scenes from the Wachowskis' *Matrix* (such as the underwater-look and the famous field of fetuses). And the *Matrix* spun off *The Animatrix* anime series.

Figure 1.20 *Battle Angel Alita*—antagonist Den's desert warriors on wheels. Mangaka Yukito Kishiro acknowledges liking *The Road Warrior* in an interview he did with Professor Hayashi for this book.[243] © Yukito Kishiro / Kodansha Ltd.

Mangaka Kishiro was also impressed with *Star Wars* but was more impacted by the *Road Warrior/ Mad Max*

Battle Angel Alita mangaka Kishiro said in an interview with Hayashi for this book that he was impressed with *Blade Runner* and *The Road Warrior* (*Mad Max 2*) and other non-Japanese entertainment like the British rock group, Deep Purple.

> **Hayashi:** Have you been influenced by *Terminator* too?
> **Kishiro:** I liked *Terminator* but not sure if I was influenced by it. I liked the B class movies like the ones by Roger Corman.
> **Hayashi:** How about *Mad Max*?
> **Kishiro:** I like *Mad Max*. The world has changed by *Mad Max*. *Star Wars* changed the way movies are made once and then *Mad Max* came out at the end of 80s which was an

---

ᶻ See the preface for background on Yoko Hayashi.

Australian film but once again the world of films has changed after. For me *Mad Max* is more important than *Blade Runner.*[aa]

Enormous Hollywood movie adaptation projects of manga and anime are on the horizon. It is hard to know far ahead of time what films will actually be produced in Hollywood because the green-lighting (approval for production) of these films is an act that takes considerable courage given these enormous budgets and thus much risk (Roy Lee, producer of the Hollywood Asian remakes *The Departed* and *The Ring*, discusses the green-light process in his interview in Chapter 10). 20th Century Fox has *Battle Angel Alita* with James Cameron attached as director in his follow-up to the *Avatar* sequels (he had originally planned to do it before *Avatar*—more on that story later in Chapter 7). This is notable in part because of Academy Award winner Cameron's status as the most commercially successful filmmaker of the modern era, which practically guarantees that, if it is produced, it will have a very significant impact. Whether or not Cameron makes *Alita*, many more large-scale Hollywood movies, while not necessarily direct adaptations, are showing intense manga/anime ancestry that are acknowledged by their creators, such as *Sucker Punch*.

Figure 1.21 *Sucker Punch*'s protagonist Baby Doll, dressed as a Japanese schoolgirl,[ab] and her female warrior comrades hit a typical manga/anime three-point fighting stance after being dropped out of an airplane into battle (Chapter 11 contains an interview with *Sucker Punch*'s screenwriter Steve Shibuya who talks in detail about the film's anime/manga/gaming influences). Director: Zack Snyder, Warner Brothers Pictures/Legendary Pictures, 2011.

[aa] This is only a fraction of the four-hour interview. Readers are encouraged to read his full interview if it is published in the future, along with Hayashi's full interviews with Matsumoto, Watanabe, and others in the Japanese manga/anime, television, and feature film industries.

[ab] A very common anime/manga trope, the sailor-type schoolgirl uniform is reflected in the title of the hit anime/manga *Sailor Moon*.

Sexy 1920s Fleischer Brothers animation star Betty Boop had a big impact on Tezuka and his most famous character, Astro Boy, as did Mighty Mouse, a cute American cartoon superhero, itself derivative of Superman. More recent sci-fi anime mega hit *Cowboy Bebop* (director: Shinichirō Watanabe, Sunrise, 1988) mixed up film noir and Hong Kong action, Blaxploitation, and more, creating a world that, according to author Susan Napier,[ac] is state-less, a short hand term I am using here for her idea, meaning non-culturally-specific, which gives global viewers an easier way into anime than most Japan-centric projects.[44] Some projects such as *The Matrix*'s anime offshoot series *The Animatrix* and American TV's *Powerpuff Girls* cartoon take this back-and-forth influence a step further. In both examples, a Japanese anime style inspires the creation of the American works which then in turn spin off Japanese anime adaptations of these Hollywood projects.[ad] All the above and more will be covered later.

American TV is also packed with animation that is heavily anime styled, to the point that it is almost the norm. This will be explored after the section about anime coming to America, beginning with *Astro Boy*. Two examples are shown here with the Fox TV shows *The Simpsons* and *The Cleveland Show*:

Figure 1.22 *The Simpsons* tribute episode to Hayao Miyazaki (the famous and successful Japanese animation director), in this image referencing *My Neighbor Totoro* ("the catbus") and *Ponyo*. 20th Century Fox Television, Gracie Films.

[ac] Napier writes that, "Despite its indisputably Japanese origins, anime exists increasingly as a nexus point in global culture—[it inhabits] an amorphous new media territory that crosses and even intermingles national boundaries" (*Anime from Akira to Howl's Moving Castle: Experiencing Contemporary Japanese Animation* (New York: Palgrave Macmillan, 2005), 22–3).

[ad] *Powerpuff Girls*'s creator Craig McCracken states that he was attempting to go back to a limited-animation style, due to the practical necessity of that show's limited budget with so many episodes to produce (and as we will learn later, the Japanese had the same reason for developing anime). Q and A with Craig McCracken (*Creating Animated Cartoons with Character by Joe Murray* (New York: Watson-Guptill Publications, 2010), 107–9).

Figure 1.23 This episode of *The Simpsons* references Miyazaki's worldwide hit *Spirited Away*, which itself represented the animism coursing through the creative veins of Japanese art and storytelling.[ae] 20th Century Fox Television, Gracie Films.

Spirited away

Miyazaki claimed that the movie's plotline about a young girl tending strange spirits at a hotel/hot spring is really a parable about the Japanese. In a 2002 interview with Tetsuya Chikushi in the *Shukan Kinobi*, (*Weekly Friday*) newspaper, he remarked, "That's why I think *Spirited Away* is something extremely local—it's from what I would call 'A land of aboriginals on the edge of East Asia,' a place never completely civilized by Confucianism, where there are lots of older local customs and Shinto rituals. It's the product of a land where there are still lots and lots of local shrine rituals."[45] Animism, the idea that non-human entities have spiritual life, has sometimes been called Japan's true native religion and informs much manga and anime, giving it a different style than Western animation. Animism takes center stage in many manga/anime, as in the worldwide megahit *Inuyasha*, whose female creator, Rumiko Takahashi, has been listed as one of the richest people in Japan. Strangely, despite its roots in Japanese religion and mythology, this fantasy series is successful outside Japan [including in America], perhaps partially due to *Inuyasha*'s "alien-ness/other-ness."

[ae] "Belief in the existence of spirits separable from bodies. Such beliefs are traditionally identified with small-scale ('primitive') societies, though they also occur in major world religions. They were first competently surveyed by Edward Burnett Tylor in *Primitive Culture* (1871). Classic animism, according to Tylor, consists of attributing conscious life to natural objects or phenomena, a practice that eventually gave rise to the notion of a soul. *See also* shaman." From "Animism," The Concise Encyclopedia, http://www.merriam-webster.com/dictionary/animism (accessed October 18, 2014).

Figure 1.24 *The Simpsons* homage to Miyazaki's *Kiki's Delivery Service*. 20th Century Fox Television, Gracie Films.

Figure 1.25 *The Simpsons* homage to several of Miyazaki's animated films, including *Howl's Moving Castle*, *Kiki's Delivery Service*, and *Princess Mononoke* (in that order). 20th Century Fox Television, Gracie Films.

Figure 1.26 *The Cleveland Show* parodies the manga/anime giant robot aesthetic, and the manga/anime technique of speed-lines, with the "Clevetron." 20th Century Fox Television.

A taste as to how far manga/anime influence on American TV animation has come is apparent in this interview:

I interviewed veteran American TV animation writer Eugene Son about this subject on the hall floor at Anime Expo[af] as cosplayers (people at manga and anime cons who dress as their favorite characters) and fans paraded by this infectiously upbeat, ebullient, and positive man (a trait common to many TV writers who need social skills to work on a writing staff). Son was a writer on American animated TV shows *Ben 10* and *Ultimate Spider-Man*. He is a favorite of my students, with whom he has generously shared his expertise on multiple occasions, and is popular within the American animated TV industry. During our interview, a number of passers-by came up to Eugene, or he called out to them, all colleagues in the business.

Davis: What have you worked on in Hollywood TV that has been influenced by anime/manga?

Son: By the time I was [writing] on *Teenage Mutant Ninja Turtles* [TV animation show] it was influenced by *Daredevil* comics, and Frank Miller [*Daredevil* and *300*'s creator and who, as we will see, is a big fan of Japanese woodblock prints and manga] was influenced by Japanese anime and manga.

[af] See definition of Anime Expo in the preface and glossary.

Davis: So what are the influences you are seeing now from manga and anime in current animated TV?

Son: They are huge. For example, to start with specifically the new artists—the current ones, doing storyboards, in terms of props, etc., are all heavily influenced in manga and anime. They are equally well versed in the Japanese directors and art styles. If you talk to the artists, the ones who are a little older than I am were heavily influenced by Tezuka. The ones who are my age are influenced by a lot of the Japanese stuff that came over at that time: *Captain Harlock*, *Macross*, and *Voltron*. The ones who are now coming up—*Evangeleon* (among others).

Davis: Do TV writers understand what is going on in manga/anime stories to make them have the impact that they have (in the best cases)?

Son: The storytelling that we were seeing in manga and anime is not so much in terms of new stories, but how far they push things, and in terms of adult stories.

Davis: What's the crossover you are seeing in terms of the Western sensibility of storytelling over in Japan? And what's an example of what writers like you are getting back from them?

Figure 1.27 Captain Harlock and other characters in his adventures. Creator Leiji Matsumoto stated in an interview that Harlock is similar in part to Errol Flynn's pirate movie persona.[46] © Leiji Matsumoto, Toei Animation

Figure 1.28 Captain Harlock's space pirate ship *Arcadia*.
© Leiji Matsumoto, Toei Animation

Son: They were being influenced in Western ways. Mangaka were looking to the West in terms of heroic characters and individuality.[ag] But one thing we were taking from them [was] that these stories could be more than just telling children's stories.

Davis: How did you get into being interested in manga/anime?

Son: My initial influence was anime that had been dubbed into English. *Voltron*,[ah] *Space Battleship Yamato* is *Star Blazers*, and *Macross* is *Robotech*. I also saw *Akira*, which was huge. People, artists are looking for new stuff. When you are with like-minded creative people and you're looking for the new stuff, someone might say, "You have to check this out." This coincided with the rise of home video and DVD and the internet.

Davis: Do you find manga and anime influence your storytelling? There is a serious depth in so much manga and anime, the story and theme "roots" like Tezuka talked about— where the story/tree is only as strong as its roots [theme/meaning/character].

[ag] For more on this, see the "Samurai and the Cowboy" section in Chapter 6.

[ah] According to the *New York Times*, massive sword wielding robot starrer *Voltron* was "localized" (a process described in chapters 6, 8 and the glossary) by American Peter Keefe, who purchased the American broadcast rights. According to the *Times*, Keefe did not have Japanese transcripts to the show's dialogue and thus invented English language scripts, guessing the plots. *Voltron* became the top syndicated show in America, with impressive merchandising sales, and was a predecessor for *Pokémon* and anime that swept America afterwards (see Niko Koppel, "Peter Keefe, Creator of Cartoon *Voltron* Dies at 57," *New York Times*, June 11, 2010). Other sources cite John Teichmann as Keefe's partner in the adaptation/American series creation, which came from *Beast King Golion* and *Armored Fleet Dairugger XV*.

Son: They can have a depth to them—even though they are kid friendly. You can dive into those dark areas, even if they are risky. Sometimes you get told you cannot do that. And sometimes you get told that you can. There are Western creators that want to do these stories that Japanese have been able to tell.

Davis: Do executives let you do more [in terms of that] now?

Son: It totally depends from network to network, executive to executive, and month to month what they allow. A couple of television executives know *Akira* better than I do. It also depends also on whether particular executives are aware of it.

Davis: Do you feel American TV is more appropriate for adaptations than features to adapt manga/anime to in part because of the long-running serialized nature?

Son: Yes, and there are bigger budgets in TV now. They do bigger stories so that you can continue on week to week. TV is more the realm of the writer than features now, while the [feature] films are being driven by the directors. I would be surprised if someday we don't see that [American TV live-action manga/anime adaptations].

Davis: What is the balance to strike between pleasing the hardcore fans of a manga or anime and the wider audience that Hollywood's expensive productions [versus anime, which are usually produced for lower budgets] needs to make a profit?

Son: If you do it right, you make both sides happy. Though the cases where you make the hardcore fans and the mainstream audience [happy] is [sic] really rare.[47]

And now HBO is developing an adaptation of *Monster* (see image on the next page), a classic manga about a doctor who saves a child who grows up to be an angelic, cold-blooded killer, for Del Toro to adapt for live-action. This deal reportedly has great creative controls for the mangaka, Naoki Urasawa, and will not extend past the original series run.[48]

Perhaps this is because, in the past, Del Toro has seen negotiations fail for Japanese properties he sought to adapt when Hollywood lawyers grappled with Japanese rights holders.[ai][49] Extremely savvy about cultural differences, he has, as we will see later, successfully negotiated the Japan–Hollywood minefield with sensitivity.[50] Such a show, if successful on American television, would mimic the Japanese system, where a large portion of live-action scripted television is based upon manga and anime, probably more so than live-action features in Japan.

Whether or not *Monster* does get made (HBO normally has a long development process and Del Toro is involved in many projects), it does represent an attempt to address some mangaka concerns about Hollywood adaptations. See a discussion about this deal in Chapter 10.

Next, we look at the additional characteristics of manga and anime that make them attractive to Hollywood.

[ai] *Domu*, by Katsuhiro Otomo (*Akira*), was the negotiation that failed and Del Toro subsequently was very careful in his negotiation for *Monster*'s adaptation rights for HBO. See Chapter 10.

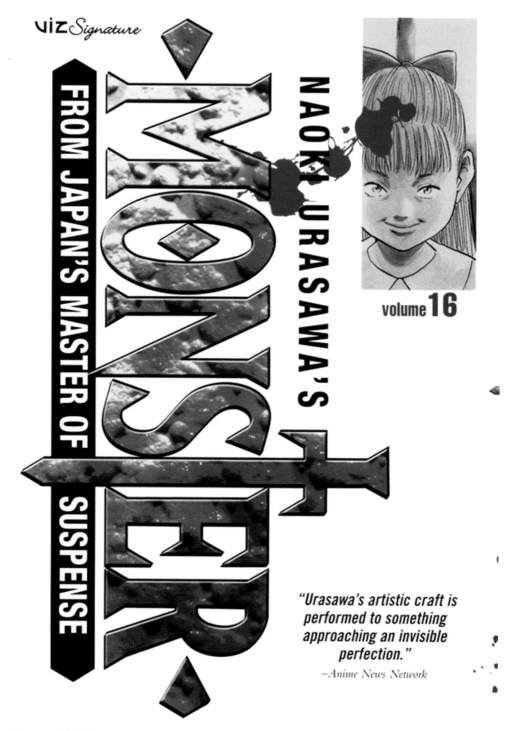

Figure 1.29 *Monster,* a project that Guillermo Del Toro is interested in adapting for American television. MONSTER © 1995 Naoki URASAWA/Studio Nuts

2

Characteristics of Manga and Anime that make them Attractive to Hollywood

I notice that people in Hollywood who are interested in adapting manga/anime to American media are very often attracted to the visual style of the characters and their attitudes, even though they usually do not know how most of the manga or anime are working on a detailed level. This is a recipe for disaster. Nobuo Masuda remarked to me that when "adapting from animation to live-action … usually the people [start] from that kind of idea—that the characters are cool and something like that."[1] And these people usually seem not to understand the story, visual style, and secret visual pointers guiding one's eyes through the frame, screen tones, character tropes, cultural cues, and so on. This ignorance may result in movies like Fox's *Dragonball Evolution*, which is controversial to many manga/anime fans and was received poorly in Japan. If the creative team had understood the visual and cultural nuances of the Japanese version of *Dragonball*, then maybe they could have been far more effective at rendering, sculpting, and freshening their own projects, or adapting ones from Japan, provided that they had the power to do so. Perhaps *Dragonball* would not have been adapted at all if the filmmakers and executives had better understood that it might be the kind of project that would be too difficult to convert to the American live-action form.

Despite this common ignorance in those adapting the works, there are a few, such as the Wachowskis, Gaeta, Arias, Darrow and their team, who were willing and able to spend the large amounts of time intensely studying the forms regarding how manga/anime operate to achieve the overall effect of emotion created in the reader or audience before making their movies. But this is very rare. This book will show why non-Japanese people are even sometimes drawn to manga/anime by the very aspects of the forms that they don't understand—its alienness. So when people want to adapt a work into live-action but do not really understand what makes the work effective (beyond some superficial elements), there is a high likelihood that the elements that made the work worthwhile in the first place will be removed in the adaptation process.

Figure 2.1 A "chibi," which is a type of "super-deformed" character where a regular character is shrunk and exaggerated in key ways. Used for comic relief in many manga series. Artist for many of this book's chibis: my student Austa Joye.

Here are what I view as some of the key characteristics (aside from the aforementioned spectacular sales) that have made manga/anime so interesting and attractive to Hollywood over the decades.

Sophisticated stories, and ...

Robert Napton is an American graphic novel writer as well as a former long-time employee at Bandai Entertainment, which, along with Sunrise, distributed the *Gundam* franchise in America. Currently Vice President and Editorial Director of Legendary Comics (Legendary Entertainment is the company that produced *Pacific Rim* and the modern Hollywood hit version of *Godzilla*—director: Gareth Edwards, Warner Brothers, 2014), Napton story-edited *Godzilla*'s graphic novel prequel. He begins with the different way the stories and characters are typically handled in manga and anime, something he could sense as a child growing up in the late 1970s/early 80s.

> **Davis:** What is it that attracts you to manga and anime in general? Is it the earnestness of the characters? The duality of the light and dark characteristics? The different religions and cultures? Fascination with an alien culture? Amazing visual styles? Serialization? Positive non-cynical values? Honor? Good guys can lose? Strong females? Emphasis on family—
>
> **Napton:** Wow. All of the above! [laughs]
>
> **Davis:** Good, question answered!
>
> **Napton:** The thing that appealed to me—when I stumbled upon *Star Blazers* and even later with *Macross* on American TV in the form of *Robotech* and I discovered the

Japanese version of *Macross*—for me, it was the storytelling. The way that the characters were portrayed. Because in children's animation in the United States at the same time, cartoons were airing that were being fed to kids that were pretty moronic, you know? You had *He-Man* … basically if you had basic intelligence you would enjoy watching those, you know? My cat would probably enjoy *He-Man* as much as I do.[a] But with anime you were engaged in a real level the way an adult is engaged in a TV series or movie. There was some story, some character, romance, death … I remember when *Robotech* aired, and the creators of that show—even

Figure 2.2 Robert Napton.

though they altered the story lines, if a character died they tried to keep that intact, and in animation in American cartoons you don't have characters dying, you know?[2]

These traits that Napton notes are found even in many children's manga and anime, where death and complex moral issues are depicted. This also applies to *Astro Boy*. Cruelly rejected by his scientist father, Astro is sold off into the circus and becomes a heart-broken orphan until rescued by a kindly scientist and given a new family.

Astro Boy's circus scenes (see Figure 2.3) also have a similarity to those of *Pinocchio*'s. And this scenario played out in *A.I. Artificial Intelligence* (director: Steven Spielberg, Warner Brothers, 2001), with its brutal fair where humans torture the robots, which was created from a project developed by Stanley Kubrick, who had earlier asked Tezuka to work on *2001: A Space Odyssey* after seeing *Astro Boy*.[b]

---

[a] Leiji Matsomuto spoke about the more complex nature of manga stories versus American comics from the early days in an interview with Takayuki Karahashi in 1996: "The art, I thought, was wonderfully meticulous and had a polish based on proper drawing skills. As drawings, they were highly complete, and they were in color, so I thought they were wonderful. But when it came to the story, comparing them even to what there was in Japan in the *Showa* [19]20's, they were still too simple. Each story's exposition–development–twist–conclusions were so short, and lacked complexity. I was more drawn towards the Japanese manga methods that were more like American movies and sophisticated French movies. I'd have to say that back when I saw American 10-cent comics, the stories felt really simple to me." This and other wonderful mangaka and anime director interviews are in a book edited by Trish Ledoux, *Anime Interviews: The First Five Years of Animerica, Anime & Manga Monthly (1992–97)* (San Francisco: Cadence Books, 1997), 154.

[b] More about Kubrick's offer to Tezuka in Chapter 6.

Figure 2.3 Astro is rescued from the circus by mentor Dr. Ochanomizu in *Astro Boy*. In the Spielberg directed, Kubrick conceptualized *A.I. Artificial Intelligence* movie, the protagonist boy is rescued from the brutal robot fair by Gigilo Joe, another artificial person who is "adult," and somewhat mentor-like.

© Tezuka Productions

As we will see in detail in Chapter 9 (the *Astro Boy* adaptation case study), that key event in his life was removed in the Summit/Imagi Hollywood adaptation, which radically altered the character. *Astro Boy* lost the plucky optimism that only seemed admirable through his upbeat overcoming of his background of parental rejection at an extremely young age and then battling evil adults and robots. (See my interview in Chapter 9 with one of the adaptation's producers, Ken Tsumura.)

The prototype for *Astro Boy* was called *Ambassador Atom* (1951).[c] The story turned out to be too complicated, and Tezuka's editor suggested simplifying it.[3]

Fred Schodt writes,

> In all of Tezuka's works, good people are easily capable of turning bad, especially if they are in positions of power—scientists, politicians, police; no one is immune. But the converse is true too. Bad people can also turn good and achieve some sort of redemption (although they may lapse again later). In reality, Tezuka was fascinated by the complexity of human nature, and it is in this sense that his best manga stories (even if, like *Astro Boy*, they were intended for children) begin to resemble Russian literature.[4]

Anime and manga characters are often portrayed in a way that emphasizes their duality. Tezuka's second most famous character, behind Astro Boy, is Black Jack, a high-priced and enormously skilled surgeon whose personality contains both light and dark aspects, which is reflected even in his appearance—the scars rip down his face "dividing him into parts."

As a child, Black Jack is torn apart by a leftover World War II bomb he finds on the beach which also kills his mother. He is then sewn back together by a mentor-figure surgeon (Black Jack is estranged from his biological father, who is a shady character). He becomes the world's highest-priced surgeon, who might let a corrupt wealthy person die if he cannot pay his outrageous fee but then in the next moment takes on a charity case.[d]

This duality is more in sync with Asian religions and cultures, particularly Japanese culture with its multiple religious outlooks. Many Japanese people adopt parts of each religious view (incuding Buddhism and Shintoism, which is perhaps Japan's true native religion, and is, in ways, a form of Animism) and their shades-of-gray methods for evaluating people's characters. Returning to the all-important definition: according to the *Dictionary of World Philosophy*, animism "refers to the belief that non-human entities are spiritual beings, or at least embody some kind of life-principle."[5]

The broad American comic book "good versus evil" simplistic moral ethic (due to the Comic Code of 1954, which we will learn about later, and lasting until the advent of the American graphic novel) that Hollywood also portrayed, particularly during the blockbuster

---

[c] Due to some conflicting accounts of when the *Astro Boy* manga was first published, I emailed expert Fred Schodt for clarification, and he replied that "The Tetsuwan Atom (Astro) character first appeared in April, 1951, in *Shonen* magazine, in the story called *Ambassador Atom* (*Atom Taishi*) which ran until March of 1952. In April, 1952, Tezuka made him the star of the renamed series (*Tetsuwan Atom*), so you could say that the *Astro Boy* serialization started in 1952, I suppose. It depends whether you want to focus on the character or the series" (email to author, April 13, 2015).

[d] In keeping with Tezuka's emphasis on the importance of theme/a moral message (as well as manga/anime's in general, particularly in the early era of the forms), *Black Jack* often critiques the corruption in the medical establishment. This has brought this issue to the Japanese public's attention. A licensed doctor in the Western style, Tezuka also had doctors in his ancestry.

Figure 2.4 Originally Tezuka's second most famous creation behind *Astro Boy*, *Black Jack* is now extremely well known in Japan, and now significantly exceeds *Astro Boy* in popularity with 176 million manga volumes sold as of March 2015, versus *Astro Boy*'s 100 million.[6] © Tezuka Productions

era ushered in by *Star Wars* and its fellow "black hat/ white hat" productions, has faded somewhat, especially in American television, which is writer-driven and currently in a golden era (for reasons we will learn later). American television shows depicting anti-heroes and protagonists with dark sides have recently proliferated and this coincides with the growth of an audience receptive to manga and anime. So it makes sense that Del Toro would try to adapt *Monster* to HBO, one of America's premiere pay channels, which is particularly adventurous in much of what it airs. Another advantage, which will be discussed later, is that since HBO doesn't work on the syndication model of American network broadcast television (see definition of syndication in Chapter 6), the company would not be pressured to extend the show past the original material's ending, solving the creative control issues that might crop up with the Japanese creator if an American TV showrunner were inventing new material after exhausting the source material.[e7] This is an issue that has proved problematic in a negotiation that myself, Hayashi, our lawyers and agents were involved in with Japanese rights holders.

Thematics, heartfelt "can do," and celebration of the value of struggle, apprenticeship, and the ordinary

Fans and readers love the fantastical sci-fi worlds painted by some manga that contain hyper detailed pages (like *Battle Angel Alita* and *Berserk*, a manga by Kentaro Miura about a wandering swordsman). But as Schodt notes, "the real triumph of manga lies in their celebration of the ordinary."[8] As American comic artist Brian Stelfreeze commented, "Comics in the United States have become such a caricature. You have to have incredible people doing incredible things, but in Japan it seems like the most popular comics are the comics of normal people doing normal things."[9]

Figure 2.5 Decades after its creation, *Black Jack* is still so popular that actor Hugh Laurie of American TV show *House* fame, whose character House has his own duality, was seen on advertising materials in Japan, where Laurie faced across at Black Jack. Black Jack's facial scar, a visual representation of his character's duality, is even more visible in his side of the image (above). *Black Jack* has had a development deal in North America as a live-action remake. © Tezuka Productions

---

[e] Though it should be noted that HBO can also later resell their shows to other networks into syndication, as happened years ago with *The Sopranos* and also with other more recent series. Showrunners are the powerful and highly-paid TV show writing/executive-producers (called "head-writers"). Often creators of shows, they also manage their daily operation.

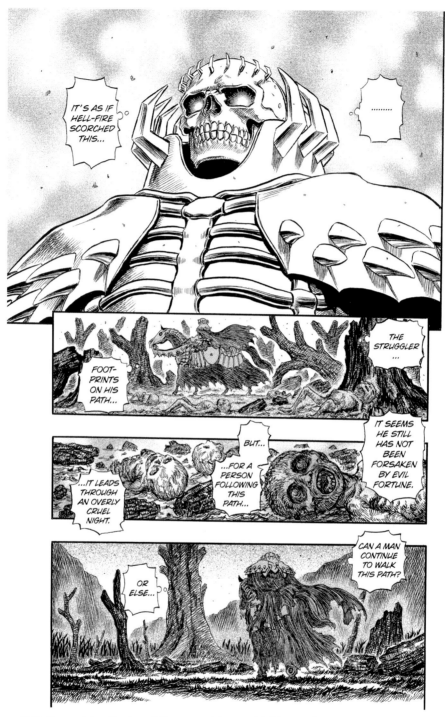

Figure 2.6 *Berserk* by Kentaro Miura combines a highly rendered world with deep philosophy as Skull Knight contemplates main character Guts's cursed path.[f]
© Kentaro Miura/Hakusensha

---

[f] And has attracted Hollywood interest, including by this author, as detailed in this book.

Even the incredible heroes of shōnen (boys') manga usually have a different emphasis than American superheroes, thus bringing them down to a certain level of identifiable reality, which creates a fresh attraction. Megahit *Bleach* (Tite Kubo, 82 million manga sold), which had a major studio development deal in Hollywood, is an example of characters that exhibit values found in Japanese society.

Ichigo, *Bleach*'s red-headed high school teen protagonist (see the tropes which describe him, "dumb is good" and "red oni/ blue oni," that his co-protagonist Rukia shares, in Chapter 7 and 8) is initially most concerned with protecting his family and friends when his home city is attacked by the same malevolent "hollows," or spirits that he discovers murdered his mother.

Figure 2.7 Ichigo, *Bleach*'s hero. BLEACH © 2001 by Tite Kubo/ SHUEISHA Inc.

Figure 2.8 The Japanese novel *All You Need Is Kill* was also made into a Hollywood movie and was adapted into a manga, with art by *Death Note* and *Bakuman*'s Takeshi Obata. ALL YOU NEED IS KILL © 2014 by Hiroshi Sakurazaka, Ryosuke Takeuchi, yoshitoshi ABe, Takeshi Obata/SHUEISHA Inc.

The producer who was attached to *Bleach*'s Hollywood live-action adaptation project, former Dreamworks executive Jason Hoffs, was also producer on the adaptation of a Japanese novel, *All You Need Is Kill* (*Edge of Tomorrow*, director: Doug Liman, Warner Brothers, 2014),[g] explains this different focus of many manga/anime heroes as follows,

> [O]ver the last decade, superhero movies have been very popular in the US. It seems like often the superhero starts as a regular person. He is battling his or her own demons, and over the course of the movie, the superhero has to decide—particularly if it's an origins story—whether to step up and become a hero with all of the obligations and sacrifice that that entails. Additionally, the hero is often more or less fighting on his own and sort of saving the world from a villain, which has been interesting on various projects to see the Japanese perspective on that specific idea. We've found that a lot of the times, if their characters have to shoulder a heroic responsibility, they're more likely to just try and take it on immediately out of a sense of duty. So all of the soul-searching "Am I up to this?" and "Is this the right thing to do?" that an American character might go through, the Japanese character might face certain challenges, but if there is a problem that they could possibly solve, their internal debate would not be extended as much or covered as much in the film, because they would feel a responsibility to just go do it and fight.[10]

Figure 2.9 Jason Hoffs, photo courtesy of VIZ Media.

Hoffs notes that there are often culturally-driven differences between the characters found in Hollywood animation/movies or American comics versus those found in Japanese manga and anime. This in turn creates somewhat different goals than would be found in a typical American superhero, more of a shading of difference than a total contrast—but significant—and if not noticed or glossed over, can lead to big trouble in an adaptation:

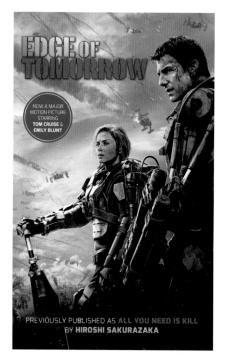

Figure 2.10 *All You Need Is Kill*

---

[g] Also, Hoffs is producer on the *Death Note* anime/manga live-action adaptation project (along with Roy Lee, Dan Lin and Masi Oka).

Jason Hoffs (cont'd):

Additionally, we've found that sometimes the Japanese character might fight for his or her family, friends, village, town, close social circle, more than facing kind of a greater, almost existential dilemma, to try to save the world, or planet, or democracy. It seems like the people that the Japanese hero is [sic] invested in seems more specific and it's about saving your family or your collective. These are not huge issues differences [sic], but they can be very significant and they only come up when you're having a very detailed discussion about how a specific character would respond to a certain situation. The Japanese might say, "Sure we like superhero movies" and stuff but this issue will only come up if they perceive that you are pursuing a kind of Americanization or superhero-ization of their character. They think that taking that direction would be causing the character to act in a way that would be fundamentally out of character with the Japanese. So again, the devil is in the details. I think that's one example of a kind of thematic difference in the cultures that can be reflected in a specific film project.[11]

Figure 2.11 ALL YOU NEED IS KILL © 2014 by Hiroshi Sakurazaka, Ryosuke Takeuchi, yoshitoshi ABe, Takeshi Obata/SHUEISHA Inc.

Figure 2.12 Michael Arias. Photograph by Sayuri Suzuki.

Without an in-depth understanding of these various manga and anime tropes, character-shadings based on Japanese culture, mythology and even foreign literary conventions, the Hollywood film and television adaptations are very likely to fail. This is echoed by Michael Arias, an anime director of the excellent *Tekkonkinkreet* (Studio 4°C, 2006) of American descent working in Japan's anime industry (a rarity) who was series producer for *The Animatrix* series.

As Arias explained,

> I think that Japanese animation is appreciated for different reasons outside of Japan than it is inside of Japan, and I think that's actually maybe a little less well understood. It can't be overstated. Japanese people have a very different way of looking at—and not saying this in a racist way—I just think that audiences here [in Japan], generalized, are a little more sophisticated when they look at animation just because by the time someone's an adult they've looked at so much comic book art and have seen so much animation that they can understand the visual language of animation and manga a little better. And I think that to a certain extent, folks overseas look at a lot of Japanese animation and they think it's cool looking, maybe, and there is definitely a different aesthetic at work. Especially the mecha [i.e. giant robot] designs. And the artwork has a distinctly alien look to it. I think that that's exciting to look at, but I also think that something in the process of doing an international co-production ends up boiling away a lot of that good stuff.[12]

That "something" is part of what this book seeks to identify.

I explained to Arias that part of the thesis of the book (as explained in the preface) was that the similarities between manga/anime and the Western forms of storytelling and filmmaking are akin to the fact that 95% of the DNA of mammals might be the same, but a kangaroo and cow are very different in that remaining percentage of genetic material. And it is by studying these differences that the major understanding of what makes each form "tick" is possible. Arias's response also alludes to the relationship back and forth across the Pacific that the American and Japanese creators have had with each other.

> **Arias:** I think the DNA metaphor is apropos, I think about it a lot actually, not just in animation but in filmmaking. I always feel that whatever I work on I exchange a little DNA with the people I work with, and if we work together again we're kind of a product of each other's creative impulses or influenced by each other. It's the same with any art form. It's the same with modern art. Picasso begot so and so begot so and so [sic]. They all admired each other from afar or preceded the guy who came next. If you look at the contents of the Museum of Modern Art, you look in there as an alien and you can see that the bear and the kangaroo are both furry and have two eyes, but it's quite difficult to classify them as biologists would in philo and species. That's maybe not a topic for someone who's in the process of making this stuff. It's like me trying to describe the difference there, or illuminate that, as a kangaroo or a bear to a human.

Tone—"We can work together (and overcome any obstacle)," and that is appealing to Hollywood

In my opinion, a charming aspect of many manga and anime is that characters often have a positive attitude that, in the words of a *Jump* editor, Hiroyuki Goto, projects the idea that if the characters work together and try hard enough, they can accomplish almost anything,

> Children know they're equal in terms of rights, but not ability. Out of ten children, perhaps one will excel in both sports and study, eight just want to do better in study or sports … They are the ones we're targeting, and the three words reflect their positive, optimistic outlook. At *Shonen Jump*, we don't believe in the aesthetics of defeat.[13]

I find it interesting that this "All American" ideal of the twentieth century is often more embedded in manga/anime than in current American scripted entertainment. There has been a refreshing lack of cynicism in much of the successful manga/anime.

Schodt's theory on this is also that "manga were merely reflecting a trend throughout Japan in the go-go economic years of the 1980's—a sort of virus that infected the whole society and still persists. 'Cheeriness' and terminal 'cutesy-ness' were 'in.' Cynicism, reflection, pessimism, introspection, seriousness, and anything 'heavy' or depressing all fell out of favor in films, novels, and intellectual life."[14]

More recently, the tables may have somewhat turned, and now American manga/anime fans may favor the innocent and pure manga/anime whereas many Japanese fans like darker material. This might be why I feel that most of the anime that come to be distributed in America are generally sunnier (though exceptions like *Death Note* and *Berserk* exist). Condry and I discussed this relative innocence of many American manga/anime fans, versus that of some Japanese ones,

> **Davis:** One of the things that really attracted me about anime and manga—at least originally—was the sincerity of it. They're not all the same, we know, and they don't fit the pattern all the time, but there is generally a more earnestness [sic] to it. My teenage daughter calls it a sweetness. When you're talking about them maybe influencing *Archer* and *Family Guy*, and getting onto Adult Swim, what those shows display is a cynicism. It's an American thing.
>
> **Condry:** One of the interesting interviews I had—and it didn't even make it into the book—was with Watanabe [Shinichirō, the anime director], who did *Cowboy Bebop* and *Samurai Champloo*, and I asked him what the difference was between these otaku and overseas otaku. And he said that the otaku in Japan are kind of twisted, scary people who have issues. American otaku tend to be very cute and pure.
>
> **Davis:** Isn't that funny?
>
> **Condry:** I thought that that was a very interesting point. I felt that too, going to anime conventions in the US versus going to them in Akihabara [the famous high tech area of Tokyo where otaku congregate].[15]

This is another example of the ping-ponging of values back and forth across the Pacific, leading to artistic configurations and observations about cultures that are very enlightening.

None of these cultural differences can be simplified into generalizations. The truism that "the devil is in the details" definitely applies here. Again, it gets down to studying that 5% difference in the "DNA" of each form and that each retain that 95% similarity, and within the 5%, carefully parsing which elements to keep and which are not appropriate. After all, a big attraction to manga and anime is its "otherness" (the 5%) and it is important to keep in mind that this small difference between the cultures has to be understood when adapting from Japan's narrative media work to other cultures. We will explore the otherness more.

It is exactly the thing that those of us who are not Japanese find interesting about manga/anime, their "otherness" and "alien-ness", that in adapting the work, we often remove as we seek to make the work more "universally acceptable" to a non-Japanese audiences. Thus, we "kill the goose that laid the golden egg" and destroy what we loved about the work, because we did not understand what it was that was attracting us to it. By making what were once the specific "differences" into a general "sameness" of other more familiar works, we lose what was special. As Michael Arias said later in the book, even location can be very important (many fans of the original anime/manga *Akira* were perturbed when press reports announced the American adaptation would be set in New York as they felt the Japanese setting was critical to the story—for more information on this, see the box below).

Casting and location—an important part of manga/anime adaptations

Ken Tsumura, a producer on the *Astro Boy* adaptation (director: David Bowers, Summit, 2009) elaborates on this as he talked to me about the fact that the Hollywood *Akira* remake project needed the original's Tokyo setting to make the story work.

Tsumura: What you hear on the Asian side is that "How can you make *Akira* with a bunch of white people in futuristic Tokyo, right?" I would defend it by saying that maybe it's not Tokyo anymore, right? I think its weird—how can you not have Japanese people in a Tokyo type of thing. That's the bad taste that the Asian market sees in how Hollywood converts these movies, and I think they [Hollywood studios] need to be more sensitive in how they make these announcements and stuff. Like when they hear that DiCaprio [Leonardo, the actor who was attached to the aborted *Akira* film adaptation] is involved, and they make an announcement that shooting has started on *Speed Racer*, or whatever, right? Or let's use *Akira*. The first thing they think is "How are they going to make this with all these famous Hollywood stars?" because they [the Japanese/Asian fans of the original manga/anime] know the original story. That is what Hollywood needs to be more careful of if they want to preserve the Asian market, which can be very big for these films. Hollywood is still very North American-centric, and it's true to a certain extent.[h] If

---

[h] However, Universal Pictures, well after this interview occurred, cast a top Bollywood (the Indian film industry) star, Irrfan Khan, in a large role in *Jurassic World*, which grossed an all-time box office record of $511 million in its first weekend (June 2015).

it does well in North America then it does well worldwide, but for some of these Japanese license products, they need to keep one eye and one ear to the Asian market.

Davis: Do you feel that Asians would accept a mixed cast?

Tsumura: It's really hard. As you know, the Asian market vs. North American or Europe is very different. What it comes down to is, in my opinion, it doesn't have to be an all-Asian cast. I worked at Disney for a couple of years, and the market has an impression that Disney is very white-bread, and they are, right? But it's the balance of trying to make it palatable for all audiences, which is a hard trick. Here's a good example, like Disney airs the series *Modern Family* on ABC, and that's a great example of what is very mixed, right? And that's what audiences want in America now. Like the movie *Up!*, right? Just by having the Cub Scout guy being Asian actually brought in more Asian people to watch the movie, and that only happened because the character designer at Pixar is Asian! So he made the old man's sidekick in *Up!* Asian. That was a good thing for Disney ultimately. Disney's direction is right. People [of all different backgrounds] don't want to see [a movie] with [for example] all African-Americans—basically you'll just get an African-American audience. To want a broad audience, you want a mix. That's what most rational people are looking for. I think that needs to be taken into consideration, and that even needs to be taken into consideration when you're making these Japanese properties.[16]

To avoid that mistake in manga/anime that has strong Japanese characteristics, including possibly casting and location (although I feel that some like *Speed Racer* and *Cowboy Bebop* are stateless—a concept, as I noted, coined by manga/anime scholar Susan Napier),[17] we must first understand the "goose."

Decompressed action sequences, thematics

Robert Napton, in having worked for the Japanese anime distributor Bandai Entertainment and as a graphic novel writer before joining Legendary Comics, closely observed the differences in manga/anime and American comics:

Napton: The art style and the aesthetic is very unique. It's a very interesting visual language that anime uses. It's borrowed heavily from Western cinema. There is a lot of trading back and forth between Western filmmaking and anime, and the history of anime. But it has a very distinct visual style, which is very appealing, so I think those two elements are what drew me to it.

Davis: You're right on the book's topic talking about cinematic style borrowed from American film that manga/anime are using. Can you give some examples?

Napton: Fred Schodt, who is kind of the grandfather of talking about manga in the US, who was also good friends with Osama Tezuka. He could speak better to the point. I know Tezuka always said that there was a heavy Western influence in his manga works, and I think that influence is a deliberate decompression—it's a comic book term. The example I'll give you is in *Superman*. In the old days in a comic you'd have four, five, six, or seven panels, kind of like, Clark Kent goes into the phone booth, the next shot is he takes off his glasses, the next shot is he rips open his shirt, the next shot is a close-up of his chest and you see the *Superman* logo. It's a very deliberate type of storytelling, but in manga, always, going back to Tezuka and the history of manga, and this also translated into the anime, you have more cinematic style. You have a thoughtful construction and a more thematic style of storytelling. For example, in a manga you can have the characters walking and he's about to transform to fly away the way Superman would, but in the Japanese comic or anime, instead of focusing on him flying away and being very literal, maybe you focus on a leaf and the wind is blowing because he's taken off. So you see the leaf goes fluttering in the air and it's very poetic and cinematic. That's more the style of manga and anime. I don't think it's a question of one being better than the other, but I think that American comics from the 30s, 40s, 50s, and 60s were a little more deliberate type of storytelling. It was just spoon-feeding, and I think that American comics have been influenced by manga now so you have more of that poetic feel in comics. I think in part that is because of manga. That's something very unique to manga, and I think it's because a lot of the manga artists were influenced by Western filmmakers and back and forth.[18]

Napton introduces a pretty significant term here—"deliberate decompression."

Deliberate decompression: Including time and spatial deformation

To give an example of traits peculiar to manga/anime that are inherent in their appeal but if not understood may lead to an adaptation disaster, Miyazaki-sensei (director of the anime feature *Spirited Away*)[i] remarked[j] on one characteristic of much manga that can make them difficult to adapt into live-action outside of Japan,

> Another hallmark of manga is that an almost unlimited deformation is possible. To give a somewhat dated example, in *Kyojin no Hoshi* (*Star of the Giants*) [a baseball manga], an entire episode concludes while the character Hyuma is throwing a pitch. Everything about life is encapsulated in that one pitch, and the artist develops a whirl of recollections in the time it takes the ball to travel. It's hard to imagine anyone other than Japanese pulling off something like this.

---

[i] Also, *Kiki's Delivery Service*, *Ponyo*, and *My Neighbor Totoro* and other works.
[j] From one of a series of interviews in the excellent two volume set encompassing Miyazaki's interviews and writings. "Miyazaki: Starting Point 1979–1996" and "Miyazaki: Turning Point 1997–2008" translated by Beth Cary and Frederik L. Schodt, published by VIZ Media.

Miyazaki went on to explain that these temporal and spatial deformations are a natural part of Japanese storytelling style since early times: "Of course infinite deformation of time and space is something that we Japanese didn't start doing with manga; it's just something we like to do. It's obvious if you listen to traditional *kodan* storytelling."[19]

After describing a famous scene from a kodan story and showing how it mirrors anime timing, Miyazaki observed, "It's because kodan stories use almost limitless distortion of time. By twisting both time and space, it becomes possible to create a more fantastic, magical world. It's one of the hallmarks of Japanese entertainment, and in manga—especially boy's manga—it also seems to me that is allows depictions of abstract human drive and tenacity to actually exceed those of real physical powers."[20]

Miyazaki concludes that this manga-centric trait of achieving physically impossible things through drive and tenacity is based on Japanese storytelling culture,

> This trend didn't start with manga; ninja used mizugumo or "water spiders"—circular pods that allowed them to walk on water—but of course Europeans would never believe this sort of thing. They'd say it violated the principles of Archimedes or some such thing. Japanese, on the other hand, tend to believe, that if we work really hard at it, we'll be able to walk on water [laughter]. It's something we Japanese just have in our blood. We like this sort of stuff. So when we obtained the techniques for making animation, and the medium of manga, you suddenly saw a huge amount of this sort of thing. It's just an extension of what we had in the old days, the kodan stories and in the fantasies about ninja.[21]

Visual effects designer John Gaeta pioneered with Lana and Andy Wachowski and the rest of their team the breakthrough techniques of the manga-and-anime-influenced *Matrix* trilogy and *Speed Racer* films. Here, Gaeta talked to me about this process of intensely studying the manga/anime originals when adapting to live-action or the hybrid forms those films represent. Gaeta, now Creative Director at Lucasfilms developing future *Star Wars* experiences, began his career learning from *2001: A Space Odyssey* and *Blade Runner* legendary special effects maestro Douglas Trumbull. He confirmed the phenomenon described in part by Miyazaki when he commented to me about this "time deformation":

> **Gaeta:** You can especially see this in any kind of complex choreography, particularly with performances in motion or fighting characters, right? Or, in *Akira*, riding bikes at breathtaking speeds through the city, or acts of supernatural phenomenon and things like that: heavy emphasis on physically based moments like radical changes in direction and dramatic pace. The pace of things varied exquisitely for maximum artistic impact—it's those types of emotional-temporal qualities that draw the audiences [in]. For us, we literally studied that stuff, we would look at how characters moved, how they were composed and juxtaposed in a singular shot and over time. How they flowed through action frame by frame; we would look at exactly how many frames it took to construct all different types of expressive moments for impact. It was more about how it made you feel, not what was real.[22]

When I asked Gaeta if they were aiming for the manga/anime style of examining a scene from many angles with the *Matrix* camera rig, he replied, "Yes absolutely … but remember we were aiming at an anime influenced movie about virtual reality. In the prior years, anime

Figure 2.13 The camera rig for *The Matrix* that replicated the anime/manga style of examining a scene from many angles and decompressing time also allowed characters to fly, in sync with anime/manga fighting styles where characters jump high and grapple mid-air.[k]

masters were experimenting with detaching the time and space of characters to the time and space of their surroundings for various reasons. So there were inspirations there that helped with the intellectual premise we wanted to get across. Only in a VR can time and space be hacked and detached from me. The 'rig' was a way to hack the look without having a true 'virtual' camera. It produced a visual trick. On the sequels, we attempted to actually make a true 'virtual' camera. Today, VR and immersive cinema is building toward this freedom. So, an anime conceptual vision helped lead toward a manifestation of the same concept."[123]

They look like us (whether the reader/audience is Asian or not) and why this is important to Hollywood

If you are Asian, you are probably already familiar with manga and anime because their penetration has been so widespread in Asia for so long, even in the People's Republic of China, despite the fact that the governments of China and Japan have had many major disagreements. When I was invited to two universities in Beijing to lecture about my manga classes and the wemakemanga.com site and research, I asked the students how many of them read manga. Nearly all the hands went up (most were *One Piece* fans).

---

[k] From the making of the *Matrix* documentary.
[l] See more from Gaeta in the *Speed Racer* Hollywood adaptation case study in Chapter 8.

Figure 2.14 The author in Beijing lecturing about manga.

But manga is very attractive to people outside of Asia, too. Why?

Napton touched on a big advantage of the physical characteristics of manga and anime characters, namely that their faces and hair generally appear non-Asian, which makes it easier for Westerners to identify with them. This familiarity helps boost overseas sales and attract Hollywood writers, directors, and producers.

> **Napton:** In the 80s this was very common—people would say [about manga and anime characters], "What do you mean it's Japanese? They don't look Japanese. They look Caucasian. They have blonde hair. They're white." That's something that's very interesting in the development of manga and anime, because when you talk about the classic animes like *Space Battle Ship Yamato*[m] or *Gundam*, the characters look international. They don't look "Asian." So I think that's something that's always been part of anime and manga in Japan. It's an aesthetic choice that became the norm. Because of that, there is a broad appeal for manga and anime outside of Japan because anyone can look at the characters and relate to them, and that's something that I'm probably not as qualified to explain why that choice was made in Japan at the time. Why Tezuka and the founders of manga and anime made that choice. Fred Schodt and guys like that would probably understand that better.[24]

---

[m] Later, Napton discusses the anime's renaming into *Star Blazers* in the USA due to its namesake being a famous World War II Japanese warship.

Schodt explains why this aesthetic choice is common in manga and anime: "When most foreigners look at manga for the first time today and see characters with huge saucer eyes, lanky legs and what appears to be blonde hair, they often want to know why there are so many 'Caucasian' people in the stories. When told that most of the characters are not 'Caucasians' but 'Japanese,' they are flabbergasted."[25] He adds that,

> Since most Japanese comics are drawn in black and white, artists have generally differentiated between Japanese characters by shading the hair of some and not of others. To foreigners, this has the effect of making some Japanese look blonde. Fans know better of course; they know the hair is really meant to be black, even when rendered in white. This Westernized or international depiction of Japanese characters has also provided the manga and anime industries with a distinct export advantage by making it easier for them to win acceptance in the United States and Europe. Many young American fans of Japanese TV shows such as *Astro Boy* in the sixties or *Robotech* in the eighties never even realized that some of their favorite characters were actually Japanese. Evolution of body shapes into leggy supermodel, and hair color choices confuse Westerners, making them think that the hair is blonde.[26]

The famous manga/anime rounded eyes further the non-Asian appeal, as do some manga characters on color covers or color pages with blonde, blue, pink, or other colored hair.[27] We will learn additional facts about Tezuka's innovations that produced that saucer-eyed style in pages to come.

It wasn't always this way ... Asian-looking faces originally proliferated in manga, but Western styles intervened

As we will see later, the early Tezuka-period character-drawing style, which came from Hollywood animation and movies, had a more early Disney-like rounded look which often did not resemble Western body proportions and was more in sync with Disney's cute animals. In fact, I had a hard time trying (and ultimately failing) to convince a Hollywood producer to adapt *Barefoot Gen*, the atomic bombing of Hiroshima manga, into a live-action production because, from the producer's point of view, the Disney-esque rounded style did not fit the dire subject matter. He thus felt that his experience reading it was being undercut by the cartoony images.

Schodt notes that pre-World War II, Japanese portrayed themselves in images "with small eyes and variable proportions" and Europeans as giant and hairy with huge noses.[28] But the American Navy Commodore Perry's arrival with steamships in Tokyo's harbor forced an isolated Japan to open up to outsiders, and then "catch up" with the foreigners' technology, forms of administration, and even art and entertainment. In doing so, the Japanese switched to the Western standard of drawing bodies at approximately an eight head-tall physique (in other words, a drawing in which a human's height equals eight or eight and a half heads).

Figure 2.15 A Japanese woodblock print of the tough negotiator American Commodore Mathew Perry, who in 1853 sailed into Tokyo's harbor and was able to threaten and get almost all his demands from the Japanese authorities at the time. The arrival of Perry's famous navy "black ships" (a term that signified the threat to the Japanese from foreign technology and military power) formed a tangential plot in the manga series *Rurouni Kenshin*. Note the big nose. Artist: Roko. Date created: 1854. Chadbourne Collection of Japanese prints. United States Library of Congress Prints and Photographs Division.

Figure 2.16 The writing on the back cover of *Rurouni Kenshin* manga volume 1 depicts the coming of the Commodore Perry American "Black Ships" era setting of the manga.[n] RUROUNI KENSHIN © 1994 by Nobuhiro Watsuki/SHUEISHA Inc

Japan's defeat in World War II caused a loss of self-confidence, and manga took the lead in adapting Western ideals of beauty, perhaps due to a "grass is greener on the other side" attitude towards other successful cultures. This Japanese cultural characteristic dated from as far back as the Heian period (AD 794 to 1185) when Japanese admiration for Buddhism, Taomism, and Korean influences peaked.

---

[n] Perry and his black ships also appear in a humor-packed textbook-like manga that encompasses 300 years of Japanese history in over 30 volumes.

Tezuka drew the wildly popular "shōjo" which is the woman/girl's genre of manga and anime, focusing on emotions and relationships (often affairs of the heart and often with its own abstract symbols and style) in the early years of that form and exaggerated his already saucer-sized eyes for those publications. Astro Boy was originally designed as a beautiful female android. But Tezuka declared in a 1978 interview that he landed a contract with a boy's magazine, and so modified the character into a male. But the long eyelashes and soft skin remained feminine. This "hint of bisexuality," as Schodt terms it, might also have come from Tezuka's mother having taken the boy to the famous all-female Takarazuka Revue in their home town of Takarazuka (near Osaka).[29] Schodt likens the boy Tezuka living near the Revue to living next door to Disneyland. Tezuka writes that, as a boy, the exotic spectacle of Parisian, Manahattan, and Broadway musicals—however second rate that they may have been in reality—made him ecstatic. The male and female roles were all played by actresses, their eyes dolled up with mascara so as to appear huge as they reflected the footlights, a trait that Tezuka later infused manga/anime with—giant window-pane shōjo eyes (for emanating emotion, as the eyes are the windows to the soul). And these characteristics flowed into shōjo,[30] beginning with Tezuka's *Princess Knight* character—the first big shōjo hit about a princess pretending to be a knight so her father's kingdom could be safe. This style was expanded upon by the female mangaka who took over the shōjo field from the men. And soon shōjo male figures became even more lanky and "Western." A few

Figure 2.17 Akihabara "Maids" in Tokyo. © Ricardo G. Willems. Akihabara (also called "Akiba" after a local shrine) is the electronics district and otaku center of Tokyo and Japan.

years ago National Geographic channel's *Taboo* series featured an attempt to find young Japanese men to work in a "maid café" (a fantasy-based café where attractive females in high heels and frilly dresses serve customers tea and sweets) in Tokyo.

At issue was whether it would be possible to find any with the right physiques or attitude—and a long-time male customer of the maid café was the only one out of over 100 applicants chosen. In the documentary, a female maid café customer admitted being attracted to the selected job applicant, despite, or perhaps because, of his dress (with her jokingly describing herself as his stalker and saying that he, who said he is heterosexual, looks great in a dress). This acting in

Figure 2.18 My student Louise Wang's comedic manga *Fujo Club* has a gender-bending theme.

different genders in the manga/anime universe and fandom doesn't carry the same stigma as it would in the real-life societies of some other nations, and perhaps dates back to the period of samurai [pre-industrial Japan] and their youthful male charges sometimes being in sexual relationships.[31] Kabuki, Japan's famous style of theater, which may have some impact on the posing of manga characters, also went through gender-bending changes. Kabuki originally featured actresses until their erotic performances were considered a threat to public morality by government officials, especially when they began serving as prostitutes on the side. So the authorities demanded that Kabuki actors be only men to counter that trend,[o] but the pretty young men chosen to replace them then did the same, and, by some accounts, were wildly pursued by audience members for prostitution, just as much as the women previously were. Finally it was ordered that the roles were to be played only by older men (who, it was correctly assumed, could not pull off such a hat trick of becoming prostitutes). And, so as to make sure, the older men were ordered to wear their hair style in a front-shaven manner making them less attractive.[32]

It should be noted that the more narrow-eyed, harder-edged *gekiga* style that developed later partially as a reaction against Tezuka's "cute" and emotionally warmer style as well as certain later women's manga (like some josei, which is an adult woman genre) have

---

[o] Women were banned as Kabuki actresses by Togugawa era officials in 1629, when male performers took over, and the men have been impersonating the female characters ever since.

readopted the more Asian look. Considering the multi-cultural and growing Asian population of America, this feature is also not as alienating to Hollywood, which continues to cast more non-Caucasian actors in its productions, as compared to previously.

Figure 2.19 Japan's defeat in World War II,ᵖ which *Barefoot Gen* depicts as the dropping of the atom bomb on Hiroshima and its aftermath—where Keiji Nakazawa, its mangaka, was a six-year-old boy—not only caused a loss of its confidence, but, correspondingly, a pursuit of the victor America's "ideals of beauty."[33]
© Keiji Nakazawa and Last Gasp (USA publisher)

ᵖThe Allied forces consisted of the United States, United Kingdom, France, the Soviet Union, China, Australia, and other countries, but defeated Japan's occupying army was mostly American. Approximately 2,620,000–3,120,000 Japanese people died as a result of World War II, out of an estimated 60–80 million deaths worldwide. The United States had approximately 420,000 war-related fatalities; France 550,000; the Soviet Union between 21,800,000 and 28,000,000; China 10,000,000–20,000,000; and Germany 5,500,000–6,900,000.

Figure 2.20 Tezuka's "star system" and use of screen tones. © Tezuka Productions

Many other visual conventions used by manga and anime are distinctive and attractive to non-Japanese and thus make the works desirable (usually without the reason being understood) for adaptation into Hollywood projects or to bring over as localized shows, such as:

An extensive set of screen tones and background detail that draw the audience into the image

Figures 2.20, 2.22 and 2.23 illustrate manga's often-extensive use of screen tones (background detailing, cross-hatching, patterns, etc.), for the buildings and the sky, which Tezuka uses to visually engage the reader. Originally, screen tones were strips applied to the paper (often by assistants).

In the Tezuka city image, the screen tones serve to pull us into the frame rather than making us passive observers—a key goal/method/technique of manga. As *Death Note*'s (an enormously popular manga[q] featuring an amoral Japanese death god named Ryuk whose appearance is inspired by the design of *Edward Scissorhands*—see Chapter 6) artist Takeshi Obata explains, "I do all the inking of the characters, even those without names, before my assistants come. Before my assistants come I try to have as many pages inked so that they can add the backgrounds. Once they arrive, I give them the pages with the most backgrounds first. So that their first day of work each week is the toughest … after that we try to go in page order."[r34]

Golgo 13's mangaka Saito performs all the page layouts based on a script prepared by his publisher's editorial department, as well as inking the faces of the main characters. His assistants draw the backgrounds and other elements.

Screen tones are a big part of backgrounds in manga

These days screen tones are often applied by the mangaka onto the page by use of computers … there are free screen tones available for the various computer programs my students use (if they wish to—some work entirely by hand, others start on paper, scan that in, manipulate the image with software and add layers using our Wacom drawing tablets). My students, when they work digital, tend to use Adobe Photoshop, Adobe Illustrator, Easy Paint Tool SAI, Firealpaca, GIMP, Paint.net and Manga Studio EX edition (the latter is exclusively a manga-creating program). Photoshop is raster based, which has its advantages in manga production, but Adobe Illustrator, which is vector based, is better with curves, as is Easy Paint Tool SAI. Illustrator also scales indefinitely in size. When visiting at Osaka Arts University in 2015, I was interested to see professors having their students use some of these programs in a similar way. Examples of electronic produced screen tones below are from one of my student's manga, *Doughnut Cop* (Akeem Roberts).

---

[q]It also spawned a critically acclaimed international hit anime, three Japanese live-action movies, two novels and a musical.
[r] From *DEATH NOTE HOW TO READ* 13 © 2006, by Tsugumi Ohba, Takeshi Obata/SHUEISHA Inc. Reprinted with permission from VIZ Media.

Figure 2.21 *Doughnut Cop*'s cover page.

Figure 2.22 Hand-drawn cross-hatchings in the background of the young man on the title page.

Figure 2.23 Computer generated screen tones on "boxing-Satan"'s body and on the doughnut's sunglasses. Several examples of my students' manga work appear in this chapter about what makes manga attractive to Hollywood (in addition to this book's over 200 top Japanese and American images). I concentrated this smaller total selection of my students' manga images most heavily in the latter part of this chapter and to a lesser extent in the final chapter (11) because these young, still-developing creators' works reflect the influence of both Japanese manga/anime and Hollywood and thus are hybrid forms that the book talks about increasing in the future. Second, because of my familiarity with my student works, having been developed in my class, they efficiently serve the dual purpose of exhibiting the type of manga characteristics that Hollywood finds attractive. Third, Hollywood is now interested in these sources—Universal Pictures produced the highly rated *Scott Pilgrim* vs. *The World* (director: Edgar Wright, 2010) from the same titled American manga/graphic novel hybrid.

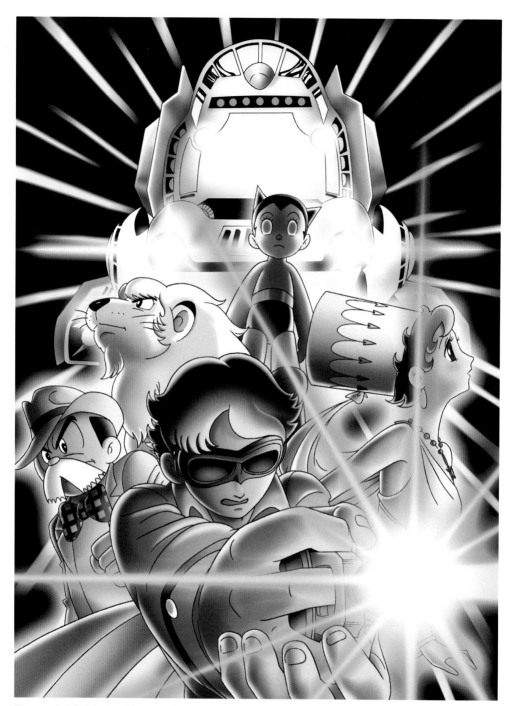

Figure 2.24 *Marine Express* featured characters from other Tezuka series, including *Astro Boy* and Mister Mustachio (English name for the character).
© Tezuka Productions

Figures 2.20 and 2.24 contain some of Tezuka's biggest "stars" and are examples of his "star system," which is based upon the classic "golden age" Hollywood star system, in which studios owned the contracts of major actors who would assume various roles in that studio's productions (usually exclusively, unless the studio allowed otherwise). These actors' appearances and characters would sometimes be modified somewhat by Tezuka from series to series, but stayed mostly within their original personality, thus remaining consistent across roles in different titles that had no story connection.

Tezuka's "star system" is somewhat similar to today's "first-look deals," (also called "overall-deals" and "housekeeping-deals") that Hollywood movie and TV studios give give major directors and stars in which the operating costs of their offices on the studio lot are paid for in exchange for the studio having first look at their projects for possible production. But the system was more binding back in the Hollywood golden era when only the studio owners were able to let a star out of his/her commitment to a studio to make a movie at another studio. Mirroring some Hollywood stars with very identifiable screen personas that they carried from role to role, Tezuka put the same characters in different manga series. As a screenwriter myself, I suspect that Tezuka knew that creating a good character takes significant time (in fact, because manga is a character-driven medium, mangaka sometimes take months to develop a character and meet with the editor to discuss and refine the character and story). He was so prolific that to keep making new characters would have slowed his productivity significantly. So he would recast them in different works (Tezuka even created a chart showing his star system and ranking his characters according to popularity—see below).

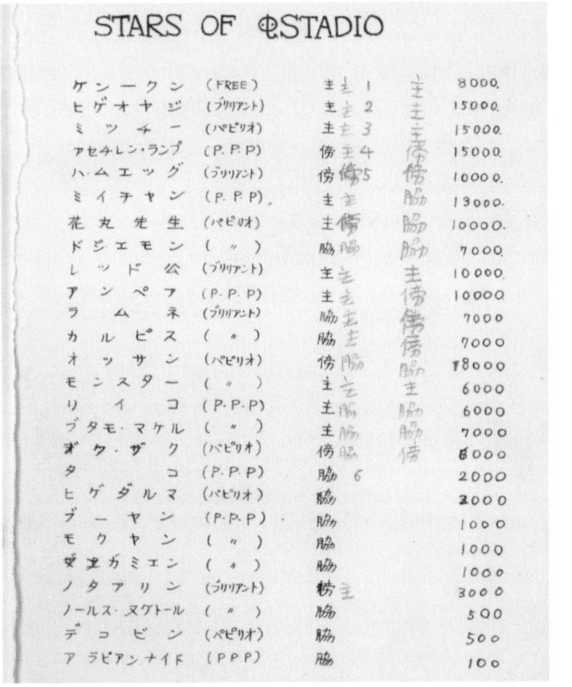

Figure 2.25 Chart reads "Stars of Mushi (虫) Studio" and lists characters that often appeared in several different Tezuka stories, such as Lamune (ラムネ), Kalpis (カルピス), and Dr. Hanamaru (花丸先生) (see Chapter 4 for descriptions of these characters and some of their Hollywood origins). Translation: Austa Joye. © Tezuka Productions

Why do mangaka need assistants?

Mangaka have to publish so many pages every week in a serialized manga in order for the stories to be long enough to incite (or inspire) deep character identification among the readers, in the same way a serialized TV show has enough air time to meet the same objective. This requires that the pages are read fast and created quickly to meet the higher quota of pages, especially when many monthlies moved to weeklies. This had a domino effect:

- The small factory-like set-up with assistants under direction of the mangaka that was developed by Tezuka to create enough pages under the enormous demand of the weekly magazines is a key difference between the American comic and Japanese manga production system.
- It also created specialization. So while one assistant might just do screen tones, another draws a particular character. Tezuka and his assistants would churn out 300 pages a month[35] (for a jaw dropping 150,000-page lifetime total)[s36] and a mangaka and ten assistants can create up to 400 to 500 pages a month[37]—and all with the mangaka still being, in reality, a creator.
- The weekly production schedule caused such a volume of pages[t] to accrue that they quickly became compiled into graphic novel volumes, which were sold separately (and in recent years to readers worldwide).

There is another reason, having to do with living space, as to why the system of production developed. In Japan, where there is a premium on space due to constricted living environments, the compilation magazines are thrown away after being read (often after being passed around first). These graphic novels can run to 300 pages or more, which, as Schodt notes, allows them to vary pacing and camera angles and to experiment. Each page is designed to be read in 3.75 seconds.[38] *Lone Wolf and Cub* (which was a movie adaptation deal in Hollywood that director Darren Aronofsky—*The Fountain*, *The Wrestler*, and *Pi*—was involved in developing at one point)[u] is over 8,000 pages long—its sword fights can last for dozens of pages. Thus the decompression that Napton and Miyazaki referred to.

Hence Schodt's observation that a group of manga artists boasted of the superiority of their artwork. But then they met a group of American comic artists, who far exceeded the

---

[s] Other estimates have ranged as high as 200,000 for his lifetime manga pages. According to Tezuka Productions, Tezuka and his team also created 21 television animated series, 12 TV animated specials, 17 theatrical animated movies, 8 original animation videos, and much more.

[t] As noted earlier, the grueling number of pages, year in and year out that mangaka have to deliver under intense time pressure is a large part of what defines a mangaka. And that to call oneself a mangaka, one has to be experienced working professionally at that volume, which even has health risks. Shōjo mangaka may have less pages, sometimes eight a week, but even then, they are outstripping most non-Japanese comic creators (except maybe syndicated newspaper comic strips), and still have to make time for story, character development and creating their rough thumbnail sketches during that week.

[u] To date, it has not been produced as a Hollywood movie, though several Japanese live-action films were made from the series, including the classic *Baby Carriage at the River Stix*.

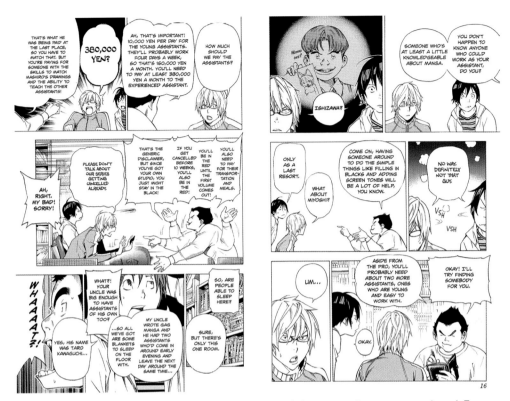

Figure 2.26 Assistants are expensive in Tokyo and the mangaka must pay them! From *Bakuman*, a wonderful "youth obtaining their dreams" manga about two high school mangaka with a meteoric career at a top manga publisher, Shueisha, created by the *Death Note* mangaka Obata and Ohba.
BAKUMAN. © 2008 by Tsugumi Ohba, Takeshi Obata/SHUEISHA Inc

mangaka's draftsmanship. The Japanese then sheepishly conceded that these Americans were superior in that respect.[39] But this does not matter because manga are meant to be read very quickly and the "assistant" system allows enough pages to be turned out that contain a visual layout not overstuffed with dialogue and lack the constant hyper-detailed background renderings that characterize many American comics. The faster that manga pages can be read (and created), the more story and, more importantly, character development (and thus empathy) can be injected in. Well-developed characters engage us and have wants and needs and weaknesses that we can empathize with, and those goals/needs then drive the characters forward, into the inevitable opposition created by other driven characters with clashing goals. Hence, conflict, empathy, and thus drama! The massively long narratives of serialized, long-running series offer the opportunity for mangaka to create many well-developed characters, which increases the likelihood that at least a few characters will resonate with almost any age or gender. These serialized stories are also naturals for adaptation into live-action television and movies series, as we will explore in greater depth shortly.

So, in terms of draftsmanship, it is all about telling the story, not about showy art (though many manga have plenty of that, as we will discuss). As Schodt puts it so well,

Figure 2.27 A notable exception: *Berserk*'s creator Miura is known for his exquisitely detailed pages. Here main chararacter Guts and his travelling companion, an apprentice witch, speak with the mysterious Skull Knight. © Kentaro Miura/Hakusensha

The cinematic style also allows manga to be far more iconographic than comics in America. Individual illustrations don't have to be particularly well executed as long as they fulfill their basic role of conveying enough information to maintain the flow of the story. And why should they be? A young American or European fan of comics may spend minutes admiring the artwork on each page of his or her favorite comic, but not as much in the case of the Japanese manga fan.[40]

Though it should be noted that mangaka, when skilled, can also pack their panels with *more* information than American comics. *Battle Angel Alita*'s mangaka Kishiro *Berserk*'s Miura dazzle with the details they pack into so many of their panels.

Battle Angel Alita has many panels that are drawn quickly and others that are marvelously detailed. The normal method is to produce enough of these more highly rendered pages to pull the reader into the environment, but then, once the "scene has been established," execute many other pages—for example, featuring talking and other actions—in a less fully rendered manner).

In summary, these story methods, along with an enormous number of tropes developed over time, help make manga/anime intoxicating and immersive to readers and audiences worldwide. The goal of manga is to get the readership to "experience" rather than "watch" a story unfold. Because serialization allows the development of deep-level stories, intense and often conflicted/complicated emotions stemming from the characters have time to develop. Emotional fireworks and often explosive action result—all attractive to the masses and thus Hollywood.

Manga have many other critical visual innovations, and these tie into emotionally engaging storytelling

Scott McCloud, a major figure of Western comics scholarship, lists some key elements of manga in the chapter "Making Manga" in his classic book, *Making Comics*. These elements include:

- "A strong sense of place,"[41] as previously discussed, including small real-world details. For instance, a person's hand might hold a steaming cup of tea as two women talk, or a wedding singer puts her hand on a microphone, pulling the reader into the scene.

Figure 2.28 I am repeating this image of *Wedding Singer* because it demonstrates the "everyday-life" stories that manga/anime often portray.

Figure 2.29 And even space creatures joking around can be portrayed as "another day in an ordinary life," so typical of manga (before their world gets ripped apart in the ensuing alien attack), in my student Paul Choate's *Project Alpha*.

Figure 2.30 *Project Alpha's* everyday life—bored aliens suiting up.

Figure 2.31 This "sense of place" that McCloud refers to can be of the exotic—such as the above *Warriors Risen* by my students Vivian Aultman and George Teague (unless you are Chinese).

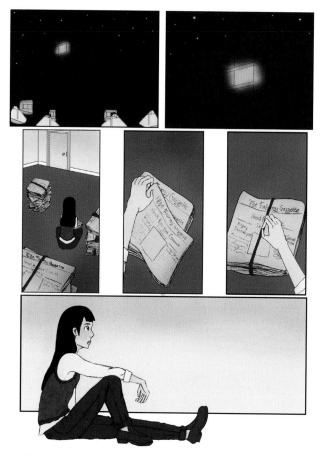

Figure 2.32 Or the "very ordinary," by my students, artist Julia Upchurch and writer Vincent Smith, in *Lulu* (above).

McCloud also defines manga characteristics of:

- "Iconic characters with simple emotive faces creating strong reader identification."[42]
- "A broad variety of character designs featuring wildly different face and body types and frequent use of recurring body archetypes"[43]

My students experiment extensively with body types in their manga. Marlowe Leverette's manga *Motherbot Connection*, below left, and Jonathan Inkley's (artist) and Andre Clemon's (writer) *Boy with the Violet Eyes*, below right, demonstrates this. And both also use different production techniques for their hybrid manga, in this case, ink and digital coloring and acrylic paints and ink.

Figure 2.33 *Motherbot Connection.*   **Figure 2.34** *Boy with the Violet Eyes.*

All-time hit manga/anime franchise *One Piece* constantly stretches the human figure into unrealistic shapes. Its protagonist Lufy has eaten the magic "gum gum" fruit, and this gives him great powers including the ability to stretch his body in extreme ways, though he also possesses a typical Achilles heel of so many manga characters, in this case, he sinks like a stone if he falls in the ocean—definitely a liability for a seafaring pirate! Other *One Piece* characters' bodies are extremely pliable in the hands of mangaka Eiichiro Oda, as these covers depict.

During the designing of the test page of my manga (adapted from my screenplay), a discussion erupted about the size of the main character's breasts. A female colleague said they were too big and thus overly sexualized the character, while an American comic/graphic novel industry veteran argued that

Figure 2.35 ONE PIECE
© 1997 by Eiichiro Oda/SHUEISHA Inc

comic artists like to draw big breasts, and so what? This is pretty common in Japan too (however, often for comedy's sake), but the bottom line is that these shapely female characters are almost a constant in traditional American comics, where the males and females usually look as if they stepped out of the gym or a bodybuilding contest. Since few of us look this way in regular life, it is not exactly a good way to build reader identification, and the super busty females can repel women readers.[v]

As previously mentioned, since 1983, when *Manga! Manga! The World of Japanese Comics* was first published (and later *Dreamland Japan*), there have been significant changes in both the American comics industry and the Japanese manga industry. This book attempts to update some of the information from these books, and build on it as well, to give a current view to build a basis for exploring the manga/

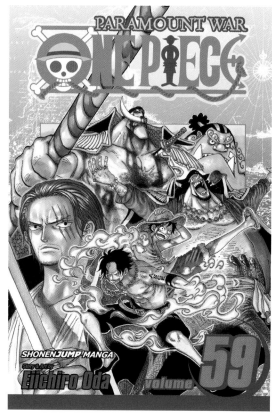

Figure 2.36 ONE PIECE
© 1997 by Eiichiro Oda/SHUEISHA Inc

anime–Hollywood relationship. One thing that has changed is that American graphic novels have come into the fore relative to DC and Marvel's often classic lantern-jawed heroes and buxom heroines with more diversity than the American comics industry had when Schodt wrote those books.[w] A large part of the emergence of graphic novels in America has been from the manga influence (see below regarding Frank Miller's importing manga's style, etc.).[x]

---

[v] As a side note, since Hollywood has based so many blockbusters on Marvel and DC superhero comics, the male actors in those movies have to now undergo staggering physical regimens to sculpt their bodies into an otherwise impossibly muscled form. Nutritionists and physical trainers supervise the actors, making sure that they are filmed on the exact days of the peak of their muscle definition and fat cutting regimen (Rebecca Keegan, "Muscle Summer—the Men of 'Captain America,' 'Thor' and 'Conan,'" *Los Angeles Times*, May 28, 2011, http://herocomplex.latimes.com/movies/muscle-summer-the-men-of-captain-america-thor-and-conan/, accessed May 29, 2011).

[w] Although superhero types continue to be far more prevalent in American comics than manga/anime—in Japan, one is more likely, for example, to read a manga about the world's greatest chef, emphasizing the value of the incredibly hard work and hazing that she went through as an apprentice. I find these classic Japanese cultural values present in so many manga very attractive, such as stressing hard work and the value of teamwork and endurance.

[x] As Robert Napton touched upon.

Figure 2.37 I have repeated this page to demonstrate that like many American comics, some manga characters are depicted in unrealistic terms. Here, as a doughnut, in my student Akeem Roberts's comedy manga *Doughnut Cop* about a policeman who turns into a doughnut and goes to hell and has to box the devil to return to his human form.

McCloud continues with his common visual elements of manga

- Paneling is a visual component to manga that I would add to McCloud's "manga traits" that becomes a separate personality in the manga. Mangaka create an enormous variety of panels and strive to create atmosphere and feelings through their shapes. American manga creator Tania Del Rio (who worked on *Sabrina*, an Archie Comic for which she was hired to "manga-ize" through new adventures, and she is one of the authors behind the book *Mangaka America: Manga by America's Hottest Artists*) gave me a PowerPoint document for use in my classes in which the many varieties of paneling are shown, helping my students move away from the simple boxes of American comics. Characters' limbs spill out of frames, which can become jagged and shattered or a variety of shapes, even flowers for shōjo, if romance is the theme. The varieties are endless.

- "Frequent use of wordless panels"[44]

One of my favorite sequences of wordless panels from Tezuka, which also illustrates his common themes of respect for living things, non-violence, and sacrifice, takes place in his *Buddha* manga. This sequence (Figures 2.38–2.41) gets to the heart of why I and so many others love quality early manga. I find that genre richness, emotion making, and theme to be among the most important elements of manga. Tezuka believed that a story was like a tree, and the theme of the story, or its meaning, was like its roots. And like a tree, if the roots were not strong, the tree would not be strong. This sequence also illustrates the animism concept of non-humans having spiritual characteristics (i.e. souls).

As with all Japanese created manga, read from right to left.

Figure 2.38 An old wise man trudging through the snowy mountains collapses. A bear, a fox, and a rabbit come across him and try to revive him. © Tezuka Productions

Figure 2.39 Communicating among themselves, the animals decide to forage to find the old man food, each setting off in their own direction in their quest. Although the bear and fox successfully find food, the rabbit, try though he does, finds none. And is rebuked by the other two for his failure. The rabbit is distraught over his shortcomings. ©Tezuka Productions

Figure 2.40 The old man begins to build a fire, and the rabbit helps gather firewood, despite his small body. The rabbit sacrifices himself onto the fire, so that the old man can eat him, and thus survive. The old man, bear, and fox are utterly shocked and the old man cannot rescue the rabbit before it dies. © Tezuka Productions

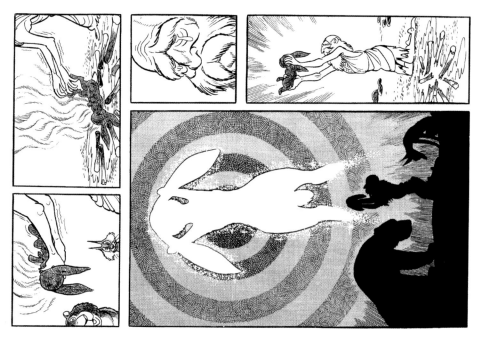

Figure 2.41 The rabbit ascends to heaven. The bear and fox lower their heads in shame and awe. © Tezuka Productions

As we can see from these pages, Tezuka succeeded in moving manga far from the mostly simple gags of previous comics into the highest level of artistic endeavor, philosophical and humanistic feeling and thought.

Figure 2.42 Hollywood director Steven Spielberg is also mentioned in Tezuka's *Buddha*.[y] © Tezuka Productions

The next few pages demonstrate how my student Louise Wang uses paneling creatively to denote anger and the emotional shattering of a woman jilted at the altar by her fiancée for another woman in her shōjo-themed *Wedding Singer* (as previously noted, shōjo is the woman/girl's genre of manga and anime, focusing on emotions and relationships—often affairs of the heart—and often with its own abstract symbols and style). Notice how as the heroine's emotional tension builds, the panel borders deviate radically from the squared-off classic American style comics. Initially, in these first pages, the frames are straighter, denoting calm. But the dialogue and sometime body parts (the characters' heads) spill over the panel border, aiding the eyes to move smoothly through the page.

---

[y] E.T. the Extraterrestrial also makes a cameo appearance in Tezuka's *Buddha* along with Yoda from *Star Wars*.

Figure 2.43 At first calmness and happiness prevails in *Wedding Singer*.

Figure 2.44 When the heroine, the wedding singer, recognizes her former fiancée, the borders become jagged, expressing her mounting anxiety upon seeing the person who previously jilted her at the altar living it up with two women at a wedding.

Figure 2.45 Panel borders become jagged and disappear entirely as she "shatters" like the glass.

Figure 2.46 Shattering into nothingness as her psyche melts down.

Figure 2.47 My student Paul Choate's *Project Alpha* demonstrates another cinematic technique used in manga. Panels can be used to break up conversations to make them more interesting by, for example, showing a close-up on a hand or eyes. A key manga trait is emphasizing the details of the physical story environment, and all these techniques are used to pull the readers into the story.

Speaking of environment, urban scenes are typical of Japan, where most people are crowded into cities such as Tokyo (see photo on the next page).

McCloud also breaks down the visual differences between manga and American comics into six transition (meaning panel to panel) forms. He found that manga tended to often use "*Moment to Moment transitions*,"[45] (italics added) which he defines as single actions portrayed in a series of moments (for instance, a man falling down steps, shown in various panels of the falling action as if it were being filmed, stretched out more than American comics would normally do). By contrast, American comics use less moment-to-moment or aspect-to-aspect sequences. Aspect-to-aspect (which manga also use extensively) is what McCloud terms "transitions from one aspect of a place, idea or mood to another."[46] An example would be a shot of the sun in the sky above peaceful trees followed directly by a close-up of a woman's face as she suns in the grass looking up in the sky, followed

Figure 2.48 Author in Tokyo (Shibuya) in a vibrant urban environment typical of many found in manga/anime. Photo: Yoko Hayashi.

Figure 2.49 My student Tonya Holladay depicts a snowy urban scene in her manga *FAS*.

Figure 2.50 *Alrik* by my student Timothy Johnson, effectively establishes a night forest scene.

by birds flying in the clouds.[47] And these taken together show a more cinematic, decompressed nature of manga over American comics.

McCloud also cites "genre maturity" as a big advantage of manga/anime[48]

Genre is particularly attractive to Hollywood, which has always been a genre-based system. Genres are not limiting but freeing, and even the most abstract storytelling movie can usually be classified into a genre.

The genres of Japanese manga/anime extend far beyond legacy American comics' limited storytelling genres—in fact, they seem to cover almost everything![z] Almost any genre is acceptable as long as the manga is popular.[aa] Here are a few examples of manga/anime that have or had Hollywood adaptation deals (though not yet produced) and their genres:[ab]

- Adventure: *Naruto* (producer, Avi Arad, director: Michael Gracey, Lionsgate Films).
- Medical mystery anti-hero: *Black Jack.*
- Science fiction: *Battle Angel Alita* (20th Century Fox, director: James Cameron, producer John Landau), *Ghost in the Shell* (Dreamworks, starring Scarlett Johansson, producers Ari and Avi Arad)**,** *Akira* (Appian Way Productions, producers Leonardo DiCaprio and Andrew Lazar)—although in 2013, after sets were built for the production, the studio shelved the project. In 2015 a new screenplay for the *Akira* adaptation project was commissioned by Warner Brothers.
- Noir (with sci-fi): *Cowboy Beebop* (producer Joshua Long who is interviewed for this book had Keanu Reeves attached at one point). Currently, as of the finishing of this book, the rights are being negotiated for by another Hollywood studio.
- Comedy: *GTO*—an ex-trucker becomes the best high school teacher in Japan by using extremely unorthodox methods.
- Food comedy: *Iron Wok Jan.*
- Samurai: *Lone Wolf and Cub* (producer Justin Lin, Kamala Films).
- Swords, teens, and monsters: *Bleach* (was a major studio's project with producer Jason Hoffs (interviewed in this book, who also produced the adaptation of the Japanese novel *All You Need Is Kill*, titled *Edge of Tomorrow*, Warner Brothers).
- Thriller/Horror: *Death Note* (producers Roy Lee [also interviewed in this book], Jason Hoffs, Dan Lin and Masi Oka, Warner Brothers).

---

[z] Manga can be "how to" as well, covering such subjects as the post-war inventions of freeze dried noodles by salarymen and scientists and Japan's first mass-produced sports car.

[aa] Unlike some film industries, critics play no role in determining a manga's success or failure. There are very few anyway. But there are other cultural/historical reasons for manga's often wild and uninhibited (and thus popular) tone. The refined manners that many non-Japanese today associate the culture with (such as the Japanese tea ceremony) are really a fairly recent development in the middle class. The "common people" of Japanese history have always had an earthy sensibility that is reflected in manga/anime—and only since the Meiji Restoration were the refined manners of the upper classes imposed down upon the "regular people." Which is why a burping, head-scratching samurai can find his home in manga/anime. And of course Hollywood too has always required that the majority of its films be populist, to give studios the greatest chance to recoup their usually expensive investments.

[ab] Other manga/anime that have had various stages of development in Hollywood that are not covered in this book, due to space limitations, include *Parasyte, Robotech, Voltron, Goth, Evangelion,* and *Blood the Last Vampire* (which was released).

My students echo the genre diversity found in manga and anime—even a superhero story is given a big twist ...

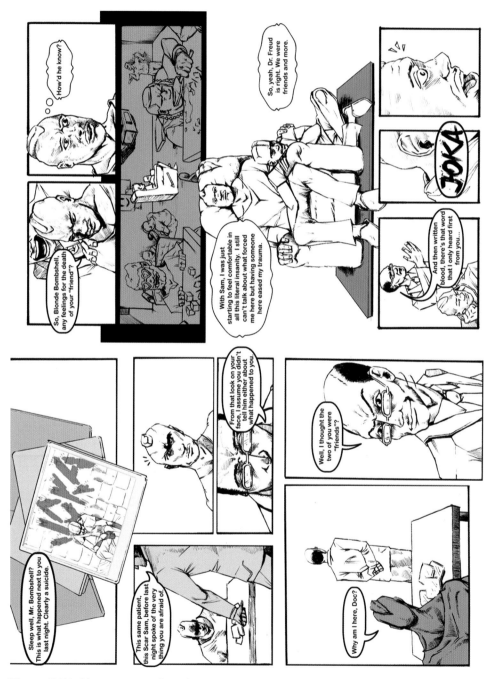

Figure 2.51 Above, genre diversity, my student Jeremy Darby's *African Dragon* features an African superhero breaking into an insane asylum to get a villain. Darby also seeks to bring more African American characters into manga.

Figure 2.52 My student Natalie Askew's ghost story *Artes Magicae*.

Below, my student Jarad Greene's *Tom Timberlan Unwitting Adventurer* brings back the Disney style to his manga, set in a family-friendly fantasy world. Disney's enormous impact upon manga will be covered in Chapter 4.

Figure 2.53 *Tom Timberlan Unwitting Adventurer* by Jarad Greene.

Figure 2.54 *Tom Timberlan Unwitting Adventurer* by Jarad Greene.

A key difference between these Japanese and American storytelling forms is that there are more genres and subgenres in Japan than in the United States. In the United States, there used to be great genre diversity in comics. But a development occurred which undercut that ... which we will read about next.

The Comics Code

One of the main reasons why the Japanese manga system encouraged such creativity and diversity compared to American comics (especially before American graphic novels began being inspired in part by manga) was the Comics Code.

The Comics Code of 1954 was a self-imposed form of strict censorship that the American comic publishers imposed on themselves in response to parental and political pressure about the content of American comics at the time. In the early 1950s, the American comics industry was thriving and quite diverse. The suppression of the American industry through the code is the main reason why Hollywood mines the superhero comics of DC and Marvel over and over again (besides their box-office success), as they were among the few major companies to survive the effects of the code because, generally speaking, the broad, relatively simplistic personalities of their superheroes would still fit within the code's extremely narrow confines of what was acceptable.

The code led to a situation in which superheroes with superficial personalities proliferated—when the only "weakness" of Superman is a gimmick, kryptonite, rather than a personality weakness (which are almost always more interesting). This distances

Figure 2.55 1954 U.S. Senate Subcommittee Hearings into Juvenile Delinquency, with a focus on comic books, which led to the restrictive Comics Code.
© Bettman/CORBIS

many readers because people do not generally like characters who appear superior to them. Even the relatively superficial James Bond, arguably the most famous cinema character ever, is defined as much by his weaknesses as his abilities as the world's greatest spy. He is handsome and has a plethora of amazing gadgets and weapons, but he is also a womanizer, a misogynist, a gambler, and an extreme loner with more than a touch of sadism and masochism. Without those weaknesses, superhuman Bond would be too one-dimensional and perfect and thus not work as a character. Thus, by ruling out these types of adult foibles in American comics, the Comics Code severely limited the appeal of American comics to wide swathes of the American

public from that point forward, until the advent of the graphic novel. This is a cautionary lesson to governments attempting to force storytellers within certain parameters: if you become too restrictive, there is almost no chance that the work will be successful overseas, and it will probably not even be successful in your own country to the degree that you would like.

So American comics became stranded in a primarily male adolescence and earlier childhood with an extremely narrow range of subject matter and mostly unrelatable

Figure 2.56 *Domo Nation* by my student Lauren Elizabeth. Vibrant and alive, spilling out of its frames.

characters and stories full of broad superheroes,[ac] animals, and gags, thus limiting readership to mostly boys. Later, American comics became a focus of collectors, who would keep wrappers unopened in the hopes of financial appreciation in coming years. Manga, on the other hand, was meant to be consumed, not held in a drawer. It was meant to be read, perhaps then handed around, read again, and maybe eventually end up in a rental "manga café."[ad] Vibrant and alive, spilling out of its frames, pushing boundaries in every direction, manga retained its diversity and creativity.

So from 1954 onward, manga's enormous popularity as a mainstay of entertainment and storytelling was never seriously challenged by American comics, which shrunk to become more of a cottage industry compared to the publishing giant that manga grew into.

Shueisha, the giant Japanese manga publisher, for example, did not cave in to protests in 1972 from outraged parents' and teachers' associations about such manga as the rebellious school children's comedy manga series *Harenchi Gakuen* (*Shameless School*) by Nagai Go, in which the students and teachers engage in naughty hijinks, which might seem innocent today. As Masuda emailed me, "*Harenchi gakuen*, yes, I read and liked the manga series when I was kid. It was quite outrageous at that time even though it might not be that bad in today's standards; flipping up a girl's skirt is a big deal or something like that."[49] The refusal to adhere to guidelines censoring artistic expression allowed Japanese manga to preserve its diversity and freedom of creative expression and leap ahead into sales territory driven by a broad acceptance by both genders and a wide variety of age groups, which American comics did not have after the code. Consequently, manga so completely dominated American comics on a worldwide-sales basis as to render them a tiny footnote.[ae][af]

The small expense is another great advantage of manga

As Schodt notes, filmmakers need to have the kind of personality that can marshal huge financial resources and a battalion of collaborators. But for becoming a mangaka, "entry level requirements for the profession consist mainly of good ideas, a certain degree of physical and intellectual stamina, and pens, pencils and paper. It isn't necessary to be a particularly good artist."[50]

[ac] A lack of human foibles also restricts characters from being able to attempt to overcome their weaknesses, and thus we are unable to admire them for striving to improve themselves. Many manga/anime characters are even aware of their own imperfections, producing a higher level of empathy from the readership/audience. I consider this "self-aware" trait indicative of a very high level of character development.

[ad] Manga cafés allow patrons to have snacks, coffee, or tea and sit and read manga that the café provides. In Japan, there are even private "couples booths."

[ae] When the *Shameless School* manga ended, according to Schodt (the manga is not distributed in America so I could not read it), "the last episode erupted in total war between the PTA and the school, with machine guns, tanks and missiles all thrown in the fray. Everyone was destroyed" (Frederik L Schodt and Osamu Tezuka, *Manga! Manga!: The World of Japanese Comics* (Tokyo and New York: Kodansha International; distributed in the US by Kodansha International/USA through Harper & Row, 1986), 123).

[af] It is important to note that in the 1980s, manga publishers did come under strong public pressure to curtail the wilder subject matter, but although there was a degree of reasonable self-censorship for a while, it did not result in a restrictive formal code like the Comics Code.

Examples abound in this book of manga created by my students who came into my class without formidable art-drafting or figure-drawing skills, but still created engaging and sometimes even philosophically mind-blowing manga. This is largely because manga is, first and foremost, a story and character form.

Figure 2.57 *EXIT*, by my students Carmen Wiggins (writer) and Andrew Williams (artist), was one of the first manga created in my class. It does not have polished art, but neither does much of manga. And *EXIT* expresses the duality of a character that must slay creatures she pities even after they kill her friend—as they are tortured souls that can only be released when she destroys them. The emphasis is upon story, and the simple yet stylish artwork conveys it well.

Figure 2.58 *EXIT.*

Figure 2.59 *EXIT.*

Figure 2.60 *EXIT.*

Figure 2.61 *EXIT.*

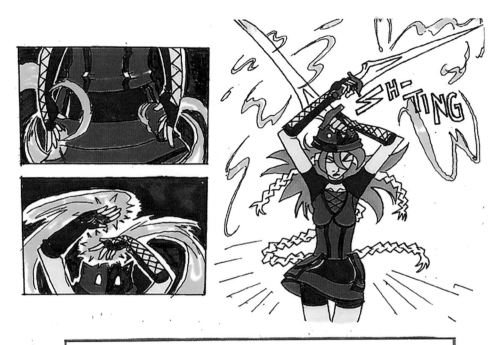

Figure 2.62 In keeping with manga's focus, *EXIT*'s protagonist's emotional dilemma is more important than polished art.

In the manga world, there is plenty of room for a talented storyteller using a simpler line.

Figure 2.63 The playful and simple lines of *Inked* by my students Natalie Askew (artist) and Robert Lipe (writer).

On the other hand, others of my students have highly developed drafting skills. Below is some of my students' black and white refined manga work—artist Frank Ellerbe has worked for major graphic novel publishers.

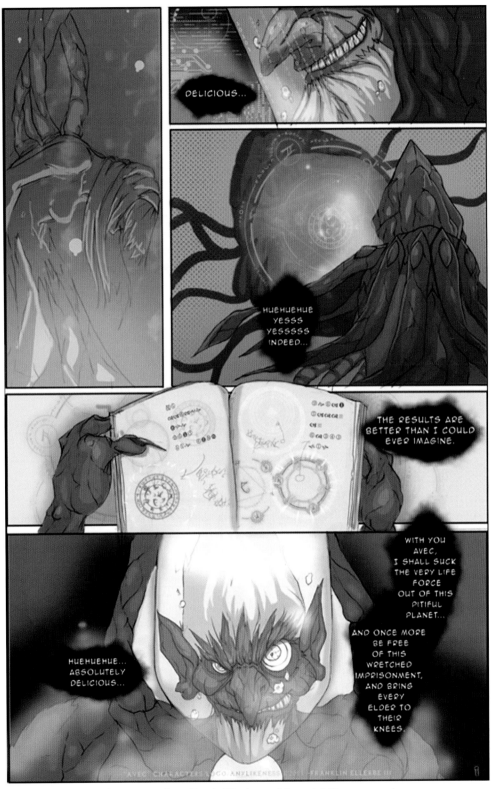

Figure 2.64 *Avec* by my student Frank Ellerbe, while exhibiting several manga characteristics, also has high quality draftsmanship, which is often found in American comics.

Figure 2.65 *Motherbot Connection* by my grad student Marlowe Leverette has classic American comic style mixed with manga's—typical of many works in my classes.

Below, *Fujo Club* and *A King's Revenge* each have a classic Japanese manga style.

Figure 2.66 *Fujo Club* by Louise Wang, like another of her series on the next page, and her *Wedding Singer*, exhibits a "pure" Japanese manga style.

Figure 2.60 Wang's art in *King's Revenge*, with story by my student John Sheridan.

Figure 2.68 "Patients in mid-city hospital's ICU are vanishing, all under the care of one doctor and his sinister *Project Afterlife*."[ag] *Afterlife* by Austa Joye (artist) and Kenneth Bragg (writer).

[ag] Manga plot summary by reporter Chris Horn, in the Spring 2015 issue of the *Carolinian* magazine—a review of my classes, my students' manga, and their career success (p. 16).

Figure 2.69 *Decrementia*, by my current student Jessica Jordan, also exhibits hybridity and a pretty high degree of artistic skill.

Examples of these technically accomplished young artists' manga are scattered throughout this book. But the truth is, as in the case of *Exit*, that more crudely or quickly drawn manga can be just as entertaining or meaningful as long as the story/character and tone work well. The Wachowskis' *Matrix* and *Speed Racer* visual designer John Gaeta explained to me about how on a technical level that same crudeness of much pre-computer-rendered anime (i.e. the earlier cell-based, drawn/inked/painted work) was used to evoke emotion and thus, as in the case of much of manga, make more of an emotional impression than more highly technically accomplished art might: "[W]hen you're watching certain animated content, particularly, you know, these great, expressive Japanese works, the real intent of the designers of a lot of these anime is to get you feeling in an expressive way: they are not trying to emulate the real world or photography or in any way, right?"[51]

Figure 2.70 *Vault 9* by my student Patrick Fowler is a hit-man turned school teacher comedy story.

Figure 2.71 *Vault 9.*

This faster-to-produce "less polished" artwork is advantageous to both the Japanese and Hollywood movie and TV industries because many more manga can be created, and Hollywood can do what it always does—cherry-pick the best ones for adaptation. The same can be true for any film, animation, or television industry worldwide.

When I was hired at the University of South Carolina as their screenwriting professor, I brought the manga classes I had been teaching at University of California, Irvine, to my new home. As a colleague at another university with a larger film school remarked to me, my manga focus was ideal because it didn't take the large resources of a film program. Thus, my students could create many quality and diverse manga stories for very little cost.

Figure 2.72 *Vault 9.*

Figure 2.73 Some of my students' work that is on my office walls. All manga requires is a pen and paper or a computer drawing pad. It does not even require particularly great draftsmanship. A sense of fun, however, is required! Photo: James Henderson.

Figure 2.74 *Defense Maiden,* a fantasy/action manga by my students Rebecca Shrom (artist) and Ryan Stevens (writer).

The same holds true of manga production as a platform for "trying out stories" before incurring the massive expense of a live-action movie, TV show, or animation project. Manga might even make more sense than comics for this purpose because its various attributes make it more effective as a storytelling platform. If its creator is talented, driven, and a good story-teller, manga presents the opportunity to take the emotions, characters, and setting of a story to their absolute limits, thereby giving the story its "best shot," all on a very small budget. For example, *Project Alpha* (seen on right) could not have been created in live-action by Paul Choate due to high expense, but in manga form with a computer and a drawing pad, he conveys the characters' and backstories (what happened before

Figure 2.75 *Project Alpha* by Paul Choate.

the story began) in an interesting way without having top-level art skills. Imagination, perseverance, and craft (understanding the form) are more important.

And that cost-effective and highly successful way to tell long form stories with deep character development, has allowed much manga to be created that has captured the imagination of its readers. Much of it became Japanese anime, live-action television shows and movies—and more recently, Hollywood adaptations. But the manga/anime and Hollywood creative universes were tied together from the beginnings of the modern manga form post-World War II. However, before telling that fascinating story, it is important to tell the equally intriguing tale of how the early DNA of manga/anime developed separately, including before the twentieth century.

Figure 2.76 *Horizon* by Andrew Williams.

Figure 2.77 *Horizon*, page "in production" by Andrew Williams.

Figure 2.78 *Life of Tony* by Zach Rothrock (writer) and Austa Joye (artist).

Figure 2.79 *Pastel White* by Austa Joye.

3

Divergent DNA: Modern Manga's Ancestry Leading up to the Beginning of Modernization of the Form by Tezuka in the World War II Era

Wind from the east: Beginnings

- Roots of manga from Japanese art/culture/literary traditions, pre-World War II history, including early scrolls and woodblock printing.
- Japanese comics are impacted by the style of British comics during the Meiji period.
- Osamu Tezuka, "the god of manga," begins to create modern manga post-World War II.

While Hollywood and American comics (including American comics based on Hollywood's work, which I will go into more detail about later) have had significant influence on Japanese manga/anime, some of manga/anime's "DNA" was derived from pre-manga Japanese history, as well as Tezuka's imaginative and revolutionary innovations, aspects of Japanese culture, and even literary styles from countries other than Japan. This is part of the "otherness" of manga/anime that is so enticing to many in Hollywood, which has always thrived on the mantra of "a little of the old, a little of the new."

Let's start with the fascinating old …

Pre-manga: China, monks, and the pleasure district

"An ocean begins with a drop of water." What has become overwhelmingly the most successful comics form in world history, with anime series like *Gundam* grossing $688 million dollars a year, arguably began with bored Japanese laborers in the sixth century.[1]

Schodt notes that doodles and caricatures were found behind walls and ceilings of two sacred temples built during the sixth and seventh centuries. The buildings were a product of the Japanese infatuation with China during that period.[2] This relationship with its Chinese roots is typical of Japanese artistic development. Because, in many ways, China—Japan's regional neighbor, a much older civilization, and the dominant power in the world for so many centuries—was the mother of Japan.

Schodt writes that "the first undisputed masterpiece of Japanese cartooning" was the famous "Toba Scrolls." These twelfth-century drawings were painted onto paper scrolls as long as 80 feet and placed in sequence to tell of legends, battles, and events from daily life. The scrolls could be funny, too. They were named after their most famous creator: an artist priest named Toba Sōjō (also called Bishop Toba) who made fun of the members of his own priesthood by turning them into monkeys, foxes, and frogs, and even showing them in farting contests (his "farting contest scroll" is called the Choujuu-jinbutsu-giga, predating the scatological/bodily function humor found in some comedy manga).[3] The drawings did not have borders or frames as manga has now, but the story could be understood sequentially by reading across the scroll. The original scrolls were a hybrid of Chinese and Japanese styles, much like the later confluence of manga/anime and Hollywood.

"Hybrid": Hybridity: "Anything of mixed ancestry: something that is formed by combining two or more things"[4]

Figure 3.1 My student Austa Joye's hybrid anime/manga/American Cartoon Network show-type characters, in various emotional poses, that enable Austa to consistently convey that character's range of emotions when re-drawing the character over and over, a process manga artists often do to prepare for drawing a new series.

There are modern manga based on Chinese myths and stories as well. The second most popular manga of all time, as of 2015, is *Dragon Ball*, which was loosely inspired by the classic Chinese tale *Journey to the West* and was, of course, made into the Hollywood *Dragonball Evolution* movie. Also, one of the first anime feature films that came to America the year before *Astro Boy* (see Chapter 6) was based upon the same myth and was the first work associated with Tezuka to appear in the USA.

Hayao Miyazaki, director of popular Japanese animated features including *Spirited Away*, *My Neighbor Totoro, Nausicaa of the Valley of the Wind*, and who is sometimes called the "Walt Disney of Japan,"[a] spoke in an interview[b] about these illustrated scrolls. They date from the Heian Period and the Kamakura Period (AD 1185–1333) during an upsurge of interest in Buddhism and the repelling of two Mongol invasions. Miyazaki said of the scrolls, "you can tell that Japanese people really believed that they could depict the human world in its entirety in this format. They thought that they could express nearly anything with drawings and words, whether it was related to politics, economics, art, religion or even erotica."[5]

As we have seen, the manga story structure is usually serialized (except in the case of "one-shots"—which are manga with single stories and a conclusive ending—or like *Astro Boy*, where episodes each end conclusively). Manga also have storytelling ancestry from Japanese literary history, which includes an inclination for very long stories. The classic epic *The Tale of Genji*, a story written circa AD 1000 about the loves and life of a character named Genji and the Heian court by a lady-in-waiting, Murasaki Shikibu, is Japan's first novel. It is also known as the world's first psychological novel and, with over 400 characters, is an example of the extreme length of some Japanese literary works.[c] This story was also turned into a scroll during the twelfth century. It is perhaps not a coincidence that Tezuka would adopt the same extremely long serialized form as a major characteristic of much of manga.

Figure 3.2 Murasaki Shikibu, illustration by Tosa Mitsuoki who did a series on *The Tale of Genji* in the seventeenth century.[d] From the Faculty of Oriental Studies at the University of Oxford website.

---

[a] An inaccurate comparison in one sense, because Disney, for most of his later career, was more of a producer than an animator.

[b] From "Miyazaki: Starting Point 1979–96," translated by Fred Schodt and Beth Cary, published by VIZ Media.

[c] Compare with the manga/anime franchise *Dragonball*, allegedly containing over 500 characters.

[d] Murasaki Shikibu found herself in competition with another women writer being sponsored within the court world in which she was kept. It might be a stretch, but a comparison could be made between that situation and what is described Chapter 5 of this book regarding the intensely competitive nature between mangaka and between their editors, within their publishers. A manga publisher owner, Hikaru Sasahara, who is Japanese, remarked to me in his interview (cited later in the book) about how competition is the key factor in one excelling.

In the mid-seventeenth century came Zen Pictures. According to Schodt, the process of creating these pictures was seen primarily as a way for the artist to attain spiritual enlightenment. Thus, the end product was not of prime importance. Achieving this detached mental state required adopting an irreverent attitude and what Schodt calls a "refined sense of the absurdity of man's 'permanent condition.'"[6] This is a trait also found in quite a few modern-day works of comedic manga and anime. A key aspect of Zen Pictures is, as Schodt notes, artistic techniques that "have enabled the Japanese painter to express in line even the most intangible and elusive shapes, without the aid of shading or color, [which is a technique that] exemplified a trait common to almost all Japanese art, including today's comics—an economy of line."[7] It is this skill that has enabled manga to mostly adopt a black and white form, all the way to the present. And it is a difficult and critical part of instruction for my manga students who, as Westerners, are usually untrained in the technique. Josiah Conder (1852–1920) was a British architect who worked as a foreign advisor to the government during the Meiji Period and is considered the father of modern Japanese architecture. Conder also studied art under a Japanese woodblock artist and cartoonist at the turn of the twentieth century and observed that "the limits imposed on the technique of his art, and the constant practice of defining form by means of line drawn with the flexible brush, have enabled the Japanese painter to express in line even the most intangible and elusive shapes, without the aid of shading or color."[8]

It is partially because of these techniques that manga has flourished into the present almost entirely as a black and white medium. Although ocassionally there are color lead-in pages to manga, doled out by the editors at the publishing companies to successful mangaka for special issues or at select intervals, in the vast majority of cases it remains a black and white medium. My students, as we have seen, have pushed the medium into color with my encouragement, partially because color manga display better in the digital form and online, which is arguably the best current method of publication when one does not have a publication deal—and, recognizing that manga is an evolving hyrid, we want to add something new to the form. Most of us also don't know Japanese flexible brush technique! That may be changing. A print-maker professor colleague of mine at the School

Figure 3.3 Associate Professor Mary Robinson, of the School of Visual Art and Design at the University of South Carolina, making a *moku hanga* Japanese woodblock print. Photo courtesy of Mary Robinson.

Figure 3.4 Fictional mangaka discuss their publisher Shueisha's practice of giving manga occasional color pages in *Bakuman*.
BAKUMAN. © 2008 by Tsugumi Ohba, Takeshi Obata/SHUEISHA Inc.

of Visual Art and Design at the University of South Carolina, Mary Robinson, has studied under an Ukiyo-e master in Japan and has instructed my students on this stage of manga's pre-history.

And as noted in the preface, I am now exposed to the renowned manga program at Kyoto Seika University, where I was invited to come learn from them and present my research, as well as Osaka Art University's excellent program, in 2015.

Ukiyo-e (manga's predecessor, the famous Japanese woodblock prints, Edo Period, May 3, 1868–July 30, 1912)

The average Japanese person of the eras before the 1800s would not have been exposed to scrolls or Zen Pictures as they were reserved for the aristocracy, religious personages, and high officials (including samurai/warrior families).[9] The growing merchant middle class of the Edo Period yearned for visual story-telling as part of that era's popular enjoyment of the arts and culture in a rapidly urbanizing Japan. In short, they now had money and wanted to spend it on entertainment. This desire was fulfilled when the most famous style of Japanese woodblock prints, Ukiyo-e, was developed. Ukiyo-e depicted the "Floating World" culture that began in the red-light district of Edo (now modern Tokyo). The "Floating World" was a celebration of the fleeting nature of life and youth before the onset of decay and death as sometimes symbolized by the cherry blossom's brief flowering and rapid disappearance. The "Floating World" culture also appeared in other cities such as Kyoto and Osaka. Included in its subject matter were the brothels, Kabuki theaters, and teahouses that were frequented by the expanding middle class. Geisha, Kabuki actors, samurai, and nature were often the subjects of these mass-produced woodblock prints. Professor Robinson has demonstrated to our students how the most exquisite of these works might have 20 or more colors—even the sky can be printed with multiple hues, each taking a separate block to print that color. The

Figure 3.5 "Yoshitoshi's (1839–died 1892) dashing woman warrior is based on the historical figure Hangaku Gozen (English: Lady Hangaku), who lived around the year 1200. She is considered one of the three woman warriors of Japan, along with Empress Jingû and Tomoe Gozen. She lived in the province of Echigo (present-day Niigata) and fought, unsuccessfully, against the Kamakura shogunate. She was sent to Kamakura for execution but was saved by a warrior who asked for her to be spared and then married her."[10] From the series *Yoshitoshi Mushuburai: A series of warriors by Yoshitoshi*, Library of Congress, prints and drawings.

blocks have to be carefully aligned so that their registration does not deviate, and thus all the colors are lined up carefully as to where they must appear. The process is quite difficult. Below and on the following page are examples of these colorful woodblock prints.

Schodt observes that Ukiyo-e were lively, topical, cheap entertainment and playful, much like modern-day manga.[11]

The Edo Period ended with the Meiji Restoration, which itself began on May 3, 1868, after the fall of Edo to the forces of the 16-year-old Meiji Emperor, and the capital was quickly renamed Tokyo. The Meiji era, as it is also called, ran until July 30, 1912, and was considered the first half of the period of Japan's transition from feudalism to its modern form.

Images below are from the very famous series *The Fifty-three Stations of the Tōkaidō Road* by Hiroshige Ando.

Figure 3.6 *Night Snow at Kanbara (Station #16)*. Kana: かんばら　よろ　の　ゆき Kanji：蒲原　夜之雪 Series Kanji：東海道五拾三次之内（保永堂版東海道）*Kanbara Yoru no Yuki. Tōkaidō Gojūsantsugi no Uchi (Hōeidō Ban Tōkaidō)*. 東海道五拾三次之内（保永堂版東海道）蒲原　夜之雪. Utagawa Hiroshige, Japanese, 1797–1858. Edo Period—Tempō, c. 1833–4. Woodblock print (Nishiki-e); ink and color on paper. Honolulu Museum of Art, Gift of James A. Michener, 1979 (17420).

Figure 3.7 *Fujikawa (Station #15)*. Kanji : 藤川 Series Kanji : 東海道五拾三次（狂歌入
東海道） *Fujikawa Tōkaidō Gojūsantsugi (Kyōka Iri Tōkaidō)*. 東海道五拾三次（狂歌入東
海道） 藤川. Utagawa Hiroshige, Japanese, 1797–1858. Edo Period—Kaei, c. 1842.
Woodblock print (Nishiki-e); ink and color on paper. Honolulu Museum of Art, Gift of
James A. Michener, 1991 (22431).

A key shared characteristic of Japanese narrative scrolls, woodblock prints, and modern
manga is their method of storytelling that clearly conveys the story without words. Unlike
the often dialogue-packed frames of traditional American comics, manga tend to use
dialogue more sparingly. The layout of the manga page and panels incorporates dialogue
organically and tends to have plenty of white space around it. This also allows it to be
read faster, while still potentially achieving substantial story and character development
due to the length of the manga, whereas American comics often cram the dialogue in the
remaining spaces not dominated by the image, slowing the reader down and making the
work feel like an illustrated short book that has to be "read" rather than "experienced."
Not like a manga, which is an integrated and distinct whole form. This is due in part to
the role of the "letterer" in American comics, who usually adds his/her work *after* the art
has been created and inked. Thus, dialogue placement sometimes becomes almost more
of an afterthought to the American comics' art, as opposed to its integration into manga
layout from the get-go.

This "white space" and sparse dialogue also makes manga storytelling more visual as
opposed to text-based. A professor visiting my manga class from Osaka Arts University's
Character Creative Arts Department, Nobuaki Hosoda, emphasized that the manga story

should be able to be understood entirely without words. Frank Miller, a famous American graphic novelist whose works were turned into such successful Hollywood films as *Sin City* (directors: Frank Miller and Robert Rodriguez—Quentin Tarantino as Guest Director, Dimension Films, 2005) and *300* (director: Zack Snyder, Legendary Pictures/Warner Brothers Pictures, 2006), said in a 1982 interview in *Comics Journal*, "Lately, I've been immersing myself in Japanese prints. They closely resemble comic book drawing, which in many ways is emblematic. People have come to recognize a certain configuration of lines being the nose. They deal with the series of images that, like comics, have to convey information." He added, "I was able to read 100 pages of the Japanese comic the other day without even becoming confused. And it was written in Japanese! *They rely totally on the visuals. They approach comics as a pure form more than American comic artists do*"[12] (my italics).

As Schodt notes, "like so much of old Japanese art, Ukiyo-e works attempted to present reality without dwelling on anatomy and perspective, they tried to capture a mood, in essence, and an impression—something also vital to caricature and cartooning."

This echoes the fact that manga artists do not have to be great at figure drawing/drafting.

Western style comics appear in Japan

The first modern era Western-style comic in Japan was the humorous and sometimes satirical *Japan Punch* (1862–87), based on the popular British *Punch* series. *Japan Punch's* was created by Charles Wirgman, an English cartoonist and illustrator (1832–91). *Japan Punch's* text was illustrated with single and double panel illustrations drawn by Wirgman, who worked as a correspondent for the *Illustrated London News* in Yokohama, Japan, where he remained until his death. Wirgman was a talented artist. He also trained Ukiyo-e artists in Western-style drawing. Soon the Japanese acquired Western printing skills and technology, which quickly made the expensive Ukiyo-e techniques outdated, and paved the way for manga's eventual rise and mass production.[13]

Paper Theaters

Another manga predecessor was "Paper Theaters" or "Paper Drama" (Kami-shibai). In this medium, a performer would display ornately drawn picture boards inserted in sequence in a frame as he narrated; he traveled between performance locations on a bicycle, onto which he would attach the frame containing the picture boards.[e]

---

[e] As the photos on the next page show, a few Kami-shibai storytellers still practice their trade. The author enjoyed a Kami-shibai performance at the wonderful Kyoto International Manga Museum in 2015, from a young, practicing Kami-shibai storyteller who, in his performance, compared some *Ôgon Bat* villain characters to American comic icons like *Spiderman's* Green Goblin. The storyteller may have been aware of *Spiderman* as it is unique among other Marvel properties that were adapted into anime—it was adapted into a Japanese live-action TV series (TV Tokyo, 1978–79).

Figure 3.8 A modern-day Kami-shibai storyteller narrating Ōgon Bat to children. Image courtesy of Tokyobling (tokyobling.wordpress.com).

Figure 3.9 A modern-day Kami-shibai storyteller. Image courtesy of Tokyobling (tokyobling.wordpress.com).

Barefoot Gen mangaka Keiji Nakazawa recalled in his autobiography a Kami-shibai storyteller from his childhood plying his trade in the ruins of Hiroshima after the atomic bomb. And if young Nakazawa's enthusiasm for Kami-shibai was any indication, it may have been a part of the reason for his development as a professional mangaka,

> The storyteller came by each night and I would watch, enthralled, my heart racing. I got to know the storyteller and took on the job of walking around clapping the clappers to summon the children. In return, I got to watch for free and was given a chopstick wrapped in pickled seaweed and dipped in malty syrup. The storyteller prided himself on narrating with seven different voices. Enraptured by his impassioned performance, I worshipped him. *Golden Bat* [*Ōgon Bat*][f] and *Little Big Man* were hits that transported the children of the ruins during the postwar period.[14]

According to manga scholar and author Paul Gravett's *Manga: Sixty Years of Japanese Comics*, Kami-shibai storytellers, who began in the 1930's, plied Japanese streets up through post-World War II, until the technology of the 1950s (especially television) made the Kami-shibai obsolete, after which many of the artists became mangaka. Schodt estimates that at one point there were 10,000 and some 5 million people per day watched a show.[15] In fact, later, the *Astro Boy* anime, due to its extremely low budget, sometimes had so few frames in an episode that it resembled a Kami-shibai. This was not a coincidence, as the creators acknowledged that the show was based upon the Kami-shibai model to save money (for more details on this, see Chapter 6 about anime's development and coming to America).[g]

Comic production and distribution methods just before Tezuka broke out with his first giant hit, *New Treasure Island*

In the 1920s, Japanese comic strips consisted of eight or so usually square panels (in the Western style), but the 1930's saw the appearance of multi-story manga magazines that featured text stories, eimonogatari (illustrated stories) and educational articles. These were compiled individually into fancy bound versions of what we would today call a "graphic novel." This evolved into the current manga-industry practice of several serialized series running in a phone-book-sized issue. This development, combined with Tezuka's later innovations, would lead to multi-year epics with deep character development. And of course, the substantial length of the series provided the opportunity to introduce legions of characters into a story over time

---

[f] This also became a manga by Tezuka in 1947.

[g] Nobuo Masuda notes that *Golden Bat* is based on a really old manga series. I've never seen the anime series. The superhero [*Golden Bat*] might be regarded as a *Batman* take-off. But he fights against an invader from outer space or something like that rather than human villains" (email to author, November 30, 2014). Director Del Toro references the series as well (see Chapter 6).

The changing political and cultural scene sets the stage for World War II, the ashes of which instigated a fertile stage for modern manga's birth and explosive growth

Because of the very real threat that the technologically advanced United States and other countries represented to the Japanese, who were watching the Western powers carve up China, the Meiji era government had to act. The Japanese authorities developed the slogan "Catch up! Overtake!" The Japanese culture and people have always had the ability to do just that. China was their first teacher, until the two countries went their separate ways; then Commodore Perry showed up in Tokyo Bay with warships—and the Japanese people were shocked to see that America and other outside powers could easily defeat their military. So then they caught up, and overtook. This process was largely an intense industrialization based on the Western model of progress (Japan already had an extremely well-developed and literate society), and also included changes in law to come in line with the modern era.

The Meiji restoration was a period of artistic flowering, a pre-war breath of liberalism, and a flirtation with more democratic ideas. Part of this process included cultural and artistic inspirations from abroad. Gravett's book shows a pre-manga Japanese comic heroine attempting to learn the Charleston.[h] American music (especially jazz) flooded Japan in the 1920s, as did Hollywood movies. There were even Japanese "flappers" (a type of women's fashion and attitude from the "Roaring 20s"—for an example, see the photograph on the next page).

This period was also the beginning of the flowering of the Japanese film industry, and many of its film jewels would then impact manga and anime, including the classic cinema director Akira Kurosawa, a giant of the industry (1910–98). Professor Hosoda explained to my students when he visited my classes that many mangaka look to Kurosawa's films for layout inspiration when they are in need of ideas.

An example of a trope that crosses over from Japanese cinema to manga and anime and on to Hollywood's productions is the famous *Seven Samurai* sword fight scene, where two opponents ran towards each other, slashed at each other, then seconds pass with wounds undisclosed, and then, after a dramatic pause, one falls dead. This trope is repeated in many manga and anime. An example of this is Figure 3.11 on the next page.

The type of trope described above then in turn affected modern Hollywood movies, such as the giant robot samurai vs. school-girl battle scene in *Sucker Punch* featuring the same type of fight move (Figure 3.12 on the next page). Screenwriter Steven Shibuya, who wrote *Sucker Punch* with Snyder, described it in an interview with me (Chapter 11), where he talked about this kind of sword slash where the top of the body of the casualty, after a beat, slides off the torso.[i][16]

---

[h] An American dance from that era.
[i] This also occurs in *Rurouni Kenshin* and Tezuka's gender-bending *Princess Knight*.

Figure 3.10 *Modern Girls in Beach Pajama Style*, (Biichi pajama sutairu no moga tachi)
Artist: Kageyama Koyo (1907–1981)
Showa era, 1928
Gelatin silver print, 30 x 21.8 cm
Courtesy of Kageyama Tomohiro
© Kegeyama Tomohiro Courtesy of Mead Art Museum, Amherst College, Amherst,
Massachusetts, Museum Purchase and Purchase with Richard Templeton (class of
1931) Photography Fund.

Figure 3.11 A similar type slashing sword fight in *Gundam*.
MOBILE SUIT GUNDAM UC
© SOTSU, SUNRISE

Figure 3.12 And the same type of manga/anime fighting move in *Sucker Punch*
(director: Zack Snyder, Warner Brothers Pictures/Legendary Pictures, 2011).

And the 1920s saw the coming of age of the parents of the future mangaka that would invent and modernize the manga and anime industries into their current form. These often liberal parents, like those of Tezuka (who was born in 1928 to a mother who encouraged him artistically) and Nakazawa (born in 1939, whose father was involved in regional theater and was politically free-thinking), gave their children a perspective that included principles of freedom and self-determination and, in many cases, an interest in new ideas, fashion, and literature from outside of Japan. This included strong influences from 1920s Hollywood movies that these parents watched and, where possible, exposed their children to.

Unfortunately, the "Catch up! Overtake!" mentality also contributed to World War II. Japan would experience horror, tragedy, and then rebirth—and the surviving young people would build the manga industry into a creative and commercial juggernaut.

War, destruction, defeat: Japan starts over and Tezuka leads the way

The brief blooming of liberal ideas during the Meiji era was snuffed out by nationalism and totalitarianism that swept and manipulated the society, and fed into the more negative aspects of the culture. It also suppressed those few who were brave enough to differ from that totalitarian path through fear of death, torture, imprisonment, and ostracism. This led to the disastrous war in the Pacific.

Tezuka begins to develop modern manga quietly while hiding out in the war years

In an interview with the manga/anime cultural magazine *Otaku USA*, Schodt summed up Tezuka's importance,

> Something that's fascinating about Tezuka and *Astro Boy* is that he created the entire framework for the anime and manga industry with that one work. You have a manga, you animate it into a 30-minute TV series, you create merchandise, you create feature films, then you keep drawing it and create this Godzilla machine ... that's where it all comes from. He didn't just create these amazing works, he also created this whole thing that all of us are indebted to.[17]

Figure 3.13 Fred Schodt at the Tezuka Museum in Takarazuka, Japan, a suburb of Osaka and hometown of Tezuka. Courtesy of Frederik L. Schodt

Perhaps what Schodt means by this is that Tezuka didn't "just" invent modern manga, and a huge number of its genres, but he also invented anime television shows that would sweep the world, helped pioneer their production processes, and even blazed new paths in international television co-financing and co-project development with American television networks.[j]

---

[j] Chapter 6 will explore in part Tezuka's revolutionary deals with American television network NBC for his *Astro Boy* and *Kimba the White Lion*.

Fortunately too young to serve in the military, medical student Tezuka (who had doctors in his ancestry) hid out from the war as he developed his style. As he came into adulthood, Tezuka worked in a factory producing asbestos slate for the military. He created manga everywhere—even in the bathrooms at his work—composing thousands of pages as he developed his craft, which would serve as the basis for modern manga. One time, another worker using the bathroom mistook Tezuka's stashed manga work for toilet paper, with the expected unfortunate results.[18]

Emerging from the factory after an American firebombing, Tezuka was shocked to see "a sea of fire" and the charred remains of civilians who had sought refuge under a collapsed bridge.[19] The fire bombings and atomic bombings were the culmination of a war in which civilians had gradually become targets for the military on both sides on an unprecedented scale. The atrocities against civilians on a mass level became a terrible feature of the war.

These events and Japan's eventual defeat would have a profound effect on Tezuka, engendering his respect for all living things, and upon Tezuka's pioneering manga colleagues whom he inspired.

For example, at the same time in Hiroshima, far to the south of Tokyo, six-year-old Keiji Nakazawa's family was cruelly ostracized for his father's outspoken opposition to the war, for which his father was imprisoned and probably tortured, and their small farm field destroyed. His later *Barefoot Gen* manga depicts how, as retribution for the family's anti-war stance, his teen sister was strip-searched by a school official and the official was then thrashed by her father. Nakazawa was as courageous as his father in denouncing the imperial system at his school; he was impressed by his father's brave pronouncements to his family and local officials that the war was not winnable because of the lack of resources in Japan compared to the Americans'.

Hiroshima was spared earlier allied bombing because it was being selected to be a pristine target so the damage would be most severe, a dire fate from the atomic bombs that would have many implications for manga and anime as an art/story form.[k][20] As noted, the never-experienced-before (or since) shock and horror of the atomic bombings would affect influential works like the manga/anime *Akira* which was many Hollywood creators' first experience with anime when it was a hit in US art houses in the 1980s, the live-action adaptation of which Leonardo DiCaprio has tried to make in Hollywood. Other anime inspired by the Allied bombing of Japan include *Grave of the Fireflies*, the heart-wrenching story of two war orphans trying unsuccessfully to survive firebombing and starvation. And many other stories in manga and anime would bear the atomic imprint which, as Nakazawa notes in his autobiography, never stops causing pain and death, generation after generation.

Eventually, Nakazawa, after becoming a successful mangaka, in his *Barefoot Gen*, sought to place the blame "where it belonged"—largely with the Japanese imperial system—though he also reserved withering criticism for the American military for having dropped the bombs on civilians. This is another example of how the medium has been

---

[k] The atomic bomb targeting committee meeting minutes have been declassified and were, at the time of this book's writing, available online. See the corresponding endnote for details.

Figure 3.14 *Barefoot Gen.* Each night Keiji Nakazawa's mother wondered why Hiroshima was not being firebombed, while neighboring cities were.
© Keiji Nakazawa. All rights reserved. Used by permission of Last Gasp.

used for serious thought and messages, which to Americans familiar with post-Comics-Code American comics, came as a fresh blast of integrity and diversity.

During the occupation, Tezuka was beaten up by some US troops in downtown Takarazuka when he was unable to explain directions to them to their satisfaction.[21] [22] Schodt states that Tezuka was horrified to realize that the government could change the nature of "reality" and create a world in which white was black, and days later black would become white.[23] But instead of becoming cynical or withdrawn after these experiences, Tezuka developed a revulsion for war, a respect for all living things, and an acknowledgment of the complexity of human nature, which would permeate all of his works.[24] McCarthy observed that the violent incident also made him "wonder how people who couldn't understand one another could ever be at peace," another enduring theme in his storytelling.[25]

There was great fear among Japanese civilians of atrocities that might be committed by the occupiers of Japan, especially as the war had become a "total war" in which civilians were now official targets. But fortunately for the Japanese people, overall the actual US occupation—coming after the mass civilian deaths and injuries of the firebombing and atom bombs—was benevolent by historical standards. (The lack of a "revenge occupation" was particularly notable since the Japanese military's behavior had often been so extreme.)

The war years were characterized by a lack of necessities—immediately post-war, Japan, in ruins, was more of an underground barter economy than anything else.

As the society rebuilt, a pent-up desire for entertainment developed. With theaters bombed out, American and other foreign films would sometimes be projected on a screen on the side of a building.[26] And the Japanese film industry was temporarily dormant.

Once Tezuka developed the modern manga form, this gave manga the opening it (and later anime) needed to become a dominant form of mass media storytelling entertainment in post-war Japan.

Osaka "red books"

Tezuka's and manga's big break also came because, despite travelling to Tokyo several times, he was unable to get work at the large traditional publishers in Tokyo which were back on their heels as they regrouped after the devastation of the war (huge swathes of Tokyo had been destroyed by firebombing raids). This destruction of infrastructure and the new beginnings that arose from the post-war devastation were critical in forming the hotbed in which manga could flourish. Several small publishers sprung up in Osaka[i] creating *akahon* books (or "red books"), which were printed on rough, cheap paper, and used red ink.[27] Tezuka, having no choice but to start at the bottom, became an akahon artist while he was in medical school. Here, developing his art and storytelling, he laid the final groundwork for modern manga.

---

[i] Osaka is nearby Takarazuka, Tezuka's home town.

4

Modern Manga is Developed, with Heavy Hollywood Movie/Animation Influences (The Examples of Similar DNA)

- The brief story of Tezuka and his early contemporaries' contributions to the development of modern manga including Hollywood's impact upon the form.

Hollywood's influence on Tezuka and other early mangaka

Even as a young boy, Tezuka's mother Fumiko encouraged him to do what made him happy, which was to draw comics.[a] His father, a successful upper middle-class engineer/salaryman,[b] had the income and interest to purchase a Pathe film projector (9.5 mm gauge—called a "Pathe baby"), and was an avid collector of American animation. They showed their son many Hollywood films,[1] which included Fleischer Brothers animation. As noted earlier, Dave and Max Fleischer were New York filmmaking brothers who created *Betty Boop*. And they produced the animated versions of *Superman* and *Popeye* (both of which Miyazaki also mentions positively). Tezuka began watching these animated films in the 1930s, both at home with his family via the projector and in theaters.[2] Tezuka was influenced by them all, and he also incorporated Walt Disney's *Bambi* and sexy 1920s icon Betty Boop's enormous eyes into his manga.[3]

---

[a] Helen McCarthy notes that "One of Fumiko's ancestors was Hanzō Hattori, a 16th century samurai sometimes erroneously depicted as a ninja in comics and pulp fiction. (Quentin Tarantino borrowed his name in his *Kill Bill* films.)" (Helen McCarthy, *The Art of Osamu Tezuka: God of Manga* (New York: Abrams ComicArts, 2009), 15).

[b] "Salaryman" is a term meaning a male office worker, who could, for example, be a corporate executive, salesman, etc.

According to manga scholar Paul Gravett, after watching a Hollywood film, Tezuka asked, "Why are American movies so different from Japanese ones? How can I draw comics that make people cry and be moved like that movie?" Gravett surmises that this was the leap of imagination that allowed Tezuka to transform Japanese comics.[4]

Tezuka loved Hollywood for its ability to convey strong emotions, and he looked for ways to express that through manga, and later, anime. He incorporated the big eyes of the Disney animated movie character Bambi into his characters, believing that the eyes are the windows to the soul. McCarthy notes that he watched *Bambi* more than 80 times after its Japanese release in 1951.[5]

Disney would prove to be the greatest visual stylistic impact upon Tezuka's development of manga. As Schodt notes, "anyone familiar with comics can see that Tezuka's biggest stylistic influence is the rounded style of Walt Disney, whose work he adored and imported into anime as well."[6]

Figure 4.1 *Betty Boop* on the author's Hacky Sack. Betty Boop © King Features Syndicate Inc., World Rights Reserved

An enormous Disney fan, when the war ended and Hollywood films were available again, the backlog from the war years plus a 1946 freeze on ticket prices caused attendance to explode, and movies were among the cheapest forms of entertainment. Tezuka saw *Snow White and the Seven Dwarfs* over 50 times.[7] He saw *Pinocchio* many times as well, a film that would heavily influence *Astro Boy*.[8]

Manga scholar Ryan Holmberg translated Tezuka's strong feelings about Disney in *The Comics Journal*:

> I liked Disney, I adored Disney, here before you is a man whose life was determined by Disney. I first encountered Mickey around second grade at an animation festival. Also my father brought home a rickety home projector called the Pathé Baby, and amongst the films he purchased was *Mickey's Choo Choo*. From that point on I became attached to Disney by a chain that could not be cut … I first followed the comics of Tagawa Suihō and Yokoyama Ryūichi. But suddenly, once I became devoted to Disney, I set out to copy and master that stuffed-animal style, eventually ending up with how I now draw.[9]

Figure 4.2 A malevolent-looking Mickey Mouse-type character in Tezuka's *Magic House*. © Tezuka Productions

Figure 4.3 *Steamboat Willie*'s Black Pete, a Disney villain who continued appearing in *Donald Duck* animation and inspired Tezuka's pirate, Buku Bukk.[10] © 1928 Disney

Figure 4.4 Buku Bukk who also plays Pirate Bowarl in *Shintakarajima* (*New Treasure Island*) © Tezuka Productions

The Japanese economy and infrastructure was in tatters and many war orphans starved in the streets. Nakazawa said that everyone was so busy just trying to survive they could think of scarcely anything else.[11] As Tezuka recalled, Walt Disney's animated films formed a welcome contrast to that struggle: "Around 1945, daily life might have been hard, but the reputation of Disney was at its highest. The voices of *Mickey Mouse* and *Donald Duck* had stabilized; *Snow White* and *Bambi* were huge hits and had received a number of international prizes. It really was like the brightness of a rising sun."[12]

Donald Duck and Scrooge McDuck—Big Tezuka influences

Figure 4.5 Scrooge McDuck and Donald Duck, two major influences on Tezuka.
© Disney

Figure 4.6 Carl Barks drawing Scrooge McDuck. Disney's *Donald Duck* had a big impact on Tezuka. Disney master artist Carl Barks drawing depictions of Donald's cheapskate rich Uncle Scrooge also had an influence on Tezuka.[13] © Disney

Tezuka even eventually met Walt Disney, whom he considered his idol, at the New York World's Fair (1964): "As the story Tezuka loved to recount goes, he spotted Mr. Disney, ran up to him excitedly like an ordinary fan, and introduced himself. To Tezuka's never-ending delight, Mr. Disney reportedly said that he was well aware of Tezuka and *Astro Boy*, and someday 'hoped to make something like it.'"[14]

Michael Arias states that Tezuka was initially "trying to copy the Disney pipeline."[15] Whatever Tezuka's intention might have been, Disney animation and comics clearly had a significant impact upon his early work and, consequently, impacted manga's "birth" and development into its modern form.

Figure 4.7 Holiday greeting card that Tezuka allegedly sent to Carl Barks.
Donald Duck © Disney
Astro Boy © Tezuka Productions

"The white man's representative": Superman

The Fleischer Brothers' animated *Superman* was the first American television series shown in Japan (1955). In 1958 the live-action *Superman*, with George Reeves as its star, was the biggest hit in Japan up to that time. Along with *Pinocchio*'s influence on *Astro Boy*'s mangaka, its lineage from *Superman* is clear. Tezuka was even a president of the *Superman* fan club of Japan.[16]

Below and following two pages, *Astro Boy*, DC's *Superman*, and Paul Terry's *Mighty Mouse* in matching red boots, trunks, and flying poses.

Figure 4.8 *Astro Boy*
© Tezuka Productions

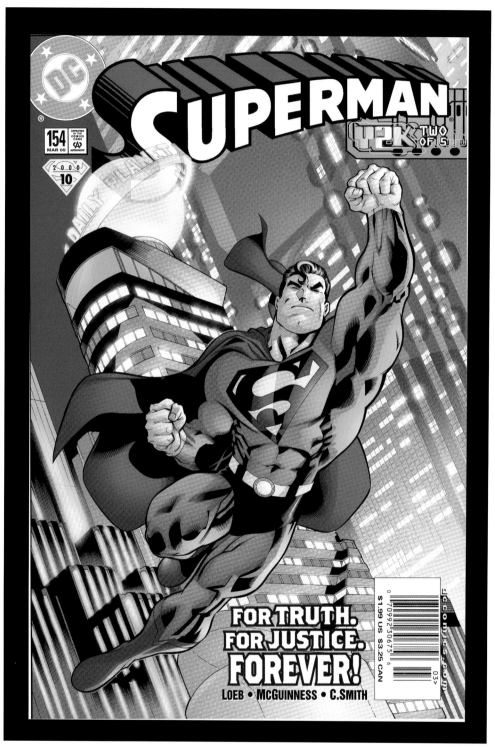

Figure 4.9 *Superman*
™ and © DC Comics

Figure 4.10 Tezuka also gave credit to Paul Terry's *Mighty Mouse*, a *Superman* parody from the same era of American comics and animation, as another source of inspiration for *Astro Boy*.[17] © Photoshot/Collection Christophel

According to Schodt's translation of Tezuka, "Atom's father was in effect *Mighty Mouse*, whose father was *Superman*. And that's the reason I used the [English] subtitle of *Mighty Atom* on the opening page when I first serialized the story. You can also see the resemblance to *Mighty Mouse* in the flying scenes, where Atom has one hand out in front of him, in a fist." Schodt continues, "And other times, Tezuka did not hesitate to speculate on the similarities between *Astro Boy* and *Mickey Mouse*."[18] According to Holmberg, Tezuka recalled that,

When *Superman* and *Batman* came to Japan, it was right after the war, right? Together with the G.I.'s. In other words, our height and theirs was completely different. We were totally overwhelmed physically, and got this complex about being unable to compete with White people. It was just then that *Superman* arrived, the White man's representative, and I thought who the hell does he think he is? And then Lois Lane, the classic American beauty. Even her outfit and her makeup were like a foreign woman's. Of course today Japanese make themselves up more like foreigners than foreigners do. Ha ha ha.[19]

Figure 4.11 The first Tezuka comic strip, *The Diary of Little Ma* (or *Ma-chan's Diary*), before his long-form manga breakthrough hit *New Treasure Island*, in which the Japanese protagonist is dwarfed by an American G.I. (1946).[20] © Tezuka Productions

When he later visited America, Tezuka finally overcame his inferiority complex about the big-framed Americans, which perhaps had been partially a result of having been beat up right after the war by a group of G.I.s.[21]

Tezuka discussed why he chose Disney's approach over that of *Superman*: "But at the time, everyone in *Superman* looked like an alien from another planet. Compared with that, Mickey Mouse was just an animal, and so was easier to use. That's the side I got consumed with. So just maybe, had I felt more in common with Superman, my drawing style would have been different."[22]

Other Tezuka characters that were directly based on Hollywood stars

According to notable manga scholar Helen McCarthy's book *The Art of Osamu Tezuka: God of Manga*, the following Tezuka characters were directly modeled on Hollywood actors.

Figure 4.12 Rommel, who appeared in *Kimba the White Lion* and *Astro Boy*, and was an antagonist other times, was patterned on German actor Erich Von Stroheim,[23] who emigrated to Hollywood and was also a major Hollywood film director (including the monumental classic feature *Greed*). © Tezuka Productions

Figure 4.13 Erich Von Stroheim in *I Was an Adventuress* (director: Gregory Ratoff, 20th Century Fox, 1940).

Figure 4.14 According to McCarthy, this character, Mason, was based upon actor James Mason, a star of many Hollywood movies in the 1950s and 60s.
© Tezuka Productions

Figure 4.15 Actor James Mason in *Five Fingers* (director: Joseph Mankiewicz, 20th Century Fox, 1952).

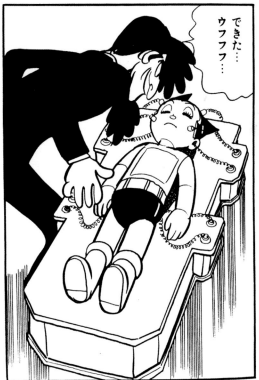

Figure 4.16 *Astro Boy*, lower left panel, Dr. Temna, Astro's creator, mans the controls to first awaken the robot boy, a pose similar to James Mason playing his undersea organ in Disney's live-action movie *20,000 Leagues Under the Sea*. © Tezuka Productions

---

James Mason played memorable roles such as the mad inventor Captain Nemo in *20,000 Leagues Under the Sea* (director: Richard Fleischer[c], Walt Disney Productions, 1954), a movie that Tezuka also possibly references when Astro Boy's partially deranged inventor father/creator appears in the same pose over his lab equipment as Mason did over his undersea organ (Figure 4.16). The scene also has shades of the classic Hollywood film adaptation of Mary Shelly's *Frankenstein* (director: James Whale, Universal Pictures, 1931).

McCarthy notes that James Mason first captured Tezuka's attention as a swashbuckling swordsman in *The Prisoner of Zenda* and that his first role in Tezuka's work was as a character named Major Zenda in *Queen Nasubi*, a 1954 girls' (shōjo) manga. She mentions that the character made appearances in several other manga, including *Black Jack*, *The Three-Eyed One* (a story about a sweet, if irritating, young boy who has a third eye covered with a bandage, and when it is removed, he wreaks havoc and becomes evil incarnate), and *Phoenix*, Tezuka's ambitious multi-decade masterwork.

Figure 4.17 Hollywood star Charles Boyer influenced this Tezuka character Monsieur Ampere (above), who also appeared in *Black Jack* and *Astro Boy* as an earl and a lawyer.[24] © Tezuka Productions

---

[c] Coincidentally, Hollywood film director Richard Fleischer was the son of animator Max Fleischer, of the Fleischer Brothers, whose work, as noted, had an impact upon Tezuka and other Japanese mangaka and animators.

Figure 4.18 Charles Boyer in *Tales of Manhattan*—based on the novel *Story of a Tailcoat* by Francisco Rojas González (director: Julien Duvivier, 20th Century Fox, 1942).

Figure 4.19 Tezuka's slapstick vampire comedy *Don Dracula*. An American indie Dracula comedy came out at the same time, *Love at First Bite* (director: Stan Dragoti, AIP, 1979), which was titled *Dorakyura Miyako e Iku* in Japan—in English, *Dracula Comes to Town*—and contains a famous "Dracula at the disco" scene which the Tezuka manga also includes. But Tezuka, perhaps playfully, claimed it was merely a coincidence.[25]
© Tezuka Productions

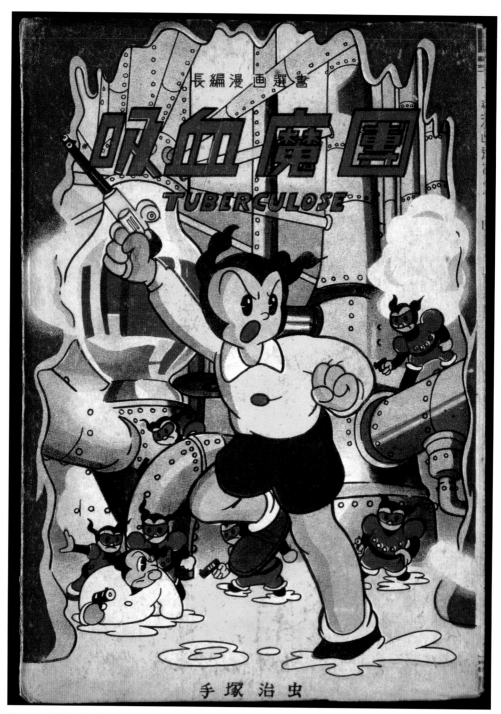

Figure 4.20 McCarthy speculated that Hollywood's feature film *Fantastic Voyage* (director: Richard Fleischer, 20th Century Fox, 1966) might have been inspired by Tezuka's *Tuberculose*. © Tezuka Productions

Figure 4.21 Tezuka's *Metropolis*.[27] © Tezuka Productions

On the other hand, Schodt writes that 20th Century Fox film studio sent a message to Tezuka about a producer "wanting to know the copyright status of a particular episode in *Astro Boy* because Fox was interested in using it for a new science-fiction film," but the producer never contacted Tezuka. Schodt explains that Tezuka felt after seeing *Fantastic Voyage* that "he'd been had."[28] Schodt notes that "Although impossible to prove, it is widely believed in Japan today that *Fantastic Voyage* is based upon Tezuka's 1964 *Astro Boy* animation episode, *Saikin butai*, broadcast in America as *The Mighty Microbe Army*."[29] And of course, "widely believed" does not necessarily mean it is true.

Tezuka's manga *Metropolis* may have taken its title directly from the Fritz Lang movie (while the classic film directed by Fritz Lang in 1926 was not produced in Hollywood, Lang later became a top Hollywood director), but Helen McCarthy writes that Tezuka had not seen the Lang movie when he started work on this version.[30] Notice the RCA Building denoting the New York City setting.

Tezuka and other early mangaka were impacted by Hollywood films in other, more general ways

Until the advent of the "graphic novel," American comics mimicked the vaudeville approach. In Tezuka's autobiography, he remarked that, "Most [old comics] were drawn as if seated in an audience viewing a stage, where the actors emerge from the wings and interact. This made it impossible to create dramatic or psychological effects, so I began to use cinematic techniques."[31] Tezuka was also impressed by vaudeville, which itself was the ancestor of Hollywood comedy.

American "vaudeville" is a form of comedy that pre-dates motion pictures and died out not long after the advent of sound in film. Vaudevillian actors and performers would go on stage, "do their bits," and exit. Performers, such as comedy trio the Three Stooges, came from a vaudeville background and successfully made the transition into films which, of course, included a sequencing of scenes that were more cinematic—employing a dollying (i.e. moving) camera, edits, and changes in perspective and location—and thus are similar to the movies and TV of today. This transition is similar to the progression from traditional comics into manga. Comics before manga played like short vaudeville skits, wherein the reader was like an audience member at a play facing a stage (the comic page) and watched passively from a distance as the action played out. Alexander Mackendrick, director of classic film comedies like *The Ladykillers* and *The Sweet Smell of Success*, told my fellow students and I at CalArts that "comedy plays in the master shot." One of Tezuka's revolutionary developments was to move the form out of that static wide shot into three dimensions. Just as vaudeville comedy moved off the flat stage and two-dimensional cinema performances into more 3-D approaches that immersed the audience, manga evolved from an often predictable 2-D comics medium into an engaging 3-D form, thanks to Tezuka and his contemporaries. As part of that cinematic revolution, Tezuka also developed the famous manga "speed lines" and other cinematic styles derived largely from Hollywood's motion-active style.

Hollywood's emphasis on action and movement was something Tezuka found that he could import into his new manga. Schodt notes,

Figure 4.23 Manga/anime speed lines in the Hollywood *Speed Racer* adaptation (directors: Lana & Andy Wachowski, Warner Brothers, 2008).

Figure 4.22 Left, Tezuka uses "Speed Lines" in the famous opening sequence of *New Treasure Island.*
© Tezuka Productions

What Osamu Tezuka did was to inject a feeling of motion into a still-life subject: He would draw a picture of Mount Fuji, Mount Moon (from *Kimba the White Lion*), or *Astro Boy*, for example, then draw the same subject a little closer, then draw another picture of the same subject even closer—as though the successive drawings were being seen through the lens of a movie camera slowly moving in for a close-up. (That way, the artist was instilling a feeling of motion to a still subject. That is how he created action in his manga and, then, in his anime.)[32]

Tezuka's first hit manga, *New Treasure Island* (*Shintakarajima*), which demonstrated these new techniques, swept the youth of Japan. It is widely regarded as the first "modern era" manga hit.

From then on, as Schodt observes, the Japanese kids could not get enough of manga.[33] In his essay for *The Comics Journal*, Holmberg translates some of the reactions of modern-day mangaka to Tezuka's first megahit, *New Treasure Island*, which sold over 400,000 copies in 1947. According to Holmberg, "Motō Abiko's autobiographical *Manga Road* (*Manga Michi*, 1970–2) shows he and Hiroshi Fujimoto (the other half of the Fujiko Fujio duo)[d] when they first read *New Treasure Island* in 1947 after swiping it from a local

---

[d]They were a mangaka pair who created the famous *Doraemon* children's manga about a robot cat and a little boy who go on adventures together, which has sold over 100 million copies and countless anime (see Figure 8.1 on page 244). In Japan, Abiko is also known as Fujiko Fujio A. As Schodt explains, "What makes all this complicated is that for years Fujiko Fujio wrote as a duo, masquerading as one person with one working pen name. Then, they had a falling out, and split their copyrights. To distinguish themselves, today they are known as Fujio F. Fujio, and Fujiko Fujio A. 'F' stands for Fujimoto. 'A' stands for Akibo. They no longer used Fujiko Fujio." (Email to author, August 31, 2015) Fujimoto is deceased. Disney is currently trying to adapt *Doraemon* into the USA TV market.

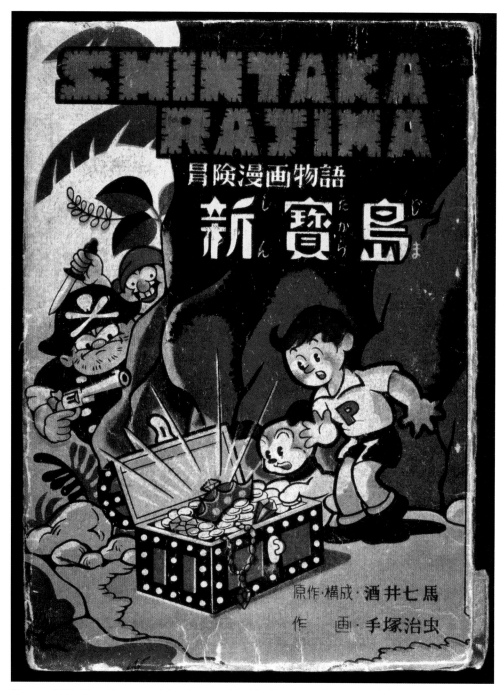

Figure 4.24 *New Treasure Island* was a big hit despite a devastated Japanese economy. © Tezuka Productions

shop." Holmberg translates Motōo Abiko's recollection in his autobiography of his and his partner's reaction to Tezuka's work as, '*What a strange name … The two boys opened the book that they had taken without asking, and received an awesome shock!!*'" According to Holmberg, Abiko subsequently explains in his autobiography that his and Fujimoto's first step as cartoonists entailed copying the entire book, all 190 pages of it.[34]

Further citing Abiko's autobiography (1975–6), Holmberg writes,

[T]he event was recounted like this [by Motōo Abiko]: "I will never forget when I first saw the book *New Treasure Island* when I was a second year middle school student in 1947 … Looking back at it now, I can see that my destiny was decided by picking up this book. When I opened to the main text, the shock was so great that I almost blacked out. At the top of the right page of the spread, there was the small title To the Sea of Adventures, and

Figure 4.25 *New Treasure Island*'s famous opening cinematic pages.
© Tezuka Productions

beneath it a boy in a cap driving a sports car from right to left … I had never seen such a manga. Two pages with nothing but driving. What was so exciting about it? I felt this biological pleasure as if it was myself in that car speeding toward the wharf … This was of course just cartoons printed and fixed on paper, but still the car was going at such speed. It was like watching a movie! That's right, this is a movie. It is a movie drawn on paper. No! Wait a minute. It's not a movie after all. Then, what is it!?"[35]

Figure 4.26 *New Treasure Island* © Tezuka Productions

Figure 4.27 *New Treasure Island* © Tezuka Productions

Tezuka's inspiration also came from American comics that were themselves influenced by Hollywood movies (in addition to *Scrooge McDuck*)

Tezuka was also influenced directly by American comics that were themselves inspired by Hollywood films. According to Holmberg, this took place after Hollywood films' initial influence upon Tezuka, who said, "Speaking of myself, when it comes to comics, from 1947 or 48, for the next fifteen or sixteen years, I was heavily influenced by American comics." Holmberg writes that Tezuka used the term "Amerika manga."[36]

But how did Tezuka get his hands on American comics? See the sidebox

Tezuka tells the fascinating story of Opera Joe[e]

It was the spring of the year after the defeat [which means the spring of 1946], and I was a student at the Osaka University Medical School. In the building next to my department was the YMCA, where they kept a piano. I would often times skip lectures and occupy that room and play it.

One day, completely in my own style, I was playing Mozart's Turkish March. All of a sudden a Black soldier entered the room. There was nothing really strange about an American soldier being at the YMCA. He took a sheet of music from the piano, and once I was finished playing began to sing in tenor.

It was something that I had heard before. It was a march. Eventually I realized that it was the aria "This Butterfly Shall Fly No More" from *The Marriage of Figaro*. To a Mozart piece, he had responded with a Mozart aria. He was a great opera fan, this intellectual Black soldier named Joe …

One day, after learning that I liked cartoons when I drew a quick caricature portrait of him, he brought me a mountain of American comic books. It was like the heavens opened and rained manna. There were absolutely no manga materials around at the time. I read through them like a worm, was overjoyed, and copied them obsessively …

My friendship with him might have been short, but it became the reason I decided to become a manga artist.[37]

According to Holmberg, Tezuka observed,

Those American comics themselves were heavily influenced by Buster Keaton's comedies, Mack Sennett, those sorts of films from the golden age of comedy. The gagmen that appeared there, for example Roscoe Arbuckle or Ben Turpin, there were lots of comics that used their style, their faces just as is. Especially Chaplin with his bowed legs and oversized shoes. Those sorts of features were used directly in comics. *In that era, all American cartoonists imitated the stars of comedy* (italics added by Davis). That is what I worked so hard at copying, and so that's why my comics are bowlegged and big-shoed. At the level of content too I was deeply influenced by the strong social caricatures of Chaplin's comedies, the tears mixed with the laughter. The biggest influence of all was the rhythm.[38]

---

[e] Translations throughout this section, of Tezuka and Akibo, are excerpts from Ryan Holmberg's excellent *The Comics Journal* articles.

American animation sprang from vaudeville?

Peter Chung, director of the *Matriculated* segment of *The Animatrix* anime and *Aeon Flux* (which he also created—an American hybrid anime series broadcast on MTV 1991–5), observed in his interview with me that,

> Animation was created in the West—it's really an American art form. It's all based on vaudeville, to create a personality that appears on-screen that you're interested in seeing because everything that happens is character-based. Animated features came about much later. Animation is based on theatrical shorts, which appeared before movies, which are based on other comedic theatrical shorts. When you used to go to a movie … you had a newsreel, you had a cartoon, you had a comedy short, you had a documentary short, and then you had your feature. That's why all those categories exist still in the Academy Awards. Even though they don't show theatrical short animations anymore, it's still a category. The whole idea of animation was completely based around the idea of creating a character that you would recognize. You didn't see the film for Charlie Chaplin—the character. You saw it for the performance. Theatrical animation is still based on that idea. *Kung Fu Panda*, etc., it's all based on characters who have personality.[39]

Nakazawa about Hollywood stars being creative inspirations

Keiji Nakazawa's career is also proof that Hollywood and vaudeville influenced manga because traces of both are clearly evident in his work as an early mangaka in the post-war years. Younger than Tezuka, Nakazawa was six years old when the atomic bomb was dropped on his home town of Hiroshima, killing most of his family and leaving him scarred.

And, after his baby sister died, initially only he and his mother were left to fend in the atomic desert of Hiroshima, with no help from practically anyone. Forced to grow up quickly under the most horrifying conditions imaginable, amidst cruelty and deprivation from all sides, Nakazawa is an incredibly inspiring individual with an equally sad life story. Yet despite it all, he eventually became a successful mangaka who also later created the classic *Barefoot Gen* manga and anime[f] about his own experiences along the way, which he did to "pin the blame where it belonged." (The imperialistic Japanese war machine at the time receives his harshest critique, but the work conveys blame to all who are guilty. In my opinion, *Barefoot Gen* is the greatest anti-war work ever.) Prominent American graphic novelist R. Crumb referred to Nakazawa as one of the great comic artists of the twentieth century.[g]

Below, Nakazwa's happy family on the night before the Hiroshima atomic bombing that killed most of them.

---

[f] Nakazawa-sensei was writer and executive producer on the two-part anime—the director was Mori Masaki.
[g] From the back cover of *Barefoot Gen*, volume 1, published by Last Gasp in the United States.

Figure 4.28 *Barefoot Gen* by Keiji Nakazawa. © Keiji Nakazawa. All rights reserved. Used by permission of Last Gasp.

In *Hiroshima: The Autobiography of Barefoot Gen*,[h] Nakazawa described how he first experienced Tezuka's magic in a makeshift school in post-war Hiroshima. His reaction is typical of Tezuka's electrifying impact upon the youth of the time. When he was living in what he termed the "atomic desert" of Hiroshima, Nakazawa discovered manga and Tezuka's work after a school friend's father gave his son a copy of *New Treasure Island* after picking it up on a business trip: "One day I encountered a terrific manga book; it changed my life." But getting ahold of the manga was not easy: "The boy who owned the book was a stinker, and he'd close the book or take forever to turn the page. I'd read along, getting angry and scolding him, 'turn the page! Open it wider!'" Nakazawa continued, "I wanted to read what happened next and couldn't wait for recess to come. To get the owner to turn the page, I toadied and flattered him. Thrilled, I lost myself in reading it."[40]

Nakazawa "wanted to read *New Treasure Island* at [his] leisure," but the boy wouldn't let him. Finally, at a small bargain bookstore at Yokogawa Station, he spotted "*New Treasure Island* on a shelf, and was madly happy." After purchasing it with money Nakazawa had saved collecting scrap metal, he recalled that "I danced my way home and immersed myself in it. I read it hundreds of times, thousands of times."[41]

Nakazawa states, "*New Treasure Island* is an important work—you simply can't write the postwar history of manga without including it … it was so dazzling that for me it might as well have been the

Figure 4.29 Humphrey Bogart in *Deadline USA*, 20th Century Fox, 1952.

Figure 4.30 Tezuka also modeled two characters, Lamune and Kalpis, on 1930s–1940s comedy stars Abbott and Costello. © Tezuka Productions

Figure 4.31 Abbott and Costello, seen here in *Abbott and Costello Go To Mars* (director: Charles Lamont, Universal Pictures, 1953).

---

[h]Edited and translated by Richard H. Minear, it is very inspiring, vivid, powerful—and well worth reading.

very first manga. Selling between four and five hundred thousand copies, it enshrined Osamu Tezuka." To Nakazawa and other young mangaka, "Osamu Tezuka was godlike."[42]

In his autobiography, Nakazawa describes his own Hollywood influences on his development into a successful mangaka,

> Gary Cooper, Tyrone Power, James Cagney, Randolph Scott, Clark Gable, Robert Taylor, Alan Ladd, Humphrey Bogart, John Wayne, Susan Hayward, June Allyson, Ava Gardner, Deborah Kerr, Piper Laurie, Martha Hayes. I stored countless names in my memory. Chaplin, the Mutt-and-Jeff combo Abbott and Costello, the Marx Brothers, Bob Hope, Danny Kaye—all were important characters useful in comic manga. As I came to love film, my desire to draw manga increased.[43]

McCarthy notes that Abbott and Costello lookalikes Lamune and Kalpis "debuted in Tezuka's version of *Golden Bat* (1947) appearing in many comics and in the animated *Astro Boy*. They work in many comics. They occasionally work solo and in drag."[44]

Nakazawa, who had seen almost every unimaginable horror in the wake of the atomic bomb, midwifed his own little sister—who was born in the hours after the detonation only to die shortly thereafter, just long enough for he and his mother to have gotten to know and love her personality—wasn't about to let any petty rules keep him from experiencing the magic artistry of golden-age Hollywood. He ignored the restrictions on youths only being able to go to films with parents or older siblings:

Figure 4.32 Groucho, Chico, and Harpo Marx of the Marx Brothers, another Nakazawa influence (here seen in *Duck Soup*, director: Leo McCarey, Paramount Pictures, 1933).

Keiji Nakazawa (cont'd):

> We were forbidden by the school [to] go watch movies alone … I hated that crazy idea so much it made me want to throw up … I watched films that forbade admission to children under eighteen that contained sexual content or violence! To say children would go amok if they saw such films! Or that seeing gangster films they would become no-goods! I had no use for such a school that had such simplistic, silly ideas![45]

The irony of this was that in 1954 the Comics Code in America would take that same "simplistic, silly" approach—that American comics were corrupting the youth.

At Hiroshima's only large (seven-story) department store's theater, Nakazawa paid for a movie ticket with his small savings from collecting possibly radioactive scrap metal and saw *Beauty and the Beast* above the panorama of Hiroshima's former "atomic desert," now filled with a sea of huts. He explains, "Three or four years earlier, this burned-out store had housed many moaning burned and injured bomb victims, but year by year it was rehabbed, and high class goods came to be displayed, more and more on the store's counter. It was a great playground for us [children]. From early morning on vacation days, we'd ride the elevator, going up and down over and over again." Nakazawa notes how the boys were dressed in no more than loincloths, to the "amazement and disgust" of the store salespeople.[46]

Even the gangsters who moved into Hiroshima, plying the black market, turning children into drug mules and even assassins,[47] and forcing a harsh reality upon the war's survivors, couldn't dim the enthusiasm and drive that Nakazawa possessed to become a successful mangaka as Hollywood films increased their creative impact upon him. As a young man, Nakazawa got an apartment in Hiroshima, and remembered "My apartment adjoined the red-light district, and women of the night and gangsters thronged the streets. It was a very raucous place: in a fight between gangsters at a nearby cabaret, dynamite exploded. Seventy millimeter films[i] made their debut, and the impact of the giant screen and the sound increased; when I saw *Ben Hur* (director: William Wyler, 1959) I was blown away—it was a great movie."[48] Despite the intimidation tactics of the thugs identifiable by sunglasses and bellybands as they dueled it out in the streets of the now gaudy and rebuilding Hiroshima, and despite privation in post-war Japan, to Nakazawa, Tezuka, and the children and young people of Japan, the future was ahead. Arising from the atomic ashes and saddled with a failed immediate past, they could form it the way they wanted to some degree.

---

[i] At that time, Hollywood began utilizing the expensive wide screen film format in large-scale epics, such as those of superstar directors David Lean (*Lawrence of Arabia*) and William Wyler (*Ben Hur*). This was partially in response to the increasing popularity of newly-invented television. The studios felt that wide-screen epics could compete with the small viewing boxes. And only the wealthy Hollywood movie studios could effectively finance, produce, and distribute them.

Figure 4.33 *Barefoot Gen* by Keiji Nakazawa. © Keiji Nakazawa. All rights reserved. Used by permission of Last Gasp.

Figure 4.34 © Keiji Nakazawa. All rights reserved. Used by permission of Last Gasp.

Manga was a big part of that fresh future. These children, who would eventually become inspired and talented pioneer mangaka and editors, would make it up as they went along and build the surprisingly successful juggernaut that would become modern manga. One of the great redeeming aspects of much early manga (especially before merchandising and corporatization became entrenched) was how emotional it was.

Early manga wasn't just a business—it was very often ethical. There was a real desire to show attitudes and character traits that were admirable but also, among quite a few, an eagerness to tell the truth about the human condition.

Tezuka had freed the form from the restrictions of the simple gag strips that American comics relied upon. And he would then, along with those who followed (like Nakazawa), go deep into character and story and change the form of what comics could achieve.

And like all artists and writers, the early mangaka needed their role models and inspiration, and at first, Disney, Barks, the Fleischer Brothers, and others from Hollywood provided that.

Figure 4.35 © Keiji Nakazawa. All rights reserved. Used by permission of Last Gasp.

Like Tezuka, Nakazawa was also heavily impressed by Disney animation

When I saw Walt Disney's *Snow White*, I couldn't forget it. For weeks afterward, scenes came to mind, one after another. Moreover, learning that it was made, in color, before the war, I was speechless at the splendor of America's power.[49]

5

The Manga Industry Today

Figure 5.1 Manga is so immersive, that you can read it on a busy city street corner.
© Ofer Wolberger

- Editors—manga's secret weapons.
- Business structure, innovative production methods and the role of competition in the manga system.
- Copyright/moral rights differences between Japan and America that aid the manga/anime forms creatively.

The editors have a lot of say in how the manga turns out

The editorial system that developed with the manga publishers in Japan is extremely different from the American comics industry. It is logical to assume that the unique way the manga publishers and editors manage the manga creators has contributed a great deal to the current enormous success of the medium worldwide.

Some of these differences between the manga industry in Japan and the American comics industry include the following:

How editors and publishers handle the creative talent

Manga editors traditionally identify new talent through either the aspiring mangaka's submission to the publisher by or in sponsoring contests.[1] New mangaka can be as young as high school age. During my 2015 visit to one of the manga universities in Japan, a professor there explained that these days Shueisha[a] prefers that new mangaka to be around 23 years old."

Underage mangaka who are put under contract naturally might need their parents' approval, if they don't live in Tokyo, to move there. And in such cases, the editors might have to convince the parents that they will be responsible for the underage creator, including getting them apartments in Tokyo.[2] As Schodt writes, in the case of a young woman mangaka new to the huge city of Tokyo, an editor could present a shoulder to cry on.[3] The relationships between editors and mangaka are frequently intimate, and sometimes even romantic. A few young female mangaka have ended up marrying their editors.[4] This would be natural because, in the high-pressured world of serialized page delivery, the editors serve many roles, including sometimes that of psychiatrist, cook, authority figure, partner—in other words, whatever it takes to get the pages done on time. Since modern manga needs to be serialized (usually) and thus hopefully long running; the editor–mangaka relationship on a hit series may enjoy equal longevity, provided that the editor does not retire, leave for another reason, or get reassigned within the companies (reassignment is a traditional Japanese corporate system of teaching an employee the major areas/departments of the company).

Fostering competition between series

Mega-publisher Shueisha encourages competition to the utmost. In his book *Manga Zombie*, manga critic Takeo Udagawa explains the formula of *Shonen Jump*[b] manga: "From the start, *Shonen Jump*'s strength lay in what was known as its 'Great Two' system. Pillar

---

[a]Reminder: the most popular manga publisher for several recent decades.
[b]Reminder: Shueisha's flagship manga magazine and historically the most successful in terms of circulation.

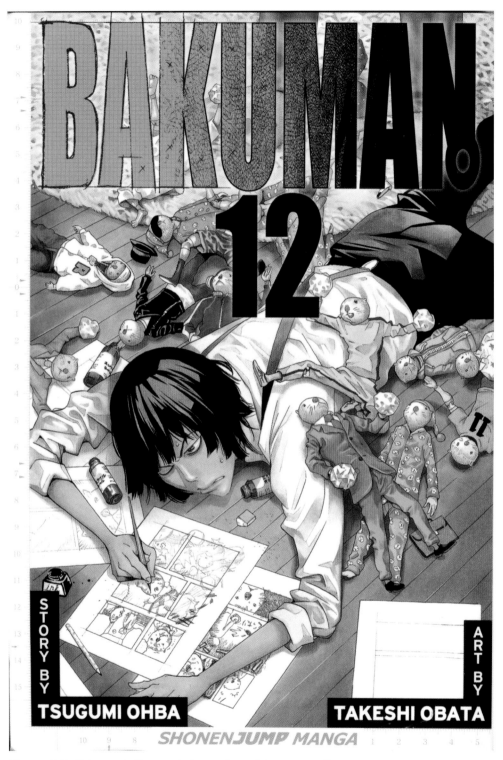

Figure 5.2 *Bakuman*'s "mangakaka protagonists are mostly young.
BAKUMAN. © 2008 by Tsugumi Ohba, Takeshi Obata/SHUEISHA Inc.

Figure 5.3 The Chief Editor in *Bakuman* explains to the novice young mangaka how Shueisha is ruthless about cutting off series with low ratings. The Japanese manga business is extremely competitive, like American TV.
BAKUMAN. © 2008 by Tsugumi Ohba, Takeshi Obata/SHUEISHA Inc.

One was watertight contracts binding artists exclusively to the publication. Pillar Two was comprehensive reader surveys; the artists had to keep high ratings in them or face the ax."[5]

Hollywood has always served as a huge filter, picking and choosing the best properties in the world for adaptation. Due to its intense competition, the manga industry potentially serves as an ideal pre-filter for Hollywood in the same way that it works as a filter for the Japanese television and movie industries as well as anime. The Japanese film and TV industries are heavily dependent upon adapting manga.

A great story can come from anywhere, but a story that has slugged it out in the intense competition of the Japanese publishing industry and has run for at least a while is clearly popular and durable, especially when we see *how* competitive the manga industry really is.

The public readership only sees the cream of the crop. For every published manga, many others are rejected. According to Hayashi, normally a mangaka will get perhaps three chances maximum, and if he/she does not produce a success, usually he/she is out for good.

From top down, the system is based on the same kind of intense internal competition to get projects published that exists in Hollywood. To convey the complexities and competitiveness of this process, I will relate my own visit to Shueisha to pitch a manga.

I arrived in Tokyo from Los Angeles for the wonderful opportunity to pitch my manga idea to Shueisha's *Ultra Jump* magazine. The interpretation/translation company that I had hired for the meeting had assigned a young man to work with me that day who previously had wanted to become a mangaka, assuming that he would best understand the system that I was attempting to broach. The morning of the meeting, we ended up at a copy shop across the street from Shueisha' famous building, both frantically copying the art so the editor would have something to look at as I pitched.

In this particular case, the Japanese artist I had employed in Los Angeles to draw the characters had repeatedly failed to meet deadlines. Like a manga editor, I finally had to go to her apartment to try to get the work from her. She still didn't have it and assured me it would be delivered to me when I got to Tokyo. I boarded the plane with much trepidation, and after I arrived in Tokyo she failed to deliver the art in the days leading up to the meeting. Finally, that morning a friend of hers brought the artwork to the interpreter, who himself was nervous about not meeting the deadline, and we dashed across the street. The kind man who had arranged the meeting, Mr. "M" (whom I had met in Los Angeles regarding my initial interest in *Battle Angel Alita* as a Hollywood adaptation project),[c] looked like he had aged ten years in three minutes because we were cutting the time so close. In Japan, to be late for such a meeting would be a significant error, especially in the case of such an exceptional invitation.

Figure 5.4 *Bakuman*'s two young mangaka heroes knock out pages over burgers and fries. BAKUMAN. © 2008 by Tsugumi Ohba, Takeshi Obata/SHUEISHA Inc.

As we rode the elevator to the main floor, I tried to compose myself. I also imagined the plight of many editors in the manga world going through similar experiences—perhaps smoking cigarettes down to the filter, gobbling ulcer medicine as they try somehow to coax, threaten, cajole or whatever it takes to get the art out of the mangaka. My experience in my own manga class since then has been as sort of the editor of all their projects, so with 25-plus student manga projects running at once each semester, my identification with manga editors has increased even more. In seven years teaching at my university, I have overseen roughly 1,000 student projects in my classes, consisting of manga, screenplays, and TV scripts. But what happens in my classes is nothing compared to the pressures of professional manga serialization. Editors have been known to cook for the mangaka,

[c] See Preface.

show up "accidentally" in coffee houses and restaurants frequented by the mangaka, go to doorsteps and beseech their wives, and even, famously, "canning" (kan-zume) them in a hotel room. This is a practice in which the mangaka is sequestered so that they will focus and finish their pages.[6] With an entire distribution system, worldwide, depending upon the mangaka to deliver their finished pages weekly, late delivery is unthinkable. Stories have circulated for years of mangaka yelling at their editors for falling asleep in the middle of the night while they worked, and of one who escaped out of their hotel window and was chased across Japan by their editor, who finally retrieved the pages. Whether or not the latter is an urban myth, it is reflective of the pressure-cooker intensity of manga serialization.

Geof Darrow, a prominent graphic novelist who worked with Frank Miller and who was also on the Wachowskis' creative teams for *Speed Racer* and *The Matrix*, talked to me about similar experiences he had in Japan,

> The first guys I made contact with over there [in Japan, happened] because I was in France working with a company formed by Moebius.[d] They had everyone on their list. They had Frank [Miller] and Liberatore [Tanino, an Italian comics author/artist] and all the best guys … they got a letter from Japan about a guy who was trying to order their stuff, and I was like, "Oh let me answer this one in English." He was an editor at Kodansha [the major publisher]. I went over there eventually and he took me to their offices. I have pictures of it and—oh my god it was a frightening place! Every day he'd go to work and he spent most of his time going from one to the other, sitting with these people, making sure they were drawing and getting these pages out of them. He had ten artists he had to keep an eye on. It was super stressful. Eventually he got out of it and started selling American toys. It's the same with animation. I was working at MadHouse [a major anime studio] and the assistants just go and sit on the doorstep, and then just kind of cajole the guys or their wives to get them to hurry up and finish these scenes that are due. It's amazing.[7]

Editors with a "hands on" (intensive) approach

Schodt notes that Tezuka, due to his enthusiasm and energy, overextended his obligations, and "like many famous Japanese comic artists he came to depend on his own staff and editors to hound him; scrambling to meet the deadline became an essential part of his daily routine."[8] Schodt recalls the story of an editor flying to San Francisco to get Tezuka, who was having too much fun on the trip to complete his work. And cursing after having finally gotten Tezuka to focus on finishing his pages.[ef9]

In the US comics industry, laggard artists are countered by a tried and true technique: a large portion of the payment for their artwork is withheld until they produce all of the

---

[d] The French artist, cartoonist, and writer. His real name was Jean Henri Gaston Giraud (1938–2012), who, incidentally, contributed storyboards and concept designs for films such as *Alien* (director: Ridley Scott) and *The Abyss* (director: James Cameron). He was admired by Miyazaki.

[e] For a good example of manga editors trying to get art out of a star mangaka, there is a video (that, as of this book's writing, was available on the internet) of Tezuka working near the end of his life, and the editors are speaking in a disparaging and frustrated way about his wily ability to hold them off. He is seen finishing pages in the taxicab parked outside the airport terminal.

[f] There is even an informative and entertaining manga about being a manga editor: *King of Editors*, by Seiki Tsuchida.

Figure 5.5 A page from *Bakuman*—the mangaka create a calendar schedule for their assistants and themselves as they produce two serialized series at one time. BAKUMAN. © 2008 by Tsugumi Ohba, Takeshi Obata/SHUEISHA Inc.

work for which they were contracted. My department accounting manager, who administers the grant I was awarded at the university where I teach, advised I withhold at least 50% as the final payment to the artist for my manga, which is not a bad strategy, considering the tendency of many comic artists to procrastinate. But, serialized mangaka are on a pressure-cooker schedule many times as intense because, for a hit series, they have to deliver so many pages weekly, month after month, and sometimes year after year.

A buffer is built in for the extremely rare event of a major illness that forces stoppage. The idea of suspending a hit series for a mental block is unthinkable. An entire industry rests on the hits, all the way down to mom-and-pop newsstands in the subway stations and the corner 7-Eleven, not to mention worldwide distribution, which is now simultaneous to Japan due to the internet.

Felipe Smith, an Argentinian who created *Peepo Choo* in Japan (which was serialized in Kodansha's *Morning* magazine, 2008–10), noted the following on a 2014 Comic-Con panel:

I've had meetings that started at 3 AM when I was getting ready to go to bed … I've got buddies who work for Marvel, DC, Image, Dark Horse; depending on the schedule, they'll start the comic before it's serialized. For most artists, a page a day is solid, but most people are doing less than that … In Japan, it's a lot more. If you're going to be putting out a monthly or a weekly, then you're having your meetings where you decide on your story, and changes that need to be made … In a seven day week, it will take four days to write the script, write it out, have your editor tell you to rewrite it. That just happens. Maybe you'll have a fight with your editor. It gets really personal. You see them more than anyone, unless you're married. You'll have just as many drinks and meals … My editor once told me, "Don't think of me as a human, think of me as a crow. I'm a savage. I need to eat." … He's a great editor; I learned a lot, but I got phone calls after meetings that we just had. We'd have meetings at 8 PM after dinner, and we'd sit down and we'd figure out pages … and he'd say, "Okay, we're done, go home. Do these pages." … I'd leave, draw a little, and get a phone call saying that he'd thought about it some more, and we should have another meeting.[10]

Assistants: Bring extra clothes and food

For the assistant of a mangaka, a position that does not really exist in the United States, the process is very arduous as well. Jamie Lynn Lano, an American who went to Tokyo to be around the anime scene but did not expect to be hired into the industry, was amazed and delighted when she fell into a situation where she worked for the mangaka of the megahit manga/anime *Prince of Tennis*.[11]

Figure 5.6 The *Prince of Tennis* is an example of mangaka being able to make almost any subject incredibly dynamic and exciting.[g]
THE PRINCE OF TENNIS © 1999 by Takeshi Konomi/SHUEISHA Inc.

---

[g] Deliberate time decompression is a key element in the arsenal mangaka/anime directors deploy to achieve this success in sports anime/manga in particular, but even in such uncinematic subjects as cooking or even Pachinko or Asian board games.

Asked by anime/manga industry journalist Deb Aoki at Comic-Con 2014 about her experiences, she explained what it was like:

Lano: I didn't move to Japan to make comics—I didn't think it was something you could do as a foreigner. I moved to Japan because I graduated college and wanted to live in the "land of anime." Sometime down the road, my friends told me that [Konomi, the creator of *Prince of Tennis*] had put out an ad for assistants, and it was non-smoking, and it said newbies were okay. I applied, and it happened. I was a huge fan of the series before, and I had considered going into comics as a profession in high school. So it just happened for me. I didn't move there with that specific intent. I just fell into it. It was hard work, but it wasn't the intent.

Aoki: What was the interview process like?

Lano: I had to send in an application, a resume in Japanese, and a photograph—this is common in Japan. I had to recreate two specific pages from *The Prince of Tennis* manga, volume 27. So I sat down and got all the materials and got the materials from the art store. I looked at it really close, and spent a couple days meticulously drawing it, even though I had no idea what I was doing. Three to four days later, I got a call from who would later become our editor at *Weekly Shonen Jump*. The editor had me come into the studio and gave me Konomi-sensei's cell phone number. "Go to this station way far. Call him, and he'll come pick you up. Here's his cell phone number." So I did, shaking the whole time, and what I thought would be a one or two hour thing ended up being three days.

Aoki: I guess the interview turned out well.

Lano: It turned into a three-day thing. When he first showed me around, he was like, "Here's a bunk you can use" and I was like, what? A bunk for what? We went to the store later that night, and he was like, "I'm going to buy you some snacks." I turned to the other assistant and asked, "Are we staying overnight?" He helped me get through the experience. It's embarrassing when you have your idol—who's really hot, by the way—he handed me a 10,000 yen bill and was like, "Buy anything you need. The [guy assistant] and me, we're going to go downstairs and shop for food." The other girl assistant was like, "Don't you need underwear?" But at the time I didn't know the word for underwear. So I didn't buy any because my Japanese sucked at the time … Apparently I was good enough to get past this; he kept me on for a long time.[12]

On the same Comic-Con panel, American manga editor Lillian Diaz-Przybyl (see her photograph on the following page) explained the more invasive nature of Japanese manga editors versus American ones.[13]

Aoki: Lillian, did you ever live in Japan?

Diaz-Przybyl: I did. I double-majored in Japanese and English, so I studied abroad in Japan for six months. I took a course in anime and manga production. It wasn't a serious course. We took tours of studios like Toei and had guest speakers. Stu Levy [founder of original American manga publisher Tokyopop] was one of the guest speakers. He mentioned that *Tokyopop* did internships, but they were unpaid and in California, and I was in the East Coast. It put it on my radar. So when I was graduating, I just applied to a junior editor position at Tokyopop on a whim. I worked more with

Figure 5.7 American manga editor Lilian Diaz-Przybyl (second from right) at Anime Expo in Los Angeles where my students and I make great connections to several manga publishing executives and researchers. One of Wemakemanga.com's original student webmasters, Mike Hughes, is on the far end to my right. *Project Alpha* is on the screen. Also pictured are Robert Napton and American manga creator Tania Del Rio. Photo: Bert Le.

Diaz-Przybyl (cont'd):

> licensed manga, and stuff coming from Japan. That was when we started doing original English language manga, so I was trained in the style of being a manga editor.
>
> **Aoki:** What is the way of editing that's different than in America?
>
> **Diaz-Przybyl:** There's an intensiveness that you can achieve in the Japanese industry just by sheer proximity. I went back and forth to Japan a bunch of times on licensing trips. I talked to a bunch of creators. If you ever read comics or watch anime where the editor knocks on the artist's door and asks for pages … that's a real thing that happens. They will sit with you until your work is done. You don't have the ability to do that in America. Everything's digital, and can be done remotely. Your ability to go and sit on somebody until they finish their work is different. It's a different way of managing talent.[14]

The "hands on" nature of the Japanese manga system is further reflected in the competition-based editor's room.

Figure 5.8 BAKUMAN. © 2008 by Tsugumi Ohba, Takeshi Obata/SHUEISHA Inc.

Even the desks in the editor's room are arranged to foster competition

Regarding my observations about pitching my own manga project at Shueisha to the *Ultra Jump* editor, when we arrived on the main floor, this is what I saw (see previous page, Figure 5.8):

As is clear in the previous *Bakuman* page above, the three groups are each underneath a separate deputy-in-chief. The three deputy editors-in-chief are under the editor-in-chief. So not only are the editors in each group competing against each other to present new manga ideas and artists or new ideas from older artists, or to keep their mangaka's series running another week, but each deputy editor is also competing against the other two. And this is for one magazine, *Shonen Jump*.[15]

This sort of intense competition throughout Shueisha has its roots in a philosophy. As Hikaru Sasahara, the Japanese owner of Digital Manga Publishing (*Berserk*, *Vampire Hunter D*, and *Yaoi* genre) and who claims to be the first person who attempted to get the *Astro Boy* live-action adaptation movie going in Hollywood, told me, "Opposition is the key to make each one excel."[16]

Figure 5.9 *Bakuman* shows caring and dedicated manga editors assigned to the fledgling or veteran mangakas doing everything they can to make the story work. The weekly serialization meeting is depicted on the upper right side page.
BAKUMAN. © 2008 by Tsugumi Ohba, Takeshi Obata/SHUEISHA Inc.

This opposition concept may be apparent in the way that Shueisha and its rival Shogakukan (which originally founded Shueisha in 1924 for the purposes of publishing entertainment magazines and then later moved into entertainment itself and became its competitor) are separate companies yet part of the same major publishing group, the Hitotsubashi Group.

So what determines whether a series stays or is dropped, or whether a new one gets picked up? Regularly, there is a high-level meeting only the group captains (and those higher up, like the editor-in-chief) can attend called the "serialization meeting." This meeting (see previous page, Figure 5.9) determines whether existing series have survived another week or if contracts will be ended and the series dropped, and whether new series will be picked up.

The method used to decide which series are dropped is partially by reader feedback solicited by the publisher, which is then tabulated, along with comments.

Below: The mangaka protagonists of *Bakuman* react to readers' polls and their editor Mr. Hattori discusses story and strategy with them.

Figure 5.10 BAKUMAN. © 2008, by Tsugumi Ohba, Takeshi Obata/SHUEISHA Inc.

Ian Condry, after his year living and studying the anime and manga industries, made the following observation:

> **Condry:** They have these big, thick manga series that come out weekly, and they put in postcards, and they get back 3–4,000 postcards a week. And they go through them. Add them up. What are the three best stories and the three worst stories in this issue? And if you're one of the worst stories you get cycled out pretty quick. There are so many manga artists ready to break into that world, and on the flipside of that, if you're successful you've battled it out year after year. They don't care if you've been nine years successful now. If you're one of the most boring, you're out too. You may get a little more time to prove that you can bring yourself back, but there's not a lot of love in that world. It's like TV pilots, you either hit or you don't.
>
> **Davis:** And it doesn't matter what you did before. You have to get to first base yourself.
>
> **Condry:** It's about the readers. On one hand, the industry is very attentive and set up this formalized feedback loop where they get thousands of responses a week.[17]

American comics editors rarely have the same kind of hands-on relationships with their charges. Nor do they have the readers' polls. As Condry said, manga production is a lot more like American TV production (for example, with the American system of "Nielson ratings" for feedback of a show's popularity) than American comics, as we will learn more about later.

Walt Disney reportedly said, "Get to know the characters before they get involved with the plot." Many successful mangaka have focused on that approach as well. And the business model of the manga publishing industry aids in fans' identification with manga characters. For example, Condry explains how the low cost of manga helps readers to become hooked on the characters,

> The other thing that makes it interesting in the manga world is that it's so cheap. It really is cheap. The thing about the manga is that you can read it for free! If you have a half-hour to wait, just flip into a convenience store and stand there and read them. Or maybe buy one and pass it along. They say that the average pass-along rate for manga is three to six people! So this stuff is really passed around. This happens to me too. Whenever I ask people what manga they like, they usually give me a couple. "You gotta read this one. And this one." So that's really the foundation, and it's through that process where you find an audience that's deeply committed to these characters. Then they're like, "Well, I'll watch it as an anime or I'll buy the toy or I'll listen to the drama CD or get some of the merchandise." It's because there's already an attachment to the characters that makes it so successful in Japan, and it's the intensity of the competition in the manga world that makes this really broad catalogue for anime to build upon.[18]

Differences in legal/copyright

The differences in legal and copyright norms between those enjoyed by the Japanese mangaka and those that affect American comics creators and writers may have also had a profound impact upon the enormous sales of manga versus the very limited sales of American comics.

Ownership: Mangaka versus American comics writers and American screen and TV

The primary differences are simple:

Mangaka: much more control over the series and any of its licensing spin-offs.
American comic artists: traditionally had no control over pretty much anything, creative or businesswise, if the funding entities don't want them to have control.

As Napton notes, the creative ownership situation in America is beginning to change: more American publishers such as Image are allowing creators to retain their ancillary rights. But, the classic American comic publishers DC and Marvel own their legacy series outright for the most part.

The American system commonly requires assignation of copyright ownership to the employer of the creator's work. For example, when I sold my speculative screenplay *Cyber Ship* to Warner Brothers, that studio assumed ownership of its copyright.[h] This means that, by owning underlying copyright, the studio can essentially do whatever it wants with it. Besides whatever my contract with Warners stipulates, I have no more rights to *Cyber Ship* outside of certain rights designated in the Writer's Guild of America's Minimum Basic Agreement (MBA) which the American movie studios and television networks are signatories to, which grants the WGA jurisdiction over limited parts of the transaction (governing such things as pension/health insurance payments and minimum allowable payments and working conditions). This copyright ownership issue has major implications for the creators of famous American comic series (*Superman*, *Batman*, etc.), especially when their comics have been made into hit movies and sold extensive merchandising. Selling a "pitch" to an American movie studio or network works the same way, in that the copyright becomes the property of the corporation that paid for the story that was pitched.[i]

For mangaka, the situation is very different. Consulted about almost everything, mangaka decide if and when anime and live-action adaptations get made (that is, *if* their editors bring them the offer—editors might turn away offers that are deemed unworthy before they get to the mangaka: the star creators are fiercely protected in terms of access). And this includes when Hollywood wants to adapt their manga/anime.[j]

---

[h] But of course I happily agreed to this in return for the possibility of it being produced, and the large amount of payment that I received. The contract that conveys copyright from the writer/creator to the studio is called the "assignment of rights" part of the agreement.

[i] As also does the writing (or rewriting) services of the screen or TV writer (after the pitch is "sold") to create the actual script. This process will be detailed later as pertains to Hollywood manga/anime adaptations.

[j] Besides Hollywood, other Asian countries have licensed the right to produce their own local language live-action versions of Japanese manga/anime series, even if those were already turned into Japanese live-action TV shows, including South Korea (that for example adapted *Hana Yori Dango* into the *Boys over Flowers* [English translation] Korean TV drama, as well as *Densha Otaku* (*Train Man*). Japanese networks have also adapted Korean scripted live-action television shows, which are known for their high quality, into Japanese language versions with Japanese actors (for example, *Hotelier*). This practice, called "formats," and like localizations of anime/manga and Hollywood movies and TV shows, takes place worldwide. For example, the American television show *The Office* was adapted from the British show, and USA's *Ugly Betty* was adapted from a Columbian telenovela *Yo soy Bett, la fea*, which itself was adapted to many countries. Showrunner Phil Rosenthal (who created the American TV hit *Everybody Loves Raymond*) even made a documentary about the process of adapting that show for Russia's television industry.

In America, mainstream comic creators, at least until fairly recently, have mostly worked under a "work for hire" agreement. And, here again, the corporation controls and owns everything. Unlike the mangaka, the American comic writer has historically been "a cog in the machine."

Robert Napton explains how this works in detail:

A lot of anime is based on manga, and the manga writers and artists have extraordinary creative control over their work in Japan. Much more so than in America. Comic artists, or comic writers—oh my God they'll probably … having worked as a comic writer for ten years I would say they're probably at the bottom of the barrel. That's changing now because you got guys like Robert Kirkman who have been really successful with his TV series, *The Walking Dead*, getting the respect he's due from the creators of that show. He's very involved in the process. But that's the exception, and that's all starting to happen now. Before, basically as a comic creator in America you'd work for Marvel or DC, they'd pay you x-amount of dollars, they'd own what you create; they would go off and exploit it elsewhere. No one would ever give you the time of day again after that. That's changing in America, but in Japan it's always been the opposite.[19]

Figure 5.11 Mangaka are paid in a few ways which reflect their power versus American comic creators. This page explains some of those.
BAKUMAN. © 2008 by Tsugumi Ohba, Takeshi Obata/SHUEISHA Inc.

So, writers for classic-era American comics hired by the big publishers are often, if not usually, simply writers for hire, not original creators who have control, and power, like the mangaka have. The American comics companies own the characters and the entire franchise. The corporation just keeps hiring new artists who, harsh to say, are usually interchangeable. Mangaka, on the other hand, usually have far more control over their own series. They have to approve and profit by any ancillary spin-offs, including the anime, live-action television shows and movies, toys, games, merchandising, and on and on. Most importantly, they usually have the determining choice in all creative decisions regarding their manga, including when to end it, if they themselves end it (rather than if it ends due to cancellation). Creative power is built-in and those with hit series accrue wealth. This is not the case for the above-mentioned American writers.

The Japanese copyright system and the emphasis on creators' rights

I interviewed Salil Mehra, an international copyright law professor at Temple University's Beasley School of Law, to discuss how the Japanese copyright system came about and the differences in the Japanese and American systems. Mehra observed,

> There are similarities; there are differences. They're an interesting case because they incorporate—first off, they're a very affluent country, a large market, and pretty developed export of cultural industries. Nothing probably like Hollywood, but pretty big cultural exports. They have a legal system that is somewhat different from ours, but that values a lot of the same things ours does. In their constitution, they have freedom of expression [which] guarantees many of the things that we would find familiar. And so, sometimes they come to similar resolutions as us, sometimes different ones, and that's what makes it interesting.[20]

"Doujinshi" is an example of the differences between Japanese creators' rights (moral rights) and American copyright laws

Before continuing with Professor Mehra's account, I want to quote Digital Manga Publishing owner Hikaru Sasahara[k] to educate the readers about *doujinshi* (a term meaning self-published manga):

Davis: Do you see any way that the United States publishing industry can be changed to make it more likely that people can create better works that are not Japanese based?

Sasahara: Yes. As you know there [have been] several really huge conventions in Japan for the last 20 or 25 years. One of the biggest is called Comiket. It attracts more than 400,000 people twice a year, summer and winter. This huge gathering [is comprised of] those people who actually create their own private comics on their own, and they make their own printout and bind them together with a local printing company. They call it doujinshi. That market is really growing big, and as the popularity grows within

---

[k] For details on Sasahara's background as regards the topic of this book, see Chapter 9.

Figure 5.12 Anime Expo, the largest North American anime con, Los Angeles. Photo: author.

Hikaru Sasahara (cont'd):

the doujinshi market, the competition grows as they try to become better and better. So this gathering, this doujinshi private manga creator event, is one of the ways the Japanese manga is really excelling compared to the comics done by the other countries. Doujinshi could not survive if it wasn't for a difference in Japanese copyright law, emphasis and practice over American copyright law. If American fans for example began drawing and selling *Mickey Mouse* comic books without authorization from Disney, the corporation would be compelled to act to enforce their copyright. Or they would risk losing it.[21]

Comparing mangaka to pro baseball players

Mehra: There's a book called *Free Culture* by the copyright expert Lawrence Lessig that explains the free culture movement in college campuses. He discusses the work I did ten years ago in his book. And the issue is, the industry developed in a way that is more like a cross between literature and, I've had Japanese economists explain to me this way, like baseball. A combination of literature and baseball. I know that sounds odd. [Laughs] The idea is that there is essentially a kind of minor league structure. For a long time it was understood, and obviously intellectual property protection is getting stronger everywhere, and that might be good or bad in the long-term, but 10–20 years ago it was understood that the doujinshi markets were actually a kind of minor league area where talent could develop and make sales rise up, get spotted. And if you got spotted, you'd get your turn to bat. You'd get to start a serial in one of the manga magazines. And if your serial caught on, you could get your own fan base. And this gives the mangaka a certain amount of power in the same way a baseball star has, and that was the idea. But it's also a power that's seen as this sort of literary—maybe not the highest literary respect—but increasingly respected. They're not like people who are making it for hire, usually. They're people who came up through this free-agent model in the same way to become Alex Rodriguez, you have to fight off a thousand other Alex Rodriguez's through the minor league markets, and then eventually you have fans. If you do a new serial, they'll latch onto it. You have your own style, and that style might incorporate design elements, storyline elements, dialogue, things they like about the way you do things. That gives you a certain amount of power. You're not fungible [i.e. interchangeable] with another author in the way. This would be somewhat akin to how the public views a very select number of film directors. Usually, these directors have a very distinct style and/or are critically acclaimed and/or have extreme commercial success over the body of their work. Thus their fanbase will go see their films no matter what. Tezuka is a unique example. That's like using Babe Ruth as the example.[22]

Professor Mehra went on to explain that in manga, the readers are often followers of the mangaka's work as a fan would be, and the mangaka may be their hero, but in film, audiences usually are not attached to the screenwriter or director in the same way, except in the case of a few superstar directors. And that thus the filmmakers can't really drive merchandising due to their relationship with the audience—but mangaka do have that kind of relationship and "are the people who should have the stronger ability to market merchandise."

> **Davis:** It's like a personality thing.
> **Mehra:** And that might be a way to understand it. The second issue is the moral rights issue.

Moral rights: In this case, an author's right to the integrity of their work

How Japanese copyright law and practice developed differently and why this impacted the power and control of the mangaka

> **Mehra:** In the US we really aren't a moral rights jurisdiction. We have very limited moral rights. We don't completely recognize moral rights as part of our copyright law. We really deal with the same issues through things like defamation and unfair competition. There are moral rights for visual artists in the United States, but it's a narrow subset— like painting and things like that—through a statute about 20 years ago. In Japan, you continue to have [moral rights]—and Japan isn't unique. A lot of civil law jurisdictions provide for inalienable rights against distortion of your work, which is prejudicial to your reputation or somehow distortive or in bad face. Law professors have argued that the distinction is because copyright in the civil law jurisdictions traditionally came out of this kind of natural law understanding that this was the artist's sweat and

toil. It was an extension of the artist's self. Whereas in the US, there was a much more utilitarian understanding that copyright was a right given to incentivize artists to create and sell, to promote a sort of economic growth, or something like that. So it's a more instrumental idea, more economically rational. If you believe the first story— the natural extension of yourself, your sweat and your toil—then inalienable moral rights against things like bad face or distortion makes sense, because it's not just the artist sold you the right and you're going to go sell a movie, it's that the artist has done something out of their own heart and soul and you're injuring them if you do it in a bad way, or you twist everything. Whereas in the US, the idea is to sell product, or to encourage creation—well you've done that, they've created because they could sell it so what's the problem, you know what I'm saying?

Davis: That's really huge.

Mehra: That could explain some of it. But there are ways to deal with it. The concern is being hit with some sort of moral rights claim … you could give them some sort of consultative role, right? Or something like that to the original author.

Davis: You know what they call that here? I find it fascinating what you just said, because in every single Japanese negotiation [that I've been involved in]—the [Hollywood] studios always say "meaningful consultation." That's very interesting because it means that the studios are trying to address that but it's not serious [if they don't want it to be].

Mehra: It's really just a way to avoid the train going off the track, or alternatively to head off a claim by the moral rights holder. If the moral rights holder [according to the tradition and law within their country] comes in and goes, "Look, I sold my copyrights to these people who remade my thing and it's a distortion and it's bad face" and the judge says, "But you were consulted on this as it was produced." Right? It's a hard argument for the right's holder.

Davis: That's brilliant. I didn't even think of that. That's why the studio lawyers are often the smartest …

Mehra: I think so.

How is this manga/Japanese copyright/moral rights system different from the American Hollywood copyright system?

Davis: It sounds like a question of shading, because you were talking about their moral rights there, right? It's more of an attitude, right?

Mehra: Right. Moral rights, I think, we shouldn't get too wrapped-up in it. The overwhelming concept of it [as] this bad face exploitation or something that might hurt the reputation of the original author. That kind of idea. Although it's an important thing, it's not as if the moral rights say that this author will always have the rights to all derivative work. It's kind of an additional concern if you're going to license anything.

Davis: That's pretty huge, because over here there's no such thing. [Here I am referring to the rights in America of the comic writer and screenwriter, as regards to having no "moral rights" etc.]

Mehra: I don't want to exaggerate it, because it's not a Japanese-only thing. You'll see in civil law, places like France, Germany, etc., there's a moral rights tradition as well. And the idea isn't simply, "Oh, they changed my work." It's that they changed your work in such a way that it's in bad face or damages your reputation.

Davis: It's just a different way of approaching everything, and I think you've given us an overview. Historically, do you know where this comes from?

Mehra: It's the European civil law transfer. It's the split. It's a number of things, not just intellectual copyright. It's one of those splits that's largely Anglo-American law versus European civil law, and Japan really absorbed it. A lot of its constitutional traditions come from American law now, a lot of its private law—like contracts, copyrights, things that deal with private individuals, draw on German civil law.

Davis: German is all about being the artisan or something?

Mehra: Something like that.

Davis: Because that would really help the readers see where this comes from.

Mehra: I think that's a big part of it. Law professors, we could be wrong, but there have been a bunch of people who have written about how it goes back ultimately to this idea of natural rights in your creation, and that being a civil law concept. Copyright is largely being about incentive for writing. Incentive for production, and that being the American consumption. People always exaggerate that it's all one or all the other, and it's probably not all one or all the other, but there is that difference in flavor.

Davis: I'm a little confused about when you say copyright as incentive for creative production … what do you mean by that?

Mehra: If you go back to the US Constitution, Jefferson drafted a constitution where we give Congress the power to establish systems of patent and copyright, "to promote progress in the useful arts." So the idea is not to recognize the toil of inventors and artists, but to create a better society. To increase GDP or something like that. Intellectual property law—patent or copyright—is a tool to an end as opposed to something that recognizes a natural right.[23]

The takeaway of this interview, it seems to me, is that there's sometimes an inherent paradox here: US copyright law is supposed to encourage production for the "greater good," yet, in the process, it sometimes disenfranchises artists, which *discourages* artistic production. So, to a certain degree, the Japanese manga publishing system actually encourages creativity and artistic production more than the US legacy comic publishing system does (or at least did, before things started changing recently). In Japan, in the manga system, the individual artist is empowered—which is in the best interest of that country's "greater good."[1]

Healthy focus on the core business first and foremost
What we can we learn about my pitch to Shueisha

In Tokyo, as I pitched my story at Shueisha's manga magazine *Ultra Jump* (in which *Battle Angel Alita* was being published at the time) and attempted to persuade them to acquire the story and develop it as a manga, I attempted to "hook" the editor with its merchandising potential. This kind of strategy is fairly common in Hollywood—I even notice my students doing the same when pitching their stories in my class (pitching also helps them hone their stories through the resulting feedback they receive and learn to explain their

---

[1] Although, as I noted, with various American publishers such as Image now letting creators keep ancillary rights, things are changing. My own publishing deal for my own manga that I will write after finishing this book has me keeping the ancillary rights.

projects quickly and simply to publishers and producers). And when they do bring up merchandising potential, I tell them what the Shueisha editor said to me when I brought up merchandising—he advised me not to think about such things. Instead, the editor emphasized that in the early stages, they only focus on making the manga a success. He stressed that they do not initially focus on the transmedia/cross-platforming, but only on making the creative work succeed in its initial form. After a manga becomes successful, he said, then the potential licensee would have to prove their trustworthiness to protect the image and reputation of the underlying brand.

I found that attitude very refreshing, and very different from the attitude of some American comics companies that seem to be acquiring work *only* because it might have Hollywood adaptation potential. This is why a company like Image Comics seems healthier, as it is focused, like Shueisha's editor was, on the core business/creativity of creating a successful comic/manga. This is not, however, to say that the manga system is not enormously entangled with merchandising, spinoffs, and every sort of ancillary market possible. But the base of the business, manga, needs to be developed properly first for any of the other aspects to work at all. And once again, this is a "shades of gray," or in Mehra's words "a difference in flavor," situation, and there are insiders in Japan who have complained in the same way American filmmakers have complained about the ancillary angles that come into play, particularly once the manga hits the anime stage. Part of this is due to the fact that anime costs more than producing the manga, so commercial pressures are bound to intensify even more (though, as we've seen, it is cut-throat already in terms of what gets cut and kept—but at the initial stage, ideally the only consideration/focus is the quality manga). More about my Shueisha meeting later. But for now, this seems to be a perfect point to go to the next part of this story.

6

Anime is Born and Invades America (and American TV goes to Japan and Influences Manga/Anime)

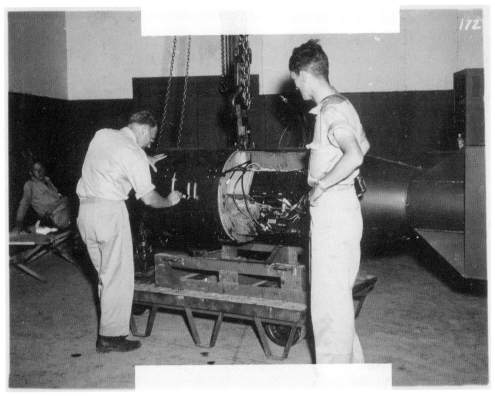

Figure 6.1 Tinian Island in the Pacific, the Little Boy atomic bomb is finished. Courtesy National Archives. Unrestricted. Note: Declassified: NND 730339 image #77-BT-172.

The atomic bombings of the Japanese cities of Hiroshima and Nagasaki marked the end of World War II and had a thematic impact on quite a few manga and anime that arose from the ashes.

And now, American television would go to Japan and make its own waves that would reflect back to America in the form of manga/anime it sometimes inspired.

American TV goes to Japan and influences manga and anime

Television, as much as film features, plays a huge role in the confluences covered in this book and potentially even more—in the future of global scripted media entertainment.

The economics of losing World War II put Japanese television development behind America by several years (pre-war Japanese experiments in TV showed promise, but the war cut off the development in resource-poor Japan). So the TV shows of America—the wealthy victor—were the first of either country's to cross the Pacific. The Fleischer Brothers' animated *Superman* was the first American series shown in Japan (1955). *Popeye*, *Huckleberry Hound*, and *The Flintstones* followed. The significant cultural and linguistic differences between the two countries did not hinder the success of American animated television shows in Japan. As Jonathan Clements and Motoko Tamamoro observe in *The Dorama Encyclopedia: A Guide to Japanese TV Drama Since 1953*, "When two cultures are very different, cartoons are often easier to transform into local products—dubbed dialogue is harder to spot, and children are less likely to notice anyway."[1] And in 1958, 74% of Japanese TV households watched the live-action *Superman* starring George Reeves, making it the biggest hit of all time in Japan.[2]

More American TV live-action comedies followed, such as *I Love Lucy*, *I Dream of Jeannie* (Japanese title: *Cute Witch Jeannie*), and *Bewitched* (*My Wife is a Witch*). After Tezuka invented the anime TV series form, the latter two shows helped create the anime genre of Magical Girls with *Comet-San* and subsequent anime serials such as *Little Witch Sally* and Tezuka's *Marvelous Melmo*.[3]

This became an example of the type of "boomerang" effect that this book repeatedly highlights, where works cross over to another country and then stimulate the creation of works there, which then come back to the original country. Clements and Tamamoro explain that "Treated as a wholly juvenile genre in Japan, the idea [the Magical Girl genre] soon split into two distinct subsets of animation—girls' stories about sorcerous minxes who could transform, Cinderella-style, into older, more sophisticated versions of themselves, and boys' stories about guys with magical girlfriends … 'the magical girlfriend' subgenre lives on in live-action Japanese scripted shows such as *Minami's Sweet-heart* and *Steel Angel Kurumi—Pure*."[4] Later, the hit *Sailor Moon* (Naoko Takeuchi), of the Magical Girl genre, would become very popular with female American fans after that anime TV show was localized for American broadcast by the same team (led by Fred Ladd) that adapted *Astro Boy*, *Kimba the White Lion*, and *Gigantor* during the early anime wave in America.[5]

Figure 6.2 Osamu Tezuka's *Marvelous Melmo*. © Tezuka Productions

American live-action TV invades Japan

When the American 1960s live-action television show *Batman* arrived in Japan, it was adapted as a manga tie-in which *Shonen King* magazine hired mangaka Jiro Kuwata to pen. Kuwata had to take cultural differences into account:

> I totally reconstructed the stories so they would appeal to Japanese readers. One example I clearly remember was when a villain posed to Batman a nonsense word riddle at an extreme life-or-death-situation. Batman was seriously trying to answer it when he was about to die! That particular scene lacked so much reality to me and seemed awfully awkward. The stories had to be more mature and real for the Japanese readers. Such a thing would have been very wrong to them.[6]

A popular American comedy, *I Love Lucy*, became a hit with recently luxury-deprived (due to World War II) and traditionally submissive Japanese housewives, who enjoyed watching the redhead, and other American actresses, boss their husbands around in comparatively opulent kitchens and homes. This benefitted the advertisers, as the Japanese housewives traditionally controlled the household budgets and thus discretionary spending.[7]

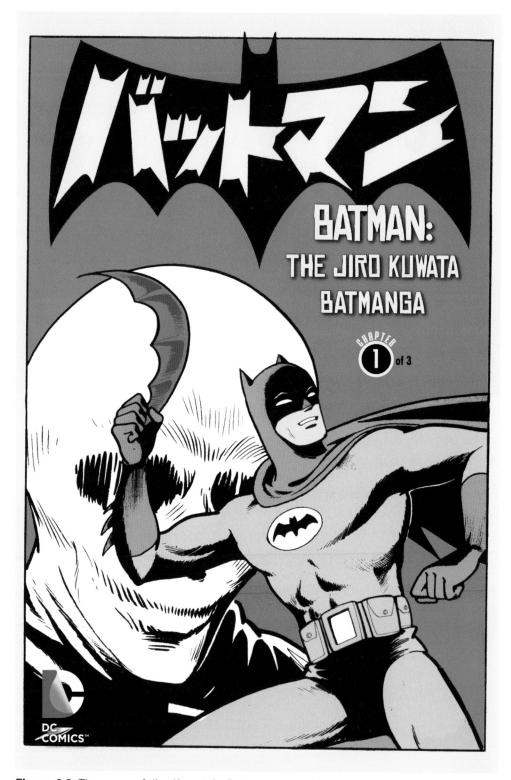

Figure 6.3 The cover of Jiro Kuwata's *Batman* manga box set.
Batman is ™ and © DC Comics

A brief summary of the development of Japanese home-grown TV shows

After watching many other American shows in various genres, such as Westerns, including the Clint Eastwood-starrer *Rawhide*, and police shows like *Dragnet*, Japanese viewers started writing their TV networks, asking why Japan didn't have its own television shows. Adding to this problem, some Japanese viewers complained that it was hard to tell the Americans apart.[8] Eventually, with the advent of industrial videotape, and remote broadcast capability, the Japanese TV production industry's technology and expertise began to compete with the Americans'.[a]

The first Japanese drama shot on video in several locations was *I Want to be a Shellfish* (*Watashi wa Kai ni Naritai*, 1958), a story of a gentle barber arrested as a C-class war criminal, who claimed to have been ordered to execute an Allied war prisoner under the threat that he'd be killed by his superiors if he didn't comply. As he awaited the gallows, he wished to be reborn as a shellfish so he would never be drafted again.[9] Initially, Japanese TV production was hobbled by the superior Japanese film industry which froze out the fledgling TV industry, refusing to let its artisans, writers, stars, and directors work in television.[10] And to further block TV's growth, the Japanese film industry did not initially allow their movies to be televised. Local television production companies gradually hired creative talent from radio and other industries, and Japanese-produced TV eventually outstripped imported American shows. 1964 was the first year in which no American TV show was in the top 20 in viewer ratings in Japan.[11] By the 1990s, the Japanese film industry, its postwar Akira Kurosawa-era heyday long behind it,[12] realized that TV was now where the profits were. Movie theaters had become little more than "loss leaders" to set up video sales. Because of this shift in economic trends, the two industries became tightly integrated.[b13]

Japan's anime television shows became the major part of Japan's exportable animation and comics to America which inspired many of today's up-and-coming Hollywood film and animation makers (with some notable exceptions like *Akira* and Miyazaki's feature animated films, which influenced filmmakers in America as well).[c]

Thus today, the Japanese television schedule is populated in large part by manga/anime shows, reality, talk, game, sports and news shows as well as other home-grown productions. Recently, however, Japanese television has experienced a ratings decline, perhaps due to video gaming and a lack of diverse scripted content that American television now broadcasts.

---

[a] The first Japanese television satellite broadcast (and the first trans-Pacific satellite broadcast) was planned to be from Dallas, Texas, with John F. Kennedy addressing the Japanese people on November 22, 1963 in a goodwill speech, highlighting this new technology. But before the transmission, he was assassinated. Instead, Japanese television viewers, who had received widespread publicity regarding the technological breakthrough, were shocked with the news of his murder transmitted via satellite. The advent of international TV news also gave the Japanese people a more accurate view of the world, dissipating many stereotypes that they previously held about other peoples. And those changed attitudes were reflected in manga/anime.

[b] Although in recent years Japanese feature filmmaking has had some what of a resurgence.

[c] Even more than manga: because anime television shows pre-dated manga in coming to America to any meaningful degree—by decades.

These American TV shows (and, as we have seen, Hollywood movies) have had a profound effect on many Japanese anime directors who came after modern-manga founder Tezuka. To the Japanese creators until fairly recently, Hollywood was a golden, glamorous industry. Professor Ian Condry, who, as noted, spent a year in Japan studying the anime industry, discussed this:

> **Davis:** Do you have some examples of anime directors or artists who noted specific influences from Hollywood or American/European films?
>
> **Condry:** Ooh, that's a good question. They all do. I'd be hard-pressed now to say whom. Some of that stuff should be out and about. Oshii Mamoru[d] talks about his influences … also, the guy who made *Cowboy Bebop*—Watanabe [Shinichirō].[e] It's safe to say that Hollywood has had a huge impact on the ways everybody sees film—any kinds of film and television entertainment."[f][14]

And as the manga boom swept Japan in the 1950s and *Astro Boy* became the biggest manga hit to date, the anime industry was about to be born, and, once again, this revolution would come from Tezuka by way of his little robot boy.

Astro Boy comes to America

The first American television airing of an anime series was *Astro Boy*—a big success in 1963 on NBC TV that was, as noted, followed by the even more popular *Gigantor*, and later in 1965 by the first color anime TV show, Tezuka's *The Jungle Emperor* (in America titled *Kimba the White Lion*). Those initial shows were eventually followed by other anime TV series such as *Speed Racer*, *Battle of the Planets*, the afore-

Figure 6.4 Tezuka visits Paramount movie studio in Hollywood in the 1980s.
© Tezuka Productions

mentioned *Sailor Moon*, and, much later, *Dragonball*, *Pokémon*, *One Piece*, *Naruto*, and so on. As we will later see in detail, the flood of anime series to America also had a big impact on much younger, future Hollywood creatives like the Wachowskis, James Cameron, and

---

[d] A director of several successful anime, including *Ghost in the Shell*.

[e] Also director of *Space Dandy*, *Samurai Champloo*, and part of *Animatrix* (with other directors). He is interviewed for this book by Yoko Hayashi.

[f] The Hollywood impact upon anime/manga can encompass homages and in-jokes. For example, *The Rocky Horror Picture Show*'s intergalactic transvestite character Dr. Frank-N-Furter (played in that live-action movie by Tim Curry) was referenced in the naming of the character Franken Von Vogler in the anime *Giant Robo* series—according to *Giant Robo*'s director Yasuhiro Imagawa in a 1994 interview with Takayuki Karahashi in *Animerica Anime & Manga Monthly* magazine. The article states that the flamboyant Imagawa is such a fan of *The Rocky Horror Picture Show* that he once went to a *Rocky Horror* screening as the wheelchair-bound Dr. Scott, a character from that movie (Karahashi, *Anime Interviews*, 78–9, 81).

others who, in most cases, first saw anime on TV as children, probably without initially knowing the shows were from Japan.

But first, anime itself had to be invented.

The story of the *Astro Boy* adaptation process between NBC and Mushi, Tezuka's anime production company, are as fascinating as they are critical to understand

Contrary to popular belief, *Astro Boy* was not the first Japanese animation to be distributed in the United States. Three Japanese animated feature films had been exhibited in America theatrically in 1961, but failed shortly before the *Astro Boy* TV series aired on NBC. *Hakujaden* (*Tale of the White Serpent*), released in Japan in 1958, was an adaptation of a fable from Chinese mythology, *Madame White Snake*. Released by American International Pictures (AIP) in 1961 and modeled after Disney films, it failed to find an audience, although in Japan it had a positive impact upon Miyazaki and caused him in part to want to become an animator.[g] The second feature, *Sarutobi Sasuke*, fared no better. An original story also told in the Disney style featuring cute animals, a ninja hero, and songs, it tanked at the box office. The third feature, *Saiyuki*, an adaptation of the manga *Boku no Son Gokū* by Osamu Tezuka, was based on possibly the most famous Chinese legend of them all, and one of the four great classical novels of Chinese literature: *Journey to the West*. Though financially supported more by its distributor (again AIP) than the first two, it also failed to find a significant audience despite being the best-remembered of the three. According to pop culture critic Terrence Canote, "Osamu Tezuka later stated that his only role on the film was as a script consultant. It would be this adaptation of his manga that would lead to his interest in animation and hence the TV series he created over the years."[15]

A little known fact is that there was an *Astro Boy* live-action TV show that Fuji had broadcast in 1959 that was produced by independent producers. With 65 aired half-hour episodes, it was apparently somewhat of a commercial success. But according to Clements and Tamamuro, Tezuka was "aghast" with the show, and his anime was a way for him to create the project his way.[16]

Astro Boy's first syndication order by American TV was a robust 52 episodes, and its final total was 104. Since NBC was one of only three major networks at the time, this ensured that *Astro Boy* would be seen all over America. It also set the stage for the initial 1960s anime explosion onto American TV that made a big impact on a handful of the current and future Hollywood directors, writers, and artists, including Stanley Kubrick who, after seeing *Astro Boy* and getting Tezuka's mailing address from NBC, offered Tezuka the job of art director on his upcoming sci-fi masterpiece *2001: A Space Odyssey*.[17] This was a high compliment indeed.

---

[g] And of course later his films were big worldwide hits and eventually became distributed through Walt Disney Studios.

Kubrick wrote Tezuka that he was very impressed with *Astro Boy*. Tezuka, although very flattered by the invitation from the already-famous Kubrick, who by then had directed *Dr. Strangelove*, *Lolita*, and *Spartacus* (Tezuka reportedly even photographed the envelope that Kubrick's invitation arrived in), declined the invitation due to the amount of time he would have had to spend in England during the production. He had too much going on with all his anime and manga projects.[18] But after *2001: A Space Odyssey* came out, "Tezuka often played the soundtrack at full volume through his long working nights."[19]

How anime "style" was created largely by financial necessity

Tezuka reportedly called manga "my wife," and anime "my mistress," because anime is comparatively very expensive—and as some mistresses do to their lovers, anime eventually helped cause Tezuka's company, Mushi, to fall into bankruptcy. But in 1963, Tezuka put together his production company Mushi (which means "insects"—Tezuka was a lifelong insect enthusiast). Right after that, Fuji TV, Japan's top network, agreed to finance him to animate his manga *Tetsuan Atom* [later titled *Astro Boy* in America]. Although Tezuka was reportedly very happy at the idea of animating his manga characters, he faced significant hurdles.

Fruitful risk-taking

Before going bankrupt, but after *Astro Boy*, Mushi was later responsible for other successful TV anime like *Princess Knight* (the first of the eventual booming girls' shōjo-style genre in manga and anime—and with a gender-bending twist, which the NBC executives of the 1960s rejected, terming it a "sex switch").[20] Mushi also produced the boxing classic *Ashita no Joe*, as well as more adult-oriented feature films such as *1001 Nights*, *Cleopatra* (the first X-rated animated film), and *The Belladonna of Sadness*.[21] And we'll learn about its big post-*Astro Boy* success in America, *Kimba the White Lion*, later in this chapter.

Necessity is the mother of anime's invention

The differences in mechanical and artistic production of anime versus American animation are in large part due to Tezuka's lack of funding. Financing for the *Tetsuan Atom* show consisted of a ridiculously small amount from Fuji TV: "according to Eiichi Yamamoto, part of the original team of six at Mushi, Fuji paid approximately 750,000 yen while production costs were estimated to be over 2,500,000 yen."[h22] There was a candy company sponsor,

---

[h] I have read other production cost estimates, including 2,100,000 yen. So I put the question as to the amount of *Astro Boy*'s budget to Associate Professor Mariko Koizumi of Kyoto Seika University's manga program, who specializes in the study of the business of the manga and anime industries. She replied that "The payment to Mushi [Tezuka's production company] from the broadcasting station [Fuji] was 550,000 yen. The average production cost at that time (30 minutes) was more than 30,000,000 yen for full animation. No [official] figure for *Astro Boy*'s production cost was revealed." (Email to author, July 27, 2015). Whatever the actual cost was, it was clearly far more than what Tezuka was receiving from Fuji.

Meiji, but there were no big income streams coming from sources like the breakfast cereal manufacturers that supported American television animated series. This budget shortfall was apparently exacerbated by the fact that Tezuka deliberately bid the price he claimed he could produce the animated shows for, hoping that then he could corner the market for anime production due to his low price and keep future competitors out.[23] Also, early animation in every country has to cut corners to make the budgets. These factors forced Tezuka and his animators to abandon Disney's heavily rendered (and very expensive) style that he so dearly loved; however, these stylistic "compromises" resulted in creative innovations that would become an important part of anime's signature aesthetic. Thus Japanese limited-animation, which is called "anime," was born. Mushi was initially set up in Tezuka's house but eventually grew to over 400 employees and revolutionized animation in Japan.

The many very expensive techniques that were used in creating the Disney style of animation were intended to give the audience the most "transparent" (i.e. not "seeing the hand of the creator") seamless experience, such as high frame-rates (either 12 or 24 per second) and separate artists for each character. As Schodt noted, "A ninety minute feature length animation produced in this fashion would require 129,600 individual drawings."[24] Since it would have taken 3,000 animators (far more than existed in Japan) and a huge budget to approximate Disney production values (*Snow White and the Seven Dwarfs'* budget was $1.4 million, an astronomical amount for that time), all kinds of innovations were discussed by the Japanese to try to compensate in order to produce the 25 minutes of anime per episode on a much lower budget.[25] So, on the suggestion of a Tezuka employee, Tezuka and his creative team implemented their own version of the "Kami-shibai" style.

Figure 6.5 Tezuka in his own studio. © Tezuka Productions

(Described earlier, it is a pre-manga form of popular entertainment somewhat similar to a primitive slide show.[26] Most Kami-shibai stories consist of 12 or 16 large [15˝ x 10.5˝] sturdy, beautifully illustrated cards.)[27]

Sometimes the confluence between manga/anime and Hollywood is imagined and not actual. In 1955, *Sazae-san*[i] was made into a short-lived scripted TV live-action show, which subsequently started the now-widespread tradition of TV live-action adaptations of manga. *I Love Lucy* was imported into Japan two years after *Sazae-san*'s live-action TV adaptation. Some Japanese viewers protested that *I Love Lucy* plagiarized *Sazae-san*.[28] They didn't understand the production cycle or length of time it took to get an idea into TV production in the USA, nor that it was extremely unlikely that Desi or Lucy Arnaz had seen *Sazae-san* and then suddenly created a show based on it.

The production work accomplished for *Astro Boy* was enormous and required weekends with people living and innovating in the production offices. Tezuka and his team pioneered techniques like holding frames for several seconds, panning across a static cell to give the impression of movement without having to redraw, and a plethora of other new stylistic methods.

Peter Chung describes the main differences between anime and American animation

Peter Chung is the Korean-American director who directed the cult-status anime that was hailed as "ahead of its time," MTV's avante-garde *Aeon Flux* (1991–5), as well as a segment of the *The Animatrix*.[j] Chung's imaginatively written and directed *The Animatrix* segment, *Matriculated*, pushes the *Matrix* universe and story perhaps as far as it can go, as a group of humans seek to socialize one of the machine empire's killer robots by introducing it to human emotions. Chung was *The Animatrix*'s one non-Japanese writer, outside of the Wachowskis' contributions, such as their *Flight of the Orsis* episode, as otherwise *The Animatrix*, a hit and a showpiece of Hollywood/anime hybridity, allowed high-end Japanese anime directors to interpret the Wachowskis' universe.

The Matrix is one of the best live-action interpretations of Japanese animation style ever. *The Animatrix* offers a fascinating view into the world of *The Matrix* outside of the films.[k]

---

[i] As noted, the classic early "four panel" comic strip (1947) by female comic pioneer Machiko Hasegawa. It was later adapted into an anime series so incredibly popular that its total run far exceeded Hollywood's all-time longest-running scripted TV series, the animated *The Simpsons*.

[j] *The Animatrix*, a nine-part direct to video anime anthology of stories based upon *The Matrix* film universe, was produced by Lana and Andy Wachowski, with series producer Michael Arias, and was financed by Village Roadshow Pictures, Warner Home Video, and produced at Madhouse, Studio 4°C, and others (2003).

[k] For example, *The Second Renaissance* parts 1 and 2 (directed by Mahiro Maeda and written by Andy and Lana Wachowski) together form a 20-minute prequel story for the *Matrix* trilogy's universe. It explains, in fascinating detail and with stunning visuals, why the *Matrix* world came to be, including the initial brutality by the humans to the robots/machines that motivated the robots to create their own society, leading to the war that the machines won. And just as art sometimes predicts the future, like with *The Matrix*, *The Second Renaissance* forms a cautionary tale years in advance of the real fears of the implications of an AI arms race upon humanity as expressed by experts including Stephen Hawking, Apple Co-Founder Steve Wozniak and Bill Gates when they called for a ban on autonomous weapons in 2015.

Chung, with the knowledge of a scholar on the subjects of anime and animation, described in his interview with me and web postings how many of Tezuka's and his Mushi colleagues' innovations that became money-saving hallmarks of anime style known worldwide, such as:

- Relying on camera pans to keep from having to draw more cells (which is the case in American full-animation).
- One Japanese artist drawing all the characters versus each character having its own artist, as in American animation. This is part of the reason for the huge list of artist credits on Pixar and Disney films, as well as a reason for those movies great expense.
- Moving layers of background images to avoid redrawing, and still creating convincing motion. In the "Making of *Animatrix*" documentary *Scrolls to Screen: The History and Culture of Anime*, graphic novelist Todd McFarlane (*Spawn*) demonstrates an example from what many consider a landmark anime, *Akira* (director Katsuhiro Otomo's 1988 adaptation of his 2,182-page manga), that hit American art-house theaters and introduced many now middle-aged Americans to anime (and is now a potential Hollywood live-action adaptation project). In *Akira*, foreground and background night buildings slide on different planes at different speeds, giving the illusion of motion. Thus, instead of having the camera track inward, the buildings slide past.[29]

This kind of effect was similar to what I remember seeing as a child. As a toddler, I remember being in my crib in New York City and watching *Astro Boy*. I felt that the way Astro moved through the streets, hovering, with buildings passing him by on both sides, was somehow different than what I was already used to in animation. It was eerie and dreamlike. In writing this book, I learned what caused that "look" and movement. Peter Chung explains,

Figure 6.6 A scene from *Akira* (director: Katsuhiro Otomo) where multiple cells slide past each other, giving the impression of a perspective shift as the "camera" "moves" closer into the cluster of buildings. © MASHROOM/AKIRA COMMITTEE All Rights Reserved.

There are even differences in the Japanese 35mm animation stands which emphasized approximation over precision and thus opened up a greater range of movement for shots like flying scenes but the downside was less accuracy in simple panning walking cycles, where the feet wouldn't be properly anchored on the background—"sliding foot syndrome." As opposed to the American system where the peg bars have increments precisely noted by the animator on the exposure sheet (x) sheet. The goal was accuracy.[30]

Tezuka and his collaborators worked around the clock, even developing ink stains and callouses on their hands.[31] "They figured out how to cheat their way through the process, and in the good moments, actually convince you that they weren't cheating," noted McFarlane in *Scrolls to Screens*, with Schodt also observing that anime "often looks like reading manga, often the frame is semi-frozen and the characters don't move as rapidly as Disney animation … freezing the frame, looking at the eyes, focusing on the emotion."[32]

This also worked for achieving spectacle. *Pacific Rim* director Del Toro recalled that, "I remember I was watching Japanese anime with Jim Cameron, because we used to show each other the latest anime back in the 90s and he said, 'What amazes me about the Japanese sci-fi anime is that they can get more value and that's why they go for animation. The budgets are not restrictive. They can get really crazy.'"[33]

These innovations were often marvelous, but also created some drawbacks compared to American animation. And these differences often contribute to the perhaps "5%" alienness of the genetic building blocks of Japanese anime and manga as opposed to other countries' animation, live-action, and comics that makes these forms attractive and interesting to non-Japanese, but can also, sometimes, distance the viewer as well. As Chung notes, they are a mixed bag. One of the primary differences is lip-syncing.

According to Chung, "The evolution of most current Japanese animated character design derives from the need to cover the imprecision of their lip sync,"[34] that is, looped as opposed to pre-recorded dialogue. Anime saves money by recording the actors after the animation was locked or nearly locked, in contrast to the way Hollywood animation, including Disney and later Pixar, records the actors first then painstakingly renders the animation through elaborate timing to match the voice track. Anime's often narrow, cute, or handsome faces possess the small chin required for anime characters' mouths to appear as little out of sync as possible to the post-recorded dialogue.

A drawback of this recording process is characters appearing less 'whole' in the way their voice is disconnected from their mouth movements. Chung cites the GGI live-action feature *Babe* (director: Chris Noonan, Universal Pictures, 1995) as an example where great care was taken to animate the mouth movements on the protagonist pig to sync up to the pre-recorded dialogue, and how this created empathy for the character. It is also an example of how audiences often emotionally connect more to characters in the best highly-rendered Hollywood animation (Disney, Pixar, etc.). This difference also illustrates the entire process of how animation as opposed to anime is created.[35] As Chung explains, "American directors will focus on the character's performance as he delivers the dialogue, to the exclusion of the other factors in a scene, such as environment lighting, camera angle and movement … the Japanese director tends to do the opposite. Both tendencies have their good and bad points."[36]

Anime director and *Animatrix* series producer Michael Arias discusses anime voice acting

Arias: [Part of the goal of anime is] to make stuff expressive with as few drawings as possible, and that was not the primary concern at the Walt Disney studios. It affects all kinds of things. It's more efficient and it gives your animators more freedom, and it costs less to record dialogue after the animation is complete, or when the animation is almost entirely finished, and makes no attempt to synchronize lip movements. The good voice actors get pretty close, when they do, they call it *afureko*, which means "after record."[l] That's how things are voiced here [in Japan]—this is just one example by the way—when it's in a nearly completed stage or when it's completely complete they will have the voices recorded for it. Kind of the way ADR[m] is done for live-action, except in live-action ADR you have the actor who actually acted the part come in and record dialogue that was already recorded once on set but the quality wasn't great, or they didn't get a great track, and they'll try to place the voice in the scene perfectly. Whereas in animation, it's hard to say whether the chicken came before the egg, but the aesthetic has evolved in Japanese animation where perfect lip sync is not a high priority. I mean it's not a priority at all. Maybe the only time when you do *puresuko*, which is "pre-scoring" of dialogue, is when you have child actors, or as an experiment, or if you're working on a co-production. For like a TV series, they try to get the lip movements spot on, so they'll have a guy who does a timing sheet, which is a symbolic representation of mouth positions for a line of dialogue and mark it out along the timeline, so the animator can place the mouth in the right shape at the right time. Which is constricting if you're an animator. It restricts the performance. It makes the animator locked into the intention of the voice actor and not the character. Animators here complain about being made to work with a timing sheet. It also splits the performance into two parts. The dialogue part and the action part. Unless it's really well done, you'll have characters whose mouths are just moving along with dialogue without necessarily any relation to the movement of their bodies or their poses.[37]

Nobuo Masuda further explains the different lip-syncing techniques

Davis: Can you explain, for those who read the book, the process of recording dialogue in Japan on an anime, and where it comes in the production, versus in America where it comes in animation?

Masuda: In Japan, actors get together and add ADR [Automatic Dialogue Replacement] to the picture.

Davis: So they [add] ADR to the picture after they've done the actual animation?

Masuda: Yeah, sometimes they do it after the animation is done, but in actuality they do it

---

[l] Arias later re-explained that afureko refers to the process of dubbing animation after production of visuals is complete, a process subordinate to the image production. This contrasts with puresuko, "pre-scoring," the technique common outside of East Asia, wherein dialogue is recorded a priori.

[m] Automatic Dialogue Replacement.

during the rough animation. Sometimes it's just the layout, sometimes the line test. The actors gather together and make recordings for the picture. In the United States, they usually record the voice first.

Davis: So you felt in the analysis on that page [a web page with Peter Chung's theories on this subject], that's one thing that makes it different, making the Japanese animated characters with the pointy chins and small mouths so the lip flap won't be too evident?

Masuda: In Japanese, the lip flap is free-mouthed. In the United States, the mouth is more complicated. Like when you throw out the F sound you have to make a certain shape with the lip. But in Japan we don't do that kind of thing.

Davis: Did you have any kind of feeling that part of the reason you have a problem with adaptations is because there is something inherent to the way the Japanese process of creating the anime and manga that's, unless you really understand it—the physical process, the cultural, what went into it—you're going to lose it when you try to adapt it to live-action?

Masuda: Yeah, probably. You're not talking about story.[38]

A final example of Peter Chung's money-saving hallmarks of anime style is ...

- "**Pay calculation:** This has a huge impact on the entire approach to production. Key animators are paid by the cut. In-betweeners are paid by the sheet. It doesn't cost more for an in-betweener to spend longer on a drawing, resulting in a tendency to produce a lower count of very detailed drawings rather than a higher count of simple ones."[39]

After Walt Disney produced lavish hyper-detailed and expensive productions, he tried to return to simplicity with Disney's *The Jungle Book* and *One Hundred and One Dalmatians*. American TV created animated shows like *Mr. Magoo*. That these developments coincided with the invention of anime might seem to indicate a shared "back to the basics" artistic movement influencing Japanese and American animators at the time. But Chung feels that it was more a matter of each side of the ocean separately grappling with cost issues and solving these technically as well as artistic trends in America influencing American animation style.[40]

Norman Klein's *Seven Minutes: The Life and Death of the American Animated Cartoon* describes how the American animation industry progressed from the early limited-animation that had such an impact on manga and thus on anime's development. A key manga story innovation was Tezuka's progression into a long "novelistic" form, which he extended into many anime. Anime, like the manga upon which its stories and characters are often based, is genre-rich. The time of day when anime airs depends on whether a show is considered family-friendly or darker themed—family shows air in the daytime, while more adult-themed shows air late at night.[n] For example, general audience *One Piece* airs during

---

[n] This practice is the same for US animation, chiefly Adult Swim but also Fox/FX animated shows like *Archer*, *Bob's Burgers*, *Family Guy*, etc.

daytime hours while the violent anime *Berserk* and the crime-filled thriller/horror *Death Note* aired late at night. However, some family-friendly programs do explore deep, and sometimes controversial, themes. Even child-friendly *Astro Boy* wasn't afraid to fight for "robot rights," which some saw as a thinly veiled reference to the American civil rights movement, even flying to Vietnam to protect Vietnamese children from United States B-52 bombers.[41]

Perhaps the more conservative later strategy by Disney (that might have been related to Klein's statement that Walt and his brother Roy used merchandising to help keep the company afloat during lean times)[o] left the door wide open for Tezuka and other mangaka and anime creators in Japan to develop the often edgy, challenging, and relatable stories and themes, even while preserving the big family audience. But even in darker manga/anime like *Black Jack* and *Berserk*, some of the characters were "cute" so that they could reach a broader readership/audience. Regardless, Disney merchandising and theme parks remain very popular in Japan.

The upshot of Tezuka's ability to produce such inexpensive anime is that financiers grew to expect shoestring budgets as the norm. Thus *Astro Boy* and later anime, with a few exceptions such as the lavishly financed *Akira* and the well-budgeted animated films of Miyazaki, started a trend that continues to the present, in which anime are often woefully underfinanced. Miyazaki specifically blames Tezuka for the chronic impoverishment of anime budgets.[42]

A quick detour: Snickering all the way to the bank—American television show *Wacky Racers'* minor impact in Japan

Klein's book also covers US animation's move back into limited-animation with TV shows such as *Mr. Magoo*, and Hanna-Barbera Studios' money-saving production processes on *The Flintstones*. Hanna-Barbera also produced *Wacky Racers* (also called *Wacky Races*), an animated television series about a group of 11 different cars racing against each other in various road rallies, with each driver hoping to win the title of the "World's Wackiest Racer." Both shows were successful in Japan. A very famous mecha anime's own parody spin-off is believed by some fans to have parodied the look of lantern-jawed villain Dick Dastardly and his sidekick Mutley the snickering dog characters from *Wacky Racers*.[p]

In Klein's interview with him, Joe Barbera talks about how he stripped out much of Disney's processes and "brought animation back to the twenties … where only certain body parts would move,"[43] thus making Hanna-Barbera incredibly prolific low-cost animators, although far less creative or elegant than Tezuka's anime. In fact, the NBC representative who first saw *Tetsuwan Atom* while watching TV in a Tokyo hotel had assumed that "since

---

[o] According to Klein, labor disputes as well as a contraction of the revenues paid in the theatrical short-film market put severe financial pressure on Walt Disney at points, and merchandising revenue became a key way to diversify and thus reduce financial risk. The theme parks of course became an excellent way to achieve this goal, leading to huge success.
[p] However, in keeping with the rigorous scholarship of this book, I am not naming the series due to lack of evidence of the creators stating that this is the case.

there was no TV animation coming from Japan in those days … because of the extremely limited-animation, the new show must be something out of Hanna-Barbera Studios."[44] However, anime and manga's best works are more sophisticated than such simplistic (if sometimes enjoyable) American made-for-TV animation, which was usually intended for kids. Though exceptions exist, the general quality difference in anime versus American TV animation of that era is also due to the essential qualities of manga, anime's predecessor, as described earlier. Manga's strengths would become anime's. That said, like *Wacky Racers*, there are many anime not meant to be decoded for deep and intense storytelling.

Wacky Racers is also illustrative of how hard it is to predict what successfully crosses over from one culture to another.

A possible explanation for the show's popularity in Japan might be the fact that "the cartoon was unusual in the large number of regular characters, twenty-four in total: the twenty-three people spread among the eleven race cars, plus the never-seen (and never identified) race announcer."[45] These large groupings of protagonists and villains are very common in manga and anime. Or, just maybe its popularity is simply because Japanese kids like snickering dogs wearing racing goggles and scarves?

So returning to 1963, where was Tezuka to get more money for the production of *Astro Boy*?

American television! Stay with me here while I explain …

Why is TV often the most ideal medium for anime adaptations

When I was in Tokyo pitching my own manga project to the editor of *Ultra Jump* (a manga magazine of top publisher Shueisha, as described in Chapter 5), my paid interpreter, who was assigned to me because his interpretation company employer knew his background as an aspiring mangaka, told me he felt that usually manga/anime were more appropriate for TV than for feature films.

I remembered that in Japan, Korea, and Taiwan, numerous hit shows based on manga air on TV each season. I explored the validity of his statement, and it turned out to be largely true. This is largely due to:

- Syndication on American TV.
- The serialized nature of most anime/manga.

- The way anime/manga plot "arcs" can conveniently line up with TV seasons and shorter sets of episodes.

Syndication in American TV: A key to anime's success and a key difference from Japan and most other nation's TV distribution systems

As we will see in detail in the case studies in the following chapters, modern Hollywood has a strong inclination toward film adaptation remakes of anime and manga. But initially *Astro Boy* and a host of other anime that followed it to America were localized (again, translated and culturally adjusted to local customs/attitudes and broadcast regulations), and then aired on network TV and/or local, syndicated television stations.

What is syndication?

Broadcasting syndication is the sale of the right to broadcast radio and television shows by multiple radio and television stations. This is often done by first airing the show on a network for a fee, which varies (but with expensive American scripted television series, this payment is usually only equivalent to a portion of the initial production cost). The Hollywood TV studio (equivalent to a bank/financier) then has to hope that the show runs long enough on the network to build up enough episodes so that it can be "syndicated." In other words, enough episodes must be produced so that people don't get tired of constant repeats as the episodes get re-broadcast on local stations.[46]

Successful syndication is a pot of gold, frequently worth billions of dollars; for instance, *The Simpsons* sold syndication rights for over $1 billion, and *Friends*, *Seinfeld*, and *The Big Bang Theory* reputedly sold for similar rates. Syndication is the end of the rainbow that almost all American primetime scripted TV aims for. It usually requires about five seasons for a show to air before it can get a syndication deal, although some hot shows can reach that point faster (*Modern Family* on USA, *The Big Bang Theory*, *Mike and Molly*, and *2 Broke Girls* on TBS, to name a few). Reflecting this, a TV profit participation contract offered by a TV studio to the rights holders and participants (actors, producers, showrunners) will typically show no profits for the participants for the first four years.[47]

The shows that often syndicate best are ones like *Astro Boy* that have story endings to each episode.[48] This is because they can be aired on local stations out of order without confusing the viewer. This is a particularly critical issue when foreign countries air other countries' shows, as they may not be properly instructed as to the correct order of the episodes. The American TV hit show *The X-Files*, which progressed its plot throughout its seasons and is thus considered "serialized," was once shown out of order in Japan, according to W. M. Penn (a pseudonym of American expatriate Kathleen Morikawa), a television critic for the huge Japanese newspaper *Yomiuri Shimbun*. Penn states that characters that had died in previous episodes were showing up alive again a week later.

When she called the station to complain, Penn was curtly told that the station had the right to order the episodes however they wanted and had ordered them according to "subject matter."[49] In 1964, Fred Ladd faced this problem of plots spanning more than one episode when localizing the next anime hit in America, *Gigantor*, or Mitsuteru Yokoyama's *Tetsujin 28-gō* (*Iron Man 28*), which was the giant-robot grandfather of worldwide blockbuster anime series *Gundam* and *Transformers*.[50]

How and why did syndication get started?

I Love Lucy's real-life married couple Lucy and Desi Arnaz wanted to stay in LA to shoot their show for the quality of their family life, rather than stage it in NYC as was the custom then. The NYC-based network agreed to the plan with the stipulation that the actor-couple would foot the additional costs required to shoot in LA versus in NYC. The couple agreed to this—in exchange for majority ownership of the show's profits after the initial NBC network airings. In the second season, Lucy Arnaz's real-life pregnancy caused the producers to rebroadcast popular shows from the first season so that she could have a break to recuperate. These "rerun" shows became an unexpected hit and eventually led to the development of the profitable syndication market—a practice that continues to this day.[51] As TV show production costs climbed due to escalating expenses, including Hollywood crews, actors, producers, writers, directors, and inflation, American TV shows became too expensive to finance simply by network fees paid to broadcast the show for a limited time. So "deficit financing" had to be employed, where TV studios became the same as banks, covering the shortfall between the broadcast fee the network paid and the show's production costs.[52] But Japan's TV market was much smaller, and without the large number of independent stations America has, the syndication system did not develop there.

Astro Boy's financing from NBC

Eighteen years after World War II ended, as had occurred with some Kaiju movies earlier, a co-financing business deal spanning the Pacific—between his production company and, this time, America's top network, NBC Television—gave new life to *Astro Boy*.

NBC TV didn't just air *Astro Boy* in exchange for paying Mushi a fee—they actually co-financed its production with Fuji TV and, indirectly, the aforementioned Japanese candy sponsor, Meiji. In other words, NBC was partially financing production of the *Astro Boy* anime television show. This is called a co-production. They were able to do this because the US has a large syndication market (Japan does not have one), which would support enough money paid by groups of stations for the rights to broadcast *Astro Boy*.[q] That is, *if* the stations liked the show once NBC paid to localize it. That was the financial risk NBC was taking.

---

[q] I.e. pay enough money to cover NBC's costs to license the broadcast rights from the Japanese plus cover that network's localization and distribution costs, etc. and still leave a profit for NBC.

Fred Ladd's fascinating story of adapting *Astro Boy* for American TV

Fred Ladd, a freelance localizer who often worked for NBC, and NBC executives were shown the *Astro Boy* anime in New York by an agent of Tezuka's company, Mushi Productions. NBC tentatively agreed to syndicate it for the US and hired Ladd to localize it for American television.[53] He was attracted to the project partly because he had worked on a different animation, *Pinocchio in Outer Space* (Fred Ladd co-produced it with Norm Prescott), that bore certain similarities—and of course *Pinocchio* had a huge influence on Tezuka's creation of *Astro Boy*. The *Pinocchio* aspect was attractive to NBC too.[54][55] And although Astro Boy knows right from wrong from the beginning, both characters were artificially created and came under the spell of evil circus-master-types (Ham Egg in *Astro Boy*, Stromboli in *Pinocchio*) but gradually prevailed. And both characters have a benevolent adopted father figure.

NBC required a pilot be created first to be sure they wanted to go to the next expensive step of hiring Ladd to localize all the episodes.[56] This "step deal" is typical of American TV and movie industries, and is also used with screen and TV writer deals, where at any point the deal can be terminated after a completed step. So Ladd had to first create an English dubbed "pilot" (usually the first episode) to prove to NBC brass that *Astro Boy* would work. After the pilot was approved, the rest of the episodes were localized, and then NBC field salesmen marketed it to TV stations in the heartlands of America without telling the local stations that the series was from Japan.[57] The year was 1963, just 18 years after the Japanese surrender, and it was believed that feelings were still too raw from World War II. Robert Napton talks about his generation that loved anime but didn't know that it was from Japan—possibly for that reason:

> **Napton:** When I was a kid, the shows that really got my interest were *Speed Racer* and *Kimba the White Lion*. Of course at that time I didn't know that they were anime. I just knew that I liked them and that there was something very different about them, but I couldn't quite put my finger on what it was. They were different from other "cartoons" that I had watched—*Scooby-Doo* or what-have-you, you know? There was just an action and cool science fiction element to the shows. Especially in the case of *Speed Racer*. Not so much in *Kimba*, but even *Kimba* had a different kind of storytelling in the way it was animated. As a kid you just took it in, and I just sensed that there was something different about it. I just didn't know what it was. Then, around 1979–80, there were two shows that happened around the same time. The first one was called *Star Blazers*. The other one was called *Battle of the Planets*. I was about 13 when those shows hit in America. I saw *Star Blazers* on a TV series that was broadcast out of the Bay Area, because I lived in northern California, and that show was called *Captain Cosmic*.[r] And that was back when kid shows in the afternoon had hosts. There were

---

[r] As Napton notes, *Star Blazers* anime television series became popular in the United States beginning in northern California when it was aired on *Captain Cosmic*, beginning in 1979. In the previous year, a feature-length anime titled *Space Battleship Yamato* (retitled *Space Cruisers*) was shown in theaters in southern California, but its exposure there was very limited.

these people hired by these TV stations to interact with the community and the kids. Of course this type of stuff is all long-since gone, but you would have these kind of science fiction themed Space Theater shows with these hosts in space suits talking to the kids. It was all very innocent and fun stuff and definitely part of my generation. Certainly nothing you would see today. But anyway, the host of that particular show, Captain Cosmic, was showing *Star Blazers*, and actually brought in a guy by the name of August Ragone, who was a local Bay Area expert on *Godzilla* and Japanese monster live-action, author of *Eiji Tsuburaya: Master of Monsters*. He basically explained to the kids watching, one of which was me, during a commercial break, "Oh the show you're watching, *Star Blazers*, was actually animated in Japan, and it's really called *Space Battleship Yamato*, and *Speed Racer* and some other shows you might have seen were animated in Japan." And that was actually the moment I discovered anime, which is crazy. And I don't know if I should thank August or hunt him down! [laughs] Because it started a lifelong involvement for me in the anime industry. But that's literally how I discovered anime.

Davis: So they tried to make these look like they were from America, which is probably why you thought "This is weird and what is this?" and the guy had to explain it to you.

Napton: That's exactly right. And the show I'm talking about, *Star Blazers*, you hit on a very specific point that's really interesting. In *Star Blazers*, I think even more than in *Speed Racer* and some of the others, a classic example of what you're talking about because, as I learned later when I saw the original episodes in Japanese and I saw the movies, in the series *Star Blazers* the hero of the show is the Yamato, which is a historical Japanese battleship. In the TV series, the naval battleship is retrofitted into becoming a spaceship that leaves Earth in defense of Earth to save Earth. It's a Japanese battleship, the Yamato, and it's very much the center of the series. In a sense—to their credit—in the very first episode they do acknowledge that the ship is named the Yamato, which in a way is kind of shocking looking back on it that they even addressed it. But they immediately say that for this mission we are renaming it the *Argo*, which is from *Jason and the Argonauts*, because the *Argo* was a great ship that went on a great quest and we're going on a great quest. So they immediately Westernized the ship itself. The ship in many ways became less important than the characters, which was different from the tone of the Japanese version. That, of course, was because of the concerns you're raising, which are, well, are American kids going to wanna watch a show about a Japanese World War II battle cruiser?

Davis: And would their parents get upset?

Napton: So that's a really, really interesting example of what you're talking about, and I absolutely say that you're 100% right. They were trying to disguise the Japanese origins, and if I hadn't been watching that kids show hosted by this guy who I later met and became friends with. I always said, "You're the reason I'm here!" If August Ragone hadn't come onto the show and explained to the kids who were watching, I would've probably never known or had found out until much later. So that's a very interesting topic.[58]

Similarly, Ladd had to make many changes to make *Astro Boy* acceptable to the network censors and the American public. He and his team preserved the original for all intents and purposes, but tackled cultural differences in a seamless manner. *Astro Boy*'s eventual American, and worldwide, success also upended the long-held Japanese notion that "things made for Japanese cannot be understood/appreciated by foreigners."[59]

Astro Boy's instances of violence and sex were pared out or creatively worked around by Fred Ladd as he grappled with cultural differences, as is evidenced in the following anecdotes:

Figure 6.7 *Star Blazer's* main ship.
STAR BLAZERS2199
© SHOJI NISHIZAKI/VOYAGER/STAR BLAZERS

- Japanese traditional forthrightness about death, even in children's entertainment, was not acceptable to NBC. So Ladd excised much of the machine gun action emanating from *Astro Boy*'s rear end.[60] Through skillful editing and dialogue additions (Ladd and even American voice actors wrote additional dialogue), a scene with a corpse was transformed into another character looking down and exclaiming, "He's unconscious!"[61] Schodt states, "to Tezuka, the most baffling aspect of Americans was their attitude towards violence. One early viewer he met claimed that he couldn't show *Astro Boy* to his children because of the violence, which made Tezuka wonder why animated *Popeye* shorts, which had even more slapstick violence, could be popular."[62]

- When Ladd visited Mushi offices in Tokyo arguing for significant changes he felt were necessary to get the project onto the air in the USA, he explained to the animators that pressing a gun against someone's head is considered violent by American viewers, though merely brandishing it is not. A young Japanese employee responded that Americans must see samurais protecting their lords as cruel and violent, but that the Japanese considered American movie gunfighters gunning down strangers the same way. Ladd was caught by surprise by this and responded by muttering something about "cultural differences," and that what is acceptable in one society may be taboo in another. Ladd admitted that he had no valid response.[63]

- An episode with a young bachelor who has a picture of a naked woman on his wall had to be excised. Tezuka was upset to learn about the nude image from NBC and returned to Tokyo to find that one of his background painters had put the image in as a stimulant to stay awake during an all-night shift.[64]

• Also cut were a crucifix and Christ's image, as well as an image involving vivisection, despite the fact that Tezuka believed that putting in Christian iconography would make his work popular in America. As Schodt observes, "from the beginning, Tezuka had made his *Mighty Atom* manga series quite culturally neutral. In making the early animation episodes, however, he had deliberately tried to anticipate the feelings of foreigners to avoid any imagery they might regard as too 'oriental' or 'exotic.' Instead of using Japan's Buddhist or Shinto symbols, for example, he often incorporated Christian motifs such as churches and crosses. Yet to his surprise, this often posed a problem with NBC because of the multi-denominational nature of the American audience and the population of minority religions."

• Schodt observes that, "Similarly, when making the animated series, Tezuka sometimes tried to take foreign viewers into account, intentionally inserting English words into background scenes of props. To his astonishment, NBC had a problem with this too, because they were afraid that many in the young audience would not be able to read the text."[65] Ladd worked around all of these uses of Christian iconography, violence, or the above example of sexuality by judiciously cutting and altering dialogue, among other methods.[66]

• In one case, he joined parts of two heavily cut episodes together to form one episode. *Gigantor*, the giant-robot anime, which would be Ladd's next anime adaptation project for NBC, had several multi-part episodes. Ladd and NBC had the anime studio shoot new endings to the episodes that originally lacked endings. The result was that now, with endings, *Astro Boy* and *Gigantor* could be "aired out of order" because, as previously stated, most episodes were self-contained, making both also ideal for foreign sales. *Astro Boy* was later sold into 23 other countries.[67]

The NBC execs and Ladd turned the *Tetsuwan Atom* title into English-friendly *Astro Boy*, by copying the "this boy" and "that boy" trend of titling comics at that time (*Superboy*, etc.), and adding the word "Astro."[68][69] The English title has since become almost as popular in Japan as the original Japanese title.

The *Tetsuwan Atomu* theme song was an orchestral march without words, composed by Tatsuo Takai. In those days, American children liked to sing along with the theme song of their favorite show. So Ladd and NBC hired Don Rockwell to write lyrics to the melody. Tezuka, upon hearing it, liked the song so much that he ended up using it on all remaining Japanese airing *Astro Boy* episodes, but with Japanese lyrics written to Takai's music. All 104 US episodes opened and closed with the English song to the Japanese music.[70]

Later, Nobuo Masuda speaks of more recent US anime localizations he produced for Sunrise. For example, he describes in his interview how a female's nipple was shown in an anime, and Cartoon Network covered it up with digitally created shower steam.[71]

Astro Boy became a big hit in the USA ("45% of the audience in Atlanta, 38% in Memphis, 37% Charleston, 30% New York City, 65% in Jackson, and top ratings in many other markets").[72] The show also spun off a 78 rpm record featuring the Takai-penned theme song with Don Rockwell's English lyrics that was extremely successful with American children of the day.[73]

Tezuka gets another 52 episodes out of NBC

Ladd recounts how NBC execs were very surprised when, a few months later, Tezuka presented NBC with 52 more episodes, and when NBC told Tezuka that they didn't want them, Tezuka threatened to take these new *Astro Boy* episodes to a competitor network. Since having the same series airing with a competitor would be unheard of, NBC capitulated and licensed the new set, running the total to an unprecedented 104 episodes.[74] And NBC's finicky nature, *after* they had made a good profit on the first 52, should have been a warning to Tezuka. But he had no way of knowing that …

Hollywood is extremely choosey—ignore this fact at your own peril!

The resounding American successes of *Astro Boy* and Tezuka's *Kimba the White Lion* (see below) apparently gave Tezuka the idea that he could continue bringing anime to the US and getting deals with NBC.[75] But like many others who initially struck gold in Hollywood and assumed that success would continue, he would painfully find out differently.

When I sold my screenplay to Warner Brothers for a significant price, I felt excited and confident about my future in Hollywood. And this sale allowed me to attract and hire a top entertainment lawyer. So, as he was far more experienced, I asked him for his career advice. He said, "keep your financial overhead low." I took his advice. I kept driving the same car, and I didn't go buy a house in expensive Los Angeles. What he meant was, "Don't assume that success and income are a straight line upward from here—you will have more creative options if you are not desperate for money." Tezuka had no way of knowing that he could not depend on any stream of future deals for his shows coming through in the future from Hollywood after his big successes with *Astro Boy* and, as we will see next, *Kimba the White Lion* in the United States.

After *Astro Boy* and *Kimba's* success, Tezuka may have thought that he now would be rewarded with a loyal long-term partner—NBC—and it is understandable that he did, as this is more in line with the style of relationship-building traditional to Japanese business, particularly in that era. So it was reasonable for him to assume they would probably be "partners for life." But Hollywood can pick and choose because almost everyone, whether they admit it or not, wants to be involved in that industry, which has the most money and prestige of any global entertainment industry. Thus Hollywood can very selectively "cherry pick" only the "'best properties" (in their minds) regardless of the rights holders' previous successes. Put another way, with a massive international distribution organization and the most bankable directors and global star actors, Hollywood is the king of world media. Therefore, they can and usually do say "no" often—including to the creators

Figure 6.8 Scene from *Jungle Emperor, Go Ahead Leo!* (*Kimba the White Lion* in America), Tezuka's hit color follow-up anime TV series to *Astro Boy*.
© Tezuka Productions

who previously made them money. And with so many people trying to sell to Hollywood, it is the ultimate buyer's market.

Tezuka, when rejected by NBC for future shows after *Kimba*, did take his shows to other networks to try to get them involved, and quickly tried to adapt to the situation by seeking out NBC's competitors. But *Princess Knight* and other later anime series that he brought to America were rejected by the networks. Perhaps part of the flaw in his strategy was that these new shows were not available to be evaluated in the script/story-treatment stage, and thus the networks' executives could not have creative input and the emotional investment from the projects' inceptions, as they did with *Kimba*. In a way, getting the American executives to "buy into" the process earlier is often the safest route. The problem also was that by going ahead and producing these follow-up shows to *Kimba* without American money, Tezuka was overextending his company financially and *had* to get an American buyer, and when they did not bite, his company was in deep trouble financially. Fortunately, despite the eventual bankruptcy, Tezuka did take that risk, because otherwise we would not have all those other wonderful anime series. Hollywood, with its vast financial resources, is aware that it is the hoped-for mark of success to creators worldwide and so is able to pick and choose from the best of the best, whether it be anime, manga, screenplays, books, and so on.[76] The old Hollywood adage, "You're only as good as your last movie (or TV show)," continues to be true. The (perhaps cultural) misperception of Tezuka that he somehow had an "in" with NBC because of *Astro Boy*'s success would lead to the downfall of his animation company, as he overcommitted to producing anime series without checking to see if Hollywood would finance and distribute them. NBC rejected most of Mushi's later work. Eventually, Mushi went bankrupt.[77] But not before a famous little white lion came to America, again from Tezuka …

Kimba the White Lion (1965)

After Ladd localized the hit giant robot anime *Tetsujin 28-gō*, which became a big hit in America as *Gigantor*, Tezuka presented Ladd and NBC with an anime project proposal, called a "story treatment," for *Kimba the White Lion* (Japanese title, *Jangaaru Taitei*, or *Jungle Emperor*).[78]

Hoping that NBC would finance *Kimba*, which was first published in *Manga Shonen* (*Comic Boy*) magazine in 1950, Tezuka presented the network with a plan of how the show would work, a listing of main characters, general storyline, tone, themes, and so on.

Figure 6.9 Scene from *Jungle Emperor* (a.k.a. *Kimba the White Lion*). The lion cub is orphaned after he and his mother are trapped on a sinking ship carrying them to a foreign zoo and his mother, caged, urges Kimba to leap out of the ship's window and swim for the African coast. The tragic relationship between Kimba and his mother contains elements of Disney's *Bambi* (which Tezuka was enamoured with).
© Tezuka Productions

The network demanded that it must be in color, stating that the era of black and white had ended. But more significantly for the escalating creative collaboration between Japan and America, Tezuka agreed with NBC's requirement that the main character, a lion cub, must not grow older during the anime series, as he had originally planned. This was very important to NBC's marketing team—they felt that it was much easier to sell a Bambi-type character that is cute and young in a children's show to the US field stations.[79] As noted, it was a big success.

Anime today in Japan

An anime deal on a manga is considered a real mark of success and, if it happens, usually occurs about two years after the manga debuts, and is more likely to occur with long-running hits. Although at Shueisha, sometimes the offer comes as early as six months after the manga's debut. At Shueisha, it is often up to the editor-in-chief whether to pass on the anime offer to the mangaka.[80]

But, an anime deal takes a great deal of the publisher's time/manpower and is impossible to do without securing a sponsor, due to the large scale of the endeavor.[81] The publisher also wants to protect the perception of the underlying manga in the case of an anime, as it will be widely seen—so care is taken in placing it with the right anime producer(s).[82]

Miyazaki complains about merchandising

Despite popular opinions to the contrary, this "go for the largest audience" phenomenon is not limited to Hollywood. In almost any situation where there is a significant budget, in a business environment, these pressures come into play, except in the luckiest of circumstances for the creators—including in Japan. Hayao Miyazaki, the famous Japanese animation director, discussed the anime television show production companies' desire to get a larger audience than the manga—an acknowledgment of the fact that, moving up the ladder from the manga, which is a singular artist's vision,[t] the anime TV series costs more to produce than the manga. And thus it's natural that the rights committee funding the anime TV show wish it to reach a wide audience, and generate more merchandising income—just as the Hollywood studios want the same for a manga/anime adaptation.

Miyazaki complained about merchandising driving creative decisions in the anime industry,

> When animated shows started airing on TV, the TV stations at first really had no idea what to do, so they basically left us alone to do as we pleased. As a result, we were able to come up with a variety of ideas and implement them, and these were the shows that were then broadcast. Now, however, we have to create shows that help sell more toys, increase profits from licensing, or help publishers make more money;

---

[s] Drama CDs and novelizations are sometimes assigned to manga series that are hits but don't seem appropriate—for instance, that maybe are not fantastical enough—for an anime adaptation format. These are often directly supervised by the publisher.

[t] Even though the creative visions of the editor and even assistants, where they are used, can come into play.

Figure 6.10 The protagonists in *Bakuman* are excited to receive an offer relayed through their editor to them for a novel adaptation and a drama CD. Notice that the chief editor also instructs their editor to ask for any specific requests they have. This illustrates the mangaka's enhanced power and financial position versus that of the legacy American comic writers. The young mangaka protagonists eagerly hope for the next possible deal, the anime TV series—a real mark of success and additional profit for them. BAKUMAN. © 2008 by Tsugumi Ohba, Takeshi Obata/SHUEISHA Inc.

we're faced with all sorts of constraints and locked into a tightly controlled system. To give you one example, nowadays the share of revenue that a show will generate from licensing is already divided up before the production even starts. If we were to earn, say, ten dollars, one group will have to get $1.50, another will get two dollars and yet another will get fifty cents.[u] And the result is that we have to choose projects that are safe and do everything possible to ensure that everyone involved gets their expected cut … For example, we can't make any changes to characters in [popular] series …[83]

Almost all media artists, if they are honest with themselves, will admit that they want the widest audience possible for the enormously hard work that they put into their creations. Nobody sets out with the intention, "I want very few people to see my work," especially when the work is financed at high cost and showing a profit will impact them being able to create another. But this is a balancing act.

How much do mangaka have to do creatively with the anime or merchandising?

They have various levels of involvement with their anime creatively, from hands-on to hands-off. In an interview with *Shonen Jump* magazine, *Bleach*'s mangaka Tite Kubo was asked, "How involved are you in making the *Bleach* animated series?" and responded, "I'm involved with the character designs. Usually the character designs are done with manga artists just overseeing, but in my case I actually draw what all the characters should look like—I am essentially drawing all of the characters that appear in the anime. It is very rare for the artist to be involved this much."[84]

Manga finally follows anime and sweeps into the American market further influencing Hollywood filmmakers

In America, the latest invasion of anime during the first decade of the twenty-first century, led by *Pokémon* and rapidly expanding into a wide variety of manga and anime, truly made it a nearly mainstream form. What characterized this wave was that, for the first time, it included manga, as fans sought to explore the often-deeper stories that the manga presented. Many publishers jumped on board and soon the American bookshops had aisles dedicated to manga. In many cases, these sections were the most popular parts of the bookstore, filled with standing people browsing through them as they do in Japan.[v]

---

[u]This practice of the financing of films and animation by a *rights committee* is a very important characteristic of Japanese entertainment and publishing, and will be explained in chapter 8.
[v]Often anime skips some story points of the manga assuming that the fans have already read the manga.

"Modern era" Japanese manga and anime creators have continued, until fairly recently, to be influenced by Hollywood, as Nobuo Masuda notes in his conversation with me

> **Davis:** We know about Tezuka's influence from Walt Disney and Warner Brothers and Hollywood movies, but what other creators were influenced by American pop culture or Hollywood?
>
> **Masuda:** It started with Tezuka's manga. *Gundam* is also heavily influenced by Western culture.[w]
>
> **Davis:** *Star Wars* is heavily influenced by *Hidden Fortress* by Kurosawa. So what this book is basically saying in part is that this stuff is washing back and forth, and has been for a really long time.
>
> **Masuda:** Even the Japanese character design, they're getting … [the designs] somewhere as well.[x][85]

For another example of this Hollywood influence on top manga/anime creators, *Berserk's* mangaka Miura is so enamored with *Star Wars* that he named one of his arcs "Millennium Falcon."[y] Furthermore, when he granted Professor Hayashi and I the right to seek an adaptation of *Berserk* in Hollywood, I successfully pitched the project and thus got 20th Century Fox/New Regency into negotiations with Miura's lawyer. At the time, Miura remarked through his editor to Hayashi, that he was happy it was Fox, as *Star Wars* was originally produced there.[z]

Speaking of robots, what about *Transformers*? weren't those movies directly from Japanese sources? Yes, but it's not that simple

The animated American *Transformers* television show in the 1980s sold enough to hit syndication. *Transformers* was also adapted by Hollywood into a blockbuster live-action movie franchise (director: Michael Bay, Dreamworks, 2007, 2009, 2011, 2013, 2014), with its first three films grossing almost $3 billion worldwide. The 1986 *Transformers* animated movie (which Peter Chung storyboarded) featured the voice acting of Eric Idle, Judd Nelson, Leonard Nimoy, Casey Kasem, and Robert Stack. It also marked the final roles for both Orson Welles and Scatman Crothers.[86] The *Transformers* TV show and animated movie

---

[w] For this book, I interviewed Syd Mead, the Hollywood *Blade Runner* and *Star Wars* designer and "visual futurist," who, as mentioned, designed the mobile suits for incarnations of two epoch-making anime, the *Turn A Gundam* and *Space Battleship Yamato/Star Blazers* series. The interview was too last-minute to fit into the book, but I may ask for his permission to publish it in the future.

[x] See Chapter 11 for how *Gundam's* design was partially inspired by *Star Wars*.

[y] The name of the rebels' space ship in the original *Star Wars* movie.

[z] Unfortunately, the negotiations were not successful.

were not anime, although a superficial analysis might assume that they qualify as such based on their Giant Robot style, and the fact that Japanese studio Toei Animation animated the series. But *Transformers* is not being covered in the feature adaptation case study chapters in this book. As a former Bandai editor and marketing chief, graphic novel writer and current vice president of Legendary Entertainment's comics division Robert Napton notes, "*Transformers* was created by Hasbro using molds from Japanese toys, so its lineage is more in the Japanese toy market than anime. Splitting hairs, but important hairs I think. *Transformers* is an example of the Japanese toy aesthetic being co-opted by Hasbro and becoming successful—but it's a Western interpretation of 'Giant Robots' in my opinion."[aa]

But the reason I am focusing on *Transformers* here is for the reason Napton states: "But it is the *preeminent* example of a Western company co-opting the Giant Robot aesthetic and making it work in the US market far better than any straight anime importation has *ever* worked. So it begs the question: Does the Japanese toy and anime sensibility have to be Westernized in order to find a mass audience? It would seem that in fact it *does*, since no anime property has achieved the success [as a live-action Hollywood adaptation] of *Transformers*."[87]

It is important to note that the above interview with Robert Napton took place before the release of the Giant Robot movie *Pacific Rim*, which reportedly grossed over $400 million worldwide and which this author thoroughly enjoyed.[ab]

Manga, Kaiju (Japanese monsters), and giant robot anime go to Hollywood together, via Mexico in *Pacific Rim*

Guillermo Del Toro is one of a handful of "A list" (top level) feature directors in Hollywood who is entrusted with huge budgets for "event" movies. Originally an experienced make-up artist, he then began making his own feature films, including the American graphic novel adaptations *Hellboy* and *Hellboy II: The Golden Army*, and is good friends with two other Mexican directors who are now major Hollywood directors: Alfonso Cuarón (*Gravity*) and Alejandro González Iñárritu (*Babel*).

Del Toro is proof of the fact that much manga and anime as well as Japanese Kaiju television shows came to Mexico, in some cases without coming to America. As noted earlier, his movie *Pacific Rim* is a direct result of those influences (see earlier Chapter 1 image comparison). I tried to land an interview with him through his manager, but his busy schedule did not permit it; instead, I did find a 2013 interview with Gina McIntyre in *The LA Times Hero Complex*, in which he directly states the manga/anime/Kaiju influences on that movie. I felt that it was important to include here:

[aa] According to Napton, *Transformers* is based on a Hasbro toy line that is itself based on the Diaclone and Microman toy lines originally created by Japanese toy manufacturer Takara.
[ab] And for which a sequel has been approved.

Del Toro: The thing with *Pacific Rim* is that all my childhood, for whatever reason, I don't know what happened but in the 60's and 70's in Mexico a lot of our entertainment was pop Japanese culture. We grew up with *Tetsujin 28* [in America, *Gigantor*], we grew up with, um, I don't know how it's called in America, it was *Captain Ultra* in Mexico. *Captain Ultra*. It was a guy that killed some guys that looked like Martians and we grew up with Tsuburaya's *Ultra Man, Ultra 7, Ultra Q*. We grew up with *Wolf Boy Ken* or *Ken the Wolf Boy* [which Miyazaki worked on], *Astro Boy, Princess Knight*, all the Tezuka animation. And in the cinemas we used to go to see the animated films, all the Kaiju and I spent a lot of time on [sic] my childhood drawing giant robots and designing the interior. And I would put my bedroom, a big kitchen, the reactor, very important, the pistons, and there would always be two features in the giant robot. There would be a cinema and a toilet. Which is pretty revealing.

McIntyre: [laughs] That's just good planning.

Del Toro: [laughs] It was good planning! And then we loved another series that was called *Space Giants*, and the fights with the Kaijus were just fantastic. And there was a cartoon called "*Golden Bat*" (Ōgon Bat) where a laughing golden skeleton used to fight Kaijus and slice them in half. So all that stuff is brimming up.[acadae88]

This echoes Nakazawa's recollection of the Kami-shibai telling that same story and Masuda's recollection of Tezuka's *Golden Bat*, as well as the photo of the Kami-shibai in Chapter 3.

A trend that developed on American television in the last two decades as a result of anime airing on them is that…

[ac] Found online at publication was a video where Del Toro, along with the female adult and child star of *Pacific Rim*, Rinko Kikuchi and Mana Ashida, lovingly visited a *Gundam* exhibit in Japan.

[ad] Interview transcribed by Amber Brown-Rodgers.

[ae] Del Toro appears to be extremely knowledgeable about the Japanese forms inspiring his work. In endorsing a contest to name the best examples of Japanese culture, called Sugoi Japan, sponsored by the largest circulation newspaper in the world, the *Yomiuri Shimbun*, Del Toro wrote:

Japan has been, and will always be, a great influence in Western art. Its impact on European painters in the 19th century was key to revitalizing Symbolism and Pre-Raphaelite art. In the same manner, anime and manga have permeated all of Western culture; their aesthetics, language and coding, their unforgettable and powerful stories have held great power for my generation of storytellers.

You can see the enormous love I have for all things Japanese in everything I do, be it *Hellboy, Pacific Rim* or *Pan's Labyrinth*, I remain keenly aware of Japanese filmmakers, Yokai legends, the engravings of Utamaro or Hokushai, the Kwaidan of Lafcadio Hearn [also known as Koizumi Yakumo, an author of books about Japan] or the anime of great masters, Miyazaki, Otomo, Go Nagai, Osamu Tezuka, Satoshi Kon and many others, the brilliant game design of Hideo Kojima, the Kaiju of Tsuburaya and the manga of Naoki Urasawa (one of which I am proud to be adapting into a TV series).

Japan has held a lure for me that remains unparalleled in my imagination. It is exciting and thrilling to see that we will witness as Japanese audiences vote for their favorite stories and storytellers, many of which, I am sure, we are not aware of in the West. The Sugoi Japan project will reveal amazing Japanese properties that will enrich the exchange of ideas, characters and stories that has connected both hemispheres of the globe for centuries now. I, for one, couldn't be more eager to discover them and be stimulated by their great creativity and originality. (Scott Green, "Guillermo Del Toro Mentions 'Monster' Adaptation in Sugoi Japan Endorsement," August -186, 1,814, http://www.crunchyroll.com/anime-news/2014/08/14/guillermo-del-toro-mentions-monster-adaptation-in-sugoi-japan-endorsement) (accessed June 22, 2015).

Adult Swim and other American animation networks began being influenced by the anime they were airing to create their own anime-influenced animated TV shows

This most recent wave of anime, I feel, also opened up the door for other more adventuresome animation to begin to be created in the United States.

Ian Condry made the following observation:

Figure 6.11 *Hi Hi Puffy Ami Yumi*, an American-aired, Japanese-created anime television show about two Japanese pop stars. SAMURAI JACK, HI HI PUFFY AMI YUMI and SYM-BIONIC TITAN and all related characters and elements are trademarks of and © Cartoon Network.

> **Condry:** [O]ne of the things that I think happened is that, what manga was able to do in reaching teenage audiences is what enabled anime to also find a sweet spot in the global market. I go back to the Comics Code from 1954, which said that comics could only be for children. They can't be too violent and they can't be too sexy. They have to promote family values. That really drove a stake into the very vibrant comic book industry in the US because of that self-regulation. So the US comic market left that out, as did the cartoons. It was a big deal when *The Simpsons* came out and it was a bit racy. Then you get even further with *South Park* and a lot of those shows! *Family Guy* and *American Dad* and *Futurama* … they keep coming and coming. When Adult Swim was all anime, everyone said, "Oh my God, look! It's Japanese animation and it's amazing and sexy and violent!" And now you have much more raunchy stuff on American TV in cartoon form. I don't think we had much of a hub a decade ago when anime came rushing in. It's also related to *Pokémon. Pokémon* was such a hit so it got a lot of TV distributors' attention, which brought in some of these other things.
>
> **Davis:** What you're saying is something I haven't thought of at all, which is that the latest wave has really blown the door open for the other people doing American animation, to push the limits in terms of content.[89]

And then the circle becomes complete, again, when American Craig McCracken's anime-influenced television show *The Powerpuff Girls* and the Wachowskis' anime-inspired *Matrix* universe got their own anime spinoffs produced in Japan: *Powerpuff Girls Z* and *The Animatrix*.

Cowboys and samurai

The popularity of Akira Kurosawa's *Rashomon* (1950 in Japan, 1951 in the USA) abroad was a surprise to the Japanese for the same reason and had happened by a fluke when Daiei, the studio that financed it, received an invitation to submit from the Venice Film Festival. Having no confidence that *Rashoman* would be understood abroad, Daiei tried to avoid sending it. Finally, they sent it to Venice, and to their shock *Rashomon* became a big international hit. It put Kurosawa and its star, Toshiro Mifune, firmly on the global cinema map. Kurosawa became almost universally regarded as a directing great, and it is widely known that George Lucas based *Star Wars* heavily on Kurosawa's *Hidden Fortress*.[90] What is less known is that Lucas particularly admired Kurosawa's ability to start epics in the middle of the fray, with little explanation up front of backstory/history, and he applied this technique in *Star Wars*.[91] Kurosawa was also influenced by American cinema and particularly by American Westerns, a compliment paid back when *The Magnificent Seven* (director: Preston Sturges, MGM, 1960), a direct remake based on Kurosawa's masterpiece *The Seven Samurai*, was produced in Hollywood. According to *Side B* magazine, a court case concluded that director Sergio Leone borrowed from Kurosawa's most popular movie *Yojimbo* (1961, also starring Mifune) for his Clint Eastwood-starring Spaghetti Western *A Fistful of Dollars*.[92]

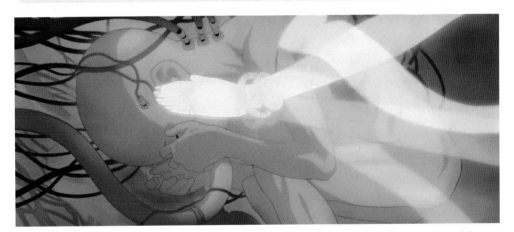

Figure 6.12 *The Animatrix* anime series episodes *The Second Renaissance* 1 and 2 (directed by Mahiro Maeda and written by Lana and Andy Wachowski) are examples of Hollywood writers and anime directors in Japan combining in yet another hybrid configuration. It explains how the *Matrix* world was established in the war between humans and machines, and why the machines were forced to derive energy by "harvesting" people—and in terms of storytelling, is as good as the original live-action film. Other *Animatrix* segments were written by the Japanese directors or, in the case of Korean-American Peter Chung's *Matriculated* segment, written and directed by Chung.[af][ag] Village Roadshow Pictures, distributed by Warner Home Video 2003.

[af] Arias notes an exception to this hybridity in the segment *Flight of the Orsis*: "none of the Japanese anime team was involved in making that episode. Even my own involvement, as producer of the entire series, was fairly minimal" (email to author, February 13, 2015).

[ag] *Aeon Flux*, Chung's MTV ground breaking anime hybrid series was referenced earlier.

In the next chapter, we will begin the "how to" part of this book. This will start in part with a fascinating dissection of a few of the differences in writing, storytelling, and production methods between the Japanese and Hollywood systems, and follow with case studies of major anime/manga adaptations from Hollywood, including interviews with the principal creative and business people in those productions, to find out how the sides worked together either successfully or unsuccessfully.

7

Adaptations of Manga and Anime to American Television and Live-Action Movies (and What Creators can Learn from Them and Apply to Their Own Works)

Why else were all these anime being produced for TV and not as theatrical features?

After all, starting in the mid-1960s, the Americans (NBC) were even giving creative input on, and co-funding *Kimba* from the story phase onward

There are creative, story, and structural reasons why TV is a natural home for anime. This is partly because "arcs" in manga and anime are often ideal for TV adaptation and localization. "Arcs" are storylines that go on for several episodes and are fairly common. Frequently in anime adapted for TV, "arcs" last for a viewing season, making them a natural fit for television.

A fairly reliable way to identify an arc is by the appearance and then disappearance of the chief villain. Some arcs are named after the villain who appears in several successive anime episodes, or for an entire TV season, and then dies off. In earlier years, it would have been problematic to "strip" arcs out of order for American syndication, but things have changed. The global marketplace has gotten more familiar with techniques for broadcasting serialized show episodes in the correct order. Also, American cable networks have become one of the prime venues for anime now, so this issue has become less of a problem. Furthermore, legal anime streaming websites like Crunchyroll and VIZ Media number the episodes in order and air them in order. Even the illegal "fansubbers"[a] number the episodes!

Anime often contains a "villain of the season" that marks the arc. Many anime and manga also contain shorter "villain arcs." Frequently anime episodes "wrap up" and end their immediate plots each episode, while a larger story arc remains to carry viewers into the next mini-arc or episode. *One Piece* and *Naruto*[b] are serialized in this manner—and thus are in sync with much of modern scripted American live-action television, even in cases of many procedural or self-contained shows. Each of these anime series has a "runner" or overarching story that follows over the course of several episodes. *One Piece* features villains who, one after another, or in groups, oppose boy-pirate Luffy and his crew of friends searching the seas for the Grand Line treasure. Villains who disappear sometimes reappear later (for instance, Buggy the Clown—a villain at the beginning who dispatches enemies and entire towns with his "Buggy Balls" cannon balls and has a disturbing ability to separate his body parts— reappears *much* later in the multi-year series again and again—a technique called "sidelining" that will be covered later in this chapter). So each episode derives tension from the story and conflict at hand, usually driven by the arc's villain, but also often "wraps up," conclusively ending that episode. Another dramatic driving force in *One Piece* is the overall progress of their pirate ship headed towards great treasure, a journey that continues throughout all the episodes, carrying us along with the characters' adventures and the mangaka's inventiveness.[c]

Characters that "travel," much like the Marvel universe

Another reason that watching an anime structured like *One Piece* "out of order" in syndication would not necessarily be as much of a problem now as it was in the time of *Astro Boy* is the same reason why Shueisha manga and the anime based upon them tend to be heavily focused on character. And story logic is a bit less critical when characters are truly stars. As Condry explained to me,

To me that is the major difference between anime and Hollywood—Hollywood is about

---

[a] Meaning fans translating and subtitling of the original anime or manga coming from Japan and putting them on the web to share (which depends on the laws of a person's home country—and uploading them is illegal in Japan). Fan subgroups often communicate through the internet, transcribing and localizing shows or movies and often morally justifying these actions when the programs are not commercially available in their own country.

[b] As noted, 205 million manga copies sold, 640 anime TV episodes produced, and its own Hollywood movie adaptation deal, as of 2015.

[c] *Star Blazers* was the first popular anime series aired on American television to have its structure based on arcs. This opened the floodgates for the many later serialized anime series to follow to America. The upshot, of course, was that, with stories "arcing" over many episodes, deeper characters could be developed and stories could be more complex.

the story. Story, story, story. That's what you need for a successful film. Whereas in Japan, I feel that their multimedia complexes are much more centered on characters—Astro Boy or Goku or whoever the character is. That's the logic of the production and the logic of the trans-media creativity. That's one of the arguments I try to make, that the collaborative creativity of anime is centered around characters, and I think that's pretty different than how Hollywood usually views a successful film or a franchise."[1]

This emphasis on the character over story is evident in the way that Marvel superheroes and villains are able to transfer to other adaptations (and media forms) using storylines not found in their original comics. In the Sheuisha and Marvel stories, whether *One Piece* or *Iron Man* (which has also been adapted into an anime), the characters *are* the stars. The story is not the star. Thus, it becomes possible to transpose the characters outside of the original storyline if done carefully. This has exciting implications for video games and merchandising, too—video games are heavily intertwined with manga/anime.[e] A Japanese publishing executive explained to me that Shueisha manga (and thus the animes based on those works) tended to be character-focused, whereas Kodansha's manga tended to be more story-focused. It is no secret that this kind of "cross-platforming" is exactly what companies like American movie studios aspire to.[f]

After a manga becomes successful, the potential licensee (including for anime and live-action adaptations) would have to prove their trustworthiness [to the publisher and mangaka] to protect the image and reputation of the underlying brand. Ian Condry affirmed, "At the manga companies, they're very touchy and careful when it comes to making anime. They've said to me directly that, 'We don't mind anime being made as long as it doesn't hurt the brand, but if it might hurt the brand then we definitely don't want it because that's the whole point of managing the brand and the characters.'"[2]

For live-action feature film manga/anime adaptations, adapting an arc into the initial feature film, especially the first arc in the origin stories, can be a good initial approach

Chief among adaptation pitfalls one must be aware of is to remember not to try to cram too much into a feature film's normally uncluttered structure. As former DreamWorks executive Jason Hoffs (and a producer of the Tom Cruise starrer *Edge of Tomorrow*, an adaptation of *All You Need Is Kill*, a Japanese sci-fi novel and the Hollywood *Death Note* adaptation) stated in his interview for this book, "Some things [manga, anime] may be

---

[d] As noted, strong character identification also makes it more likely that readers and audiences can drop into a multi-decade story (many people having been born years after the manga/anime's inception) and allows the characters to develop their own followings with the new readers.

[e] More on a Hollywood film that was influenced by anime *and* computer games by its co-screenwriter in Chapter 11.

[f] As we have seen, Tezuka did this with his "star system," where his characters appeared in stories other than their own original ones.

better [adapted] as short stories, or books, or video games, or cartoons. The format of a live-action movie is very specific. Very visual. It's somewhat spare."[3]

This derives from the fact that:

- An audience has to go home eventually, and so films that run more than two hours push the limit.
- The more films per day a theater can show, the more money they can make, all other things being equal.
- Hollywood has tended to focus on rapidly forward-driving, tight plots in its story structure, which we will see later is illustrative of the difference between Asian and American cultures.

These limits inherent in adapting manga/anime to film were reinforced to me as I tried to figure out how to adapt *Berserk*. I realized that manga tend to often "wander off the story spine." *Berserk*'s medieval bio-horror plot of young anti-hero swordsman Guts and his fellow orphans in the mercenary Band of Hawks, led by his best friend Griffith, initially drives hard on a fairly linear path, until the Eclipse Arc where Griffith joins forces with the evil "Godhand" group of supernatural overlords. Griffith exchanges his soul and the lives of his friends for ultimate power. He enrages Guts—who barely escapes the demons' hellish attack (emerging minus one eye and hand and now with a huge chip on his shoulder). Then Guts, his hand replaced with a nasty built-in repeater crossbow and wielding a 7ft sword, embarks on a path of revenge (and possible spiritual enlightenment). But his journey at this point tends to wander near and far, making adaptation of these sections to a feature film very challenging. Screenwriter Steve Shibuya (*Sucker Punch*, director: Zack Snyder, Warner Brothers, 2011) also tried to tackle *Berserk* when he approached Zack Snyder with it and found the same. Every good story is somewhat different, but dividing the arcs into three acts—or, if the arcs are long, even into separate movies for each arc—might be a way to combat overcrowding the story. In the case of *Berserk*, this could be done by ending the first movie with the Eclipse event and Guts's vow of revenge.

Bleach (Tite Kubo) is one of the many examples of hit Japanese manga that sets its story up fantastically and is ideal to be adapted by Hollywood, where it was in studio development until recently. The story is attractive to Hollywood because audiences will likely identify more with protagonist Ichigo, who fights for his family and friends, than with the more abstract "world saving" American superheroes.

For instance, the first *Bleach* arc features the Grand Fisher Hollow (hollows are malevolent spirits of formerly ordinary humans that feed on the souls of humans by killing them) who killed Ichigo's beloved mother.

Using extensions hidden inside the fingers of one of his claws, the Grand Fisher can pierce an opponent's body and look into their memories, searching for a relationship that is dear to the person being attached, even if that beloved person is dead. Then, with the other hand, he transforms his lure into that something.[4] This is a highly inventive way to integrate the classic dramatic principle of introducing "personal stakes" or "internal personal goals" (Ichigo's love for his mother, evoked by her image), and combining that with the action goal (Ichigo must try to stop the Grand Fisher and the other Hollows from hurting his living family) in a visual manner.

Figure 7.1 *Bleach* The Grand Fisher confronts Ichigo while holding Ichigo's sister in the form of a "lure" he uses to deceive victims. © Tite Kubo/Shueisha, TV TOKYO, dentsu, Pierrot

Figure 7.2 *Bleach* Grand Fisher impales Ichigo with his memory-searching claw. © Tite Kubo/Shueisha, TV TOKYO, dentsu, Pierrot

When Ichigo defeats the Grand Fisher, the arc ends. Then a new major arc is set up when Ichigo's Hollow-fighting female partner Rukia is kidnapped back into the Soul Society from whence she originally came as punishment by her people for breaking the law that Soul Reapers (Hollow hunters) must avoid becoming too involved with a human. Ichigo, with Rukia's special powers (which she accidentally gives him), must organize a group of his best friends to go to this other world and rescue Rukia before she is executed. Focusing on this arc in a film script would be an excellent way to adapt this work into a feature film: the death of the Grand Fisher when Ichigo's sword-wielding father saves Ichigo and his sisters, but leaving Rukia needing to be rescued, and thus setting up a sequel film. As this *Bleach* example illustrates, those adapting must pick carefully and not try to compress into one film an entire story that may run for years and dozens of volumes.

In her essay "What Boys Will Be: A Study of Shōnen Manga,"[g] Angela Drummond-Mathews observes that *Dragonball* was ingenious in the way it handled arcs. She writes that mangaka Toriyama chose each plot point in such a way that it stood directly in the path of both internal and external goals for more than one character: "their goals were clearly defined and the trials or obstacles referred directly to them … in order for the story not to appear trivial by only having external goals, the characters must have internal goals."[5] These internal personal goals are a hallmark of the best manga—or any story—because they give it meaning and theme. Otherwise, stories are just action (or empty plot, devoid of psychological motivation) and lack depth.

Differences in DNA—it's not a matter of absolutes, but a matter of "shading"

Of course, personal/internal goals versus action goals are a well-known technique in both Japan and Hollywood. But the use of a technique is more about "shading or weighting"—that is, how much a certain technique is emphasized in Japan versus America/Hollywood.

Applying Joseph Campbell's mythology to *Bleach*

Drummond-Mathews compares the narrative structure of the universal "hero's journey" myth, described by Joseph Campbell in his classic book *The Hero with a Thousand Faces*, to successful manga/anime series, focusing largely upon *Bleach*. Her analysis illuminates the degree to which the Japanese shade their storytelling to massively favor the Campbell-described "initiation phase," or middle section, of the story (in the traditional three-act Hollywood feature structure, this would be "Act 2") where the universal hero has left the "ordinary world" to pursue their goal and face their trials. Thus the American/Hollywood feature structure tends to be more streamlined and "end-goal" oriented than the Japanese forms. By contrast, as Drummond-Mathews notes, the manga/anime tend to focus the majority of the time on the middle of the story, "on the experience of the journey,"[6] where "the manga hero will have grown, matured and learns something that not only enriches

[g]Part of an anthology, *Manga*, edited by Toni Johnson-Woods, Bloomsbury Academic.

herself but the world around her."[7] Hollywood feature films have traditionally emphasized more about "getting to the end goal." Whereas part of this difference is a function of serialized versus feature-length, this "shading/weighting" involves a cultural bias as well and ties into our religions and overall approaches to life. At the risk of oversimplifying, one of the many differences between these two cultures might be the difference between an emphasis on goal versus emphasis on process. In turn, it's reflected in how our storytelling is oriented.

Another important story issue in manga/anime: Filler arcs

When weekly television's voracious airtime appetite for episodes of a hit anime series becomes a serious problem, often lower quality imposters called "filler arcs" are employed.

Anime series often "get ahead" of the manga story on which they are based due to the faster rate anime is produced for TV. Scores of animators progress more quickly than the more artisan-like set-up of the mangaka and their much smaller team of assistants who rush to keep up with the anime team's faster production. To combat this, the anime producers may have to create their own "arcs" to stall for time while the mangaka and their team catches up. "Fighting arcs" are a typical method used in shōnen anime to fill this void, or to stall for mangaka who have run out of ideas. Endless fights and a dearth of character and story development are typical of many of these "fighting arcs." The point is that if one is trying to adapt a Japanese anime into another country's live-action TV show or feature (after securing the rights—we'll learn about that later), it is important to be able to recognize filler arcs and arcs in general in order to know what to use and how to structure the adaptation. Also, structuring your own original narrative work using arcs and other techniques outlined in this book in a creative way that transposes well with Hollywood might lead to more distribution opportunities in the domestic and international markets one is targeting. There are a very large number of techniques that go into making manga and anime series work for years and years. These methods can be utilized by American and other countries' serialized television, either for adaptations or for one's own creative work. These tropes and techniques number in the hundreds, if not thousands, but a couple of them include the following:

"Character shot-gunning"

This a term invented by one of my manga class students, Andrew Cross, for the frequent practice of mangaka on long-running shōnen series of hurling battalions of new characters into the plot, presumably hoping that one or two will hook the readership (see Andrew, who is in the closely-linked video game industry, and young mangaka Paul Choate's discussion of this concept later in this chapter). *Bleach* mangaka Tite Kubo, who is known for throwing large numbers of characters into the story when he gets creatively blocked, added,

> **Kubo:** Sometimes I can't think of any new characters. Then other times, I come up with 10 or more new characters.
>
> **Q:** Are there any characters that you thought fans would love but didn't, or a character that caught on with fans in a way that you didn't expect?

Figure 7.3 *Bleach*'s mangaka Tite Kubo at work. Photo by permission of Deb Aoki and VIZ Media.

> **Kubo:** I don't really recall any characters that I've created that I thought fans would love
> but didn't, but usually I notice that when I start describing a character's personality
> or back story, the fans start to really respond to them, and really start liking them.
> However, in the case of Suhei Hisagi [Lieutenant/Acting Captain of Squad 9], fans
> got hooked on him before I even started describing his personality, so that was very
> unusual.[8]

Often, "character shot-gunning" is so successful that it builds momentum where it otherwise might be slowing and sometimes even makes the reader jump the rails and care less about the original characters as the story surges into a new "arc" and become involved with the new characters mixed in with the original characters.

"Battle manga"

The "battle manga" genre often uses "character shot-gunning." In this genre, the hero and their posse often battle through martial arts or other battle tournaments. These battles can either be wonderfully inventive or stimulate important character growth and story development, as in the case of *Battle Angel Alita*, or endless and repetitive to an intelligent adult sensibility. For example, *Yu Yu Hakusho* by Yoshihiro Togashi is initially a charming and well-plotted hit manga/anime about a tough juvenile delinquent with a neglectful mother who dies while selflessly saving a child from being killed in a traffic accident and becomes a spirit with the task of righting wrongs on Earth. The story eventually lapses into a one-dimensional monster/freak-of-the-week battle manga.

In a quality battle manga sequence, Alita "finds herself" through battle in the motorball arena, where contestants hurtle down a track at insane speeds to catch the motorball using mind-blowing combat techniques and weaponry. Fans get to wear special helmets so they can be in the mind of their favorite contestant. True to the genre's tropes, Alita gathers her own motley group of teammates.

This discussion of battle manga brings us to the film adaptation of *Battle Angel Alita* that James Cameron plans to direct after *Avatar 4*. He will reportedly adapt the manga by taking the love story and the Makaku sections about a monster that was created by the evil cyber surgeon Desty Nova who opposes Alita in the series, and fleshing out the father–daughter relationship while working in the extreme sport Alita is known for—motorball.[9] But to make the story work for film, he'll need to pull out some material. Part of *Battle Angel Alita*'s attractiveness as a property for Hollywood adaptation stems from its highly relatable father–daughter relationship. Also advantageous is *BAA*'s high-concept sci-fi setting that also sets up a marketing angle regarding the "motorball" circuit where Alita and her cyborg antagonists battle it out. Kishiro hopes Cameron uses motorball, and Cameron said he will.[10] Extremely well-developed characters, even the smallest bit players, with wonderful idealism and violent duality in Alita and her father figure, Doc Ido, and others, help keep things fascinating. Both their good and bad traits create repercussions down the line, as in life.

Figure 7.4 From Yukito Kishiro's phenomenal manga *Battle Angel Alita*, kindly cyber-surgeon Doc Ido discovers Alita's living brain and spinal cord in a scrap heap after she mysteriously fell out of the elitist floating city above (Tripares).
© Yukito Kishiro / Kodansha Ltd.

Alita ("Gally" in the Japanese version) is extremely courageous and under the worst sort of pressure. We admire her for her quest to step out of her comfort zone after Doc Ido adopts her (a surprising number of Japanese manga/anime and TV characters are orphaned [like Astro Boy] as a way to create instant empathy—and then some are lovingly adopted) and go on a quest to find her origins. Her duality is relatable in that we are all complex, layered creatures who are driven by sometimes-contradictory desires, strengths, weaknesses and fears—something that many manga and anime focus on. Alita will obsessively pursue her personal goal amidst great violence to find out who she really is (when I first discovered the manga, the comics store owner bluntly stated an unusual aspect of *Battle Angel Alita*—that "Alita, the female hero, is a killer"), despite the fact that kindly cyber-surgeon Doc Ido has given her a loving home when he rebuilds her body, after finding only her head and spinal column in a garbage heap.

But instead of living within that warm, unsullied cocoon and considering herself lucky (the scrap heap world is full of struggling orphans), she rebels like a teen daughter and immediately follows him out into the dangerous city to discover Ido's dark side (he enjoys slaughtering dangerous psychopaths with a rocket powered hammer weapon). She then decides that she too will find her own way, and becomes motorball queen in the death slaughter of that "sport" because it challenges her and helps her regain her memories. And, like a petulant adolescent girl, she says that if Ido doesn't like it then "that's tough!" Cameron remarked on the fact that since he has two daughters, he can relate to her character even more.[11]

As Cameron said about Alita, "It would have to be pried out of my cold dead fingers, *Battle Angel Alita* is just a great, kick-ass story."[h][12]

In the interview with Hayashi, Kishiro also cited Douglas Trumbull, who designed special effects on *2001: A Space Odyssey* and *Blade Runner*, as an influence. And Kishiro stated to Hayashi that the murderous computer HAL from *2001* showed him that each character could justify his point of view, no matter whether an observer judged them as morally "evil."[13] I found this especially interesting, since it was manga/anime, particularly *Battle Angel Alita*, that taught me as a Westerner, that particular dramatic idea. Speaking of *Blade Runner*, at least a part of "the look" of that classic was derived by director Ridley Scott from his trips to urban Asia during his first career as a commercial director where the cacophony of neon and "things built upon things" impressed him.[14] "I was spending a lot of time in New York," Scott said. "The city back then seemed to be dismantling itself. It was marginally out of control. I'd also shot some commercials in Hong Kong. This was before the skyscrapers. The streets seemed medieval. There were 4,000 junks in the harbor, and the harbor was filthy. You wouldn't want to fall in; you'd never get out alive."[15] Scott

---

[h]The raw (initial) translation of the original *Battle Angel Alita* manga series in the US when it was published by VIZ (Kishiro later moved to Kodansha, which publishes the *BAA* sequel series, *Last Order*) was by Matt Thorn (who later was involved founding the Kyoto Seika University manga program and now is an associate professor there) and the rewrite was by Fred Burke (who, according to Thorn, came up with the name "Alita") and Sterling Bell. They did an excellent job—illustrating that the quality of a manga translation, like with anime, is of course instrumental as to whether the story and characters will be fully understood by its readers in the new culture. Readers that can include Hollywood producers, directors wishing to adapt them.

had wanted to shoot *Blade Runner* in Hong Kong, but couldn't afford to.[16] A *Blade Runner* visual influence (though I may be mistaken) is being possibly reflected in some of *Battle Angel Alita*'s scrapyard city scenes.

In terms of personal experience influencing his work, in his interview with Hayashi for this book, Kishiro talks about his relaxation and creativity techniques, including hanging out in junkyards.[i] It's no accident that several key Alita scenes take place in junkyards, and in some sense, the whole "scrapyard city" is a junkyard. This junk piled upon junk idea was also central to French artist Moebius's approach when he had a major hand in *Blade Runner*'s look, which I found out around the time when Ridley Scott had a phone meeting with me about possibly working on a screenplay for a Moebius project about a satellite boy, *Starwatcher* (I was told that Scott had read and liked my Warner Brothers-owned space script). And *Blade Runner*'s design of buildings

Figure 7.5 Doc Ido adopts Alita as his daughter and builds her a new body, combat-ready to help her survive in the often-brutal dog-eat-dog surface-dweller world.

© Yukito Kishiro / Kodansha Ltd.

built upon buildings is a technique which Kishiro uses for his cityscapes in Alita. Ironically, one of the buildings in the cityscape over which Deckard (played by Harrison Ford) flies in *Blade Runner* was constructed by Trumbull's team out of a model of the *Star Wars*' Millennium Falcon space ship turned on its side! As noted earlier, Syd Mead, who designed the *Blade Runner* "spinner car," also redesigned the mobile suits for a *Gundam* series (*Turn A Gundam*) and the updated ship for *Space Battle Ship Yamato*. And in Chapter 11, one of the early architects of *Gundam* alleges the series' *Star Wars* inspiration. So, once again, these trans-Pacific ideas and influences all mix into wonderful new stories.

Another key to *Alita*'s adaptability as a Hollywood feature is its limited number of characters, unlike many long-running manga. As the adapting screenwriter/producer/director, one must carefully choose which personalities to emphasize. *Alita* has quite a

---

[i] Which is why my theory about *Blade Runner*'s possible influence on *Alita* also might be incorrect. And because *Blade Runner* itself is influenced visually in part by an Asian city, Hong Kong, and Kishiro is an urban-dwelling Asian (a resident of Tokyo).

few characters that shift in and out of focus as the story progresses, but it's not at all like a multi-year-running manga with possibly hundreds of individuals. The limited number of characters, coupled with clear antagonists and Alita's driving quest, tends to "center its story spine" so it is more linear and "Western" than the typical manga, thus more feature-friendly. This was an especially striking aspect that attracted me to the project, as from my screenwriting background I knew this linearity to be critical to the success of the adaptation.

Because long-running manga normally have so many characters, they must be "herded"

Mangaka have developed ways to handle the massive number of characters often found in a long serialized manga. Some manga have characters that total over 500. Allegedly, *Dragon Ball* had so many characters eventually its mangaka Toriyama could not remember all their names. Thus, the much-maligned (by many manga/anime fans) *Dragonball Evolution* adaptation faced a huge hurdle from the beginning.

The negative implications for adapting such manga/anime series into live-action feature films are self-evident: often one cannot include even most of the stories or characters, or too much screen time will be eaten up by too many characters, resulting in many severely underdeveloped characters that all fight for screen time during the limited duration of a feature film. One mangaka spoofed this by cramming all her characters in one room as they fight for lines of dialogue. So how do mangaka handle these big groups?

Sidelining characters

One way is by taking them out of the action or story for a while, and sometimes a very long time. This risks alienating fans of that particular character. Aspiring American mangaka Paul Choate (see more of his *Project Alpha* at right and below) explains ways mangaka playfully apologize to fans for sidelining characters.

Choate's manga from my class, *Project Alpha*, contains a large cast of alien characters and takes place during

Figure 7.6 My student Paul Choate's work exhibits manga-style-like limbs crossing the panels, very creative use of paneling, chibi characters for comic relief, and adds bursting colors.

Figure 7.7 A love of Choate's own imagined technological world inhabits his work.

Figure 7.8 *Project Alpha* is typical of manga's allowance for a distinct artistic style, as long as it is engaging to the readership.

an intergalactic war. So he had to learn techniques to manage all of the characters, such as sidelining some of them. I encouraged Choate and other students to begin their stories with just a few key characters and then expand out later.[j] Andrew Cross, who created the comedy manga *Head Asplode* in the class, is also well versed in manga/anime tropes,

> **Choate:** In *Bleach* and *Naruto*, they make it a point to give each character screen time, and if they don't then in the extra sections at the end of the show they'll even have some characters complain about not getting screen time. They'll break the 4th wall in the extras and just kind of acknowledge that they haven't given the character screen time. I remember Naruto [the character], at the end of one of the episodes, looking from one upcoming script to the next, and he complained that he wasn't anywhere in them and that he was the main character of the show. Which is really surreal and funny! [laughs]
>
> **Cross:** They did that in *The World God Only Knows*. It hasn't been translated yet, but at the end of the first season in the comic there is this character that comes in much later that everybody was a big fan of. But she wasn't in the first season of the show at all, and so at the end of the first season, on the last episode, she does the 'On the Next Episode' thing. And she's like "Finally I get to show up! And you guys get to see me because I'm awesome!" [laughs][17]

---

[j] See the end of the book for an example of "character relationship charts" that I have my students fill out to keep their manga from being overcrowded as they do not have the luxury of a long-running series that pro mangaka in Japan do … yet.

Figure 7.9 *Head Asplode*, a comedy manga by my student Andrew Cross, deals with office workers in a search for toner ink.

Figure 7.10 *Head Asplode.*

If you look closely at the form, there is an almost bottomless well of amazing techniques in manga and animes that, when successfully used, can cross over to American film and TV. Some of these techniques are already known by our top TV and movie writers. By being exposed to them in manga, one can transpose them into your own storytelling, thereby expanding your skills. Here are a few that you might find useful:

Dealing with large numbers of characters

Let's say you are not adapting or creating your own manga or anime but rather writing a TV show or a young adult novel (the shōjo manga and young adult (YA) scene are very intertwined with similar tropes and character archetypes) with a large number of characters, and you are finding it difficult to balance screen time for each one. Studying how manga handles and utilizes large groups of characters to energize the storylines "mid-season" can help. For example:

Character herding

Another useful trick top mangaka use for handling large numbers of characters is to herd character groups through various methods. W. M. Penn, who, as previously mentioned, writes about the world of Japanese TV, which is largely based upon manga adaptations, notes, "math ability is definitely a boon to understanding [Japanese] romantic dramas."[18] The same goes for manga and anime. It's not a stretch to conjecture that much of this ability to handle large groups in

Figure 7.11 *Head Asplode.*

dramatic and comedy situation stems from Japanese culture's traditional focus on group dynamics. Here are two ways of putting characters into geometrical grouping (herding) structures associated with comedies:

Love dodecahedron

A love triangle, especially unrequited love, tends to involve heartbreak and frustration due to the unrequited love in the relationship. But by making it into a large number of characters—so that, for example, A loves B, but B loves C, and C loves D, and so on—then it becomes a comedy. There is usually a pivotal character in these manga/anime who, for reasons of honor or general wishy-washiness, does not commit to the person who loves them; and when they do commit, everyone else may realize that "love the one you're with" is the best course, or the situation may remain a mess indefinitely. The "love dodecahedron" also works as an American comedy technique.

Unwanted harem

This popular comedy genre involves a lone man with several attractive women fighting for his attention. The pivotal character may think like a chaste hero, missing the point that he is in an enviable position, or see it as an obstacle between him and the girl he truly likes. Perhaps the most famous example of this trope is in the hit *Tenchi Muyo!*, where the lead has an unwanted harem of space alien ladies (who look like attractive young women); as he grows through the series from a carefree boy into a man, he comes to protect them, and they eventually end up with their own mates and offspring. Some more recent popular examples include *Negima, Love Hina, High School of the Dead*, and *Rosario the Vampire*.

Tropes can be deployed for other uses, such as "Dumb is Good"—where a character without much intelligence is often morally good.

These last three tropes were taken from the TV Tropes.org website: if you are interested in exploring this subject more, this website is a place to go for an incredible number of manga/anime tropes. You can look up a particular show or movie and see many tropes found within it. Knowing these methods is very helpful for creators and anyone involved in fictional narrative media, and the site covers almost every genre and major title imaginable.

Endings: Put this manga (or American TV show) out of its misery!

The above feeling of many readers or viewers may be symptomatic of many series that were strong when they started off but seemed to lose their way. Whether for income or other reasons, as long as these series hold up in the ratings, the mangaka and editors often keep them going with "no end in sight." This is similar to American TV shows that run too many seasons, because sometimes enough of a fan base remains even when the creative spark has dissipated.[k] Then it becomes a financial decision to keep the series grinding out, despite the lack of quality. Though very rarely, an American TV show that has dropped in the ratings and has held on by a thread will subsequently rise from the ashes (like *Smallville*) and run creatively successfully several more seasons.

Lack of a conclusive ending, or an ending at all, is a part of what I call manga/anime's "wandering spine" syndrome—a tendency to stray off the dramatic story spine. This is partially cultural (as we've seen) but also partially because manga writers usually initially only plan a certain amount of the story, and rarely plan the ending (*Death Note*, as we will see, is a partial exception—with the end planned but the middle parts not worked out, leading Ohba to say he got into a bind several times).

When an American TV pilot is "picked up" and episodes ordered, the showrunner has to quickly plan out the episodes for the season. Similarly, when a manga is picked up for serialization by a publisher, the mangaka has to invent more story at a much faster rate under intense pressure from their editor. *Bleach*'s Kubo demonstrates this "fly by the stick"

---

[k] Modern scripted Japanese TV series usually run single seasons, with some notable exceptions.

approach and "make it up as you go along" that characterizes so much serialized development on both sides of the Pacific:

Deb Aoki: You're already up to 33 volumes of *Bleach*—how much longer do you think this story will go?

Kubo: I can't really say how long this story will be by the time it ends, but I have a few more stories that I want to tell, so this series will go on for a while. [laughs]

In an interview with *Puff, Tsunami* magazines, *Battle Angel Alita* mangaka Kishiro discusses his intentional—rather than accidental—way of keeping plotting loose:

It had been a few years since I had imagined a "space" version of the series. Gally [Alita in the American translation] would go up to Zalem [the floating utopian city above the scrapyard] and continue her adventures in space. External and personal circumstances made it difficult to continue the series. I then decided to end it. I wasn't forced to do it; I made the decision after some painful thought. Since the beginning, I made it a rule for *Gunnm* [Japanese title of *Battle Angel Alita,* which means "dream" in Japanese] not to plan ahead or organize the story beforehand, so as to keep it "free." I frequently had the bad idea of planning an episode's outcome and having to find completely unexpected solutions. To conclude *Gunnm* I didn't change the way I had worked until I finally had to do something definitive: Gally had to save Zalem, which is about to fall. But I didn't know how. During the development of the action I theoretically couldn't let the heroine die. The editors [at Shueisha] and myself discussed it a lot. Finally, after thinking about it all night long, I decided to resuscitate Gally in the epilogue.[19]

Besides the nature of serialization, there is another reason why these manga stories often "wander," as Jason Hoffs and I discussed:

Davis: That's one of the things that I noticed about [*Battle Angel*] *Alita*, how conclusive the ending [of the original manga series] was even though it is in its own way ambiguous but clear. And that is unusual—and are you ready for this? This is a fascinating insight that Joshua [Long[l]] had. He said that the reason that this happens is that the mangakas are so busy—and he said he was told this by an editor in Japan—that the mangakas are so busy just trying to get the one-shot [which is often the form of the manga story at the beginning stage] to work that they never think past a certain point, and so that is why so many mangas begin great and then just wander and kind of fill in time.

Hoffs: That's right! They're not necessarily plotting out the beginning, middle, and the end of the arc because it could be a one-shot or it could run at 60 Tankōbon volumes.[m] They don't know.

Davis: Which is fascinating!

Hoffs: Also, remember the audience in a manga has a lot of feedback. I'm not really sure, but the mangaka could also be expecting to be getting feedback from the audience. Maybe he's not even sure where it's going to go. Maybe it's the readership. He obviously drives it, but his readership helps define in some ways the course of the piece.[20]

---

[l] At the time of writing this book, Joshua Long was a producer on the gestating *Cowboy Beebop* Hollywood adaptation and discusses "chain of title" and "E/O" insurance in Chapter 9.

[m] As noted, Tankōbon each contain one volume of a manga series, rather than running several different series at once like manga magazines do.

This process contrasts with how Hollywood feature screenwriters are supposed to work. Knowing the ending when beginning a feature screenplay is critical, as audiences expect a quality ending—a certain inevitability, but also a surprise. As we've seen, the short running-time of a feature film does not give the writer the ability to explore and wander as much as they might be able to in a novel. A feature plot eventually drives toward a specific conclusion, even if [sometimes] ambiguous in interpretation. Feature endings are crucial, and a mediocre film with a great ending tends to find success, whereas a good film with a mediocre ending is often destined to fail.

The "perfect ending" has long been the hallmark of great movies—especially those with worldwide appeal—and drama, going back to the beginnings of storytelling. And this characteristic makes some rare manga/anime mesh well with Hollywood and worldwide film for feature adaptations. *Death Note*, for example, has a "perfect ending."

As explained earlier, *Death Note* is a masterful thriller about Light, an overachieving high school student who finds a notebook dropped into the human world by a bored Japanese death god (Shinigami) named Ryuk. The Death Notebook allows anyone who possesses it to kill anyone whose name they write down in it. The young man proceeds to utilize it to rid the world of criminals and later, less idealistically, law enforcement figures trying to locate him as he goes mad with power. Light's companion in the story is Ryuk.

Figure 7.12 *Death Note*'s amoral death god (Shinigami) observer Ryuk.
© Tsugumi Ohba, Takeshi Obata/Shueisha
© DNDP, VAP, Shueisha, Madhouse

The reason the latter dropped the Death Notebook into the human world was to get some entertainment by watching humans fight over it. Ryuk comes down to Earth to be an amoral observer.

Death Note manga artist Takeshi Obata was interviewed by *Death Note* writer Tsugumi Ohba in *Death Note, Vol. 13: How to Read*, also cited in *The Matrix*

Ohba: Have you gotten ideas from movies?

Obata: In terms of character design, a little bit from *The Matrix*—Ryuk is inspired by *Edward Scissorhands*.

Ohba: I love *Edward Scissorhands* too. I like most of Tim Burton's movies.[21]

Figure 7.13 Notice the similarities between Ryuk (Figure 7.12) and Edward Scissorhands. *Edward Scissorhands* (director: Tim Burton, 20th Century Fox, 1990).

Currently a Warner Brothers adaptation project *Death Note* is unusual in that its writer, Tsugumi Ohba, planned the ending ahead: "When writing a story, I start with the ending. I think about the story as a whole and how much I can fit into one chapter. With the end in mind, I start creating the thumbnails. However, I only work this way because I lack confidence—especially when the series first starts".[n]

---

[n]From DEATH NOTE HOW TO READ 13 © 2006 by Tsugumi Ohba, Takeshi Obata/SHUEISHA Inc. Reprinted by permission of VIZ Media.

Regarding endings of Japanese manga/anime, Michael Arias explained to me how abstract they can become, and how this creates a challenge, in those cases, for adapting them for the West:

> **Davis:** A lot of people say that Americans just want to get to the end of the plot. They want to get to the goal in terms of storytelling. And the Japanese want to experience the journey. It's all about the journey.
>
> **Arias:** Yeah!
>
> **Davis:** So maybe it's a little like that?
>
> **Arias:** Maybe it is. It may be a part of just a general sensibility, a part of Japanese animation that takes you off into Never Never Land in the same way that the final reel of *2001: A Space Odyssey* does. You know, a lot of my movie tries to go there.
>
> **Davis:** It does go there.
>
> **Arias:** And *Akira* and a lot of Japanese movies that end in a tunnel of plasma or whatever it is, and that is obviously a metaphor for the character's inner transformation.[22]

Figure 7.14 Speed goes "into the tunnel of plasma (light)," as his character transforms. Austa Joye describes this moment of Speed's character change: "He is facing the world, against all odds and doing the impossible. He's going into a bleak dog-eat-dog world with his idealistic mindset—challenged to maintain a Zen-like attitude, not to be swayed by immorality. The reason this sequence is different is because he knows this and still is going out there, threatened to be ripped apart—but his goal is to maintain [this attitude] and apply his dignity to his love for racing and not stop and back down from it."[23] *Speed Racer*, Warner Brothers, 2008.

Arias: It's not always spelled out. It'd be tough to explain on paper in a lot of ways. I'm struggling with a comic I love right now which ends in metaphysical territory as well, where the first half of it was spot on and great. Great characters, great storytelling, and it almost felt Western, but as soon as I was looking at it that way it kind of ran off the rails and went deep into metaphysical deep space. And it never comes back and it makes no attempt to resolve it logically. I think that's maybe a little more acceptable here [in Japan], to end something with an enormous explosive or spectacular question mark. A question mark nonetheless, whereas Westerners are a little less ready to digest.°

Now that we've sampled the many differences in emphasis between manga/anime and Hollywood storytelling, we are equipped with the tools to examine the critical ways that manga/anime adaptations have succeeded and failed by looking at two major case studies.

° Jason Hoffs told me in his interview that "a sort of frustration on the American side [in adaptations] could be looking at a wonderful piece of source material that does have a very clear concept and character but in ending it's a little more anamorphic because it's not as important to them [the Japanese]."

8

Hollywood Adaptation Case Study #1: In Defense of *Speed Racer*

- Why the *Speed Racer* live-action remake is the most successful Hollywood live-action adaptation so far of a manga or anime

The biggest anime hit in America at the time

As children, Lana and Andy Wachowski and other current Hollywood filmmakers often saw their first anime on American television. One of these was *Speed Racer* (Japanese title, *Mach Go Go Go*. "Go" means "five" in Japanese, hence the name of Speed's racecar), which arrived in the USA in 1967.[1] As author Patrick Drazen[a] summarizes, "Teenager Go Mifune[b] circled the globe driving the Mach 5, a highly advanced racecar, accompanied by his father, little brother, and girlfriend."[c2] A smash anime success in America, *Speed Racer* was riding the initial 1960s wave of anime hits in the US which included *Astro Boy*; Mitsuteru Yokohama's *Gigantor*, which premiered on Japanese TV the same year as *Astro Boy*, but did not arrive in the US until the following year (1965)—followed by *Marine Boy*; and Tezuka's *Wonder 3*[d] and of course his *Kimba the White Lion*. *Speed Racer* was the biggest hit of them all, topping *Gigantor*, which was the American champion to date. To this day, *Speed Racer* remains the anime series that even non-anime fans remember warmly.[3] All of these series followed the practice of commercial kids-friendly manga, spinning-off merchandising. But this was before Japanese manga/anime merchandising became big globally decades later, especially with the *Pokémon* boom. Robert Napton

---

[a] As noted, the author of *Anime Explosion: The What? Why & Wow of Japanese Animation*.

[b] Go Mifune, the Japanese original manga/anime's protagonist's name, was allegedly based upon that of the famous Japanese actor (and Kurosawa film regular) Toshiro Mifune.

[c] Girly and tomboy Trixie is a resourceful helicopter pilot who often shadows Speed during the cross-country races. Unlike the many passive female animated characters of that era, Trixie will fight if physically cornered and never begs villains. She sometimes rescued Speed and others.

[d] Tezuka began *Wonder 3* as an anime then created the manga afterwards. It utilized the Disney production method of each character having its own animator assigned to it, as Tezuka admired that technique (*Astro Boy and Anime Come to the Americas*, 73).

remembers pining for the *Speed Racer* toy car, as the Mach 5 was a big attraction for children,

> It's funny because *Speed Racer* was such a nostalgic thing, especially for my age. I was kind of the first generation who watched it in syndication in the 70s. I was under ten when I first saw it. When I was a kid I was obsessed with the idea, "Why can't I go to a toy store and buy a Mach 5 toy? Why are there no toys?" I didn't understand. There were toys in Japan, but not in the US. I remember the first time I saw a Mach 5 toy from Japan, and I bought it when I was an adult and I was like, "Wow, it took me 20 years to find this!" [*laughs*][4]

The creators of the series, Tatsuo, Kenji, and Toyoharu Yoshida (a.k.a the Tatsunoko brothers), set out to make something that would be popular in America,[5] which is a different approach than most manga and anime, which were, and still are, usually intended first and foremost for domestic Japanese audiences and readers. In some ways "produce only for the Japanese market" remains a strategy. For example, in 2014, when Disney announced they were going to localize the massively successful *Doraemon* TV show for America, I was approached as a person with some knowledge on the subject by a reporter from Japan's largest newspaper for a comment. I understood the interview would revolve around the big question of "What makes an American company think they can adapt such a Japanese-centric show in America?"[c]

Figure 8.1 *Doraemon*. Over 100 million manga sold.

---

[c] However, the interview was canceled.

As we saw earlier, *Astro Boy*'s American premiere came more from the fact that Tezuka had a financial shortfall that needed to be filled and, almost by accident, an erudite-sounding intermediary (Ken Fujita) offered to try selling it to the US networks and then traveled to America and met with NBC executives—Kiyoshi Fujita closed the deal with NBC.[6] By the time *Speed Racer* came along, the *Astro Boy* foreign sales success story had swept Japan. According to journalist Patrick Macias, who interviewed the youngest brother, Toyoharu Yoshida, who went by the pen name Ippei Kuri and who was its main producer and came up with its wonderful storylines and sequences, said, "We had a big intention to sell it to America right from the beginning."[7]

The reason for the original anime's popularity in the US may be partially due to its American origins

The Tatsunoko brothers (Tatsuo was the main visual designer) were inspired by superhero comic books given to Yoshida and brothers Kenji and Toyoharu by American soldiers after the defeat of Japan in World War II.[f8] As stated earlier, direct influences upon *Speed Racer* were allegedly the Elvis Presley film *Viva Las Vegas* and James Bond's *Goldfinger*, Hollywood smashes in Japan in 1965. Elvis's racing attire provided inspiration for Speed's outfit, along with his pompadour.[9] The Mach Five car was based on a combination of Bond's gadget-filled Aston Martin and possibly some of the cars in the Elvis movie.[g10] The balancing act that the brothers faced in trying to make the anime popular in Japan and America was complicated by the car accidents, which added danger and drama.[11] At the time, the American consumer watchdog group Action For Children's Television called *Speed Racer* an "animated monstrosity" and the "ultimate in crime, evil characters, cruelty, and destruction."[12] But Kuri said, "We intentionally tried to make a show that was peaceful and not violent. For instance, there is no evil organization that the heroes have to fight. There are villains, of course, sometimes with guns, but they never kill anyone. Still, we heard some complaints later that *Speed Racer* was considered a little too violent in the USA. But in Japan, it was actually conservative and not violent at all."[13] Kuri also remarked, "The hard part was that we needed to have the show be popular in Japan first in order to sell it to America. Facing that dilemma, we tried to compromise and make something that was simply feel-good entertainment."[14]

---

[f] A more detailed breakdown of the other brothers and their roles, besides Ippei Kuri (the youngest), is: Kenji Yoshida (anime producer and illustrator), and Tatsuo Yoshida (the founder), who came up with the production company's name. Tatsuo also created the *Speed Racer* manga that preceded the anime.

[g] One of the *Speed Racer*'s best villain-vehicles is "The Mammoth Car," a massive train-like car constructed from gold, which it is thereby disguising and smuggling—the same method used by James Bond's legendary villain Goldfinger utilizing his solid gold Rolls Royce. A similar, but non-gold-type vehicle was used in the Wachowskis' adaptation.

Their strategy succeeded beyond their wildest imaginations when, violent or not (the American cartoons of that era, *Bugs Bunny, Road Runner, Tom and Jerry, Heckle and Jeckle, Deputy Droopy*, and *Popeye*, to name just a few, were often exceedingly violent), it became a smash hit in the United States after it was localized, leading to its worldwide syndication. It has played almost continuously since, with its characters being featured in commercials as well. Unfortunately, the Tatsunoko brothers didn't see much profit, at least at first. Kuri noted that, "At the beginning of the syndication, *Speed Racer* didn't bring in much of a profit. I'm sorry to say that the middle man on the Japanese side of the deal was kind of sloppy about his work."[15] Still, he viewed it as a success due to its worldwide popularity.[16]

How *Speed Racer* was altered by its US localizer and became almost a second version—which the Wachowskis then based their movie partially upon

Peter Fernandez, who was first hired by *Astro Boy*'s American localizer Fred Ladd to write scripts at 100 dollars apiece and dub lines for *Astro Boy* and *Gigantor*,[17] became a central figure in *Speed Racer*'s success in the US after Ladd was shown the pilot. Ladd was intrigued with elements like Racer X's character and the pressured-filled timeline of each episode, and he wanted to localize the series when it was brought to him from Japan by Ken Fujita, but was unable to take it on due to his work commitments on other anime series. Ladd then handed it over to Delphi Associates, which employed Fernandez to write the localization scripts, voice main parts, and direct the other voice actors.[18] Fernandez said, "My only instructions for *Speed Racer* were to 'Americanize' the Japanese version. I was given free rein to come up with the script. The translations I got were very sparse, so I had to make up a lot of the dialogue."[19] Fernandez also worked hard to infuse tremendous energy into his voice cast to match the original Japanese mouth movements. Fernandez's 2010 *LA Times* obituary reports that "Corinne Orr, the only surviving member of the dubbing cast, recalled that 'he sent us through the Crooked Strait and wrote rapid-fire dialogue to try to match the English to the fast-paced Japanese mouth flaps … he loved his wordplay.'"[20] Fernandez said, "I tried to match the energy levels of what was on the screen and whip everyone up into a frenzy."[21] Fernandez explained that *Speed Racer*'s snappy dialogue was sometimes oiled by alcohol at lunchtime: "In those days, Jack Dempsey, the fighter, had a restaurant across the street from our studio. We'd have an hour for lunch and I'd have two or three whiskey sours, and I guess that helped me with the rest of the afternoon."[22]

Fernandez would write the localization scripts in two days and record in one. He was the voice of Speed and Speed's mysterious missing brother Racer X, who had had a dispute with his father and run away. Rex repeatedly returns and saves Speed and Trixie and protects the family.

His *New York Times* obituary quotes Fernandez as saying, "I could name all the characters and write the dialogue the way I wanted,"[23] and that "naming the characters was the most fun." "Fernandez called villains Cruncher Block and Guts Buster [names that the Wachowskis kept in their adaptation], and he delighted in writing such lines as 'The secret film was filmed secretly.'"[24] The result was hyped-up delivery and creative writing that energized the American localization of *Speed Racer* to levels higher than the Japanese original, which is not nearly as beloved in Japan as it is in the United States. In fact, Japanese anime fans are often perplexed at *Speed Racer*'s giant US success.[25] One of the two main producers of the Wachowskis' version, Grant Hill, speaks in his interview below about how the Wachowskis were really creating a hybrid from two versions—the Japanese original and the American localized version.[26]

Fernandez is widely recognized by fans for his key role in the anime localization. Orr said, "he got such joy later in life appearing at cartoon conventions all over the country, where people worshiped the fact he was the voice of Speed Racer and Racer X."[27] He was asked by the Wachowskis to make a cameo as a racetrack newscaster in their adaptation. "When I met the Wachowskis, they couldn't be nicer," Fernandez said. "When they were kids, they confessed, they would run home from school to watch *Speed Racer*."[28] As Hill said to me, "They had been interested in [the anime TV show] … for a long time—since they were kids."

Speed Racer's Hollywood adaptation is as visually dazzling as anything ever put to film. Creatively speaking, *Speed Racer* (directors: Lana and Andy Wachowski, Warner Brothers, 2008) is the most successful direct adaptation of a manga/anime by Hollywood thus far. As Peter Fernandez noted, "To me the feature is faithful to the original in the most important ways and also it brings the style and imagination up to today and beyond."[29]

Figure 8.2 Speed takes the Mach 5 into the drift in a car-racing scene in the Wachowskis' movie. Visual Effects Supervisor John Gaeta talked with me about the team designing a technique to mirror the same effect one gets in anime, which is of a background repeating over and over as it slides by (simulating the anime process of reusing backgrounds to save money), but in the *Speed Racer* live-action hybrid form. This form was also, according to Gaeta and as this image's color scheme demonstrates, pop-art influenced. And "poptimistic" is the term that the Wachowskis' team invented to describe the style.[30] *Speed Racer*, Warner Brothers, 2008.

Figure 8.3 This image demonstrates what Gaeta described as one of the processes the team developed to achieve an anime look but in live-action: "We would take the real world, treat it as if it was animation layers, repaint, recompose, but in our version of it we would add some other stuff. We would add really super fancy 3D in the foreground like cars, crazy cars, and we wanted the crazy cars so that we could do outrageous action [like often occurs in managa/anime]."[31] *Speed Racer*, Warner Brothers, 2008.

Speed Racer is an utterly inspired and near-perfect adaptation of the original anime, and in fact, it is almost impossible to imagine how the film could be any better than it is. First and foremost, the Wachowskis, who come from a strong family unit themselves, made that underlying theme of the adaptation movie similar to that of the original anime. Fernandez elaborated that "I believe those original 52 episodes of *Speed Racer* still hold up so well because of two things. CARS, almost every kid has played with toy cars. And because of the family of Speed who care for him and are closely involved in every story. We care about them. And there are certain values to be found in their relationship."[32] And as Kuri noted, perhaps the anime's adherence to family values came at a perfect time as America was shifting gears socially, and the show represented nostalgia: "I think the timing may have been one of the reasons why 'Speed' became so popular in the West. The US had become a happy and prosperous nation after winning World War II, but all that began to change during the Vietnam era. The family unit started collapsing. People began protesting and criticizing their own government. But at that time, *Speed Racer* was still reflecting the image of the good old days."[33] And Fernandez said that he "always tried to get across a subtle message of some kind about decency or fair play."[34]

One of the features that I discovered from watching *Speed Racer* was how well the Wachowskis understood every aspect of the original anime, including Fernandez's main theme (their adaptation is very much about fair play). Which is another way of saying that the Wachowskis' *Speed Racer* does everything that an adaptation into another medium should do, and more. Part of the reason why the film works so well is that it hews closely to the morals and structure of the original series, keeping the characters, look, and ideas, but adding in a level of eyeball-peeling, fantastically creative production value that blurs the line between live-action and animation, creating a hybrid form (which aligns with the very essence of manga and anime). Writer and journalist Analee Newitz (*Wired, San*

Francisco Bay Guardian) observes how *Speed Racer* captures what it is like to have a child's imagination before adulthood often clamps down on creativity, which is right in line with an episode of the anime where little boy Spritle imagines he is a gunfighter in the Old West and rides a horse past beautiful static images of iconographic gunfighter scenery frozen in painterly anime hold frames … and the live-action movie's Spritle and chimp Chim Chim jacked up on their favorite candies, dancing to their own eccentric, joyous, and eye-popping beat. The film successfully combines this world of childlike imagination with the sense that race cars are transporters to freedom which offer you the chance to take your skills as far as they can go … all in a beautiful, psychedelic setting.[35]

The movie adaptation's plot adheres tightly to the original manga/anime

Plot synopsis of the Wachowskis' film:

How faithful to the original material are the filmmakers being is attested by the film's plot and characters. Speed (Emil Hirsch) is from a "Mom and Pop" small shop racing family; his supportive and ethical father, well-played by John Goodman, is nicknamed "Pops," and his loving mother is played by Susan Sarandon. From childhood on, Speed dreams of being a champion race car driver and is aided in this quest by his tomboy girlfriend Trixie (Christina Ricci). Speed's older brother, Rex (played perfectly by Matthew Fox), whom he admires and emulates, disappears in a legendary cross-country race and is presumed dead. Speed takes Rex's place in a series of races against challengers financed by a powerful and corrupt businessman (Roger Allum) who lies and uses dirty tricks, and who Speed spurns when the businessman tries to hire him over. As in the original manga and anime television show, "Racer X," a mysterious person who turns out to be Speed's long-lost brother Rex, works undercover to help him.

Figure 8.4 The myserious Racer X in the original anime was kept in the remake.
MACH GO GO GO(SPEED RACER) © Tatsunoko Production

Figure 8.5 Rex (Racer X) in the Wachowskis' version. The characters were identical, and served the same purpose in the plots, although in the Wachowskis' version, a bit older. *Speed Racer*, Warner Brothers 2008.

Figure 8.6 Trixie's character also keeps her basic style from the anime original, with flawless color-coordinated attire down to her nail polish, even when she flies her helicopter. *Speed Racer*, Warner Brothers 2008.

Figure 8.7 In *Viva Las Vegas* (director: George Sidney, MGM, 1964), Anne Margaret's character also flies in a helicopter over Elvis and his fellow racers as they follow a cross-country route through multiple terrains, just like Trixie (and often Speed's father Pops and mechanic Sparky) regularly does in the original *Speed Racer* and the Wachowskis' adaptation. It is speculation, but it seems likely to me that the two characters with her in the helicopter might have been partial models for the *Speed Racer* characters Pops and Sparky.

Below, in the Wachowskis' adaptation, Speed needs all the help he can get, with many nasty racer opponents willing to do anything to win. Gaeta explained to me that photographers were sent around the world to grab backgrounds like this desert, where a full film crew would have been impossible to afford. The images were then processed into digital cells to replicate anime's characteristics but in a new, hybrid form.[36]

Figure 8.8 Gaeta talked about scenes like the one displayed here that would have been financially or logistically impossible to do in reality or with a full crew. Instead, a few people were dispatched worldwide to photograph images in places like exotic deserts, museums, or castles where perhaps only special entry for maybe one sock-footed photographer would be allowed: "Why should we have some animators try to figure it out: we'll just augment it. We'll get what is out there in reality, which is already wild, and then we'll just pop it up and add crazy stuff to it, and that, I think, is a recipe for a lot of cool films to come."[37] *Speed Racer*, Warner Brothers, 2008.

None of the original manga and anime's major story and character elements have been altered in any significant way—the original work was exciting and fun

Figure 8.9 John Gaeta, Visual Effects Designer for the Wachowskis' *Speed Racer* and *The Matrix* trilogy.

The Wachowskis took the heart of the original and plugged it into a thrilling, visually stunning, and well-acted "go for broke" approach which incorporated the sincerity and refreshing lack of postmodernist cynicism that are hallmarks of the original *Speed Racer* manga/anime. John Goodman's performance served as an anchoring force amidst the swirling visuals and helped to create a family that you can care about. As further noted by Newitz in her article titled "10 Reasons Why *Speed Racer* is an Unsung Masterpiece," John Goodman knows how to embody a cartoon character physically, but bring an emotional edge to his performance that feels nuanced and human. He's done this repeatedly during his career, from his standout performance in *The Big Lebowski* to his show-stealing role on *Community*. Bringing him into the *Speed Racer* mix—along with Susan Sarandon as Speed's mom—turned this movie from a silly smashup story into a tale where you actually care about the fate of Speed's family."[38] Newitz states that *Speed Racer* presents:

[a] **pretty realistic picture of what it's like inside a kid's head** … when Speed and Spridle are watching cartoons (*anime*, of course), they jump inside the TV and become cartoons themselves. Every background landscape looks like a churning, whirling kid's imagination, colored spastically in crayon. This is a movie that loves kids for what they really are—little maniacs who are hopped up on adrenaline and adventurousness, who inhabit stories fully rather than from a dispassionate, ironic distance. I love that Rex takes young Speed for a completely dangerous race car ride. That scene is in the spirit of this movie, which understands that children are terrific allies on any heroic quest.[39]

Scott Holeran, of the website Box Office Mojo, which reports on the business of the Hollywood movie industry, emphasizes the "anti-cheating/fair play" theme that the Wachowskis took from the original in his review "Cartoon Remake Crosses Finish Line in Style," after stating that "*Speed Racer* is built for families, not for fanboys":[40]

Trying to beat the businessman's bought drivers, Speed teams with red-hot Racer X and an Oriental punk (an actor named Rain in a catastrophic debut). He upgrades the Mach 5 to perform fabulously impossible automotive feats—remember those cheesy jing-jing sound effects from the show?—and he takes the track at the tropical Casa Cristo 5000 competition, dreaming of acing the Grand Prix.

There isn't enough about the mechanics of improving a car's racing performance and subplots tend to overlap in confusing ways, especially during the first 45 minutes. But Speed accelerates on the curve—with underused Trixie (Christina Ricci) getting a Gothic look—and he pulls into a thrilling final lap.

"Stop steering and start driving," Rex instructs his younger brother early in the action and the remainder of *Speed Racer* cashes in on that simple advice. Mom (Miss Sarandon in milk and cookies mode) and Pops (always reliable Goodman) and their brood—also Trixie and Sparky—have an encouraging and highly positive effect on passive Speed.

Speed Racer is a stylized cartoon with live actors and spurts and streaks of stimulating sounds, colors and action. In spite of its anti-business bent, it is an exciting piece of entertainment—an emotional embrace of family as the fuel of one's highest aspirations. Ultimately, *Speed Racer* is a dazzling depiction of a young man, oiled by his family's values, who is driven to be his best.[41]

Thus, the adaptation has the thematic "strong story roots" that Tezuka so valued.

Figure 8.10 Speed triumphs and reaches his full potential as in the original anime/manga and also very much in sync with shōnen manga/anime tone where a group working earnestly together, with a humble lead young male protagonist, triumphs over odds through hard work and grit. *Speed Racer*, Warner Brothers, 2008.

Audience reception

Total lifetime grosses[h]

Domestic:	$43,945,766	46.8%
+ Foreign:	$50,000,000	53.2%
= Worldwide:	**$93,945,766**	

[h]Budget: $120 million.

Domestic summary

Opening Weekend: $18,561,337

(#3 rank, 3,606 theaters, $5,147 average)
% of total gross: 42.2%

Widest release: 3,606 theaters
Close date: August 7, 2008
In release: 91 days / 13 weeks

(Source: Box Office Mojo)

Financial misfire: All cylinders fired except the marketing ones

Part of this book's emphasis is on "how to properly adapt a work from Japan." And in evaluating success, the financial profit of the project usually comes into the equation, given the nature of how business works and the cost of these films. Michael Arias told me, "I think *Speed Racer* was a success and quite true to its roots. I think that the marketing on that was quite disastrous. I don't know in the US, but in Japan it was largely a failure of marketing. They tried to have it ride the coat tails of the Wachowskis rather than just pitching it as a kid's movie. Which it was in the same way the Pixar movies are, where you can go as a family and there's a nice cotton candy experience."[42]

Grant Hill on the attitude of the creative team making *Speed Racer* and the marketing

Relatively unknown outside Hollywood with the wider public, Grant Hill is a producer of very large-scale Hollywood films that also have the rare distinction of being artistic motion pictures with a singular vision, rather than the "committee-created" norm for big budget fare. Hill also produced the Wachowskis' *Cloud Atlas*, *V for Vendetta*, the two *Matrix* sequels, and *Speed Racer* (the latter two with Joel Silver as principal producer), and was principal producer on the Wachowskis' *Jupiter Ascending* (2015). The low-key Australian also works regularly with other high-end critically respected directors such as Terrence Malick, as principal producer on *The Thin Red Line*, and was a co-producer on *Titanic*, directed by James Cameron. Hill was nominated for two Academy Awards for *The Thin Red Line* and *Tree of Life* and won a Director's Guild of America award for *Titanic* (shared with principal producer Jon Landau and James Cameron).

In my living room in Los Angeles several years ago as we discussed one of my screenplays that we were developing, Grant noticed the *Battle Angel Alita* manga on my coffee table. I explained that I was trying to secure the adaptation rights, my first foray into this area after falling in love with the manga. He remarked to me that I'd be lucky if I ever got the rights and warned me about the difficulty of getting rights to manga/anime—he knew what I had to learn the hard way, and he pretty much guaranteed that I'd waste enormous amounts of time. He'd seen it happen to others.

An imposing man physically, he is both artistically idealistic and professionally accomplished as is required to produce such enormous movies and manage elements that can derail writer/directors—so as to protect their ability to create their art. Growing up on a farm in Perth, Australia, he began as a professional ocean diver, has a law degree, and later became one of the "go to" men in Hollywood as a unit production manager (UPM), with his specialty originally being coordinating massive resources together in short order for very large film productions. I spoke to him via phone about the *Speed Racer* project when he was in Germany working on pre-production for *Cloud Atlas*.

I began by telling Hill how amazing I felt that his credits are, especially in that there has been very little publicity on him compared to some other producers with comparable high-profile work, and he responded modestly, "Thank you. I like to keep busy."

> **Davis:** It seems like the approach you use is basically go with the vision that you've chosen to be involved with and see where it leads you rather than—I remember reading a quote by Hitchcock where an actress said something like, "Let's guarantee ahead of time that we have a hit," and Hitchcock said to her "There's no way to do that. You've just got to do your best."
>
> **Hill:** Yeah, I mean there is no way to do that. Whether you're approaching it from a very commercial perspective or an artistic one, or somewhere in the middle—you just never know. There is success and failure on each level. I guess for me it's been [sic] lucky enough to be associated with very strong, very different, very driven directors, whether it be the Wachowskis or Cameron or Terry Malick. They have all had that singular approach to these things, and there is some sort of purity to it. That's a spectrum of people. Obviously Cameron is instinctually more commercially inclined than Terry, and probably the Wachowskis are somewhere in the middle. The strength of attachment to a singular vision is sort of similar.
>
> **Davis:** I remember you sitting in my living room and you saw my *Battle Angel Alita* manga and saying, "Well good luck on that, in getting those rights because it's so difficult"—and it is so difficult, you were right, as usual. In the case of *Speed Racer*, were the rights already in the United States? In other words, it was already secured when you came onboard, I would assume?
>
> **Hill:** That was the thing. It had been secured and I forget what the process was, but basically Warner had the rights I believe ... or if they didn't have them they had access to them. I remember them expressing an interest in doing it. So, it was relatively straightforward to secure them. They [the Wachowskis] had been interested in that sort of character film for a long time—since they were kids, so they felt very strongly and that was very helpful.

Hill discusses marketing problems that may have led to the financial failure of *Speed Racer* despite its creative success

Warner Brothers had very little time to develop a marketing campaign, a theme of my interview with Hill:

> **Davis:** I saw it with my daughter in the theater, and at the time she was ten, and I said, "Why aren't there more people in here?" because we both really loved this film, and she responded, "Because it was marketed wrong." And I was amazed to hear a ten-year-old say that. I heard that around some, and I was wondering, as a producer do you get involved in that, or is that something that other people do?
>
> **Hill:** It depends on project by project. Yes, we were involved. The principal producer on that was Joel Silver and Joel is very strongly involved in marketing. You know, there are many different accounts of what—there was a sort of disconnect between the marketing and the way it was pitched, and in some cases the level of marketing wasn't even out there. Everybody has their theory, and I think that … it's sort of a shocking turnaround on that, because we had a pretty tight deadline to make, and when we eventually finished the movie, we tested the movie finished—which hadn't been done very often, because you test it before you finish so that there is some chance of clarifying what the issue is. Because we had a fixed release date and we were very close to it, we only had the opportunity to test it quickly after we'd sort of basically started to make the print, and when it was tested I think it got the highest applause that they ever got.[i] I mean, it was remarkable, I remember. So they were ecstatic about it. I think if there was a problem, the problem was two-fold. One is we had agreed or—the time between when we handed over the picture and when it was released was much too small, because it's such a conceptual movie. If you've looked at the comic books and even if you're just familiar with it, you can imagine an endless number of interpretations of that character. And so it was very difficult—and because it was sort of so much of the computer CGI, a significant amount of it was computer generated or at least enhanced—there wasn't really an opportunity to show the movie to the marketing people halfway through where they would get it. I think that by the time they saw it, they didn't really have time to properly strategize and re-orient themselves to capitalize on the previews that they received.
>
> **Davis:** I didn't mean it as any sort of criticism—it's all Greek to me. But I was just stunned by how good the movie was and then that happened, so I think that it's good for the people to know what happened from the inside.
>
> **Hill:** It's certainly not a criticism. It was bewildering to us at the time and somewhat frustrating, because we loved the movie and we love it now. It's a movie where [not a] week goes by where one or all of us get a call that's like, "Hey! I saw this movie on DVD or I saw it somewhere else. That's fantastic! When was it released?"
>
> **Davis:** Oh my god!

---

[i] Hollywood studios "test" the audiences to make decisions on movies and TV pilots just as manga publishers survey their readers for creative input and rankings.

Hill: [laughs] There wasn't, in many places, the marketing materials, and even if you have a good picture and a really good marketing campaign, it takes time to be directed and do its work.

Davis: I heard Disney starts years in advance.

Hill: They do. They're the other extreme. Yes, anyway. We're incredibly proud of it, making it, and you know you just want more people to have seen it.

A key to successful manga/anime live-action adaptations is a core group of filmmakers working with a shared fairly singular vision who fully understand the source material and have strong but open-minded collaborative leaders—who have the power

Earlier in the book, Gaeta described how the Wachowskis' team carefully studied the way the anime form works, frame by frame. Hill elaborated on how, in terms of creating the film, they were a tight-knit smaller group who were all, in Michael Arias's words "drinking the Kool-Aid":

Davis: Regarding your choices as a producer and how it ties into *Speed Racer*, it seems like you have chosen to be involved with people where not only do they have a singular visions and are top-tier filmmakers, but also it seems like the decision-making group is smaller and tighter maybe?—am I putting words in your mouth in saying that that it might lead to a purer vision in those cases? In other words, you work with writer/ directors a whole lot.

Hill: No, I guess that's true. Also, as well as being writers/directors, most of those directors have a very tight team around them. I mean, Terry has Jack Fisk who's worked on every movie with him. Billy Weber has edited all of his movies until the most recent one. On *Tree of Life* he was overall supervising editor. So, the Wachowskis are sort of the same. A lot of their close crew has been the same through their career. They had a crew that had already survived three *Matrix* movies with them, and that's also significant. Cameron's the same as well. I think what that does is … yeah, it makes it more focused because there is an understanding between the department head and an ability to interpret the vision or direction. It always comes from the director but then if you work with somebody a lot, you never fully formed the outfit, there's a lot of work that comes into taking that germ of an idea or vision and actually actualizing it. I think if you've got around you people presumably good at their job and know the sort of sensibility of the director, it makes the process a lot more focused and faster and singular in its direction.

Davis: I think this gets around to the book, the subject of dealing with—the Japanese are afraid of [a poor quality adaptation] happening and it seems like the approach that you all used was the correct one in having a very singular vision that's not being pulled from the outside. And they [the Wachowskis] so understood the way the *Speed Racer* story structure works, and how the characters work-that …

Hill: The Japanese are understandably protective of their characters. But at the same time, if you are trying to interpret it or take it to a larger audience, there are some aspects of their characters that don't translate that widely past the Japanese audience in their original form. So there is some delicacy in modernizing, changing, editing … whatever you like to call it. I think that's where, as a director, you have to have a strength of belief in the material that allows you to be confident enough to think that you can interpret in a way that's going to not detract [from] the essence of the original.

Regarding the collaborators on the Japanese side

Hill: We were very pleased with the response we got from the Japanese [for *Speed Racer*]. A lot of the people that we dealt with in the first instance were on the organization level. One of the original animators in Japan we had access to and he did some work for us. It worked very well. We were very happy.

Davis: Oh really? Did you screen it at the end, and they were happy? Okay.

Hill: They were happy and we didn't have anyone working week in and week out. It was in the early phases when we were investigating ways to do the project, and to be true to it all. We went to Japan and we contacted a number of the animators. We gave them some of our material and asked them for concept sketches of some of the elements based on what we had shown them, and they were very useful.

Davis: Was that while the script was being written, or before, or after?

Hill: It would have been while it was being written. We had a very long lead time on that because there was so much design work and so much technology that at that point had to be worked out. I think we started at least a year before we started filming. We didn't have any idea actually how we were going to achieve it. We looked at practical cars, practical courses. We went to Japan to talk to them about it. There was a lot of time spent. We were also lucky because one of our … the lead conceptual artist who is probably one of the American comic book world's most recognized and most loved figures and most talented people, a guy called Geoffrey Darrow. Geof has worked with Wachowskis on all their films. He was the original lead conceptual person on *The Matrix*. And he has spent a lot of time in Japan and he speaks Japanese and they were very aware of his work. And the fact that they are aware of his work: he spoke Japanese and that also made the whole interaction so easy. And Geof, more than any person on the planet that I have ever met just knows the history and the material of Japanese manga like back to front and knows a lot of the original manga personalities. So that certainly opened the door for us.

Davis: But yet you didn't have to do that. You did it for the real creative input and the respect. It wasn't contractually required.

Hill: Absolutely. It was definitely a desire to protect the integrity of it.

Hybridization: The meshing of the *Speed Racer* Japanese manga/anime and American localized anime TV series into the live-action Hollywood movie

Hill: Now, having said that, there's also sort of a weird cross-cultural line to deal with as well. While it was originally a Japanese manga that was successful, in the US you had the additional complication that the TV [anime] series became an incredibly popular thing for a time. That's actually how the Wachowskis first came in contact with it and maintained interest in it, because they watched it as kids.

Hill described how the hybrid story form of the Wachowski project developed from different sources: "The TV series is a totally different entity in its style than the manga, so you have two slightly different expectations and audiences because they viewed the same things in different medias, in a way. So that was something that we were trying to work through as well … I think that we in a sense styled it with an advantage, because we styled it to a hybrid—we had the original and then we had an Americanized version of it. So the trick was to retain the authenticity of the original but also make it a little more approachable in a way that the TV series did. It's a very fine line to tread".[43]

Of course, when Hill refers to an "American version," he means the American localized version of the Japanese anime TV show. Like the work that Fred Ladd did to localize the original *Astro Boy* anime TV show in America, the *Speed Racer* localization process

Figure 8.11 In their faithfulness to the original anime and manga, the *Speed Racer* adaptation team closely mirrored the basic design cues of the main components of the original anime/manga, but in other ways pushed far beyond and created a new hybrid form that, as Gaeta told me, involved intensive research and development utilizing digital technology to take it to the next level.
MACH GO GO GO(SPEED RACER) © Tatsunoko Production

Figure 8.12 The warm family aspect of *Speed Racer*'s anime.
MACH GO GO GO(SPEED RACER) © Tatsunoko Production

Figure 8.13 This warm and ethical family-focused tone was also adhered to in the adaption, which helped anchor the Wachowskis' film amidst the swirling visuals.
Speed Racer, Warner Brothers, 2008

created the version of the work that the Wachowskis first saw. That version was deliberately adapted to make the show more accessible to American audiences and fit within American cultural norms.

The "localization to make more accessible" process has another result—that locally voiced and edited anime in any non-Japanese country are sometimes very different from the original creation as it was exhibited in Japan. This impacts the American adapters of the anime (or manga) into live-action, because the source they are attracted to is not "pure"— and is its own kind of hybrid. The quality of the localization thus becomes a potentially big factor in the live-action adaptations that are using such localizations as their source material. Localizations also can be low quality, or contain inexplicable changes from the Japanese language original, that perhaps could be explained by the localizers. For example, *Robotech*, part of the second wave of anime that came to America and which is currently a Hollywood adaptation development deal, has a tortured adaptation and localization history. Author Antonia Levi, who has lived in Japan off and on since the 1970s, explains in *Samurai from Outer Space: Understanding Japanese Animation* as regards the 1980s *Space Battleship Yamato* that, "*Yamato* and *Macross* made their first appearance on American television. Retitled *Star Blazers* and *Robotech*, respectively, they were heavily edited to accommodate American tastes and sensitivities. The names of all main characters were changed to make them less foreign and easier to understand."[44] As we have seen in the case of Ladd and Fernandez's localization of *Astro Boy* and *Speed Racer* to American tastes, this is a normal procedure. Levi explains that on *Macross*:

> Some characters underwent more significant changes. Dr. Sado, the hard-drinking medical officer of the *Space Battleship Yamato*, must have attended A.A. [Alcoholics Anonymous meetings] before signing on as Dr. Sand of *Star Blazers*. Yellow Dancer, a campy transvestite who played a supporting role in the Japanese original, underwent an even more drastic transformation for *Robotech*. The censors cut as much as they could, and then rewrote the script to make him a secret agent. His periodic appearances in drag were thus explained [as] a disguise to allow him to infiltrate enemy lines as a female pop star. Why did he need to be a female pop star? Don't ask.[45]

Robotech comes from a complicated lineage. As Drazen explains, "three different Japanese TV series were collected and edited together to produce this 1985 series that is still hailed as a major leap forward in science-fiction broadcasting, live or animated."[46] This might have contributed to some of the above decisions. Due to its background, the chain of title[j] and unification of all parties into a business agreement on the live-action adaptation project for this series was rumored to be difficult by even Japanese rights standards, and clearing it to the point that the American studio was satisfied was reportedly very difficult.[k]

These changes raise the question of what is truly the "real show" that the American filmmakers are inspired to adapt into live-action, if the American localization of the anime TV series was significantly altered to try and make it line up to the values of the culture in which it is being presented? This is the process of the "sort of a weird cross-cultural line" to which Hill referred.

American fans' suspicions about radical changes caused them to guess (and sometimes investigate) what exactly the original anime was like. Errors in localization can go uncorrected due to the fact that the Japanese creators usually don't know other languages, so they can't check the foreign localizations for accuracy. Any time a film is adapted for a different culture and language, there's a considerable risk that the essence of the movie will be "lost in translation." Director Stanley Kubrick got around this issue by having filmmakers he

---

[j] Chain of title is described in detail in Chapter 9.
[k] Napton explained that *Robotech* (the English name of the series) was a combination of the anime *Macross*, *Southern Cross*, and *Mospeada*. The first 36 episodes of *Robotech* is the *Macross* TV series.

trusted perform foreign language dubs of his films.[47] Presumably the reason was that they would have the taste to match the foreign language version to Kubrick's artistic vision. But often, the original creators have little or nothing to do with the foreign language versions and just hope for the best.

Much of the level of care given to the localization will be determined by the opinions of the local market distribution company that licenses the right to distribute the work as to its potential profitability. High quality voice acting and translations cost more. The very few artists/creators who are able to preserve their artistic vision across foreign territories and are simultaneously commercially successful in their large-scale productions (like Stanley Kubrick in his day) are rare. It not only takes real time, but, given the number of languages and cultures in the world, an attention to detail and willpower that is almost superhuman. So to a degree, hybrid versions are created as the works are localized into various cultures and languages.

Getting back specifically to *Speed Racer*, and generally to the Hollywood adaptations of manga/anime, there are other reasons why the original mangaka may not be welcome to give their input beyond the "meaningful consultation" clause put in their contracts. This clause, as Professor Mehra and I speculated, may in fact exist to stave off lawsuits based on creators' rights, but may also be an attempt to try to mollify the original creators who know that the contract does not normally give them final say[48] (as previously noted, the Del Toro *Monster*/HBO adaptation project is reportedly a notable exception to this norm).

One of the *Speed Racer* and *The Matrix*'s designers, Geof Darrow, discusses the internal workings of the creative decision-making on those films

Figure 8.14 *The Matrix*'s Geof Darrow-designed field of fetuses. Darrow, who established the highly original underwater look of several key sequences also has first-hand experience in the Japanese manga world which was complementary to his work on the Wachowskis' *Speed Racer* adaptation. As noted, *The Matrix* also heavily uses anime styling—some people feel some other parts of the film's "look" is specifically derived from *Ghost in the Shell*.

Geoffrey Darrow is a highly respected graphic novel artist who has first-hand knowledge about the manga industry and who worked with the Wachowskis and Frank Miller. On *Speed Racer* and *The Matrix* he served as a lead conceptual person (in Hill's words). Some of his breakthrough designs include the pods in *The Matrix* that contained human beings like Neo being harvested for their energy by the machine empire. John Gaeta explained to me, "Geof was brought in for extraordinary, high, singular concepts, right? Geof will do a few seminal drawings that wind up translating into a logic, if you will. On *The Matrix*, he was the first person to really start drilling into the sort of biomechanical, undersea look that tends to be pervasive in both architecture and creatures. Because he's got such a far-out, wild imagination for detail, and he's famous for it—and there's a reason: he puts in detail that nobody else would ever consider and he also applies such an intensity of sort of a tone, attitude, emotional craziness, and you get that too, so he's not in there to bang out a lot of drawings. He's in there to come up with the super high concept, relevant ideas that we can create a logic from."[49]

Darrow echoed the themes of the rarity of a pure artistic vision and he emphasizes the Wachowskis' management style of seeking creative input constantly from a team who, as Hill also notes, had worked together for a long time, versus the normally highly stratified pecking order of a large Hollywood movie. And he makes insightful points about the original creators of manga/anime usually not being welcome to give input on Hollywood adaptations:

> **Davis:** When you were working on *Speed Racer*, the Wachowskis wanted to work with you and design things, and you dealt directly with them?
>
> **Darrow:** That's an odd thing. I'm working on a movie now, and I've never talked to a director. It depends on the director, but a lot of times you see the production designer, and depending on the ego of the production designer, they don't want you to have any contact with the director because sometimes they want the director to think it's all them doing all this stuff.
>
> **Davis:** Oh, I see.
>
> **Darrow:** But with the Wachowskis I had never worked on a movie [before] when I worked with them. There are other guys who have worked on movies and whenever they would walk into the room, they would just freeze up, because they've never ever had contact with the directors. But they [the Wachowskis] do. They'll pick—you go into their office, and they look at what you do. They tell you what they think, what they want you to do. They're really hands-on. I understand that it's very rare in Hollywood.[i]
>
> **Davis:** I felt like what Grant [Hill] was saying was that that kind of director essentially gets a pure, cleaner vision.
>
> **Darrow:** Otherwise, you're throwing spaghetti on the walls—what sticks? Everybody else I've ever worked for, you can do ten versions of something and they'll take one of this, one of that, and one of that. But with them, they save a lot of money because they know exactly what they want, and they tell you, "OK, I want this to look like this." Or at

---

[i] Gaeta echoed to me Darrow's assessment of the Wachowskis' collaborative spirit: "[G]reat directors understand that the folks they surround themselves with are, at times, able to conceptualize even further than themselves and, if they're great directors, they sort of observe the best of ideas and they channel the best of ideas and so … what's great about the Wachowskis is that they are very humble beings and they do allow a lot of discussion and interaction and creative freedom of the people that surround them."

least give me an idea of what they want. A lot of these directors are like, "Well, I don't know, see what you can come up with."

Davis: I've heard that over and over again from assistant directors.

Darrow: I remember one time, someone called me up and wanted me to work on one of these *X-Men* movies—the first one. "We want you to storyboard this sequence, blah blah blah, you have completely free rein, because the director doesn't like action." So I said that basically I'd be directing that, and asked if he was going to pay me like the director. [Laughs] And I said, "nah, I don't think so." But that's the way a lot of it is. They say, "here I want an action scene and this is what happens." You put it together and they get the credit for it. They still have to deal with a lot of the logistics but …

Davis: Do you feel like these certain directors, the rare ones who give the creative people direct access to them, that they're the better bet for the Japanese to go with if they have a choice for an adaptation for a work?

Darrow: Whenever anyone buys a property, the first thing they want to do is make it their own. The last guy that went around was the guy who came up with it. If they turn to you and go, "So tell me, Mr. Tezuka, would Astro Boy really do that?" and if he said no, then after a while they just decide to buy the property and do what they want with it. Ridley Scott, when I worked with him, was like, "Here's my number, call me anytime." And the producer was like, "Oh no no no, if you want to talk to Mr. Scott, you have to go through me." But he gave me his home number, and I wouldn't bother him at all, but just the fact that he gave that to me showed me how involved he was, and he was really involved. But with the producer it was just a pecking order.[50]

Michael Arias added, "The reason *Speed Racer*—if it worked—I think it's largely a testament for the Wachowskis' love for the original. And their general taste and I'm sure they had to go through the mouth for it. They were riding a pretty big wave when they got off *The Matrix* and so they were able, to a certain extent, to flex their muscles as producers of *Speed Racer*. They had a crew that had already survived three *Matrix* movies with them, and that's also significant."[51]

Addendum to *Speed Racer* case study: Two other prominent manga/anime adaptation producers in Hollywood discuss the process on other major adaptation projects currently in development

In their attempts to make changes to try and reach a larger audience outside that of the source material, the studio usually has the power if they want to exercise it.

Roy Lee is a successful Hollywood producer who has specialized in Asian remakes. *The Ring*, a remake of a Japanese horror movie, began his career in Hollywood and,

The Departed (director: Martin Scorsese) received the Academy Award for Best Motion Picture in 2007. He is a principal producer of the *Death Note*[m] adaptation project from the hit manga/anime, also set up in development at Warner Brothers.

As a high-level Hollywood producer, Lee is able to shed light on the creative issues and the acquisition and development process of these manga/anime projects. He also is privy to how studios decide to greenlight movies (meaning the all-important decision to begin production, the "holy grail" for filmmakers and something that Japanese rights holders are often frustrated to see not happening)—and he explains why the Japanese rights holders are often kept "in the dark" about progress later.

Roy Lee on dealing with notes from the studios

Davis: When you're producing and a studio gives you some notes, or to whoever's involved, do you find that if there are some notes that are really destructive, how do you deal with that?

Lee: The goal for everyone is to make the best movie possible. So, you have to take the notes into account, especially if they're coming from the studio saying that they want certain things done to the property. They may not be the best in maintaining the integrity of it, so you just have to work with the studio and the writer to make the best possible movie within the confines of what the studio's requesting.[52]

The studios are the buyers and are taking an enormous financial risk on each movie. Their good will is, from a producer's point of view, extremely important, and a producer will likely have to come back to that studio again and again to try to get funding for projects—because there are only a few major Hollywood movie studios (the "majors" are currently Paramount, Sony, Universal, Warner Brothers, Disney and 20th Century Fox).[n] Thus, following the studio executives' creative notes, even when they may not be the best at maintaining the integrity of it, is something producers are apt to feel would be wise to do. There are those who would argue that always following the studio executives' notes may be a recipe for some muddled projects, but the studios, as financiers, are well aware of their power and will exercise it when they can and want to and see that as a valid right to protect their enormous investment. Seeking commercial success is understandable and necessary, given the tremendous stakes involved. The irony is that even if a producer and director follow studio notes slavishly (which, as we will see later, is practically the only choice for most screenwriters in the studio system), or in the opposite case of powerful filmmakers that are occasionally left mostly to their own devices, neither is a guarantee that the film will be a commercial success. It is *very* hard to make a successful film or television show. Showrunner Phil Rosenthal (*Everybody Loves Raymond*) quoted show

---

[m] As Dan Lin, Jason Hoffs and Masi Oka are also presumably principal producers, this means that they probably all get the coveted "Produced By" title.

[n] Historically, United Artists and MGM were also considered major studios, but in recent years, for various reasons, their produced output has been lower. And New Line Cinema also became less prolific. Despite their hits, the overall trend in feature films is fewer "buyers" for projects due to vertical-integration of the Hollywood movie industry through mergers and acquisitions and more reliance on big-budget, and thus less numerous, "tent-pole" or "event" movies.

runner Ed Weinberger's advice, "[D]o the show you want to do, because in the end, they are going to cancel you anyway."[53] Veteran screenwriter William Goldman's (*Butch Cassidy and the Sundance Kid*) famous quote regarding this matter is "nobody knows anything" in Hollywood (presumably meaning that no one knows what will be successful).[54] A complicated set of factors, personalities, and luck influence each decision. One truism, however, is that critically acclaimed, A-list directors with a history of commercial and artistic success (particularly if it occurred recently) are more likely to be able to exert more creative leverage—which is important to artists who wish to have a specific vision in their work.

On the question of creative consultation

Davis: The fans are more hardcore than some of these mangaka about maintaining what [the original manga] was exactly.

Lee: It varies from project to project and creator to creator, because some creators have a stronger desire to maintain the integrity of the original art, and others are willing to let the studios adapt it to how they feel will work best for the different audience the movie would be trying to reach.

Davis: And are you these days, when you make a deal, is it always going to be the way the studio wanted that contractual "We Will Give Our Best Efforts in Consultation," or are people getting actually creative controls in there still?

Lee: Creative controls still are not possible on the studio level. It could be done on an independent film, but it's rare for a studio to give creative controls when there is so much money on the line for development and production. I'm trying to think of the last thing I saw that had creative controls ... there [have] been one or two instances, but I can't even remember what they are. But normally not.[55]

Jason Hoffs expresses his strategy regarding pleasing original fans versus gaining the additional audience required for Hollywood studio profitability

Davis: So, another question was, what [are] your plans for attracting and keeping the hardcore fans? Because, as you said, not to put words in your mouth, the really larger audiences [are] the one[s] that Hollywood needs to get.

Hoffs: I think that for the mangaka, there will always be a calculation of "[W]ill I likely alienate my fans if something appears to be very different, if the ethnicity of the character changes, or the age of a character, or if a character might behave in a way that the fans might not consider consistent with their manga persona?" Some of these issues are often a risk. I think we try to deal with it sensitively. We also don't want to anger or upset or let down any fan base and try to be as careful as possible. There might be certain situations, particularly if there is a really big property where we might decide not to pursue it because doing a live-action film might be too different. So I think it's an important point to realize that it's not just essential to choose the biggest, most famous properties to try to make movies out of. Often we would choose obscure properties, often properties that have never been published in the US and may not have been big sellers in Japan. But if there is a big property that may have tens of millions of fans worldwide, you have to make a very careful calculation whether you're going to upset them. Also, as far as the buzz for the movie, they also have an outsized voice, and they'll either get behind something or criticize something [and that] could have some effect on how the larger film-going diaspora is going to view it. If the fans manage to create a bad buzz, or say that this isn't an authentic representation—it's certainly the fan's right to have that voice, and they do more than ever. They end up becoming co-creators, almost, a lot more than they used to be.

Davis: I've noticed that kind of the hardcore otaku can do a lot of complaining.

Hoffs: But anybody in any business also learns, you can't make everybody happy all the time. At some point LeBron James just has to try to put the basketball in the hoop.

Davis: In some ways what you said, I'm not putting words in your mouth, might favor properties that aren't so enormous but are very suitable.

Hoffs: Absolutely.

Davis: Like *Battle Angel Alita*.

Hoffs: If something is branded and it makes it easier to sell it and maybe find an audience, that's fine. But really we're looking for the properties that are most suitable, and we'll get many big-branded properties that may have up to a billion dollars or more in worldwide revenue that we don't think would make great Hollywood films. It doesn't mean that we like them or not, but it's just they're great in the format that they're in. There may be other properties that literally sold 500 copies in Japan that nobody has ever heard of here that we think will make a beautiful and successful film.[56]

Michael Arias, who directed the critically acclaimed anime *Tekkonkinkreet* from the manga, talked about the *Berserk* films with me. In writing a proposal to adapt the manga to film, I had tried to find a way to adapt the story to the more linear form of Hollywood live-action narrative films, as noted earlier.°

Davis: We found that [after one point] the plot just … it goes all over the place.

Arias: I haven't read the original. I know it's quite popular, but I've only seen the tiniest sample of the animation. I didn't know that there was an attempt …

Davis: I was just echoing what you were saying about how things can get very, very abstract in certain series, or the A action line can just wander a lot.[57]

I explained to Arias how linear and thus "Western" the *Battle Angel Alita* plot is and that that was part of what attracted me to the story as a possible adaptation.

Davis: Given that a lot of these plots are not this tight Western plot, do you think that it's valid that people choose to adapt the project and the mangaka agrees to the contract of course to basically simplify it or [W]esternize it? Otherwise people will never be able to leave the movie theater because it'll be a four-hour movie. They have to make choices.

Arias: I think that there's a way to do that well, where it's not just a watered down, stripping away of all the cool stuff that adds richness to it. Filmmaking is enough of

---

°In the process of being given the okay to try to find a director/studio by its very talented mangaka.

an octopus kind of process in itself. It never really ends up like the original. Someone who's been through the whole "read the novel, read the manga" is never going to have the same perspective on a film. It's too different. There [are] so many more dimensions in film. I think you can be respectful and faithful to the original, but you're working with a completely different palette of tools. It's very hard. Have you seen the behind-the-scenes documentary that's with the specials [extras] of *Blade Runner*?[p]

Davis: No, I haven't.

Arias: It's one of the best filmmaking documentaries I've ever seen. That and maybe *Hearts of Darkness* are the best I've seen. It's really good, and it actually talks about when they had a long interview with [Ridley] Scott's editor about the whole process of cutting out bits and pieces to squeeze the movie in. He talks about how the editing process—and I think this also applies to the process of adaptation—it's such a violent process because you cut away all the stuff that gives something it's texture. It's like peeling skin off the chicken. It's still a chicken but it's missing something, a particular flavor that doesn't seem like an integral part of the whole thing, but when it's gone you miss it.

Davis: In other words, to preserve forward momentum.

Arias: In the rush to make a streamlined plot that goes from A to B to C as linearly as possible, it's easy when you're just sitting there cutting out frames or, for that matter, if you're adapting something, dropping characters. We did this with *Tekkon*. There's these whole subplots which we trimmed just to get it down to a manageable length, and I don't think we were entirely successful—with our choices, anyway. But there was a certain amount of scenes where there's not a lot going on, but they're great scenes that when you're reading it they add so much to have multiple digressions. It's very tough to do in a feature film unless you're Terrence Malick[q] and you can just riff. I love that stuff. I actually talked to Grant [Hill] quite a bit about working that way. But it's tough when you're adapting, especially comic books, because they tend to be just sprawling, some of the really good series. *Tekkon* was easy—it was just three books. But if you were going from *Akira*—it was only because [Katsuhiro] Otomo was the guy doing it that he was able to turn it into a film that made any sense, and even then there are a lot of fans of the original who don't like the movie because it's kind of a reimagining of the whole thing to fit it into two hours.

Davis: It's like there's too much greatness to jack into a movie, so you're going to have to cut all this great stuff out.

Arias: But I think there's a way to do that. There's a way to do that and use the tools that you have in film to produce an experience that, if not a carbon copy, it's at least an analogue or it leaves you with the same taste in your mouth. You kind of mix your DNA with the DNA of the original comic book, and come out with something that's a synthesis of both that contains some kind of different interpretation or a different aspect of the original source.

Davis: So basically the million-dollar question that's been lurking during this whole

---

[p]*Dangerous Days*, which I watched after this interview. It shows, for instance, how, in trying to cut down the movie's length, the Rachel–Deckard love scene turned into something more violent, rather than the more passionate/intimate way it appeared in earlier longer cuts, just from trimming the scene tightly.

[q]Director of the critically-lauded feature films *The Thin Red Line* and *Tree of Life*, which Grant Hill was a producer on.

interview is: so you're not against the idea of Hollywood adapting these, you're just hoping that whoever does it does a good job?

Arias: Yeah. Although we've all seen some flat-footed attempts, and with—god, I haven't seen *Dragonball Evolution* [the 2009 Hollywood adaption of manga/anime hit *Dragonball*]. I just think that if you don't get what makes the source material great, then you won't be able to turn it into something that stands on its own.

Davis: And part of the point that the book is making, which is echoed by you and Grant, is that the more cooks there are in the kitchen that aren't unified and are pulling against each other—

Arias: Yeah, that never helps.

Davis: The central group on the inside has to understand the DNA.

Arias: It has to be drinking the Kool-Aid, in a sense. I think that the source really needs a champion who is deeply embedded in the process so it won't run off the rails. I think that people gravitate towards the elements. About the same time that they're praising the elements they gravitate toward the most familiar elements, so you end up with this very pastiche of the original. I'm speaking in a very theoretical sense. That's a danger that awaits anyone adapting any source material, not just Japanese material—but particularly with adaptations of Japanese material—you're talking about relocating to a different cultural context.

Davis: Like moving it to New York or something.

Arias: Yeah! Changing the names. Location is relevant. Location—not just in the physical sense but in the cultural sense. There is a reason why these movies make sense here [in Japan], and make sense in a different way here than someone who is coming at them from the United States, or even [is] reading them in translation. It's already one generation from the source.[58]

The tofu whistle as an example of an environmental/cultural characteristic of many anime

Davis: One thing that my students and I talk about is the tofu whistle. [After I read about a tofu whistle that goes off in Japan to indicate that the tofu is ready, that crops up in anime.] Americans watching the anime are not going to know what that whistle means, but Japanese people will know. A lot of those differences are the charming aspects of anime, but you need to understand them when you're dealing with them, or you lose what's good about the original version.

Arias: There's one in *Tekkon*.

Davis: People here are like, "What was that?"

Arias: It [had] a certain domesticity.[59]

I asked Nobuo Masuda, because he is a Japanese person who is middle-aged, "What is a tofu whistle or tofu horn?"

Masuda: When I was a kid, they were peddling tofu. They were selling it from a cart.

Davis: That was one more thing that was in the writings that I read, was that you have to be Japanese to know what it is. Are you aware of the concept of red-oni and blue-oni?

Masuda: I really don't know about the colors. To me red-oni is scary.

Davis: [explaining red-oni/blue-oni theory][r]
Masuda: It reminds me of stand-up comics, manza. Usually it's one person here, right? In Japan it's two. Like one person is more hotheaded, like Groucho Marx.[60]

There are an almost endless number of characteristics in anime and manga that relate to Japanese culture; these elements are often attractive to non-Japanese audiences because of their alien-ness, but these audiences usually won't understand the nuances of the references because they only have a superficial understanding of Japanese culture. If the screenwriter, director, or producer do not understand these references, they may get eliminated in the conga-line of rewriters and creative voices in the adaptation process, especially if people on the non-Japanese end seek to reduce the elements down to the familiar in an attempt to make them universal (and, they hope, profitable to the audiences of the world, most of whom are not Japanese). On the other hand, some tropes may be understood and deliberately removed so that the adaptation will not have elements that are simply "weird" and incomprehensible to non-Japanese audiences. After all, every Hollywood movie audience member does not go see the film to become a scholar on Japanese culture. Several interviewed in this book seem to be at least advocating that the tropes are understood, so the decisions about them are not made by mistake. Regarding the long process from the time he was initially interested in a work until its production, Stanley Kubrick said he sought to constantly remind himself of what interested him in the piece in the first place. It therefore seems critical for the adapter to understand what it was that initially attracted them to the piece, and if that includes a Japanese trope that seems alien or unfamiliar, they should keep it in. Keeping it in is usually easier when they understand why it existed in the first place, which is simpler if they have knowledge of the cultural references and tropes in Japanese works or someone on their team does and can explain them.

Christine Yoo, who co-wrote on the hit anime *Afro Samurai*, which aired in America but was produced in Japan by GDH/Gonzo for America's Spike TV and Japan's Fuji TV networks, and voiced by Samuel L. Jackson, agrees that if people don't realize what made the original manga/anime work, then they might be in deep trouble. Then she takes this whole adaptation cross-cultural hybridity discussion further. She argues that adaptations should keep in the Asian elements that seem so alien to non-Asians in order to make Asians less foreign to the rest of the world. It is an interesting thesis, since so much of the world has been remodeled on the American model. For example, director Dr. George Miller (*Mad Max: Fury Road*, *Mad Max*, *The Road Warrior/Mad Max 2*, *Babe*, and *Happy Feet*) lamented that his own country, Australia, is becoming like one big suburb of America, losing its own culture.[61] Personally, I found it disturbing to find a Kentucky Fried Chicken by the Great Wall of China. It felt like a keystone of that great nation's cultural heritage was being Americanized and almost becoming like Walt Disney World.

---

[r] "Red-oni, blue-oni" is the Japanese manga/anime technique of pairing a passionate "act first, think later" character (red-oni—often with red hair or clothes) with a cooler (blue-oni, with blue tinting, perhaps of their eyeglasses or their clothes) character. This pairing almost always works, as the pair clashes, even as dual protagonists.

On the other hand, opening American franchises in foreign countries is a sensible decision because they are successful, and they give Americans comfort in a very different land. In another sense, however, preservation of different cultures is a big part of what makes the world interesting to live in. For one thing, when you travel international, isn't it just like staying in your own country if you are able to eat at the same restaurants that you normally visit when at home? The same goes with entertainment and storytelling. And once early viewers of anime figured out that it even *was* from Japan (which would have been in the 1980s when early anime cons started sprouting up in the US and more study-abroad students chose to go to Japan), they delighted in discovering things about Japanese culture from anime and manga. They still do. A few examples are:

Figure 8.15 The author at a Kentucky Fried Chicken at the Great Wall of China.

- Christianity, Christmas, and Valentine's Day are depicted very differently in anime/manga compared to their American versions. In Japan, Christmas is a time for romance. A man asking a woman on a date for Christmas Eve is considered a serious overture and their New Year's Day is more akin to the American Christian's Christmas Day—that is, a family celebration.
- Valentine's Day in Japan is more similar to the American Sadie Hawkins Day, where women make the overture (confess to the men/give them chocolates). They send the man they like candies, and if the man responds, it indicates that he anticipates that their relationship may become serious. On White Day, a month later, men reciprocate with a nice gift or marshmallows.
- Since relatively few people in Japan are Christians, Christianity is not well understood and is sometimes viewed negatively.
- A lack of physical privacy. With wood and paper construction, traditional Japanese homes prevented Japanese people from having a sense of privacy and thus helped somewhat merge their sense of individual self into the collective. When I went to Japan, I noticed a distinct lack of privacy, and the host family I stayed with constantly had family meetings and seemed extremely involved in each other's lives. As well as mine!

On the other hand, I am not so sure about applying Yoo's idea to all adaptations. Some things are better "without a specific cultural feel" to them. For example, outside of the shōnen trope of the group working together to achieve a very difficult goal, I feel that there was not so much really Japanese about *Speed Racer*, compared to the very Japanese-ness of many other anime series, at least in the case of that anime's localized dub that was aired in the United States. And I am happy that Japanese elements, if there were some that were "alien" to us, were not carried over into the Hollywood version—that is not what it seemed *Speed Racer* was all about. *Speed Racer* seems to occupy a different realm versus the Japanese-ness of many manga/anime (such as, for instance, *Inuyasha* with its nearly endless references to animism, which enriches this very popular series to viewers in the US—an argument in favor of Yoo's view). *Cowboy Bebop* has the same stateless characteristic as *Speed Racer*'s American-localized anime. And as we have seen, many others feel that the transfer went well in the Wachowskis' American film, due to there being nothing really cultural to cut.

But, Yoo believes it is important to retain the Asian-ness of Asian works and thus build an understanding between cultures:

> **Yoo:** [H]ow Asians are presented in the media—China—always has this real foreign element … the obstacles I feel more have to do with cultural things, which are cultural misunderstandings born out of fear or being afraid to ask about people's culture or really understand it … And that's just because the exposure still in a lot of ways is very superficial. So I think it's just a really gradual process. A lot of the properties that have been remade here, and a lot of people don't necessarily know that they're based on Korean films.
>
> **Davis:** Oh no, not at all.
>
> **Yoo:** Why not?
>
> **Davis:** They often don't want people to know that?
>
> **Yoo:** They're not really thinking about that. They're only in the microcosm that they're pushing, when not actually realizing that if they actually highlight the original content of it too, you're going to attract more people—I think. You're bringing more people into the fold to understand the product. It's like true engagement with the product from a marketing level, true exposure is engagement with the product. It's piquing someone's curiosity to motivate them. To inspire them. To go and seek out more information. And I think with a lot of these remake properties, why not highlight the fact that they're Asian films? Is it Hollywood's little secret? What, that they don't have any original ideas so they're taking films from Asia? I don't know what that's about. They probably haven't really thought about how they could actually engage more people into that. And then maybe people can appreciate the remake better and even make more money.[s62]

This ties into the idea that anime fans have learned so much about Japanese culture from anime. Again, the tofu whistle (also called tofu horn) idea. But during the process of adapting an anime or manga into a live-action film, who decides what characteristics of Japanese culture are kept and what gets removed in the localization process. Nobuo Masuda's job, in part, as was stated, is to supervise localization of the anime to English

---

[s] The studio response to this argument might be that the Hollywood storytelling model has been proven to be enormously successful, and that since the world contains hundreds of cultures, to focus on any one culture's storytelling characteristics in such an expensive project requiring massive financial profits could alienate other cultures' audiences for the film/show.

language dubs for Sunrise for distribution in North America. Masuda's IMDb credits are extensive and he is thus very experienced in these situations.

Davis: Don't you do supervision of the actual English script?

Masuda: That's what I do! [laughs]

Davis: So when you find things that are Japanese cultural references or maybe cultural jokes, what are the kinds of things you're having to change or adapt? What are you looking out for? Basically things that Americans would not understand?

Masuda: I just make it up each case! What else can you do?

Davis: There will be times in certain fansubs where they will go "He's talking about Japanese tofu ceremony"—I'm just making something up—but sometimes fansubs will explain something that has been referenced in the anime that we wouldn't understand. Because you're commercial and fansubs are illegal and everything—

Masuda: We don't do that kind of thing. We're trying to adapt it for Americans.

Davis: Make it universal, right.

Masuda: We localize.

Davis: Certain concepts like sarcasm do not really exist in Japanese culture? [i.e. the many manga and anime stressing positive human values without sarcasm or post-modernistic irony]

Masuda: There are some sarcastic voices in Japan as well, like *Lupin*.[t]

Davis: Are there other things that you feel that Americans cannot understand because they are very cultural, that are happening in anime that just fly right over our heads?

Masuda: I have to think about it. I really … don't know. Japanese culture started being introduced into the Western world relatively new. It's like anime is new here [America], like 20 years ago. Oriental culture is being exposed to everyone relatively recently. It takes time for Americans to understand.

Davis: When you are localizing, can you give us examples of decisions you have made to delete or change something because Americans won't understand it?

Masuda: Sometimes Japanese stories are based on some kind of word-pun. Recently, we've just tried to make it make sense. Bandai always tried to stick to the Japanese originals. Different companies do different styles.[63]

Sometimes there is a tolerance for nudity in children's programming, to some degree, that would not be found in other countries like America. Masuda seems to attribute this less to the difference in cultures and more to the Japanese parents' dislike of complaining.

Masuda: Occasionally there will be something—especially with TV stuff. Nudity is a no-no. In Japan, nudity is OK.

Davis: Like the idea of kids taking baths with their parents. Here if you did that you'd get arrested. [Note: children taking baths with their parents is a Japanese tradition.]

Masuda: And girls taking showers, fanservice.[u]

Davis: When I'm reading *Air Gear* [a manga written and illustrated by Ito "Oh Great"

---

[t] Mangaka Monkey Punch's successful spy/comedy caper squad adventures of a rather adult sensibility about the world's greatest thief and his team and the policeman chasing them. According to Dark Horizons, a comic/movie industry *news website*, Steven Spielberg was once interested in possibly adapting it.

[u] "Fanservice" is a term that means the practice of some manga artists appealing in a sexual manner to male readers.

Ōgure], for instance, there's a lot of fanservice [underwear, revealing clothing, or nudity] in there, and sometimes an underage girl is in the shower with them [women who appear to be over 18], and in America [for anime broadcast] that is a no-no.

Masuda: No good for American TV. You cannot show nipples and stuff. Sometimes you can hide nipples by adding steam or something, then it'll be TV-14.

Davis: Have you had to do that? Like add steam or something?

Masuda: Yeah, I think we did do that once. *Code Geass*, I think.

Davis: Oh, so you added the steam in the anime!

Masuda: Yeah, to hide a nipple. Cartoon Network did it.

Davis: Is there some list of what can and can't be shown?

Masuda: Each TV station has a standard practice. Sometimes it's kind of subjective, too.

Davis: Can you explain to me, as a Japanese person, what is the difference in [attitudes toward] nudity? Here, people would feel that because there are kids reading these mangas and they would say that it's not good to show nudity.

Masuda: That's the same in Japan—lots of violence, and Americans blame Japanese horror movies. [laughs] The people here, in America, think that there is too much blood in anime. So I feel like America and Japan are blaming each other.

Davis: So we blame each other. So there's nudity in America and nudity in Japan, it's just in different places.

Masuda: Probably so.

Davis: That whole violence issue is very interesting. In the Fred Ladd book, he went to Japan and at Tezuka's studio he said, "Look, on *Astro Boy* we have to cut this out because ..."

Masuda: It was too violent?

Davis: Something like that. And a young Japanese animator said something like, "You know, from our point of view, it's more disturbing that ..." there was an aspect to American violence that was more disturbing. And Ladd said that this young person made a good point. Getting back to the nudity thing, why is it in Japanese society that girl nudity [is] OK? Because there is a free expression available to the creators? And they're not trying to censor them? A religious thing?

Masuda: Parents speak up louder in the United States. When kids are watching indecent cartoons, they call up the network, right? In Japan, very few parents would call the network even if they're offended.

Davis: So it's not wanting to cause trouble? OK, I understand that.

Masuda: Tolerance is higher in Japan.[64]

9

Hollywood Adaptation Case Study #2: *Astro Boy*

- The origin story of the *Astro Boy* character.

As I explained in Chapter 2, *Astro Boy* is the story of a human-like robot boy who is invented by a scientist to replace his son Tobio who died in an auto accident. The father, Dr. Temna, a brilliant but emotionally unstable scientist, trains him to act like a human being and his surrogate son. But, after a brief period of happiness with Astro, Temna becomes frustrated that Astro cannot grow and accuses him of being a puppet and a freak. He then sells him to an evil circus ringmaster, Ham Egg (Mr. Cacciatore in the anime, a character who is another star system regular in Tezuka's manga/anime universe). Astro is enslaved and forced to do tricks until he is rescued by the kindly Professor Ochanomizu,[a] who becomes his new father figure (and who creates a robot father, mother and a sister for Astro). Soon thereafter Astro becomes a fighter for justice and robots' rights.

Astro even travels to the moon in one segment, and each story has an ending. And as stated by Schodt, that creates an opportunity to tell many complete stories, and thus the show allowed Tezuka to explore a wide array of subject matter and many different stories.[1] The original manga series sold over 100 million copies and is arguably the most famous golden-era manga. As we have seen, it also was the first anime TV series to come to America and many other countries. It is safe to say that *Astro Boy* did more to create the manga/anime industries than any other work and is a national treasure of Japan. As such, it was a risky property to adapt because the Japanese hold it so dear to their hearts. This feeds into what Hoffs inferred earlier, which is that some works are so successful that they actually might not be viable due to the sensitivity of their fans to the American adaptations.

The very young Astro of the original manga and anime has pluck, charm, and innocence. A boy too young to wear a shirt but flying about saving the world was a key aspect of his character. He showed such bravery, especially given that he was rejected cruelly by his father and gamely became part of an adopted family that the kindly professor set him up with after rescuing Astro from the circus. As Fred Ladd said in a 1993 interview

---

[a] Head of the Ministry of Science, he is also known in various English adaptations as Dr. Packadermus J. Elefun, Professor Peabody, and Dr. O'Sha. Prof. Ochanomizu places Astro in a family of other normal-looking and acting, robot parents, desiring that Astro have a normal child's life to offset his dangerous and exciting missions.

Figure 9.1 Temna is initially pleased with Astro Boy's progress in becoming a more human-like replacement for his dead son. As noted earlier, *Pinocchio* had a strong influence upon the story. © Tezuka Productions

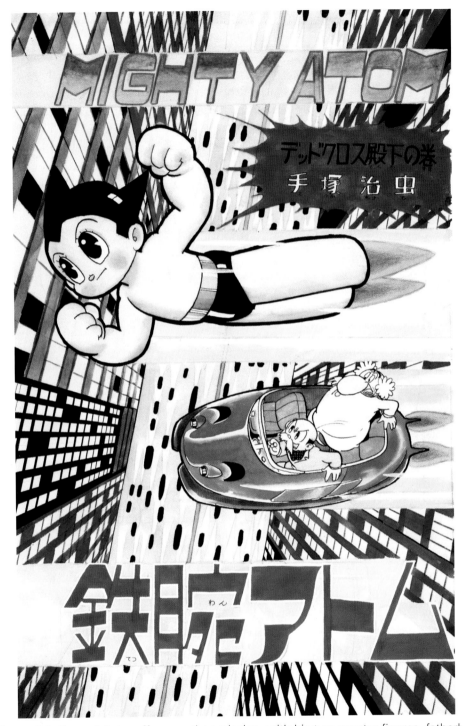

Figure 9.2 Earnest Astro off on another mission, with his two mentor figures, fatherly frizzy-haired Professor Ochanomizu and his teacher Mr. Mustachio (both regulars in Tezuka's star system), rushing to keep pace, offering comic relief. The car itself has eyes like a mechanical creature, and this brave new world where machines had personalities was part of the tapestry. © Tezuka Productions

with Schodt, "It succeeded for the same reasons *Pinocchio* succeeded and *Home Alone* succeeded—there's an empowered youngster outperforming the adult bad guys."[2] This origin story was altered in important ways in the David Bowers (*Flushed Away*) directed 2009 remake movie—something that many reviewers did not pick up on, perhaps due to not being very familiar with the original. The Bowers remake adheres to the original story superficially but, on closer examination, makes major changes that have wide-ranging impact.

Budgeted at an estimated $65 million,[b] the adaptation movie was released by Summit Entertainment, which has a deal with Universal Pictures. The *Astro Boy* movie earned an estimated $40 million worldwide. One of its production companies went bankrupt, the Hong Kong based Imagi Animation, which had previously had a hit with *Teenage Mutant Ninja Turtles* (director: Kevin Munroe, Warner Bros., 2007).

Audience reception

Total lifetime grosses

Domestic:	$19,551,067	49.0%
+ Foreign:	$20,335,919	51.0%

= Worldwide: $39,886,986

Domestic summary

Opening Weekend: $6,702,923
(#6 rank, 3,014 theaters, $2,224 average)
% of Total Gross: 34.3%

Widest release: 3,020 theaters
Close date: January 21, 2010
In release: 91 days / 13 weeks

(Source: Box Office Mojo)

On the website Rotten Tomatoes, *Astro Boy*'s audience "positive" rating was 49% and its critical reviews were roughly split, at 51%. Two of the differences between *Astro Boy* and *Speed Racer*'s adaptations are their budgets (*Speed Racer* was roughly twice the cost, though its revenues were also well over double *Astro Boy*'s) and *Speed Racer*'s audience liked the movie 20% more than that of *Astro Boy* or either film's critics.[c] Like Hikaru Sasahara (who, as we will see in the interview below, claims to have started the *Astro Boy* adaptation process), people can be opinionated on the film's quality. Regarding Hollywood adaptations of anime, Ian Condry said, "And there have been some bad examples. *Astro Boy* is another not-so-successful example! [laughs] And when you watch that production you think that these people didn't understand *Astro Boy* at all! They really didn't get it. It's like that American production of *Godzilla* too (the 1997 version). In Japan they were like, 'That

---

[b] Source: Box Office Mojo.
[c] As of writing this book.

wasn't *Godzilla*. If you called it Lizard-zilla, that's one thing, but that's not *Godzilla*."[3] Perhaps Condry's comment references how Bowers and his team changed the character for the adaptation, which will be detailed below. Other anime/manga industry pros like Masuda feel that *Astro Boy* succeeds on various levels—as its own film versus *Astro Boy* (the original). That is, they feel that it was its own work almost separate from the original.

Whether you have a positive or negative opinion about the Bowers adaptation, I will show how a few changes to the original *Astro Boy* story had a big impact on the adaptation's effectiveness, as did the design decisions the adaptation's team made to alter the look and age of Astro. And we will hear from one of its producers why this decision to change the character in several key ways was made, over the initial objections of Hong Kong-based Imagi. Additionally, we'll examine the sequencing of the original *Astro Boy* "origin story" and examine key aspects of the original that were altered. That each strand of a film's story, if removed or altered, can produce a domino effect with far-ranging implications is well known to professional screenwriters, and will be demonstrated in this case study.

Of course, if someone likes the film, they would not necessarily agree that these artistic decisions were mistakes. But it will still be educational for such readers to understand the process of how decisions regarding making changes to the original during the process of adaptation took place, including the pressure that comes to bear when so much money is at stake. This insight will come primarily from two insiders intimately involved—one a producer and an executive at Imagi, and the other a Japanese owner of a manga publisher who alleges that he was behind the original attempt to set up the movie project in Hollywood.

Let's begin with how the remake rights to the property were acquired in the first place, and thus look more into the important "rights committee" issue in Japan, chain of title, and the studio forms that Hollywood studios want the copyright owners to sign off on (which is also applicable to anyone trying to sell their script, novel, or comic in Hollywood), and more …

Business culture attitudes, legal differences/similarities, conflicts and solutions—how the *Astro Boy* Hollywood adaptation got pitched, sold and produced

Hikaru Sasahara explained how he was the first person to try to set up a Hollywood adaptation of *Astro Boy*. He is the president of American manga publisher Digital Manga Publishing (DMP). In America, DMP distributes the hit manga titles *Berserk* (with Dark Horse), *Vampire Hunter D*, and *Yaoi* (or "Boys' Love," genre titles popular with many girls and young women and typical of manga/anime's long history of gender play). As I previously noted, the gender-bending nature of some manga and anime (ever since Tezuka started the trend with *Princess Knight*) does have predecessors in Japanese culture and in Tezuka's exposure to the Takarazuka Review. However, the androgynous appearance of Astro may simply be explained in that Tezuka originally designed the character to be a female, but then switched to a male when he got a deal in a boy's magazine for the series, but did not remove the long eyelashes and softer figure of the character.[4] This adrogeny never came into play in the Bowers adaptation because the filmmakers removed these elements, as we will see.

A colorful character, Sasahara was a member of a Japanese Beatles tribute band, is an avid surfer, and was a favorite guest speaker of my manga/anime classes at UC Irvine. He possesses an innovative business sense,[d] and his generous and detailed breakdowns of the manga/anime business gave my students invaluable information from a publishing owner who has survived financial competition from much larger publishers.

> **Davis:** My first question is how did you get into this field of being a manga publisher? I'd heard that you were originally in San Francisco [having moved there as an adult from Japan], but would you mind filling me in a little on your background?
>
> **Sasahara:** Of course, of course! I don't remember exactly. It was a long time ago when I got into this industry. Maybe 13 years ago or so, when I went to Tezuka Productions in Tokyo and I found out that that they were interested in turning their properties into movies. That's [turning *Astro Boy* into a Hollywood film] one of the biggest dreams that Mr. Tezuka, when he was alive, was contemplating. And his employees decided to take his concept into reality. But the problem is that [*Astro Boy*] was very old. Not the story, but all of the character design and background was pretty old. So, there were some aesthetic problems before we could trigger the interest of any Hollywood industry. I remember that I suggested to Tezuka[e] that we needed to remake [the *Astro Boy*] manga to be more for the US audience, and also for the movie producers and scriptwriters and people of that nature. But they weren't willing to change any of it. It's part of the Japanese mentality that they wanted to carry on the way that it was created by the original author, even though the original author wanted to make it into a Hollywood movie, all of his apprentices and employees didn't want to touch anything. So I saw that as a problem, and I did actually present an idea to CAA [the top Hollywood talent agency] back then, and I remember that Nicolas Cage's [the Hollywood actor who is also known as a big comics collector] production company got interested in making a live-action *Astro Boy* film, and Nick Cage was really interested to personally become the producer for that. So I was briefly in the communication between Tezuka Prods and CAA, and it was a very interesting experience for me. I was the first one, the [agents at] CAA told me—a Japanese guy who came to CAA to try to get involved in the live-action film deal based on the comics. But at the end, the deal didn't come true for various reasons. One is the rights

[d] For example, Sasahara founded DMP in part with profits from a successful restaurant he started with his wife called the Sawtelle Kitchen, which for many years, even after he sold it, was a mainstay on the west side of Los Angeles's Sawtelle Japanese area (interview by author, November 15, 2013).

[e] Meaning Tezuka Productions; Tezuka died earlier in 1989 at the age of 60.

issue. Usually the rights of any properties in Japan, either anime or manga, there are more than three or four rights holders involved in one particular property. That will make it very complicated for anyone to go to Japan and pick up source material, because they need to talk to several people. Usually, a company like a bank is involved and the TV company who aired the show and invested the money into it, and the publishing company also are usually involved. And sometimes an advertising agency— it was kind of strange to me, but they [are] also involved as investors. In order to get one single property you need to talk to at least four or five people, or companies, to clear the way. It's a very time-consuming process and none of those guys have all the authorization—the power—to make a decision. The people in Hollywood always get dismayed by the fact that there is no executive producer for each and every title. So every time the opportunity arose, I bumped into the same problems until I finally gave up on this type of business. I thought "that's how I tap into a Hollywood deal, with the Japanese manga or anime properties." At the end there are so many problems associated with acquisition due to the rights issues and the lack of an executive producer, I finally gave up on this. Then I switched my business over to manga publishing instead.[5]

Entertainment lawyer Joyce Jun paints a more optimistic picture of rights committees as she discusses the way she approaches the Japanese mangaka and rights holders during Hollywood remake rights negotiations

Davis: I know Roy Lee recommends you; you are an expert in this legal area between the two countries. I know some major entertainment lawyers and they really don't do the intersection like you do. They're on the American side—you are really at the intersection of that with your law practice, and I was wondering what made you decide to get into that area of focus?

Jun: It was really not a conscious effort on my part at all. You know, I speak Japanese and I lived in the country. I studied as an entertainment lawyer. It's just one thing just led to another. Obviously I have an affinity for the culture and understand the culture, so my clients were Japanese entertainment companies. When that started to happen, which really began to happen in a major way with *Pokémon*, and the remake of the anime from manga properties started about 10 years ago. So I was really doing my thing, but because of my clientele and what I was doing for them, it just became a natural evolution.

Davis: Do you have an approach you use, or does it depend on the situation?

Jun: It completely depends on the situation. It's not any different than if you're approaching filmmakers here. I mean, there's A+ authors, [and] there's [sic] authors who aren't as well known. If you're approaching Spielberg as opposed to someone's [sic] who [is] just trying to get into the business, obviously you are going to approach them differently. So this is no different. I think there is a cultural difference in the sense that, here, or at least in Hollywood, film is the most revered form of entertainment—the visual—and I go back to money because the most money is made from that industry. In Japan, manga has for a long time been the most revered form of entertainment because it started everything. You know, they start with manga and then they create anime from it, then they create a movie from it, and then they create a TV series from it. So, I think that Japanese manga artists are respected, especially the popular manga authors—the powerful authors are considered the rock stars, as we consider the affluent actors [to be] here. So if you look at it that way, obviously you are going to insist on some things because they think that their form of expression, their medium—culturally speaking—is most important. I'll say this though, I think that all authors are compelled by a desire to express themselves, and Hollywood is the Holy Grail for everyone in the industry. So if you can get this across to the authors that we're not trying to destroy or kill your manga or anime. If there is a creative connection there, then the rest of it is very easy. Obviously anything in Hollywood, a lot of middle people cause problems. [laughs] The reps and whatnot, and that have nothing to do with the authors themselves, but I don't find it that difficult, honestly. It's just that you have to know the author, and what he likes. How free he is and what really actually speaks to him … It's really no different than how you approach Spielberg or Cameron or whoever.

Entertainment lawyer Jun describes the studio rights form (A standardized document that the studios try to adhere to when obtaining the rights to make movies and television shows from underlying works like books and comics into movies)

Davis: So, in that you have this wonderful niche, do you suggest that your producers that are your clients, that they have a certain form of agreement? Let's say your own type of agreement that you'd like your clients to sign with the mangaka? How does it usually work when you get involved in these? Or are you asked to tie down the rights yourself?[6]

Jun: No, I'm in the service profession, so I serve the Japanese side or the US buyers. Whoever. There are certain hybrid forms that I use, but I don't try to force that upon them—especially the US side—because no matter who the producer is, they are going to end up having the studios and financing to buy these rights and they are just not going to sign off on anything that is less than [the] *studio form*. So my job really is convincing the Japanese, or other Asians, or the rights holders, to sign off on this and why it has to be this way. For example, studios are very used to [the practice that] once they exercise an option they own the property. The Japanese side is very used to [the Hollywood studio] owning [the adaptation rights] for a while; you can borrow them for a while, but if you don't make a movie then the rights go back. I think I've convinced most of the American buyers that I work with that if you exercise the option but if you're not going to make the movie in the next five years, the rights revert back.[7]

This is an important point for all original media creators, including writers, which is that an option should not be negotiated in a way that it ties up your rights indefinitely without the project being produced. An option should be an "option to purchase," usually with 10% of the negotiated purchase price paid up-front, non-refundable, and repeated payments over time for "renewals."[f] If and when the script goes into production, the rights holder of the manga, who is the creator of either the original script, book, and/or comic, receives the [usually] 90% remaining payment. That way, if it doesn't get produced during the option period, the rights revert back to you, if you are the rights holder. And so then you have the right to find another partner, and you get to keep the initial option payment(s).

>**Davis:** So in other words the studios may come to you and say, "We would like to secure this. Will you go secure it for us?" And you do it?
>
>**Jun:** More than half of my work is really the US buyers—the producers or studios or whatnot—coming to me and saying "Can you get it?" I think that mainly studios come to me because … they don't know who are the right people to talk to. And then the process from the purely American classically trained people is too painful. [laughs] It's not too painful if you know what you're doing![8]

Sasahara details the entities that make up the Japanese rights committees

>**Davis:** If something has just been a manga and not an anime or TV show, would then the rights be simpler?
>
>**Sasahara:** Yes and no, because even in manga properties without anime or other market attached to it, there are at least two entities you need to go through. One is the original creator and then he has a representative, which happens to be the publisher. You have to at least deal with those two people. Usually those two guys—the original creator and the publisher who represents the creator—do not necessarily have the same concept or idea. I bumped into the situation where the original creator was very interested in getting into Hollywood, but the publisher was not so interested because—simply—they are afraid to bump into a lot of the legal problems dealing with Hollywood, because the publisher simply represents the manga creator and the property. I find that this is really bad because if the creator is really interested in going into Hollywood to make [an] adaptation, the publisher is not so interested because they are simply scared, [afraid] about making mistakes for his representation business. So there is definitely a conflict between publisher and the creator, and the publisher is supposed to be stimulating the property and the idea of making it into a movie or TV show or a musical or whatever. The publisher is acting as the creative agent, but it seems as though, perhaps it's just the Japanese mentality, but they are very afraid to make a mistake. So they are just happy with confining the property within the land of Japan and do not necessarily want you to take it out to Hollywood. That's another problem. But the manga is definitely a

---

[f] Lawyers representing rights holders may try to shorten the option periods to get paid more often for option renewals, while the studio/production company, knowing that the script development, casting, pre-production processes take much time (often many years), tend to push for longer option periods. Disagreements over these terms can scuttle negotiations.

very potential source for the movie and TV show and game industry, but because of the rights issue and the representation problems from the publisher, it's very difficult. Another difficulty is that they don't want to change so much of the aesthetics. They want to stick to the original story, timeline, background; everything has to be kept, the contents intact, which is totally wrong. To me, for Hollywood to take someone's property, they should be able to take it in whatever way they see fit for the US market or international market. That's not usually permitted by the content providers. [Note that, as we will see, *Astro Boy*'s core character *was* permitted by the Tezuka organization, after the American side pushed them, to be changed to try to appeal to the American market, in terms of character design and age (in my opinion, with bad results).]

Davis: Roy Lee said in an interview for the book that a studio [Universal Pictures, on its highly-rated American manga/graphic novel adaptation *Scott Pilgrim vs. The World*] hadn't marketed properly to the wider audience and had focused too much on the core fanbase of the original work. So he and you would be in sync on that … the publishers wanted to keep the mangaka sequestered away, out of access, because they didn't want to lose them.

Sasahara: Their publisher is their agent, and they are very afraid that anyone will circumvent them and go directly to the creator.

Davis: Then they say "you came to us through 'the window' into the rights holder, and thus you can't go around now."[g] Did you ever have a situation where the creators have come to you and have gone, "Look, Hikaru, I don't like what the publisher is doing. I want to just do Hollywood myself." Couldn't they just start insisting on that in their contracts with the publishers that they retain those rights?

Sasahara: Only once it happened to me. He didn't come to me, I did come to him. Hideyuki Kikuchi, for *Vampire Hunter D*. Unfortunately he is still in a contract with a French producer for a few more years. He just recently renewed it. He's a very rare case where he holds the rights all by himself and he can make his own decision to go with anyone he wants to. But they are very rare cases. It's not always like that. So Kikuchi's one of the very rare cases where he has all the power himself. He's a very nice guy, very casual. He's very open to almost any idea.[9]

Chain of title

What everyone is talking about here is "chain of title." What is chain of title? Just like a bank giving a loan to finance a property wants to know that the seller indeed has the full and sole right to convey the title to the property upon sale to the buyer, the movie studio/financier needs to know the same about the movie or TV adaptation rights for

---

[g] This means that, for example, if a Hollywood entity approaches a Japanese television network about trying to obtain remake rights for a Japanese live-action TV show that itself is a manga adaptation, then the Hollywood entity is sometimes pressured by the Japanese network to only communicate with that network during the ensuing negotiation, because the network is the "window" to the underlying rights holder (mangaka/publisher). Instead of the Hollywood entity simultaneously directly negotiating with the network and publisher/mangaka for each of their portions of the remake rights. This "window" method can destroy the negotiation if the network and publisher do not get along and thus cannot allocate each of their portions amicably.

the manga or anime. Otherwise, the studio could get sued by someone who claims later that they are owners of the property and should have a say in whether or not the movie was to be produced. Producer Joshua Long, who has been involved in the long gestating *Cowboy Bebop* Hollywood adaptation project, sheds light on the sometimes murky world of manga, anime, TV, and movie chain of title. The project had Keanu Reeves attached to it at one point.

Long explained to me about how the studio's Errors and Omissions insurance policy comes into play.

Errors and omissions insurance policy—a key to getting a studio to "sign off" on the Japanese chain of title, and a part of the process that is good for screenwriters, TV writers, and authors to know about as well

Before we get to Long's definition, what is an "errors and omissions" insurance policy? As a screenwriter, I learned about it when I sold my script to Warner Brothers and asked why I needed to pay an attorney 5% of the purchase price, $12,500 up-front cost for a deal that had already been made by my agent (who received 10% ($25,000) from me) and my manager (15% = $37,500). Already out $62,500 from the get-go, I naturally wanted to know what I would be getting that was beneficial from an entertainment lawyer. After all, hadn't the agent already negotiated the deal with the studio? One of the entertainment lawyers, whom I interviewed about possibly doing the fine-print legal work on my screenplay contract, explained that the added benefits of a lawyer parsing through the contract issued by the studio and negotiated in broad terms with the agent and the studios' business affairs lawyer with a fine tooth comb were manyfold. For one thing, the attorney could make sure that I was put on the studio's errors and omissions insurance policy, a standard practice, which would mean the studio—not I—would have to defend any frivolous lawsuits of the type that can crop up in the case of a hit (i.e. claims by others that the original writer stole their idea). The theory is that the studio and its insurance policy are better financed to fight such lawsuits than the (as we will see later) usually cash-strapped feature screenwriter. Simply adding the screenwriter, after doing due diligence, to their policy is the right thing to do. It would likely be impossible to make a living as a professional screenwriter if scribes had to defend lawsuits, or worse, indemnify the studio/network. The errors and omissions policy protects the studio against these problems as well.

Below, Long, discusses the chain of title on a particular Japanese project. First, he talks about a simple situation, like *Astro Boy*, where all rights were owned by one company, and then he addresses a far more complex situation—the classic "wandering samurai" manga

Lone Wolf and Cub that had been made into a successful series of Japanese live-action movies, including the classic *Baby Carriage at the River Stix*.[h]

> **Long:** There is a technical way that you do ensure against that [chain of title problems that crop up later after the optioning or purchase of the adaptation rights] with E&O [errors and omissions] insurance. With E&O insurance, your financier will come in and they will do their diligence on the chain of title and they will inspect all of the chain of title items. In order for them to ensure making the movie, they will do that. So we always go into this knowing that we have to pass [with] the studio, but more importantly the E&O insurance carrier. So actually it's the insurance lawyers who will review all of the chain of title documents to be satisfied. In the case of *Space Invaders* [a Japanese video game] it was very, very simple. Taito created it, owned it. They were wholly owned by Square Enix so we got the rights from Taito Corporation, which is wholly a subsidiary of Square Enix. Square Enix has all of these processes in place, so it took a long time, but there were never any problems. It was just executives and stuff like that. That was a very smooth process, but there was never any problem with the chain of title because it was extraordinarily clear, so in that case there were no issues. A corporation created it, owned it. We got it directly from that corporation. With an individual work, with an individual personal thing like Koike's [Kazuo, the writer of the series], what we really did is, because there were seven movies and TV series and all that stuff, before a certain time period, none of these contracts were written down and if they were written down they don't exist anymore. So you have to do a lot. This took a very long time to figure out if there were any possible distributable contracts that would give people the impressions that they might have certain rights. We knew that they weren't granted, and artists can only represent a warrant so much. You still need to check and make sure there was not an act of omission or oversight, or whether somebody else might think that they also have those rights.[10]

Since there is no official Japanese media "clearing house," many people find the chain of title process complicated and difficult. Joyce Jun, on the other hand, said that it is not so hard if you know what you are doing (very few do). Sometimes companies even go out of business with the chain of title they owned now unclear, which goes to show how muddy rights can be in Japan. However, *Astro Boy* was one of those rights situations that was (allegedly) not complex.

---

[h] *Baby Carriage at the River Stix* was part of a series of Japanese live-action movies adapted from the classic manga *Lone Wolf and Cub*. Its plot is that a wandering samurai anti-hero pushes his infant boy around Japan in a wooden baby carriage seeking revenge for the unjust death of his wife by corrupt authorities. And his stoic baby is not above assisting his father, sometimes deploying lethal weaponry built into the baby carriage to help defend them against hordes of attackers. More recently, the Hollywood adaptation rights were reputedly acquired by Justin Lin (who directed *The Fast and the Furious: Tokyo Drift*, Universal Pictures, 2006) for Kamala Films. A photograph of *Lone Wolf and Cub's* writer Kazuo Koike is on page xxviii (preface).

How, why, and what they changed in the *Astro Boy* characters and story

Sasahara puts forth an interesting argument below, which is that Hollywood should *not* be faithful in adapting Japanese manga/anime to Hollywood. I found this interesting, in that he is Japanese.

> **Davis:** So you feel that *Speed Racer* and *Dragon Ball* and *Astro Boy*—if you did see them— you felt they adhered too tightly to the story?
>
> **Sasahara:** They tried to keep the original storyline, character aspect, as much as the Japanese people wanted, and that's exactly how they failed. Once it's adapted by Hollywood, it should be the Hollywood way all the way. That's the whole idea, but the Japanese companies won't let them do it. Like I said earlier, there is more than one person involved in every property and some guys work for the banking company, the financial company. They rarely come to America and they don't speak the Hollywood language at all. It's very important for anyone who wants to acquire the property, they have to physically be there and negotiate one by one, and it's almost impossible.
>
> **Davis:** I believe it. I've been in this and you know what I've been through and [what] we've [Hayashi and I and our lawyers/agents] been through.
>
> **Sasahara:** They need to elect an executive producer who is given the authority to make any adaptation surrounding each and every property but there is no such role. They don't see to change it. I don't think that any deal is going to come up and [be] successful in the next five years or so, unless they finally change their mind and realize that what they've been doing is wrong. Then they'll finally elect just one single guy as the executive producer, and he'll run around the USA instead of waiting for people to come to Japan to make the deal and have the freedom to do whatever they want to.[11]

As Sasahara exited the *Astro Boy* movie project, at one point it moved to Sony Pictures Animation where it stalled and then was taken over to Summit which produced it.[i][12] Actor Nicholas Cage stayed involved and ended up voicing Astro Boy's father, Dr. Temna, in the adaptation movie.

---

[i] Along with Hong Kong based production company Imagi.

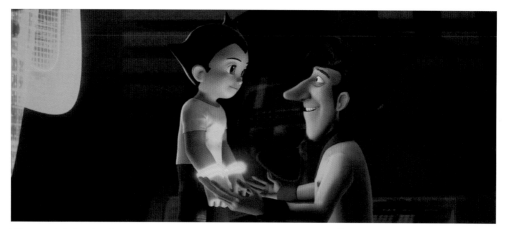

Figure 9.3 In the David Bowers-directed *Astro Boy* adaptation (Imagi, Summit, 2009), the Nicolas Cage-voiced Dr. Temna shows his love for his "son" and this seems superficially similar to the original story (but I will endeavor to demonstrate that the details of the origin stories of the two versions are quite different in key ways that changed the way that an audience would feel about the new vs. old versions). Notice how much older Astro is in this version than the original.

Figure 9.4 The Bowers' Astro's age is even older in the image above—the baby fat and androgynous look are completely gone. *Astro Boy*, director: David Bowers, Imagi/ Summit 2009.

Figure 9.5 Many aspects of the original *Astro Boy* were kept for the Bowers adaptation, like the Osamu Tezuka character making a cameo appearance, as Dr. Tezuka liked to do in his manga and anime. *Astro Boy*, director: David Bowers, Imagi/Summit 2009.

Figure 9.6 A cameo from a comical creature named Patchgourd, that Tezuka liked to put randomly into many series, appears on a billboard (shown to the left) as *Astro Boy* is chased. *Astro Boy*, director: David Bowers, Imagi/Summit 2009.

Attitudes/feelings on both sides about the collaboration—how faithful to the original material are the filmmakers being?

One of the *Astro Boy* movie's producers, Ken Tsumura, spoke about the *Astro Boy* movie in a no-holds-barred interview. An industry veteran who later was an executive on the DisneyToon Studios *Planes* project, he then worked at a premiere Taiwanese company, NEXT Animation. Tsumura is accessible and generous—and as with all of the interviewees herein, I was fortunate that he shared his thoughts about the process.

Davis: So, I was going to ask you just a few clarifications about *Astro Boy*?

Tsumura: OK.

Davis: So you were saying that, Doctor Temna, the original creator and "father figure" of Astro Boy, that they had audience-tested the idea of him saying "You are no longer my son" and being really severe about it, and American parents, or the people who saw it, were like "Don't do that, that's too much, rejecting your child like that." Is that a correct interpretation of what you said?

Tsumura: Yeah, you are aware of the *Astro Boy* original story and basically yeah … he literally creates this surrogate son to replace his lost son, and creates *Astro Boy*, and realizes that no robot can replace a real son. There is that scene where he rejects his robot and says you're not my son, and is very strict about it. The director, David Bowers, had interpreted it as per what Tezuka had intended, but when we actually tested it in Orange County [California], the reaction was "Wow that's very harsh, that's actually too harsh for kids" and we kept the essence in, but we toned down the intensity of the father rejecting the new robot.[13]

I feel that the people polled were reacting to a father rejecting a boy and, understandably, were not happy with that harshness. But, part of the point of fairy tales (which *Astro Boy* is, coming partially from *Pinocchio*) is that life IS often harsh. Even for children. But there is also joy. This depiction of the complexities of real life is the nature of fairy tales. In fairy tales, there are cautionary and tragic scenes. Like the mentor figure Jiminy Cricket in *Pinocchio*, Professor Ochanomizu, who believes that robots are self-aware and thus should have a good life and robots-rights, and Astro's teacher Mr. Mustachio, serve a purpose to illuminate the way to the light from the darkness for the child. As a screenwriter, I would argue that this change of minimizing Ochanomizu's (and Mr. Mustachio's) roles in the adaptation are a radical departure from the original *Astro Boy* story. In the original, a plucky, very young boy who, although initially sad and devastated after being rejected by his "father," is resourceful and upbeat enough to make a go of it with his new family and mentors and become a hero. This is admirable, and the appeal of the Tezuka Astro Boy has a lot to do with his being in his early youth … unlike Summit's teenage *Astro Boy*. For example, the image of the original Astro making a go of trying to control a space ship with his sister (figure 9.10, p. 294), and leading his adult mentors into an adventure, are more impressive due to his being a child.

Removing major plot points like the auto crash that killed the son and creating a sequence where Temna's original son is killed in a freak vaporization accident cause the story to feel less grounded. Also changed in the adaptation, the new robot body built by Doctor Temna retains the memories of the dead son, muddling Tezuka's original story's cleanly-delineated setup and leading some to wonder whether Tobio is *really* dead, or is Astro in some sense partially Tobio? Even the type of accident in the adaptation version hurts the story. A car wreck (i.e. the accident in the original version) is the kind of tragedy that can happen to anyone, which makes it more frightening and relatable for audiences.

This car accident was changed in the adaptation to a freak vaporization accident, which, again, doesn't ground the story. Such an accident is presumably less likely than being struck by lightning, so it is hard to relate to as a truly tragic death.

Figure 9.7 *Astro Boy* manga where his father, Dr. Temna, is bashing Astro over the head with a shovel because the robot boy was not growing, and then negotiates to sell him to the circus owner—a story point that was radically softened in the Hollywood remake due to the results of American audience test-surveys. © Tezuka Productions

Figure 9.8 Father figure Temna selling Astro to the circus master (played by Tezuka's "regular cast-member" Ham Egg) and Astro being sent away with the junked robots to the circus. This plot element was also removed in the remake. But there is a sinister element (for example, the circus master in the original and the Bowers remake—voiced by Nathan Lane) that sometimes creeps into both versions.
© Tezuka Productions

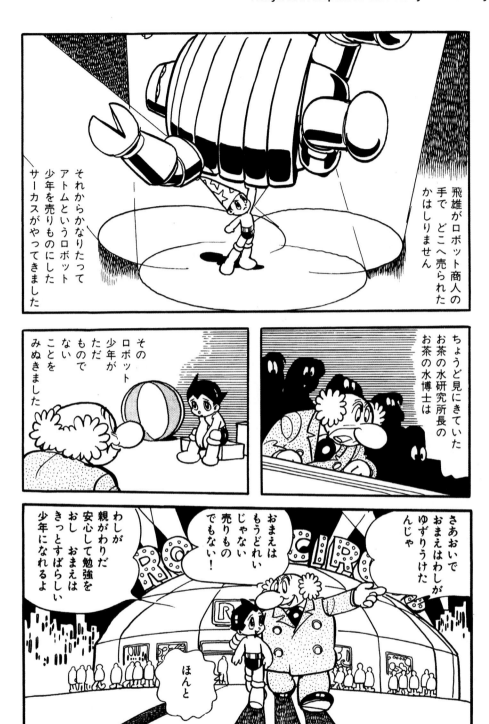

Figure 9.9 Astro being rescued and given his own warm robot family. This sense of the movement into the bright world of a new family's embrace and the strong emphasis on the professor and Astro's teacher's responsible and supportive adult mentorship is missing from the Bowers remake, making it radically different from the original.
© Tezuka Productions

Figure 9.10 This image shows Astro Boy's original design—a small boy, the friendly face with pluck and charm, the baby fat mixed with slightly feminine features, the young sister tomboy Uran, who Dr. Ochanomizu had created so that Astro would have a sibling. *Astro Boy*'s "world" was one of bright optimism, despite foes that had to be defeated and others that needed to be enlightened. © Tezuka Productions

Figure 9.11 As all to commonly occurs with young drivers, Tobio, Temna's original son, is speeding. © Tezuka Productions

Figure 9.12 The speeding boy sees the large vehicle too late. Tezuka's intensely cinematic style with speed lines and a crash jump cut. © Tezuka Productions

Figure 9.13 Temna is shattered by the loss of his human son in an all too common, and thus relateably human, way, rather than the emotionally abstract freak vaporization accident in the remake. © Tezuka Productions

I continued my interview with Tsumura, focusing on the changed relationship between Astro and his father Temna that the adaptation created:

> **Davis:** And then I noticed that in the [CG movie adaptation] story as it goes on, Astro Boy—although for a while he goes off with those kids, and the circus master turns out to be an evil guy—he [Astro] seems to be orbiting his father a lot more than in the original manga, where basically once he is rejected he is completely separated from his father. I don't remember the father again showing up in the manga series. So when the movie was shown, it wasn't like you went back and rewrote the script and reshot it to have Astro Boy sort of circling his Dad a lot more in the movie? It's just that [that] one rejection scene got toned down?
>
> **Tsumura:** Yes, exactly.[14]

Compare this with the original Astro's father figure Dr. Tenma's violent reaction to a much younger-looking character's inability to grow, shown in the original Tezuka manga sequence here.

As Tsumura states in his interview below, at least one person from Tezuka Productions felt *A.I.* was loosely based on *Astro Boy*. Whether or not that is the case, Stanley Kubrick and Steven Spielberg apparently valued this story point as well in *A.I. Artificial Intelligence*, in which the A.I. boy David, played wonderfully by Haley Joel Osment, is cruelly rejected by his adopted mother and exiled to the forest as a wanderer with other A.I.s who are brutally hunted and tortured by the humans. Astro Boy's rescue from the circus by the kindly Dr. Ochanomizu mirrors the A.I. boy's rescue by Gigolo Joe. In the adaptation, there is nothing really to rescue Astro from. He is already with Temna in parts of the middle of the movie, so it is a very different story than the original. This negates the meaningful and emotionally attractive story element of the original, where the good man [Dr. Ochanomizu] rescues the innocent child [Astro] from the abusive and rejecting 'father' [Dr. Temna] and circus master and thus becomes the new guardian, and is karmically repaid, as is the society, by the child's later good deeds. Put another way, the charming bravery in Astro's overcoming his original parent's rejection of him, adoption into a new warm family and subsequently deciding to fight for justice in the larger society is no longer part of the Bowers-version story. This reduces many audience members' empathy and admiration for the character.

Figure 9.14 Beginning with love and wonder, and a tip of the hat to Frankenstein's creation, Dr. Temna creates a replacement for his beloved dead son Tobio, culminating in Temna rejecting his new "son" Astro when he doesn't grow like a real boy, and selling Astro away to the circus. © Tezuka Productions

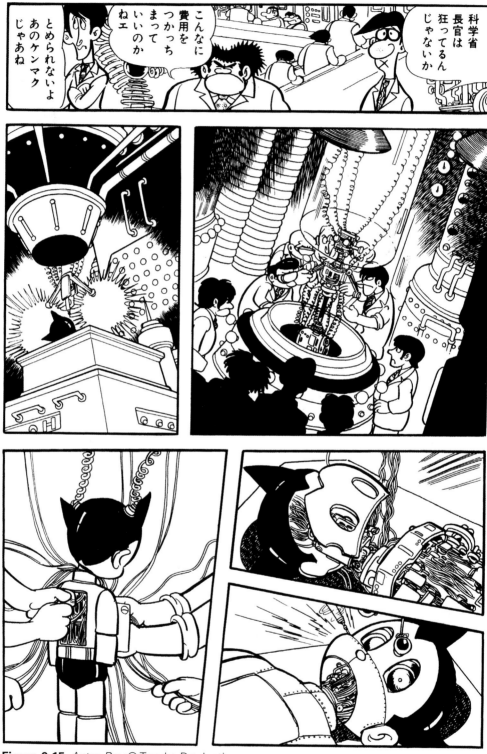

Figure 9.15 *Astro Boy* © Tezuka Productions

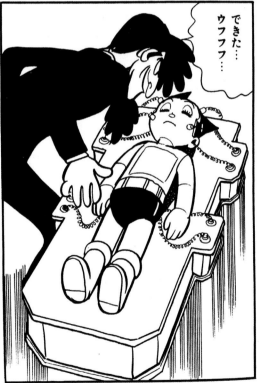

Figure 9.16 *Astro Boy* © Tezuka Productions

Figure 9.17 *Astro Boy* © Tezuka Productions

Figure 9.18 *Astro Boy* © Tezuka Productions

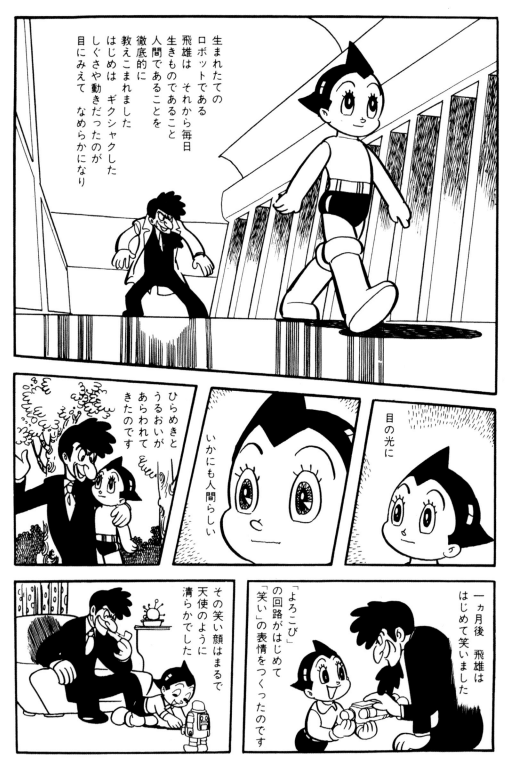

Figure 9.19 At first things go along swimmingly, Temna is initially delighted with his new "son" Astro. © Tezuka Productions

Figure 9.20 *Astro Boy* robot-child-abuse that was removed from the remake's storyline.
© Tezuka Productions

Producer Tsumura explains how the American team was allowed to change the character so radically— and why they wanted to

Davis: And who is driving the story development? One thing we're running into is the idea that if there isn't one central really powerful person, like James Cameron, who're fighting off the notes or beating the notes away, that these things can get very convoluted because there are so many fingers in the script—it's the old story, you know, so many cooks in the kitchen [i.e. all the different people making notes on a movie or TV project]. Was anyone in the driver's seat or was it like a push and pull? Who was controlling the story development? Or was it just sort of the group?

Tsumura: No no, it was definitely controlled by David Bowers, the director. Actually, the Tezuka estate, and his son, had told us from the beginning, "Please, we are not experts in making content for world consumption" but he had mentioned that *A.I.* [the *A.I. Artificial Intelligence* movie] is loosely based off the *Astro Boy* story, right? And he said that it was softened, and he said that, please do what you need to do to make this successful. He said, you [the adaptation team] need to have interpretation rights to make it palatable for a world audience. And that's the reason why they were licensing it to a Hong Kong or American studio is because they didn't have the know-how to interpret it for an international audience.

Davis: Did the Tezuka people, after the project's failure to get made at Sony, blame their own reluctance to compromise, and then go the other way with the new group? Perhaps even swayed by Sasahara's comments (presumably to them) years before?

Tsumura: Maybe they had gone through—this is not fact—they had maybe … gone through the Sony experience and realized that it takes awhile to make something successful in Hollywood and take it to the finish line, we have to be more hands-off. They had to loosen up.

Davis: It sounds exactly like that. So, under this one director, was there just one writer or was he the writer?

Tsumura: No, we worked through several directors and writers. There was an original director when I first started, I actually forgot his name, but basically Imagi made the decision to change directors, and come up with someone who really had a major feature under his belt. David Bowers had just directed *Flushed Away* … and someone who had the confidence and conviction to drive it, versus the original director who Imagi had chosen was more … he was more consensus oriented and what his weakness was, was when we watched the story reel, it was more like "Wow, I can remember Jane asking for this note and I asked for this note, someone else asked for this note." It didn't feel like it was directed, but consolidated. So we brought on David Bowers who drove the movie in his way, good or bad, and that took it to the finish line in his interpretation. Which, the Tezuka people appreciated, I think. The only thing that the Tezuka people were very picky on was the actual design. They really wanted the rights—because obviously in licensing and merchandising, they said, "You know you guys are making one movie and it will come and eventually go, but the asset of the design lives forever" and that's what [they felt] is forever valuable for them. They gave us rights to change the design to fit Western audiences, but they just wanted final approval on that and stuff. And we did show them but, ultimately, they weren't particularly picky on it.

Davis: So they had consultation rights or approval rights?

Tsumura: On design they had approval rights. But on story they had consultation only.[15]

Tsumura explains how these various contractual obligations and restrictions regarding creative decision-making on the *Astro Boy* movie adaptation played out in reality and talks about the attitudes/feelings on all three sides about this aspect of the collaboration

Davis: I want to quote you on the aging up of Astro Boy … I think you had said the Americans wanted him older because of the thing about young boys like older boys to look up to? Is that correct?

Tsumura: Yes.

Davis: And that's a big jump. He's not really a boy, but a young man/boy. Were the Tezuka people reacting negatively to that? Or did they just accept that this is the American market?

Tsumura: They accepted, I think, that it's the American market. It was actually the Hong Kong team who were closer to the original source material, who were really at first

Figure 9.21 Ken Tsumura, one of *Astro Boy*'s producers (center), Nobuo Masuda (left), and the author (right) on a panel at Anime Expo. Photo: Bert Le.

disheartened by the original design the LA team had submitted. It actually, the version that you see on the screen, is a compromise version. The original version, he was an adolescent. The version you see on screen is an 11/12-year-old boy. So the original manga, Astro Boy was about seven or eight, right? So we aged him up about five years … but the original LA version we had aged him up to about 14, and the Hong Kong team basically said, before we showed it to the Tezuka people, said that we lost the cuteness, the charm, that it will not do well in Asia. Ultimately, I think even at 12, it was never engaging to the Asian market, because if you ask people now in Asia, they basically say "Yeah your character was not very appealing" …[that] was a comment I sometimes hear.

In an attempt to be objective about the *Astro Boy* adaptation, I want to also note that some of these practices are also replicated in Japan

In the 2003 anime of *Astro Boy*, the Japanese production team *also* aged *Astro Boy* up. So, it was not only a Hollywood decision. Nobuo Masuda makes another observation, that from the Japanese point of view, their culture/values accepts much younger protagonists in their media stories than ours usually does.

As Masuda wrote me in an email,

Another comparison that occurred to me afterwards [our interview] is that main characters tend to be younger in Japanese manga than in American counterparts. In Japanese mecha-action anime, for instance, their rule of thumb is that the main characters should be teenage boys while most of those American superheroes are grown-ups. *Cowboy Bebop*, for instance, is an exception where creators purposefully went against the above rule and achieved a phenomenal success [among anime fans in both countries]. I was once involved in producing an American version of a *Street Fighter*[j] animated TV series [produced by an American company and initially aired on USA Network]. In that, the main character is a grown-up American operative, while in Japanese anime versions, the teenage duo of Ken and Ryu tend to play more leading roles. The American producer explained to me that they use Guile [who is older] as a lead.[16]

So the argument could be made that the *Astro Boy* remake took this approach for logical reasons, which are the demands of the American market and the difference between the cultures. But for *emotional* reasons, which I say are far more important, this change creates a less empathetic, older boy character who also does not bravely triumph over parental rejection at a tender age like Tezuka's original character does; it is much more impressive for a young boy to do the things Astro Boy does, as they take great courage.

---

[j] A Japanese gaming franchise that has many spin-offs.

10

The Screenplay and Television Script's Crucial Role in Adaptations, plus Pitching and The Green-Light (studio approval for production)

- Pitching.
- Commissioning and writing of the screenplay: the most crucial, and problematic, part of the process.
- The Green-Light (studio approval for production).

Step one: Pitching

Let's say that you have secured an option or shopping rights on a manga or anime that you are in love with and feel would make a wonderful movie or television show in Hollywood; what is the next step? Probably, you need to "pitch" it, which means to introduce the project and interest your movie/show's potential financing partners (often a studio) enough to commit large amounts of their money to this complicated and risky endeavor.

If it is a theatrical feature that you seek, you are asking the movie studio to commit their money to:

a) option the manga or anime during the duration of the script-development, casting, and pre-production process;

b) pay to have a feature film screenplay written and upon its hopefully satisfactory completion,

c) decide to use that screenplay to attach a director and actors, and

d) make the movie.

In American broadcast and cable television, outside of the "pay TV" model of HBO,

Showtime, and a few others, the process would be the same as step "A" above, but the TV studio would:

b) pay to have a *pilot script* written, and then, hopefully

c) the television network and TV studio funds the pilot to be produced,

d) and then, if the pilot show was evaluated as excellent or promising enough, that would hopefully lead to the production of the first season, or part of it, and the show's broadcast on domestic American TV—for at least a few episodes.

e) If enough viewers like the episodes that they saw (as delineated by the show's Nielson's ratings) to justify continued broadcast—as advertising revenue, that is, commercials, are directly related to high ratings—then the show will, with a very large amount of luck and talent, run for several seasons and achieve syndication. Otherwise, it will be cancelled.[a]

TV studios are more likely these days to try to pre-sell foreign rights to help fund the show's production because the network is only going to give them a percentage of the show's cost in exchange for American broadcast rights for a period of time. And the TV studio's ability to pre-sell foreign rights depends on whether:

a) the network has agreed to license the show for American broadcast in the first place, and

b) the show is viewed as attractive by foreign television networks.

As the globe "shrinks," the American TV industry has simultaneously premiered some series abroad, whereas previously they tended to first air shows in the USA and then try to sell them abroad after they were "proven entities" in the American television market.[b]

There is now a trend developing in American TV of skipping the pilot process entirely, and in rare instances, of ordering multiple seasons from the beginning in an attempt to get to syndication as fast as possible and avoid the flawed pilot process. This no-pilot full season(s) order would tend to be used with more established executive producers of previously hit TV series. And there is speculation that it might become more common.

---

[a] Pay-TV like HBO/Showtime does not have commercials but nonetheless also values high audience viewership numbers, for obvious reasons. HBO shows sometimes also get re-purposed for broadcast on networks with commercials, and thus syndication can also be a factor on pay TV.

[b] Worldwide premieres naturally would also include those series introduced to the public over the internet. For example, Netflix or Hulu premiering on the Web, HBO Go, and HBO Now, etc.

The Pay-TV model

As has been noted, Del Toro may have also found a way around various problems inherent in the syndication model for manga/anime adaptations by having HBO produce *Monster* (if it is produced—he speaks about the project below in the 2013 interview with Gina McIntyre for *The LA Times Hero Complex* Film Festival):

> I had pursued another property in Japan, *Domu* (*A Child's Dream*) by Katsushiro Otomo. I met Otomo-san, I was very respectful, I pitched it and then when the deal making happened, it was so awkward because the American lawyers don't understand respect. They don't understand the proper distance that you have to have with a creator of that caliber, and it went south. We stayed friends, Otomo and I, and that's a big blessing for me because I'm a huge fan, but with Urasawa (*Monster*'s mangaka), I knew I needed to. I heard it was acquired to make into a feature, and I thought, "That's horrible. You cannot compress *Monster* into a feature." So I watched, very vigilantly, until the feature [option agreement] expired and we started a dialogue with Urasawa and said we want to make it into a cable series, but properly. The book, not spin-offs, it's not gonna go for five more seasons than it needs to, it's gonna be the books. And he asked, out of respect, that I would show him the entire first season, in writing. The chapters, how they would be, so I would come in. And, you know, that's a big commitment in writing, but I did it. And I sent it to him, I said this would be the first season, and you can see how respectful it is.

Figure 10.1 MONSTER KANZENBAN © 2008 Naoki URASAWA/Studio Nuts

Del Toro further noted that, "We submitted it last week on Friday to HBO, so they're reading. I don't know what's gonna happen, if they wanna do it or not. But it was done very, very respectfully. When I go to Japan to present *Pacific Rim*, it's my hope that I will meet with Urasawa-san and I will bow like a monk, because he is a genius."[1]

[c] Transcription by Amber Brown-Rodgers.

Thus the *Monster* series can be produced without worries of the syndication issues, so that, in the case of mangaka who want to make sure their storyline is adhered to, the show ends when their original series ended. There is no worry that extra new episodes will be written by the American writers/producers in an attempt to "reach syndication" and thus possibly violate the quality of the mangaka's stories. Professor Hayashi and I ran into this problem during a negotiation and she suggested HBO as a solution, as opposed to the TV studio/network that was involved in the negotiation by the showrunner's excellent agent, who was not aware of the Japanese publishers', networks', and mangaka's "one season" bias. But at the time, based on advice I was getting that it was too far down the road with a network to switch directions, we did not. The negotiation failed for other reasons, but it was all of our (including the agent and showrunner's) first experience with this issue.[d]

So here are my pitching tips for feature projects (but remember, everyone pitches differently and the feature film industry has somewhat different pitching practices than the TV industry):

#1. DEVELOP YOUR LOGLINE. Create a succinct description of the project. For example, the logline for the big space movie spec script that I wrote and sold to Warner Brothers ended up being *The Treasure of the Sierra Madre* in space. This combination of movie ideas set in different arenas from the original story can make an effective logline, but it's just one approach.

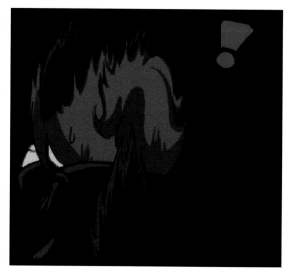

#2. WRITE A ONE-PAGER. I personally like to write the story in three paragraphs, or five, depending on the number of acts in the story. This keeps me focused on the story's spine, and helps to find the major beats. You may work differently. It also comes in handy to keep you focused on the story once you are hired to write the script (if you are going to be the screenwriter) and even when you are pitching.

I write the actual text of the pitch on oversized, single-lined paper, and it can reach up to three *large* (think artist's easel paper) pages. But that's my style, very detailed. I blow through it very fast when I make my pitch. You may decide you want to paint broader strokes, but from my experience, they want to know you have it really worked out.

---

[d]In either case, TV or feature film, if you optioned the material from the Japanese rights holders yourself, you could then transfer the option, if it is agreeable to your Japanese partners, to the movie or TV studio that acquires the remake rights. A lawyer will be helpful in this, because you may not understand what rights the studio needs. See Joyce Jun's interview in Chapter 9.

#3. PRACTICE IT. Pitch it until you have it pretty much memorized. I say "pretty much" because you want to make sure it still has a feeling of spontaneity. Pitch it in front of the mirror, maybe video yourself pitching it (then ask yourself: would you buy this pitch?). And pitch to your friends. Let them give you honest feedback. Make them know they will not be penalized for telling you the truth, but also make sure they are not there to deflate your confidence (if they are your friends, they shouldn't be!). My rule for creative input by others is "If two or three people independently agree, it might be good to assume they may be right." A comment from one person, I take with a grain of salt unless I agree with it. Refine it so there are no dead areas in it. You are giving a performance.

#4. KEEP IT TO 15 MINUTES MAX. These people are *busy* and it is hard to keep their focus longer than that.

#5. AGENTS ARE BEST, BUT ARE NOT REQUIRED. They give you credibility and can get you in doors, provided you have the goods. It's always best to have an agent set up the pitch meeting, but it is possible to pitch without an agent. If the studio then offers you and your rights holders a deal on it, for your own fee negotiation you would simply call a new agent and they will close the deal.

#6. DON'T EVER BE LATE! Give yourself time to park in the far away lot the studio may assign you, and to get lost a couple of times. If you arrive way too early, go hang in the studio commissary or walk around rather than lurking for 45 minutes in the exec's anteroom. Studios can be very cool places. As your passion is movies, and studios are chock full of past history and current filming projects, they are fun to tour when you have a few minutes to burn. And if you keep a low profile, and stay out of areas where you should not be, you should be fine.

#7. VISUAL AIDS CAN WORK. Especially when they are coming from the manga/anime. In fact, they are pretty much required for pitching such a project.

#8. GO FOR IT. When I sold a pitch of my own story to a major studio, I went in with maps of the fictional galaxy I had created and timelines of the history of these civilizations before the story began. When I am pitching, my eyes light up with fire, and I blast through the story with verve and enjoyment, making it entertaining, showing I am *prepared*, enthusiastic, and, above all, *confident* in it and myself.

#9. HOW DO I DRESS? As a manager said to me, you can drive an old car and look like a monster, but if you have the script or story (in this case, manga/anime) that they want, it won't matter. Some writers look like they just fell out of bed. Too slick can make people suspicious. But looking like a street-person may not be so bright an idea, either. Hollywood is fairly corporate; however, the screenwriter is not expected to look like the accountant. Some say dress just a little bit more casual than the exec. This is difficult, as who knows what the exec is going to wear? But choose a style that fits you.

It is important to note that if you are pitching the project, the studio needs to know who the writer will be. The writer needs a sample of their work to prove that they can write an excellent screenplay. It is rare, though not impossible, to get the writer hired without a writing sample (an exception: my first pitch was sold without the producer or studio seeing a script sample, as my agents at the time did not feel like I had anything good enough).[e]

Step two: The treatment

Part of the process of pitching is presenting a treatment. A treatment is a written document that can take many forms. Television treatments are often structured differently from feature treatments. I wrote a treatment for *Barefoot Gen* to try and set it up into development as a feature film. This was after I, and my partner at the time, Professor Hayashi, had gotten the mangaka of *Gen*, Keiji Nakazawa, to sign a "shopping agreement" giving us exclusive rights to find a production company, director, and so on, for the Hollywood remake. This is part of the materials (along with a trailer made in part from the manga/anime) that the agent with whom I worked on this (and other projects) presented to potential directors and financiers.

So let's assume that, after pitching, you found a "buyer" in Hollywood and they optioned the manga/anime:

Step three: Writing the screenplay

The next hurdle in the process is the big problem of actually getting an excellent screenplay written. Because the works (anime and manga) have to be optioned first, the screenplay can only be written by the writer that has been hired by the optioning company (the studio or network). This is an expensive process, particularly if it is a successful screenwriter, because even Writer's Guild of America's—the screenwriter's union/

---

[e] However, this extremely successful producer cautiously structured the deal as paying me to write an outline, followed by a treatment, followed by a first draft, and at any point if he felt I had not delivered quality work, he could cut me off at that stage without incurring further cost.

guild—minimum screenwriting fees for a high budget theatrical feature project are nothing to sneeze at ($127,295, including treatment).[f2] And if the writer fails to meet the expectations of the group, it could kill off the whole project right there, as it is another significant expense to hire a rewriter and then, usually, to extend the option period for the next writer. This really is "putting all your eggs into one basket" because in buying a "spec screenplay" on the open market, the studio can choose from a huge number of spec scripts written every year, but not with this "hire one writer and hope the screenplay turns out great" strategy.

As I have noted, many screenwriters in Hollywood may not have studied the manga/anime (nor the culture from which it comes) to the degree needed in order to understand it and make the adaptation screenplay work. Even without that problem, there are other matters to consider ...

Writing a good screenplay is very hard and screenplays good enough to be made are extremely rare

Nobuo Masuda discusses his opinion of the difficulty of the screenwriting stage:

Davis: OK, so there's a two-part solution [meaning first to get the anime/manga optioned so the screenplay can be commissioned and, second, hiring the screenwriter]. Now, another problem is, why does it take so long? And do you have any ideas about that?

Masuda: Simply, it's hard to come up with a screenplay. Every project I have been involved with, it's never gone beyond that stage.

Davis: It never goes beyond the screenplay stage.

Masuda: That's my personal experience.

Davis: Did you honestly feel that way because the screenplays weren't good enough?

Masuda: Yeah, it's hard to write a good screenplay.

Davis: It's really hard to write a good screenplay. It's also very hard to write one when you're the one screenwriter for a project. To buy a spec, they can chose from all the scripts written—thousands of them. But when you've chosen one writer ... the chances are low.

Masuda: You just need to pick up a good screenplay, not just a good property.[g]

---

[f] As of through May 1, 2015 (and historically these writing employment fees have escalated in price for each subsequent period).

[g] After I pitched an adaptation of a manga/anime to a major studio I was told by the studio executive, "Bring us a good script adaptation of it *and* the option rights." Before pitching it, Hayashi had secured the shopping rights from the

Davis: In other words, it's backwards. What they maybe should have done is waited for a really great screenplay to come along that tells that story or uses that character, but they can't do that.[3]

Let's assume that you succeed in optioning the manga/anime to the Hollywood studio and the writer (you or someone else) has been hired—what now? Prepare to wait, possibly a very long time. For example, if as he plans, James Cameron currently directs the *Battle Angel Alita* project (the film project is currently titled *Battle Angel*) after *Avatar 4*, which is currently slated to be released in December 2019, then *BAA* will be produced beginning in 2020. If that occurs, 20 years will then have elapsed from Cameron/Fox securing the Hollywood rights.[h]

Masuda: Japanese executives—company people—think that the screenplay is one step. If you decide to make a movie based on this book, hire some screenplay writer … it's kinda just one of the steps and should be done on a schedule or something.
Davis: Right.
Masuda: In the United States the producers wait.[4]

As Masuda notes, in Japan, the commissioning of the writing of a screenplay is considered a mechanical step towards production. In other words, the production is going to happen if the script is being written. In Hollywood, the script being written does not necessarily remotely mean that the film or TV show will be produced.

Roy Lee addresses this issue of producers in Hollywood "waiting," which is a source of frustration on the Japanese rights holders' side. He explains that this is due to the enormous stakes involved in Hollywood movies.

Davis: We thought that because the Japanese are going to be very interested in this book, we would ask some of the top producers—you, really—in Hollywood. So, the first question that they had was they were wondering why it takes so long to get a movie made, and why there are so many things that happen but never go through as movies. I was wondering if you would mind breaking that down a little bit. I know it's a big question.

---

mangaka. But the studio executive explained that, for him to have confidence in this particular project, he needed me to present him with an excellent screenplay based on the work, and for me to control all the rights, before doing the deal. I didn't believe it was feasible to do it that way. But later, Jason Hoffs did just this, when he and others convinced a high-end screenwriter to write *All You Need Is Kill*'s adaptation script on spec, while they had optioned the movie rights to the book, and they sold the screenplay for over $1,000,000 to Warner Brothers, a great payday for the writer. During that time, they had secured the rights of the novel.
[h] It is important to note here that the manga/anime projects that Hollywood has pursued so far are often large-scale productions (manga/anime, after all, often depict actions that would require expensive special effects to adapt into live-action). And that due to their sometimes enormous production costs (and thus very high financial risk) and military-campaign-level logistics, even non-manga/anime based Hollywood movies can occasionally take decades to make. For example, *Mad Max: Fury Road* (Warner Brothers, 2015), despite already having the advantage of being a sequel to the financially successful *Mad Max* trilogy, and even with those films' very talented director Dr. George Miller helming *Mad Max: Fury Road*, it still took 37 years from the original *Mad Max* in 1978 to *Mad Max: Fury Road*'s release. Miller was 70 years old upon *Mad Max: Fury Road*'s release, having been 33 when the original *Mad Max* movie was released. This time-line, frustrating as it is for all concerned, is often compounded by the fact that such in-demand A-list Hollywood film directors as Cameron and Miller are professionally very busy with many other projects to choose from, each taking years to produce.

Lee: There's two parts to that. The first part is that, because of the studio system here in the United States, the properties here that are developed, the cost[s] are so enormous compared to an independent film where they can ring up to 100 million dollars as well as the marketing expenses that add on even more millions of dollars, they are very cautious as to what projects they move forward. They do tremendous studies as they're developing it—market studies—to see if it'll be appealing to the audience. That's the first part of it. The second part of it is that there is always the margin of error for the actual quality of the adaptation. Because, there are often times that something is announced that is going to be developed, and they try to get the script adapted the way that the studio feels will be appealing to the English language audience, but sometimes the script doesn't turn out OK or it just needs further development. That just takes time.[5]

Miniature case study: Anime adaptation to Hollywood movie screenplay—dead on arrival

Davis: Just for fun, do you have any horror stories of a negotiation that you can share? Or you might not be able to share any, frankly, and keep your job at the same time! [laughs]

Robert Napton: [laughs] I don't … You know, I don't have horror stories. I have an interesting story, and I'll try to make it brief—cut me off if I'm giving you detail that you don't need, please. When I first got into anime and manga, the anime industry that I was working for—my current boss at his first company—he had a company called LA Hero, which is the first company he started in LA to bring anime to the US. This was in the early 1990s. During that time he had the opportunity to take the *Macross* TV series and turn it into a live-action movie. So he approached an American company, and for the purpose of this it'll remain nameless because they had good intentions and they were fans of *Macross*, and we got as far as everyone agreeing to a screenwriter who wrote a script that ultimately everyone disliked and the project fell apart. But what I learned a lot about in that process which relates directly to the topic of your book, which is why I'm bringing this up, because it's actually the only time I've actually been involved in trying to take an anime and turn it into an American movie, even though it was a failure. We didn't get the job done. What I learned from that process of what happened is that the expectations of what the creators in Japan wanted from a *Macross* movie and what the American producers wanted was really different, and we weren't on the same page. We were in the middle of trying to get everyone on the same page, and that was really challenging. The creator of *Macross* in Japan, Shoji Kawamori,[i]

---

[i] Kawamori-sensei, who is known for his mecha designs, and was originally an industrial designer, said in a 1995 interview in *Animerica Anime & Manga Monthly* magazine that he was a fan as a child of design elements of the 1960s-era British children's television action puppet show, *Thunderbirds* (Oshiguchi, *Anime Interviews*, 115–16). *Thunderbirds* (produced by Gerry Anderson, ITC), was later remade into a Hollywood movie.

who is a really, really nice guy and a really creative guy, he was very flexible and understanding. Mr. Kawamori, when he heard that we wanted to make an American movie and that there was an American producer wanting to make a movie, he wrote a treatment of what he thought the American movie should be, and it was very different from the *Macross* TV series. He wanted to basically reinvent the wheel. He wanted to make it very different, very new and very fresh. His new perspective on his own work, because it had been some years later since he'd done the TV series, he'd been given this opportunity to write a treatment for what could be an American movie, and he actually wanted to change it quite a bit. The American producer wanted an exact replica of the TV series that they fell in love with, which was his original story. So it was really the opposite of what you would expect! You would expect that the Japanese creator would want it to be 100% faithful, and the American company would want to take it in another direction, and it was the opposite! It made it very difficult, because in a sense Kawamori-san wrote his treatment and we were like, "Well this is a really cool story. It's kind of different from *Macross* TV series, and that's what we want to turn into a movie" and he was fine with that but he was kind of like, "Well I don't understand, we should do something new. We should push the envelope."

Davis: Oh wow!

Napton: So that was an interesting process, and then we hired an American screenwriter. We all interviewed with him. Kawamori-san came to the US. We all met with him, and we chose a screenwriter, and the screenwriter had a completely different idea. He turned in a script that everyone was not enthusiastic about—I won't mention his name. And that killed the project. Everyone was so disheartened with the screenplay and it had taken so long to get the screenplay written. And then it just … it wasn't what any of us wanted. It literally killed the process right there. That's the only occasion where I was actually involved in what you're talking about, the topic of your book. I just found it so fascinating because it was the reverse of what you would expect. The point I'd like to make is, and the punch line of the horror story is, you never know what you're going to get when you go to try to bring Japan and Hollywood together. You never know how it's going to play out, and I think every road is different, and that's what makes it so challenging and so difficult, because you have different agendas and different goals. If you're in the middle, as I was and my boss—Ken Iyadomi—was, you're in a challenging role, trying to bridge a lot of different desires and a lot of different expectations. That makes it really difficult.

Davis: So did the screenwriter just kind of steamroll it? Like, basically insist on his way?

Napton: He was given the treatment, and he had enough clout … he wasn't a superstar screenwriter, but he was a decent writer and he'd been produced and done some pretty big movies. This was in the early 90s. He was given the treatment that we'd all finally agreed upon, going back and forth with Kawamori-san and ourselves and the producers in the US, that had a little bit of everything. And then the screenwriter, because of his stature, just wanted to put his own take on it and then it just wasn't good. It wasn't a well-written screenplay. A sizable amount of money was spent on the screenplay and everyone was kind of like, "Wow … if this is how it's going to go and we've already spent X-amount of dollars and we're back to where we started then it's not worth it." So that's what killed it for everyone. We spent about two years to get to the point where we could get a screenplay written, and then it was like a turd being dropped in the middle of the room, you know? It was like, "Uh-oh!" And we were just standing there staring at each other trying to smile, but everyone kind of knew it was dead on arrival. So it was kind of a heartbreaker because we all had this dream of making a *Macross* movie. This was before the whole *Robotech* thing, and now they're trying to make a *Robotech* movie, which will involve some elements of *Macross*, 20 years later. But this was back when it was hot and were like "Wow, we're going to do something really amazing here!" and then it just fizzled out. It was definitely a heartbreaker for sure.

Davis: That was really interesting. So, in terms of screenwriters, how could you tell whether or not this screenwriter was really enthusiastic or just needed the job? Because we know that 99.9% of screenwriters just need the job.

Napton: Well, that's a great question. Again, going back to that experience with the live-action *Macross* movie that never happened, we interviewed about 20 screenwriters, all of us. They all had some familiarity with *Macross*, because they'd either seen *Robotech*—the first 36 episodes of *Robotech* is the *Macross* TV series—so most of them had seen that or were familiar with the basic story, and then we gave them the Japanese version to consider. It was a really interesting process because for once I was sorta on the other side of the chair, even though I didn't have a huge voice and they had me at all the pitch meetings sitting there and listening to the writers. This list of really top-level writers—circa 1992—were coming in one after the other, amazing people who had written great movies that I'd admired, and a lot of them had really original takes and you could see when they were enthused. A lot of them clearly had learned about it just before they walked into the meeting and were trying to B.S. their way through it. You could tell the difference, which was kind of interesting to me. One of the writers who came in, and I don't even know if he'd remember this now, was J. Michael Straczynski, who went on to create *Babylon 5* and now he's a very famous comic book writer.[j] He wrote the [feature film] *The Changeling*, which Clint Eastwood directed. So he's a very good writer, and he came in and pitched. In hindsight it probably would've been better to go with him than the one who ended up writing it, but his take was very unique and very different, but it was a take. It was a real take. He'd thought about and processed *Macross*, and gave a take as to how an American *Macross* movie should work. And that's when I learned what real writers do verses people who are just looking for a job—they come in and really have a voice and a perspective on a piece of material. Now maybe you don't agree with that perspective and maybe that perspective is wrong for a certain project, and ultimately we told Mr. Straczynski that his perspective was interesting but not quite right for this particular *Macross* that everyone was trying to make. But the point is that he had a take. A lot of the writers who came in didn't have a take, and they just kind of floundered through it, and if you said something they'd agree with you. You know, you can really … you could see the difference. So the lesson in that is, if you're going to go into a situation like that you can be desperate for a job, but as a writer you have to say what you feel and give your perspective on a project, and if you're right for it they'll agree with you and if not then you're out of luck. But I think that's better than trying to go in and just play ball with

---

[j] As comic book writer, Stracynski wrote on *The Amazing Spiderman, Thor* and *Superman*, and the Wachowskis' television series, *Sense8* (as showrunner).

whatever anyone says. And that's where things fall apart in Hollywood—it becomes this process of "Oh, I'm not going to be the guy who says no because I need this job or I don't want to get fired or piss someone off, so I'm just going to go along with the role of the community." I think that's where films get into trouble. You have to have people with a strong vision.

Davis: But those people who get fired … A lot of people feel—and I definitely feel it when I am working [on some studio projects]—that if you become too disruptive and argue and if you stand on your point you're gone. You're fired.

Napton: There's a lot of fear, and that's understandable. People are trying to have careers and make a living, but at the same time that's why there are so many bad movies.[6]

Step four: Contracts

How some rewriters who are unethical may be incentivized to rewrite the original writer's script as much as possible can be seen in a simple breakdown of my screenwriting contracts

My screenwriting contracts with Warner Brothers, Sony/Columbia and 20th Century Fox contain definitions of the "back end production bonus" which awards bonus money for a writer hired to rewrite my script (it is extremely common for rewriters to be hired on major studio projects) if they are awarded the shared credit on the script with me. For example, a bonus could be $225,000 if I am awarded sole credit, and $75,000 if I am awarded shared credit. Rewriters can also be awarded sole writing credit, possibly making the original writer lose their production bonus

entirely. As I mentioned, this happened on *All You Need Is Kill*/*Edge of Tomorrow*. The likelihood of the original writer having their credit and back end bonus taken away entirely is greater on these manga/anime adaptations (or any adaptation, such as from a book, comic book, etc.) than would be the case for original spec screenplays. These ratios/thresholds are set by the WGA and the decisions on who is awarded credit is often made in secret arbitration at the WGA. Initially, the studio will assign the credits, but any writer is free to challenge them through arbitration. The identities of members on any particular arbitration committee are kept secret. The committee members read the various drafts and weigh other pertinent information to try to determine what percentage of the final script was written by whom. Several writers may have been employed rewriting the original writer's work. A great amount is at stake in these decisions, both in terms of whether a writer will receive credit and potentially large sums of production bonus money *at all*.

Additionally, there are many other ways that scripts can go off track

In particular, Masuda talks about how the second draft of another Hollywood adaptation of an anime script was poorly received, and thus resulted in the studio abandoning the project:

> **Davis:** Do you see the process of selecting a screenplay taking a very long time? And the process of selecting the screenwriter? And the process of negotiation the original deal? How long are these things taking?
>
> **Masuda:** They take time.

Masuda then described to me the multi-month search for a successful screenwriter, who was then contracted to write the screenplay. According to Masuda, the studio felt the first draft was decent.

> **Masuda:** But then everybody gives the notes. I don't know what kind of notes [the studio] gave him.
>
> **Davis:** This brings up another interesting thing. I talked to [a producer, name redacted]. The guy works with filmmakers who really have a vision, and what he said was that it's critical in this process of these adaptations for the filmmakers to have a very strong vision, and develop it, and not have all these people involved giving different notes. His job is to block the notes.
>
> **Masuda:** Ah, that's good!
>
> **Davis:** They use him for protection, partially. He has to negotiate that to a certain degree. Just when you started to describe this whole thing, I'm listening and I was like, "Whoa, where's the really powerful person with the vision in this?"
>
> **Masuda:** I don't know what kind of system of notes they have.
>
> **Davis:** You can be sure that their system is a bunch of notes. It's a creative executive, and the executive.
>
> **Masuda:** It wasn't that [the producer] and them didn't have a creative foundation …
>
> **Davis:** For instance, it could be a less powerful director, right? But they can have protection of a powerful producer. And they can have the protection to follow their vision and that person can interfere with their vision from being derailed by a bunch of different notes.
>
> **Masuda:** Exactly. That's right.
>
> **Davis:** How many months did it take to get the draft out of the writer?
>
> **Masuda:** Oooh, I have to go back over the emails. Like half a year to find a writer. Then he writes the first draft.
>
> **Davis:** So in a way they're getting what they … why are the Japanese rights holders upset? If they're optioning it then they know that it might not get made.
>
> **Masuda:** That's a different corporate culture, right? There are so many projects that are

just dormant. Not only Japanese properties. Like Bradbury's *Martian Chronicles*. They have been trying to make a live-action feature for two decades or something.

I mention an incident when a major studio executive told me about a typical script owned by his studio being, maybe one of 600 projects it owns—and then warned me of the extremely long odds of production.

Masuda: [laughs] You need to explain that to the Japanese.

Davis: It's almost like part of their frustration is that at their publisher, they're number one. In their culture they're at the top. But Hollywood has the whole world to choose from. It must be so frustrating.

Masuda: The studios think of themselves as empires. We are starting with a [new] director now. In the case of [the project] I hated the script. There was a good direction in the first draft, but somehow it went off. The problems with writers is that when you have conflicting notes, they follow the ones from the studio.

Davis: Exactly, great point.[7]

Step five: Launching the production

Roy Lee discusses the goal here, the all important Hollywood "green light," and explains how the decision is made for putting the film into production

Launching a space ship may be easier than launching a Hollywood movie!

Davis: Just breaking that down a little more, who ends up deciding that the script is either ready or not ready? Is that the president of production? Or does it depend on the studio? I heard at one studio it's higher than the studio president, it's the next up the line [chairman].

Lee: Oh absolutely. It's more of a collective group meeting between the marketing, the production, and the businesses that go into releasing a film, and kind of derive any type of revenue from. It's more like a group oath that actually green-lights movies. It could be one person, but with bigger, more expensive movies, it becomes a corporate decision. Also, many people don't realize that the studios buy hundreds—or at least option—hundreds of different properties each year, and only make about 10 to 20 per studio. So, the chances of any project moving forward at each studio is maybe 5 to10 % from when they actually announce it.

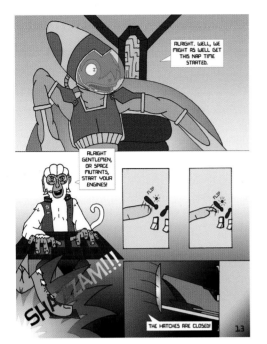

Figure 10.2 *Project Alpha* by Paul Choate. Launching a space ship may be easier than launching a Hollywood movie or television show!

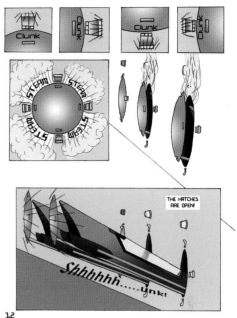

Figure 10.3 *Project Alpha.*

Figure 10.4 *Project Alpha.*

Figure 10.5 *Project Alpha.*

Davis: From when they announce that they made the deal for the option?

Lee: Yes, when they put it into development.

Davis: That's such a high bar just to get there. In your role as a producer, how are you trying to manage this? Through your relationships, checking in with them? And they're updating you at the studio as to when they're making these decisions? Are you trying to see if they need another element and then do you try to get that element from CAA? What is your role once it's in the system after its [the manga/anime] been optioned?

Lee: There are various ways of involvement, from working with the studio to hiring the writer. Or, in some cases, you bring the writer on and present the version to the studio, and then they hire the writer. Either it can be that or the initial development, but once that first script is written, it's more like working with the writer and developing the screenplay than working with the studio to package each element that makes it appealing for the studio to want to green-light the movie. Say I get a script for *Battle Angel Alita*, then I would work with the studio to find the director. Say if James Cameron said he wanted to direct it, then that would factor into the decision of the studio green-lighting the movie as opposed to some up-and-coming director that they've never heard of.

Davis: Do you find that these days, as opposed to way back when—maybe 10 or 20 years ago—that it's more oriented towards the director or the writer instead of the actors? What do you find is the element when you have these overseas properties, that you're interested in producing, to be the most important to the studios for a positive decision?

Lee: It ranges from which actors to which directors. Say if Will Smith said he wanted to star in it, that pretty much guarantees that at least—at this moment of time in Hollywood—that you will get your movie green-lit. Same thing if James Cameron says he'll direct it, or Michael Bay says he'll direct it, then that pretty much guarantees it. So it changes with the talent as people's careers escalate and fall.

Davis: In other words, there are actors who are still very important, but it's a very short list I'm imagining? I had been hearing that it's more oriented towards directors now for these Japanese manga because they need someone with a vision, and the writer. But maybe, like you said, when it's a huge actor it trumps all of that.

Lee: Yeah.

Davis: One thing that we've been hearing from the Japanese is a little bit like, "We feel out of the loop." In other words, some of the mangaka are feeling like they've made a deal but then they don't really hear anything. One of them [their editor] actually asked me to go find information on his own deal and what's happening with the project. What do you think this is? Is it sort of like everybody is really busy? Are they afraid to communicate? Is that correct that that's happening, and if so why would that be happening?

Lee: Probably, if they start not hearing anything, [it] is because it became less of a priority for the studio in terms of the project moving forward, so there really isn't any forward momentum, or anything new to update. So unless there is something that is new to the development process—say they hired a new director, or a new actor—giving them an update saying that they've worked on the script some more isn't much of an update. That is a reason why there is radio silence in the development in terms of what the author hears from the studios here in the US.

Davis: You had talked at that panel ["How to Transform Manga into Movie Mega-Bucks" at the American Film Market] you were on with Jason [Hoffs], Joyce Jun, and Don Murphy [a producer of the 2007 *Transformers*]—you were quoted as saying that often

Figure 10.6 My student Jessica Jordan's *Decrementia* page above could just as well be describing the many pitfalls of these processes.

a problem is that these deals take so long to negotiate, because Kishiro's [Yukito, *Battle Angel Alita*'s mangaka] deal took a long time [for Fox to negotiate with him], and I know *Death Note* did too—that the studio head, or whoever was originally interested at the studio, may no longer have their job anymore. How do you deal, if you have a project that you really love, and it's optioned or purchased by the studio, and it cools because of that personnel leaving, do you try to move it somewhere else? Or what is your strategy?

Lee: It depends. You just hope that it will fall to someone else who believed in it as much as the person originally hired at the studio and was overseeing it [and that the new studio executive] loves it as much. You go to the other executives—or go to the other studios—and say that this project is dormant there, and this is what we found and this is why we loved it. And hopefully you find another party to do that.[8]

Now that we are done with these two major case studies, let us move on to what the future may hold for this fascinating intersection between manga/anime and Hollywood.

11
The Future of this Hybridity

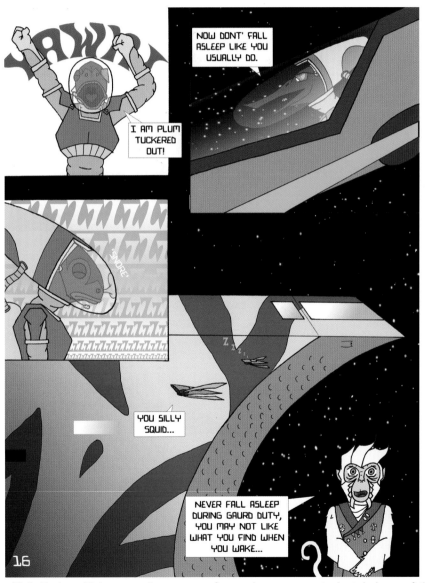

Figure 11.1 *Project Alpha* as well as some of my other manga students' views of the future in the next few images.

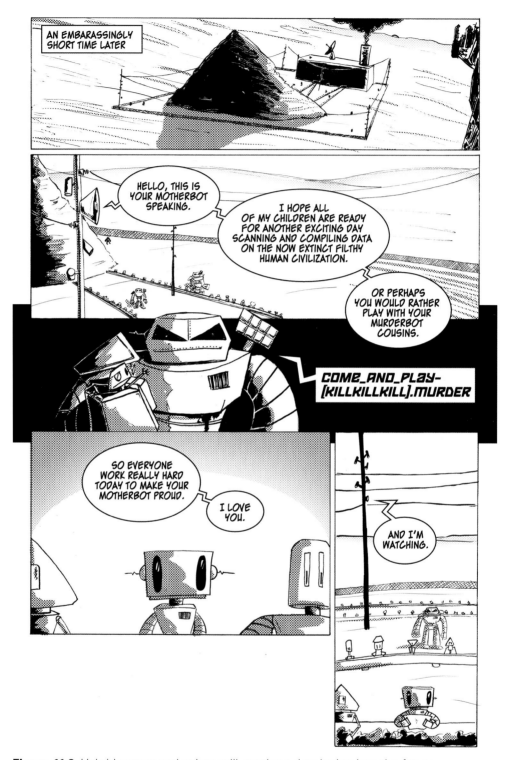

Figure 11.2 Hybrid manga and anime will continue developing into the future. *Motherbot Connection* (above) by Marlowe Leverette, like other examples of my students' manga in this book, including those in this final chapter, show the impact of the hybrity between anime, manga, and American comics/animation and movies.

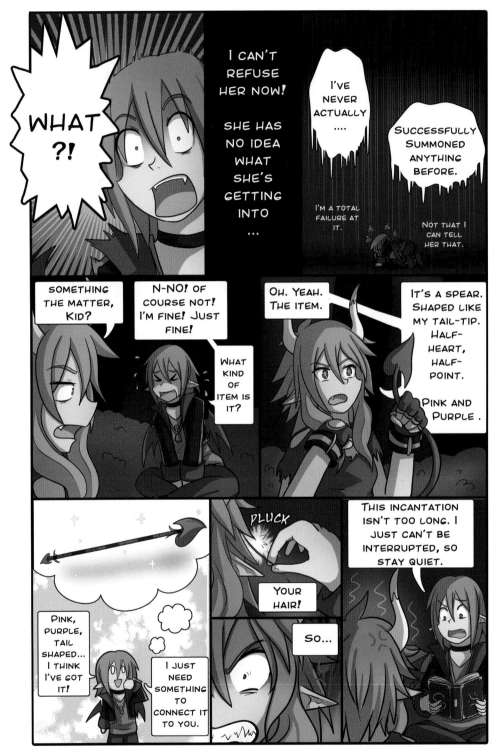

Figure 11.3 Jessica Jordan's *Decrementia* is an example of the digital future of manga production/distribution and mixing of American and Japanese styles. The internet allows Hollywood to seek manga that is only available published online, for possible adaption purposes, part of the idea behind Wemakemanga.com.

Figure 11.4 Lauren Elizabeth's *Domo Nation*.

Figure 11.5 *American Kensho: Leviathan Awake* by my grad student Alice Aaron Wyrd (writer) and Lucas T. Sams (artist) combines manga with American graphic-novel style.

My central point:

Hybridization is the past, present, and future of scripted mass media entertainment

Manga and anime were never a pure form to begin with, what with their Japanese cultural, pictorial, and literary ancestry mixing in with Hollywood influences and even Russian novels, which were favored partially for their long-form story structure that facilitates richly developed characters. And as this book makes clear, in all likelihood future movies, works of animation, and television will often consist of creators picking the best attributes of various forms from other cultures and countries because they are suitable for their storytelling requirements.

And a significant component of this book's argument is that "the devil is in the details." Or, stated in a different way by Arias, "I just think that if you don't get what makes the source material great, then you won't be able to turn it into something that stands on its own."[1] This means that media programs, universities, and governments/entertainment industries worldwide need to focus on learning the history and characteristics of manga and anime as my students and I have.

It is, of course, impossible to make this book all-encompassing. But, I went deep and wide in my research—addressing all that I felt was important for now

And in completing my account, it is important to observe that in recent years there have been major successes of manga/anime-influenced USA animated television shows. I feel that this is important to note, because otherwise the reader might be left thinking that since *Speed Racer* and *Astro Boy* were not blockbuster financial successes, that these American adaptations or manga/anime stories were tales of financial failure. This is incorrect. American animation TV shows deriving their style from anime/manga have arguably been more financially successful than direct Hollywood feature adaptations of manga/anime.

Figure 11.6 *Samurai Jack* (above) and *Sym-Bionic Titan* are two of the many California Institute of the Arts's (CalArts) graduates' manga/anime-inspired shows that are based on original storylines and characters created by Americans—interesting because CalArts was founded by funding from Walt Disney's will.[a] SAMURAI JACK, HI HI PUFFY AMI YUMI and SYM-BIONIC TITAN and all related characters and elements are trademarks of and © Cartoon Network.

It is important to note that these big TV successes were *not* direct adaptations, but rather original stories influenced by manga/anime characteristics.[b] This also raises another question, which is whether it is wiser to import the characteristics and methods of manga/anime but not the entire storylines, because the storylines themselves are possibly highly dependent upon the manga/anime visual stylistics to "hold them up" (for example, "deliberate decompression") and, in some cases, could not survive in the medium of live-action with its different rules. The Japanese stories also, as we have seen, often have many cultural characteristics that can be difficult to translate to other cultures. So an argument in favor of using the "style" but not the "story/characters" is that the American TV animated shows that have taken this approach have in many cases been successes.[c]

As Eugene Son noted in his interview (Chapter 1), there are many other examples of American animation being influenced by anime, including *Teen Titans*, which is notable because it is a spin-off from DC's *Batman*.

---

[a] These CalArts alumni include Genndy Tartakovsky, creator of the anime-influenced American shows *Samurai Jack* (above), *Sym-Bionic Titan* (next page) and *Dexter's Laboratory*. As noted in Chapter 6, CalArts alumnus Craig McCracken, created the anime-styled *Powerpuff Girls*—which, after becoming a US and international hit itself, was transformed into a separate Japanese anime series, *Powerpuff Girls Z* (produced by Japan's Toei animation) and broadcast in Japan.

[b] It is not possible to provide statistics here because comparing television and film success is like comparing "apples and oranges," but with these shows running multiple seasons, and having wide recognition among the young demographic at the time among American (and in several cases, global) viewers, this indicates success.

[c] Another advantage for the American studios and networks producing animation that is manga/anime-influenced but not based on an existing Japanese owned storyline/characters is that they then own the entire show and do not have to license the story from the Japanese.

Figure 11.7 *Sym-Bionic Titan*. SAMURAI JACK, HI HI PUFFY AMI YUMI and SYM-BIONIC TITAN and all related characters and elements are trademarks of and © Cartoon Network.

Last but not Least: Miyazaki's enormous influence upon Pixar

And, in this vein of not adapting the actual stories and characters, but instead other stylistic elements from the Japanese sources, Miyazaki's animated films have had an enormous impact upon Pixar's classic movies as explained by Pixar's founder and Chief Creative Officer John Lasseter. This is of great importance for the theme of this book, because Pixar is arguably the most successful Hollywood animation producer (or of any country) of the modern era in terms of both quality and revenue.

At an appearance at the Tokyo International Film Festival in 2014, Lasseter recalled his feelings upon viewing Miyazaki's first feature, *The Castle of Cagliostro*:[d] "I was absolutely

---

[d] A *Lupin* animated movie. Hayao Miyazaki was also co-director of the famous (in Japan) *Lupin III* television series. Which is one of the many series found within the *Lupin* franchise. As a reminder, screen-grabs of *The Simpsons*' TV show's tribute to Miyazaki-sensei's masterful work are on pages 27–9.

Figure 11.8 *Decrementia.*

blown away. It had a very strong effect on me because I felt that this was the first animated feature film I had seen that had a vision to entertain for all ages. It made me feel that I was not alone in the world. It filled my soul with a drive that said 'this is what I want to create.'" He added that "Whenever we get stuck at Pixar or Disney, I put on a Miyazaki film sequence or two, just to get us inspired again."[2]

The future

In this book, I have used manga/anime and Hollywood as the prime example of this hybridity.

Since "the future" is part of my thesis statement, let me dwell on that briefly—but very briefly, because only a fool thinks they can predict the future with absolute certainty. Anything can and will happen. But some trends can probably be predicted with relative safety.

- The "genetic" material of manga/anime will continue to develop in some distinct strands, but generally it will intertwine between cultures and countries more and more.
- Globalization is causing everything to mix together at an accelerated rate. Countries that fight to keep their own cultures will be the most likely to have visual storytelling that has enough unique characteristics of value to Hollywood. However, countries with both a distinct culture *and* a deep catalogue of visual storytelling that translate well to other cultures are extremely rare.
- For that reason, Japan will thus continue to be a leader in the hybridity this book discusses for a long time to come. This is because the manga/anime library is very deep and the culture still remains very intact. This is partially because Japanese people and their government find it very important to preserve their own culture. This will continue to give their work a distinctive quality.

Ian Condry gave a deeper look into the future possibilities

Davis: Do you see any future centers in anime and manga outside of Japan? Or do you see some future competitor to Hollywood?

Condry: It'll be interesting to see. I don't know for sure, of course. The process of outsourcing animated productions has been underway for a while. America had their own animation industry with the Fleischer Brothers and Disney, but then in the 60s they started outsourcing to Japan, and then Japan was doing a lot of the animation, and then that became too expensive. Then it went to Taiwan and the Philippines. A lot of the other anime studios started working with Korea. You're certainly in a situation where the people who can do animation are in other countries. Japanese studios are certainly complaining about this—it's harder and harder to find and train animators.

Usually animators would start with the in-between[e] animations and then key frames,[f] and then those who were good would become directors and oversee the whole process, from storyboards all the way down. Since the bottom part has been cut off and there isn't much in-betweens in the animation market, those jobs have disappeared in Japan. Anime studios expect the anime schools—the technical schools—to do that training. But it means that a lot of kids coming out of these schools just haven't done the drawing that even these younger in-betweeners in Korea, the Philippines, Taiwan, and China have done. So that bodes ill for the anime industry. On the other hand— and quite frankly I think this is more important—Japan produces the majority of the world's TV broadcast animation, at least according to some—I wish I was more confident that that number was right! [laughs] I think Japan will remain stronger than Korea and China because what makes the animation successful is the incredible manga market in Japan. They've got an epic catalogue.[3]

Figure 11.9 *One Piece* anime, definitely part of Japan's "epic catalogue" that should keep them strong for many years.
© Eiichiro Oda/Shueisha, Toei Animation. Licensed by FUN.

Most manga titles have not even been published outside of Japan, but as previously stated, an active fansubbing community exists, though the Japanese government and distributor and publishers are making a concerted effort to crack down legally on that to protect their ability to keep making the works (i.e. staying in business).

I feel that many more Japanese titles will come to influence future Hollywood creators. It was clear that Gaeta believes that the real anime/manga movement hasn't even begun in earnest yet when he told me, "*Manga and Anime Go to Hollywood*, to me, sounds as if we're in its peak or it has peaked and I don't feel that yet. I feel like anime has been knocking on the door for 15 years."[4]

---

[e] In-betweeners, before the advent of computer animation, created the many animation cells "in between" the main key frames

[f] Key frames are the main reference frames often created in Japan or the United States. They can be based upon images from the manga.

Figure 11.10 *Alrik* by my student Timothy Johnson.

Vive la différence!

As Franklin Roosevelt said during the dark days of World War II, despite the setbacks that may occur, the overall trend of human development is always up, and so it makes sense that the two art forms are going to mix together more and more, and what is surprising to me is how long they have been doing just that. But it really should have been evident logically that they were. People often look to other cultures and countries for new trends, and this crosses media. And the impressionists were influenced by Ukiyo-e, and even the most successful anime of all time was derived in part from Hollywood. In a 1993 interview in *Animerica* magazine with James Matsuzaki and Fred Schodt, Yoshiyuki Tomino, who has been called the "father of *Gundam*," specifically cited *Star Wars*: "The space colony concept and *Star Wars* were very much an influence on me; in fact, you could say they are the basis of the whole *Gundam* drama."[5] But as we saw, *Star Wars* itself was inspired in part by Kurosawa's epics. So it goes back and forth again and again, and it will continue to do

Figure 11.11 In *Pirate Feeney in the Smoke* by my student Max Blair, emotion and experimentation with form is prioritized over drafting accuracy.

Figure 11.12 Louise Wang and John Sheridan's *A King's Revenge* is the type of traditional (for lack of a better word) Japanese-style manga/anime that will continue to have a strong attraction. Current high-profile Hollywood adaptation projects center on these. But I feel that gradually Hollywood will shift into a worldwide search for manga adaptations.

so in the future, but at an accelerated rate due to the internet, more world travel, and an ever-increasing interaction between the media industries worldwide.[g]

Gaeta notes that "It's a visual art form and in its evolution they've concocted this—they've created their own form of cinematography, if you will. The idea of moving through the world is expressed in so many ways that are more emotional than physical." Thus the non-Japanese filmmakers cannot merely clone the anime/manga story and characters without learning how the forms operate. To not understand and utilize the reasons for anime/manga's appeal is to throw the baby out with the bath water.

---

[g] Ryosuki Takahashi—another high-end Sunrise anime director, writer, and producer, who along with Tomino-sensei and Takeyuki Kanda, directed a large portion of the successful 1980s mecha TV anime shows—is known for the gritty mecha series *Armored Trooper Votoms*. He said in a 1996 interview with Takayuki Karahashi that that anime's premise was partially inspired by an American rodeo movie, *Junior Bonner* (director: Sam Peckinpah; starring Steve McQueen, Cinema Releasing Corporation, 1972), (Karahashi, *Anime Interviews*, 164–6).

Future influence of Hollywood on manga/anime

Hollywood is currently successful, particularly American television, and of course as long as it remains so, it will continue to create a lot of globally targeted, large-scale theatrical movies and a diverse slate of scripted television shows. Therefore, many of these works will continue to come to Japan.

Another trend is that Hollywood film and animation's influence on Japanese manga/anime creators may be generational—and perhaps the younger generation is not as impressed by Hollywood's work as its predecessors were. When Yoko Hayashi interviewed Shinichirō Watanabe for this book he explained to her that,

> I have been influenced by so called B-class American action films. For instance, the directors, Sam Peckinpah and Don Siegel. I was heavily influenced by them. Don Siegel is well known for *Dirty Harry* and Sam Peckinpah is known for *The Getaway* [as well as *Straw Dogs* and *The Wild Bunch*]. Both are from 70s. These action films from [the] 70s are not simple action films but portrayed with in-depth description of characters. I can say they are tasteful B-class American films although they are not mega-scale films. I was heavily influenced by them. And also *Taxi Driver* [director: Martin Scorcese, Columbia Pictures, 1976] which was often shown on TV in Japan … I admired a film like *The Godfather* [director: Francis Ford Coppola, Paramount Pictures, 1972] a lot and was very much influenced by them. You know when you are in middle school, kids draw pictures on their textbooks. I was drawing the character played by [actor Robert] DeNiro in *The Godfather 2* while others were drawing the girls' bathing suits.[h6]

However, it is unknown whether Japanese anime and manga creators will continue to be as affected by works from Hollywood as they were in the past. According to Watanabe, the new generation of anime and manga creators have looked more inward, to Miyazaki, for example, for their influences. He explained to Hayashi:

> Speaking about films, your question whether there is an influence of Hollywood films in Japanese anime or not, it differs from generation to generation. At the time of Tezuka, they had a serious complex about Disney animation, rather than Hollywood. That was the first generation who built the foundation of Japanese anime. The first generation anime were created to catch up with Disney animations. The next generation [of] anime creators were not so concerned with Disney but rather influenced by live-action Hollywood films and I was one of them. Then the next generation, the today's anime creators, have not even watched Hollywood films. What they have been watching are Japanese anime.[i7]

Perhaps this is similar to the tendency of Japanese young people to no longer travel abroad as much as they did decades ago (starting at the end of the Japanese economic bubble that began in the 1980s), and who instead turned inward to explore their own beautiful and fascinating country. Echoing this, Japanese live-action filmmakers have also come back to

---

[h] Translation by Yoko Hayashi.
[i] Translation by Yoko Hayashi. This was made clear to me as I showed *The Simpsons* Miyazaki tribute images to a big class of students when I was invited to present my research at the top manga program of Kyoto Seika University. They seemed most fascinated by these American references to Miyazaki's masterpieces out of all the images I projected from this book. I quoted what Watanabe-sensei explained to Professor Hayashi—about current Japanese youth's focus on anime to the exclusion of Hollywood's works—and several students shook their heads in agreement.

Figure 11.13 *Doughnut Cop* by my student Akeem Roberts displays an influence here from *One Piece* (the skeleton character, see Figure 11.9).

the fore to a degree, after the long downward spiral of the Japanese film industry from its Akira Kurosawa heyday, and Japanese audiences have increasingly preferred the work of native filmmakers to Hollywood's. A typical Japanese movie multiplex, which 20 years ago might have exhibited several Hollywood movies and just one Japanese film, now might show a majority of Japanese films and perhaps one or two Hollywood and Korean movies.

One of the newest trends is American studios making local language films in Japan to compete with the other local language films. Sanford Panitch, President of International Film and Television at Sony Pictures Entertainment, has been on the forefront of this movement and explained to me that "The Japanese market is very challenging for Hollywood films, which has changed from the way it was ten years ago. Local films make up over 50%–60% of the overall market share in Japan. While China has surpassed Japan as the second largest film market outside of the US, it [Japan] is still a hugely important market and a vibrant source of originality for intellectual property, and I believe will always be so."[8]

Eventually, such hybridity will expand even more from that Hollywood/manga and anime axis. Here is an example of how it already has:

Computer gaming

Computer gaming is a very big and successful industry. *Sucker Punch* is an example of a film that uses *both* anime and computer gaming influences. I interviewed Steve Shibuya, the co-writer of *Sucker Punch* (along with its director Zack Snyder), and he spoke about the mix of these influences. Shibuya is a third generation American citizen of Japanese descent.[j]

> **Davis:** There's a couple scenes [in *Sucker Punch*] that have some anime tropes. When she's fighting those giant samurai robots? The crouch she goes down into? That's an anime thing.
>
> **Shibuya:** Definitely! Like when they drop from the sky and hit the ground, and kind of hit that pose? (see p. 26, Figure 1.21)
>
> **Davis:** That knee on the ground thing? So when that happened, is that you putting that in the script, or is that him doing an elaboration on what's already there in the script and him as the director putting that last touch on it?
>
> **Shibuya:** That was never directly written, when they drop from the sky and hit that pose. Those came in the development and Zack really liked that. What I know of Zack is that anime was never [earlier in his career] a very big influence on him, but in developing this [*Sucker Punch*] he worked with different artists. There was an artist—I don't remember his name but I remember early in the development of *Sucker Punch* Zack was talking to this guy. That's where that came from … but he was one of these guys

---

[j] Shibuya and I had previously discussed how to adapt *Barefoot Gen* and his father had insights about that era in Japan and how dangerous it was to speak out against government policies.

who did a lot of the pre-visualization that bring in these visual elements to the project that comes in through the production designer.

Davis: Another anime trope I noticed—is when they run past their opponent with the sword. Remember *The Seven Samurai*? That real zen swordsman? He runs past the guy and you don't know who's injured but then one guy does that slow-motion keel-over? Ever since Kurosawa did that, many sword-fighting anime have that scene.

Shibuya: Yeah, because you don't know.

Davis: And it's very beautiful.

Shibuya: Then they look at each there and half of one guy's body kinda slides off. [Laughs]

Davis: I thought she ran past one of those [robots].

Shibuya: Yeah, the last guy, she did that to [slashed, as she passed by him]. They kind of meet and then she lands on the ground in that pose, and he's way in the distance and kind of falls.

Davis: One question would be, since you weren't such a big anime and manga dude, I think at one point I introduced it to you.

Shibuya: You were the first person to define it for me, and then I kind of started to put them into the category where they fit. Anything that's done well is something we gravitated towards, whether it's an action sequence or an anime or [computer gaming] cut scenes or a movie or artwork—wherever! It's the artwork that drew us, and a lot of times it was anime.[9]

Figure 11.14 Pictured with the gun in this *Sucker Punch* image are "charms" which are a part of Japanese culture and are sometime depicted in manga/anime (director: Zack Snyder, Warner Brothers Pictures/Legendary Pictures, 2011).

Also, Shibuya mentioned one of *Sucker Punch*'s computer gaming influences:

Shibuya: *Metal Gear Solid*, some of the cut scenes in there are anime-influenced …[10]

The gaming industry is tightly tied in with the anime industry in Japan and there is generally a lot of cross-over, in both countries, between gaming and animation.

Dreamworks animation has been very adept at handling the melding of cultures, something that other producers, writers, and directors should also study

Figure 11.15 Ken Tsumura observed that Dreamworks and Disney are successful in bridging cultures in terms of actors, and in other ways, which is notable in part due to Dreamworks's great success in importing Chinese culture/art into *Kung Fu Panda*. This points to a more global hybrid storytelling in the future.

Tsumura: *Kung Fu Panda* was developed by Dreamworks, an American company. It has the sensibilities of … I can understand when you look at the components of *Kung Fu Panda*, why it's so successful. It has all the elements of making it into an entertaining film in America, and in China, especially when you replace all of the voices and stuff, it feels like a great Chinese movie, right?

Davis: Can you break that down? How it is that it can work for America as a story, and how is it that it can work for China as a story?

Tsumura: Ultimately, the reason why Pixar is so successful, and Dreamworks too, is because they're great storytellers. *Toy Story*, and the feelings from the toys and the stories they tell, it's international. Well, *Kung Fu Panda,* in particular in Asian markets, was extraordinarily a success, but ultimately it comes down to engaging characters and engaging stories. I can understand what Peter Chung is saying, that you have to take these properties … I don't think "making them into Hollywood movies" is the right term … I think you have to make them into intriguing stories with compelling characters, and ultimately that's what Hollywood does well. Those are the movies that do well. You look at the *Avengers*. It's a billion dollar property. It's not because the effects are really good, but it's really because the movies and characters are good.

Davis: Yet *Kung Fu Panda* wasn't a pre-existing manga, so it doesn't have that going against it, whereas all the original people who read it in their childhood could criticize it because it's being made by Americans … interesting in a way these remakes are almost hobbled in the comparison.

Tsumura: I think the North American audiences are very forgiving because the Asian properties are unknown to them and stuff. But, yeah, I think to an extent, it can have a handicap in the Asian market where the audience … where you think is built-in, but it's [the] reverse. Like if you don't fulfill their expectations, then they kind of shy away from you.

Davis: It was near and dear to them and you'll never measure up to it. One last thing, are you aware that Katzenberg [Jeffrey, CEO of Dreamworks movie studio] brought artists to China and made a big deal of going to those certain areas and got government and local officials involved in hosting them. They went on a trip to research what the look was there. Do you think that kind of engagement can be helpful in these sort of projects?

Tsumura: I think [it is] what Jeffrey does really well. He's a genius in marketing, and looking at the end product of *Kung Fu Panda*, you can probably find all the scenery on the internet … but Jeffery is really smart in not just doing this for research, but "hey, if we sent all these people to China, then it is authentic." These artists are there. They touched the surfaces, they scanned the mountains with their own eyes and stuff, and when you can say that to the Chinese, and in marketing, they automatically think that the product is more palatable because they've done all their homework. As you know, Jeffrey and Dreamworks has ventured into China in a big way with the joint venture with the Shanghai government and stuff, and that was his ultimate goal. He's very smart in not just thinking of one picture, but thinking of the global advantages of making these things, and what it takes to make it to the finish line successfully.[11]

The subject of *Kung Fu Panda* brings us to manga and China

Figure 11.16 *Heavy Gauntlet Origins* by my student Frank Ellerbe.

China

- In the final part of this book's final chapter, Hollywood's hybridity with China's culture will be discussed.

Part of what makes hybridization work is that there have to be differences between the cultures—otherwise, there is no hybridity, but rather duplication. Mainland China has fought hard to keep its own culture. Therefore, it serves as my final prediction of what might happen.

Figure 11.17 Big American TV animation hit show *Avatar the Last Airbender* and its sequel show *The Legend of Korra* have a huge Chinese influence and also both combine anime and American animation styles. One of *Avatar the Last Airbender*'s creators is Asian-American. © 2004 Viacom International, Inc. All rights reserved. Nickelodeon, all related titles, characters and logos are trademarks owned by Viacom Media Networks, a division of Viacom International Inc.

Not confined to the Japanese/American relationship, this hybridity expands to entertainment industries globally. For example, in 2011, I was invited to China's newest animation university program to speak about Hollywood projects that had been influenced by Chinese culture and storytelling—animated movies like *Kung Fu Panda* and television shows like *Avatar the Last Airbender* (which fuses Japanese anime, American animation, and Chinese martial arts).

Chinese professors had seen my students' manga (on the Wemakemanga.com website), and they were aware of my research and writing on this subject of the back-and-forth flow of creative influences across the Pacific as well as my background as a Hollywood screenwriter.[k] They recognized that my students were creating hybrid forms between manga and American graphic novels and comics and that the mainland Chinese needed to develop their own form that is distinct, yet globally popular—and that to do so, the Chinese creators/educators also needed to study the American animation and Japanese manga/anime forms to "find their own hybrid styles" if they were to develop their manga/comics

---

[k] For those who did not read the preface, it probably helped that although there are perhaps thousands of screen and TV writing classes at United States' universities, there is, as of yet, only one manga production class at a United States university, which is mine at the University of South Carolina (a class which I started at the University of California, Irvine).

industries to the point of high enough quality to compete commercially domestically and globally as well as to be adapted into their live-action and television and animation industries.

Examples of manga that my Chinese hosts liked on the wemakemanga.com site

Figure 11.18 *Decrementia*.

Vault 9, next page, by my student Patrick Fowler was influenced by *Grappler Baki*, a hit manga, anime, and video game series about the world of grappling.

Figure 11.19 *Vault 9*, a populist manga by my student Patrick Fowler.

Figure 11.20 *Vault 9*

Figure 11.21 *Vault 9*.

Figure 11.22 *Vault 9*.

Figure 11.23 *Kung Fu Panda 2* poster in Chinese. *Kung Fu Panda* was the box-office record holder in the People's Republic of China until *Kung Fu Panda 2* shattered that record. As both films utilize elements of Chinese culture, they set off a spirited debate due to the disappointment that they had not been created by a Chinese company. Kung Fu Panda 2 © 2011 Dreamworks Animation LLC. All rights reserved.

There was common ground for discussion. I sat at a big table with several Chinese professors as we tried to figure out what was the solution to finding ways that their students could tell animated stories that would relate to Chinese culture but still be engaging to non-Chinese people and present wonderful diverse stories and characters, all in a fresh, new style. Particularly striking to them was how each one of my students' manga had its own distinct style. They recognized that this "manga/comic artists with their own individual style" characteristic would need to develop, perhaps through the educational system, in their own country. A big issue had to do with the Chinese's frustration that Dreamworks was able to export and process their own culture and sell it back to them, making *Kung Fu Panda* and its sequel the most successful pair of movies in Chinese history. "Why can't we do that with our own culture" (i.e. make animation and films and comics that are universally successful both in China and globally)? What was the secret, they wondered? The answer I found in writing this book, which is, of course, that the DNA strands governing the characteristics of the Japanese and Hollywood forms have to be studied and dissected, as this book has begun to do. My own goal in traveling to Japan, bringing Japanese creators' knowledge here and studying American animation/live-action, is to learn from the masters of these hybrid forms of manga/anime, comics and American animation—and use that knowledge to help my students and my own creativity and also perhaps develop a curriculum that other universities, schools and creators worldwide can use to obtain similar results. One of the things I emphasized to my Chinese hosts is that their government needs to be open to a wide range of creative expression to develop vibrant commercial comic and animation industries.

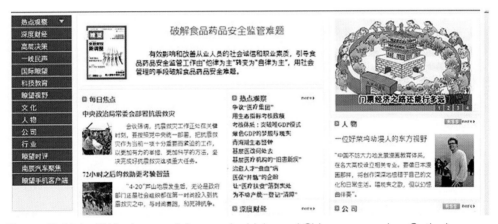

Figure 11.24 In 2013, the prestigious and widely read Chinese magazine *Outlook Weekly* ran a very positive feature article on my research and teaching, and our manga website.

But it was with the Chinese students that the exciting nature of the future of this hybridity became delightfully clear, and their youthful enthusiasm, including for their own country's future, was very intoxicating. The room went wild with discussion as the students and I tried to sort out the future of the Chinese animation, film, and television industries and their relationship to America and Japan's entertainment juggernauts when

Figure 11.25 In Beijing, at one of five presentations on my research including at China's newest animation school. A fascinating and exuberant discussion took place with the students about global hybridity.

Figure 11.26 In Beijing, hybridity is the future.

a young Chinese man suddenly spoke from the edge of the stage in perfect English with a New York accent, identifying himself as a martial artist. So, I invited him to demonstrate the kicks and sweeps of the various Chinese fighting styles that, combined with those of anime/manga, Chinese painting, and American animation, drive the story and world of *Avatar the Last Airbender* as a young lady from the audience pronounced them in Chinese from my notes.

It was a moment of spontaneous and giddy hybridity, and I expect this to continue as people from around the world develop their own entertainment industries and look to *all* of these dominant forms for inspiration and as a jumping-off point for their hopefully successful adventures in storytelling.

Figure 11.27 Image from *Buddha*. Tezuka was very concerned about the sanctity of all life. May we all be. © Tezuka Productions

And so we come to the end of the main part of this account.

Whether it is an African superhero story (*African Dragon*, by Jeremy Darby), or a post-apocalyptic comedy (*Bad Things Come in Threes* by Hannah Mitchell) …

Figure 11.28 … or rabbits in an interstellar romance (*Space Bunnies* by my student Nicole Ramirez), or my own project, the future is wide open for the mixing field of hybridity in manga/anime/Hollywood film and animation.

In brief summary going forward

Our current Wemakemanga upgrade experiment is to add voice actors' performances to a few of the manga, coordinated by me, WMM student-group president Anna Edwards, Theater professor Erica Tobolski and Media Arts/Computer Science double-major web-master Emily Shea. We also collaborate with the Japanese and English programs. Students I mentor from my scriptwriting classes like recent grad Gregory Goetz have blazed into Hollywood careers, in his case as script coordinator on Steven Spielberg's *The Whispers, True Detective, Tyrant,* the ABC/Shondaland series *The Catch* and *Salem,* as well as writer's-room assistant, traditionally one step away from TV staff writer, on the Fox TV network show *Gangland.* My scriptwriting class grad Brook Driver sold an option to his feature screenplay to a *Harry Potter* producer. For my students and I, the sky is not the limit… (even if it is an alien sky, see below). We are always seeking new ways to elevate and improve what we are doing.

Figure 11.29 A test page for my earlier manga project based on my 20th Century Fox-owned screenplay. Pre-coloring stage. Illustration by Kriss Sison and Brian Vileza.

For more projects by my students, please visit wemakemanga.com.

While you are there, please look at my students' manga work, as they exhibit the hybridity that is influencing our young people in their storytelling. As a very lucky professor, I have gotten more back from them than I could ever hope, and I am very proud of them.

Figure 11.30 At Anime Expo's Anime and Manga Studies Symposium in Los Angeles, where I have spoken each year over the July 4th weekend for many years.
Photo: Bert Le.

Afterword: Manga in Education— The Practical Benefits of Creating Manga; Two Manga Production Teaching Examples

As an example of the usefulness of learning how to create manga and hybrid manga, *Bad Things Happen In Threes*'s Hannah Mitchell took the manga class. She had learned how to use various software to create her manga, and that ability got her hired in a government

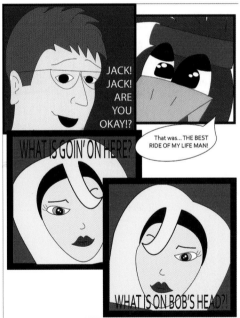

Figure A.1 Hybridity—as Hollywood's Frankenstein monster design and the bright colors typical of many of my students' work combine in Mitchell's manga.

Figure A.2 Mitchell is not trained as an artist, but learned the Adobe Illustrator program to create her manga, and so developed a graphically simple yet arresting style for the comedy about a chirpy optimistic Southern belle trying to find a boyfriend (and having to "settle" on a zombie) in the apocalypse.

job in a different media field. The students also learn to work on large-scale creative projects in groups, which is very important for preparing them for the "real world" of their creative careers, including advertising, storyboarding.

Figure A.3 *FAS*'s creator Tonya Holladay learned to create "wire frames" for websites using Manga Studio software, while creating her manga for my class.[a]

---

[a] Holladay used the wire frames for various things, including web and application design for easier user interface.

Figure A.4 With some of the many students that I mentor, Jarad Greene; Ashley Poston (Wemakemanga writer and a graduate of my TV writing class), who had her first novel, *The Sound of Us* (Bloomsbury Children), at the age of 23, and her second, *We Own the Night*, at the age of 25 (Bloomsbury, 2015); and Amy Jumper. We are videoconferencing an ex-student working in the movie industry in Los Angeles, so that they can all network and learn from students in the field, as well as share knowledge and thereby reach their goals. Ashley and Louise Wang took an NYC-based internship I established in conjunction with American manga publisher Kodansha USA, a division of the giant US publisher Random House, for my students. In 2015, Ashley was hired full-time by the *Harry Potter* publisher in NYC. Both she and Brook also have top agency representation. As noted in the preface, Louise Wang was hired full-time by Taiwan's respected NEXT animation as an animation assistant. Photo: author.

Our classes are structured in sequence, so that students can develop their stories and characters in an earlier class, then work the kinks out and hone them into their final form in the production class (in this case, a manga class, but it can also be my advanced screenwriting and TV writing classes). I also encourage the students to cross-platform their stories into other forms.

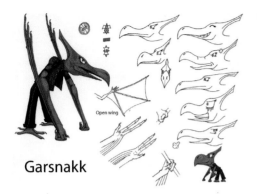

Garsnakk

Lintak

Figure A.5 *Project Alpha* character emotion and physical characteristics chart (Paul Choate).

Figure A.6 These can include props, chibis and even teddy bears (Paul Choate).

Types of Relationship Charts

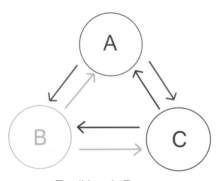

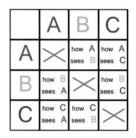

Traditional Format

This type of chart uses character portraits, arrows, and shapes to demonstrate the relationships of a small character cast. Not all characters are connected and overlap can be confusing, but line color and portrait shapes can communicate feelings without many words.

Grid Format

The grid relies less on pictures and requires a key (such as the one above) to understand, but is more efficient in giving a brief synopsis of each relationship. The grid relies on words and occasionally colors to show a variety of feelings among a large group of characters.

Figure A.7 Some students even document what I teach for the benefit of future class students (for example, this character relationship chart method I developed to make all the characters' attitudes towards each other clear)—and also so that student-led innovations can be preserved for future students on our digital backboard system. Chart by Jessica Jordan.

Quite a few of my students speak Japanese, and have been to Japan, including living in Osaka and Tokyo. For example, Louise Wang currently is living in Tokyo trying to break into the Japanese manga industry.

Glossary

To avoid repetition but allow some sort of chapter breakdown, terms and names have been placed in the chapters where they were used most prominently, or sometimes where they were first introduced.

Preface

Anime: Japanese limited-animation, rivals American animation in success and is often based upon manga sources.

Anime Expo: the largest anime con in North America, which has been held for years in Los Angeles, CA. In 2015, peak daily attendance broke all previous records and topped 90,500, and the turnstile admissions for its four days exceeded 260,700. A major part of **Anime Expo**'s programming is the Anime and Manga Studies Symposium, a track of presentations and panel discussions dedicated to the academic study of these art forms run by scholar Mikhail Koulikov.

Anime News Network (ANN): the largest anime/manga/news/information/journalistic website in the world. The site was founded in 1998 by anime/manga expert Justin Sevakis and is now maintained by a group of over 20 editors and journalists. Former editor-in-chief Christopher Macdonald is the current publisher and CEO.

Astro Boy (in Japanese, **Tetsuan Atom**; direct translation, **Mighty Atom**): the American name of **Tezuka**'s famous robot boy, originally a manga (beginning in 1954), and later adapted by him into an anime television show that was the first to come to American television and was broadcast on the NBC network beginning in 1963. During that process, **Tezuka** and his colleagues invented the televised anime series form. Probably the most legendary anime/manga.

Battle Angel Alita (known as **Gunnm** in Japan): brilliant manga by **Yukito Kishiro** (an anime was also produced) that James Cameron has long-planned to make as a major Hollywood movie.

Chibi: "Super deformed" style of regular manga/anime characters, usually used for comic relief and many times for the purpose of parody. **To the right is a chibi my student Austa Joye created of Osamu Tezuka.**

Columbia, SC: the capital of South Carolina and a center of a lot of comic/manga activity. Currently the city hosts four annual cons as well as being home for several prominent Marvel/DC artists including, for example, Sanford Greene (*Spider Man*).

Cowboy Beebop: 1988 hit anime series directed by **Shinichirō Watanabe**, with significant influences from various Hollywood genres as well as Hong Kong action movies and blaxploitation. Produced by **Sunrise**.

Patrick Drazen: author of the book *Anime Explosion: The What? Why & Wow of Japanese Animation*.

Gigantor (***Tetsujin 28-gō***, 1964): Mitsuteru Yokohama's famous giant robot is controlled by a boy with a remote controller (and an early example of **mecha**). Another anime hit on American television in the mid-60s. Alleged to be partially influenced by *Frankenstein*.

Hybridization: in this case, means creators taking the elements of each form and combining them—one work building on the other, and then the next generation builds on that work, ping-ponging back and forth across the Pacific Ocean.

Manga: modern Japanese comics, easily the most successful comic art form/business in the world.

Mangaka: Professional manga creator. Can be a writer/artist or one or the other. Some would argue that only when one has achieved a long-term professional reputation under the intense serialization schedule that creators of manga face at Japanese publishers, can they be accurately called a **mangaka**.

Nobuo Masuda: a consultant and point man for **Sunrise**'s (the large anime studio that produces ***Gundam*** and ***Cowboy Beebop***) Hollywood movie deals. **Masuda** also has a large IMDb list of many major anime that he has been the localizing producer on for the American market.

Helen McCarthy: highly regarded author of the excellent book *The Art of Osamu Tezuka, God of Manga*, and other scholarly writings on manga/anime.

Nashi Club: the large student-run anime club at the University of South Carolina, a feature typical of so many colleges, high schools, middle schools, and even elementary schools worldwide. Their annual con, Nashi Con, in Columbia, SC, has grown in size exponentially. Professor Northrop Davis is the faculty advisor for the group.

Frederik L. Schodt: author of landmark scholarly manga and anime studies books such as *Manga! Manga! The World of Japanese Comics*, *The Astro Boy Essays*, and *Dreamland Japan*. He is perhaps the most acclaimed writer in the manga and anime studies field and was awarded the Japanese government's prestigious Order of the Rising Sun, Gold Rays with Rosette for his manga/anime scholarship. **Schodt** translated ***Astro Boy*** (for Dark Horse) as well as many other important Japanese works.

Shopping agreement: Where the rights holder agrees to let the producer/writer/director "shop" the adaptation rights. It may take the form of an option agreement.

Shueisha: along with Kodansha and Shogakukan, the largest Japanese manga publishers. Other big publishers include Kodakawa.

Sunrise: the large Japanese anime studio that produces ***Gundam*** and ***Cowboy Beebop*** and many other famous series. Part of the Namco Bandai Group.

Osamu Tezuka (1928–89): the legendary "father-creator" of modern manga and anime television series as well as a producer, newspaper columnist, and licensed medical doctor. His influence upon the manga/anime field is enormous, and extends to Hollywood, including modern-day American animated television and graphic novels.

Tropes: defined here as conventions, expectations, and devices.

Ultra jump: a **Shueisha** magazine with an edgier, **seinen** side (marketed to boys and men old enough to read kanji, a Japanese system of characters adopted from Chinese writing), as opposed, for example, to **Shueisha**'s mainstream ***Weekly Shonen Jump*** flagship magazine. **Battle Angel Alita** appeared in **Ultra Jump** until **mangaka Kishiro** moved to Kodansha. It also publishes megahit *JoJo's Bizarre Adventure*.

University of South Carolina's School of Visual Art and Design (SVAD): at the University of South Carolina's flagship main campus in Columbia, SC, where Northrop Davis's manga, story, and screenwriting classes are held.

Wemakemanga.com: the website for Northrop Davis's mostly American students' manga. Many other manga have been created in his classes that are not on the site. Davis's students' manga works are examples of the hybridity that this book focuses on.

Chapter 1

Akira: director Katsushiro Otomo's anime feature, a big hit in the American theatrical market (Tokyo Movie Shinsha 1988), inspired several of that era's up-and-coming Hollywood creators. Was also a manga.

Ambassador Magma: a **Tezuka** manga that later became a live-action television show (titled *Space Giants* in America).

The Animatrix: A 2003 nine-part direct-to-video anime series based on The **Matrix** universe, produced by **Lana** and **Andy Wachowski**, and series producer **Michael Arias**, directed by mostly high-level Japanese anime directors with several episodes written by the **Wachowskis**, financed by Village Roadshow Pictures, Warner Home Video, and produced at Madhouse, Studio 4°C, and others.

Chibi of *Ambassador Magma/Space Giants* (or perhaps a **mecha**/giant robot **chibi**).

Animism: the idea that non-human entities have spiritual life. Has been called by some Japan's true native religion and informs much manga and anime.

Michael Arias: American-born director of the excellent anime **Tekkonkinkreet** (Studio 4°C 2006) and series producer for **The Animatrix**.

Bakuman: a 2008 manga (and later, anime) by Tsugumi Ohba (writer) and Takeshi Obata (artist). A fictional youth-obtaining-their-dream story about the rise to the top of the manga publishing world by two young **mangaka** published by **Shueisha**. A terrific insider's view of the industry.

Bunraku: a form of traditional Japanese puppetry. Relates to **suitmation**.

Captain Harlock: manga and anime series created by **Leiji Matsumoto** about the adventures of a space pirate. The titular character was partially modeled off of Hollywood Errol Flynn's pirate-movie persona.

Captain Ultra: a Japanese live-action television show featuring a space-patrol battling **Kaijus** (produced by Toei).

Guillermo Del Toro: Mexican director who emigrated to Hollywood (**Pacific Rim**, *Hellboy*). He was significantly influenced by anime/manga, which he experienced as he grew up in Mexico. Extremely knowledgeable about the forms.

Ghost in the Shell: a multi-media franchise based upon the "**seinen**" manga of the same title by Masamune Shirow (published Kodansha). Besides the anime feature, an anime television series was produced as well, titled *Ghost in the Shell: Stand Alone Complex*. According to **The Matrix/Speed Racer** producer Joel Silver, *G.I.T.S.* had a significant impact upon *The Matrix*.

Godzilla: the original **Kaiju** film features a nuclear-birthed monster partially inspired by **King Kong** (director: Ishiro Hondo, Toho Films 1954). **Godzilla**, the brain-child of legendary special effects master Eiji Tsuburya, was remade both by Toho and Hollywood in later years, including a hit Hollywood version in 2014 (Legendary Pictures/Warner Brothers) that also spawned sequels.

Chibi of a rampaging **Kaiju** and its hapless victim.

King Kong vs. Godzilla (1962): an example of Hollywood–Japanese co-production in the **Kaiju** genre, which preceded American TV networks' financial backing of some anime productions beginning with **Astro Boy**. Highly entertaining, fast paced, scenic with fun performances, it was hugely successful in Japan, although the American version was marred by a clumsy and unneccessary play-by-play narration with white actors and excised Japanese scenes, hurting its reputation in America.

Golgo 13: Takao Saito's manga about an amoral and laconic hit-man has sold over 200 million copies in over 45 years of continuous publication. Originally published in Shogakukan's *Big Comic Magazine* in 1968. **Golgo 13** also has anime incarnations.

Gundam: an extremely successful anime series and multi-media franchise featuring giant flying "mobile suits," produced by **Sunrise**.

Josei manga: type of manga targeting young women in their late teens into middle age. The female version of **seinen** manga.

Kaiju: translated as "strange beast" (the giant monster version is called *Daikaiju*). A Japanese genre of successful films and TV shows employing monsters as antagonists and sometimes even as protagonists that began with **Godzilla** in 1954.

King Kong: the most famous giant-ape movie (directors: Merian C. Cooper and Ernest B. Schoedsack, RKO Pictures 1933) was an inspiration for the 1954 **Godzilla**. Later fought Godzilla in the excellent **King Kong vs. Godzilla** (the American version was compromised by hack inserts of American actors).

Yukito Kishiro: brilliant **mangaka** of **Battle Angel Alita** and its sequel series, *Battle Angel Alita: Last Order* (published by Kodansha) and *Aqua Knight*. **Battle Angel Alita** was also made into an **OAV** anime. James Cameron and Fox control the film rights to **Battle Angel** (the movie project's working title).

Akira Kurosawa: legendary Japanese director whose great movies (such as *The Seven Samurai*) many **mangaka** look to for inspiration in their paneling and pacing. Also had a big impact on George Lucas (*Star Wars*) and other famous American filmmakers, whose resulting movies were often distributed in Japan and in turn influenced anime/manga creators.

Macross: created by Shoji Kawamori and a major, influential anime series as well as being subjected to an aborted Hollywood adaptation attempt. In America, titled **Robotech**.

Leiji Matsumoto: legendary **mangaka** and anime director of several manga/anime classics, including *Galaxy Express 999* and **Captain Harlock**. He began his career working with **Tezuka**.

Scott McCloud: respected American author of several famous and excellent books on comics creation including *Making Comics* and *Understanding Comics*.

Syd Mead: the Hollywood *Blade Runner* and *Tron* designer and "visual futurist" who redesigned the mobile suits and the main ship for incarnations of two epoch-making anime, *Turn A Gundam* and **Space Battleship Yamato/Star Blazers**.

Mecha: can mean robots or humanoid shaped machines, including those controlled by people.

Mighty Mouse: a cute American cartoon superhero, derivative of *Superman* and an influence on **Astro Boy**. **Tezuka** once called **Mighty Mouse** the "father" of **Astro Boy**, and **Superman** the "father" of **Mighty Mouse**.

George Miller: Australian film director and physician whose **Mad Max/Road Warrior** features impressed **Battle Angel Alita**'s **mangaka Kishiro**.

Hayao Miyazaki: famous, brilliantly insightful, grumpy, and highly influential Japanese animation director responsible for many critically acclaimed and commercially successful animated feature films, including *My Neighbor Totoro*, *Spirited Away* and *Nausicaa of the Valley of the Wind* as well as co-director on the classic *Lupin III* anime television show. Has had a very large impact on the current generation of Japanese animators. Miyazaki's influence in America, especially upon Hollywood animation powerhouse Pixar's founder **John Lasseter**, is large and his **Studio Gibili** has a business relationship with **Disney**.

Monster: Naoki Urasawa's masterpiece manga/anime (anime produced by Studio Nuts). Director **Guillermo Del Toro** has contracted with Urasawa and attempted to adapt it for HBO in America.

Haruo Nakajima: one of **Godzilla**'s suit-wearing actors. An athlete, he also played several other monsters for Toho and appeared in such productions as the **Ultra Man** television series.

One Piece: an enormously popular family-friendly pirate manga/anime and media empire. At the time of this book's publication, it has 345 million copies in print worldwide. Eiichiro Oda's manga is published in over 25 countries. Volume 69, released in March of 2013, sold 3,147,224 copies. The manga series has grossed over US $1,404,220,000 in revenue. Over 700 half-hour anime episodes have been produced and aired for the **One Piece** anime show for television. In 2015 the *Guinness World Records* committee certified the **One Piece** manga as the comic book with the most copies ever published.

One-shot: manga with a single story and conclusive ending. Some one-shots turn into serialized stories later, as happened with **Death Note**. During the interim, the story was improved before going to serialization, and the protagonist was "**aged-up**."

Katsuhiro Otomo: legendary anime director of such classics as **Akira** and *Domu* (*A Child's Dream*), the latter of which **Del Toro** has focused on adapting.

Pacific Rim: director **Guillermo Del Toro's** feature film featuring giant **mecha** and **Kaiju** (Warner Brothers Pictures, Legendary Pictures, 2013).

Powerpuff Girls: anime-styled American television animated series created by Craig McCracken. Later adapted into a Japanese anime, **Powerpuff Girls Z**.

August Ragone: American author who wrote the biography about the genius of **Kaiju** special effects, *Eiji Tsuburaya: Master of Monsters: Defending the Earth with Ultraman, Godzilla, and Friends in the Golden Age of Japanese Science Fiction Film*.

Robotech: English name of the **Macross** anime series. **Robotech** consists of the first 36 episodes of **Macross** and also two other series: *Southern Cross* and *Mospeada*.

Sazae-san: a family comedy comic that began shortly after World War II by female **mangaka** pioneer Machiko Hasegawa. Its anime is the longest-running scripted television show in world history as certified by the Guinness World Records committee (it began airing in 1969).

Seinin: a manga genre meaning "young man" of 17 into his 40s. The female version of **seinen** manga is **josei manga.**

Serialized: in this case, serialized means stories that develop over an "arc"—a multi-episode period. Serialized schedules are very grueling in the manga industry due to the large number of pages due every week.

Steve Shibuya: co-writer of ***Sucker Punch*** with **Zack Snyder**.

Joel Silver: a successful Hollywood producer who was principal producer on ***The Matrix*** trilogy and the **Wachowskis'** ***Speed Racer*** adaptation.

Zack Snyder: director of the Warner Brothers feature ***Sucker Punch*** (which is partially influenced by anime and computer games).

Eugene Son: a writer on such American animated TV shows as *Ben 10* and *Ultimate Spider-Man*.

Space Battleship Yamato: a major anime series that was influential for Hollywood creators and important in the positive impact it had on a generation of anime directors and animators as well as for its introduction of the serialized story form (**arcs**) of legions of successful anime localized into America after that. In America, the modern title is ***Star Blazers***.

Chibi of an exhausted **mangaka** staying up late with the help of cigarettes and an energy drink to make a serialization deadline.

Studio Gibili: **Hayao Miyazaki**'s production company/studio. Produced a series of very successful and critically acclaimed animated features including *Spirited Away*.

suitmation: a type of cinematic genre featuring monster suits manned by actors and possibly descended from a type of traditional Japanese puppetry (**Bunraku**). **Suitmation** is often used in **Kaiju** and **tokusatsu** shows. Hollywood movies such as *Where the Wild Things Are* (2009) also used **suitmation**.

Tankōbon: individual graphic novels that are compiled from successful manga that are previously published in larger format magazines that run several series simultaneously.

Tokusatsu: Japanese live-action films or television shows that employ extensive special effects (**Tokusatsu** literally translates as "special filming") and are often typified by the science fiction or horror genres. They are known for their use of **suitmation**.

Chibi of an expired **Kaiju** and its equally exhausted "victim."

Tsuburaya Productions: the production company of Eiji Tsuburaya, the "master of monsters." As Eiji Tsuburaya became famous, this company also produced several television shows.

Ultra Q: a Japanese live-action television show that was similar to the classic USA shows *The Outer Limits* and *The Twilight Zone* and originally had a monster-of-the-week-type format.

Voltron: massive sword-wielding-robot-starring anime was **localized** by American Peter Keefe, who purchased the American broadcast rights. Keefe did not have Japanese transcripts to the show's dialogue and thus invented English language scripts, guessing the plots. **Voltron** became the top syndicated show in America, with impressive merchandising sales.

Shinichirō Watanabe: director of **Cowboy Beebop**, a 1988 film noir/sci-fi anime series that was a big hit, including in America, and also *Space Dandy* and *Samurai Champloo*.

Weekly Shonen Jump: the flagship and most popular weekly manga magazine in the world, published by **Shueisha**, established in 1968. Its circulation peaked at 6.53 million in 1995.

Chapter 2

A.I. Artificial Intelligence: A long-time Stanley Kubrick project before he died, this highly underrated, disturbing, and compelling movie (director: Steven Spielberg, Warner Brothers, 2001) has some touches that resemble **Astro Boy**, which Kubrick had been impressed with earlier in his career.

Akihabara: the famous electronics products district in Tokyo where many **otaku** congregate. It is named after a local shrine.

All You Need Is Kill: a Japanese novel that was adapted into *Edge of Tomorrow*, a Tom Cruise starring Warner Brothers movie in 2013 as well as a manga with art by **Death Note**/**Bakuman**'s superstar manga artist Takeshi Obata.

Barefoot Gen: a ten-volume manga and two-part feature-length anime that depicts a family enduring the dropping of the atom bomb on Hiroshima and its aftermath—where **Keiji Nakazawa**, its **mangaka**, was a little boy. Brave and irrepressible protagonist "Gen" is modeled after **Nakazawa**. One of the greatest anti-war stories ever told. The manga has sold over 10 million copies.

Berserk: the manga/anime creation of Kentaro Miura, about a lone wandering swordsman in an alternate world filled with violence, an expression of the philosophical concept of causality.

Black Jack: now **Tezuka**'s most popular creation. As a boy, he was torn apart by the same bomb that kills his mother and is then sewn back together by a father figure/mentor surgeon. As an adult, Black Jack becomes the world's highest-priced surgeon, with a fascinating morally ambiguous nature.

Bleach: a very successful anime/manga franchise about a young man and his friends' adventures in the world of spirits mixed with school life (Tite Kubo).

The Comics Code: the code of 1954 was a self-imposed form of strict censorship that the American comics publishers placed on themselves in response to parental and political concerns about the content of certain American comics at the time. It severely damaged the

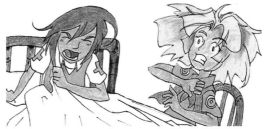

American comics industry by almost entirely destroying diversity and eliminating most interesting storytelling and characters. Though under similar pressure at times, Japanese publishers never created such a constricting code and were able to maintain a broad variety of stories/characters.

Death Note: one of the greatest thriller stories ever, this popular manga/anime features an amoral Japanese death god named Ryuk whose design is influenced by the look of *Edward Scissorhands*. Ryuk, bored with the drudgery of hell, decides to create some entertainment for himself when he drops a notebook into the human world that allows the owner to kill anyone whose name he writes in it. An absolutely fascinating plot ensues when the Death Note is found by a high-performing high school student who decides to use it to rid the world of criminals and goes power-mad with a "god complex" in the process. Ryuk, traveling to Earth to watch this play out, is thoroughly amused. By Tsugumi Ohba (writer) and Takeshi Obata (artist) (**Shueisha**).

Deliberate decompression: time and spatial deformation which comes from Japanese storytelling and infuses the manga/anime forms, giving them part of their distinct Japanese characteristics.

Dragonball: enormously successful Japanese manga/anime franchise that was adapted into a Hollywood film, ***Dragonball Evolution*** (director: James Wong, 20th Century Fox, 2009).

Jason Hoffs: a producer of *Edge of Tomorrow* and the ***Death Note*** Hollywood adaptation. A former executive of DreamWorks.

Robert Napton: an American graphic novel writer as well as a former editor at Bandai Entertainment, which, along with **Sunrise**, distributed the ***Gundam*** franchise in America. Currently Vice President and Editorial Director of Legendary Comics (Legendary Entertainment is the company that produced ***Pacific Rim*** and the modern Hollywood hit version of ***Godzilla***—director: Gareth Edwards, along with Warner Brothers Pictures, 2014). **Napton** story-edited ***Godzilla***'s graphic novel prequel.

Otaku: in Japan, the term often refers to people who are obsessive about manga/anime, but in America it generally has a more benign and friendly meaning, akin to "a big manga/anime fan." In Japan, **otaku** have a lot of financial buying power, to which the marketplace tries to cater.

Commodore Matthew Perry: in 1853, this American sailed into Tokyo's harbor and was able to get almost all his demands from the Japanese authorities at the time. The arrival of Perry's famous navy "black ships" (a term that also signified the threat to the Japanese from foreign technology) opened up Japan to foreign influences, forced the Japanese to rush to "catch up and overtake," and formed a tangential or main plot to some manga/anime such as *Rurouni Kenshin*.

Princess Knight: **Tezuka**'s first big **shōjo** hit about a princess pretending to be a knight so her father's kingdom could be safe (he had no sons).

Shōjo: the wildly popular female-oriented manga/anime genre focusing on "affairs of the heart" and thus dealing heavily with emotions and relationships and often with its own abstract symbols and style. Pioneered by **Tezuka** but later taken over by mostly female creators, several of whom became the most successful **mangaka**.

Takarazuka Revue: the famous all-women musical revue that had a big impact on **Tezuka**'s development of manga, particularly the **shōjo** genre, as well as the gender ambiguity of some of his characters. Located in **Tezuka**'s home city of Takarazuka. His mother took him to shows there as a child, deeply impressing the boy with their often over-the-top performances of global stories (everything from musical adaptations of Hollywood films to Parisian revues). The actresses' mascara-lined eyes, combined with footlights that made their pupils appear huge, along with other influences like *Betty Boop* and **Disney** movie classic character Bambi's eyes, inspired **Tezuka** to invent the window-pane-sized eyes characteristic of manga/anime, designed to enable audiences to relate to the characters' powerful emotions ("the eyes are the windows to the soul").

Tezuka's "star system": instead of isolating his characters to one manga series, **Tezuka** frequently would recast them in different works. Their visual designs would remain the same, but their personalities might or might not be altered. Similar to the classic-era Hollywood star system.

VIZ Media: the most successful publisher of manga in North America. Also, a major distributor of anime. Located in San Francisco and founded by American manga publishing industry pioneer Seiji Horibuchi

Chapter 3

akahon books: also known as "red books," printed on rough, cheap paper, and used red ink. Immediately after World War II ended, several red book publishers sprung up in Osaka, near **Tezuka**'s home town, and were instrumental in giving him his first chance to begin publishing his manga after he was initially rejected by Tokyo publishers. Later, the Tokyo publishers embraced him and he moved there.

Betty Boop: sexy 1920s big-eyed female created by the Fleischer brothers. Had a big impact on many early **mangaka**. Besides her huge eyes' impact on manga and anime characters, **Betty Boop**'s high-pitched voice may also have influenced that of many anime females.

Black Pete: a **Disney** villain who continued appearing in *Donald Duck* and inspired **Tezuka**'s pirate Buku Bukk and who also plays Pirate Bowarl in *Shintakarajima* (*New Treasure Island*).

Peter Chung: director of the *Matriculated* segment of the *The Animatrix* anime and the avante-garde *Aeon Flux* (which he also created) for MTV—an early hybrid anime broadcast on American television.

The Diary of Little Ma: an example of **Tezuka**'s early comic work before his break-out "story manga" *New Treasure Island*.

Walt Disney: the legendary founder of the famous **Disney** family of characters and its movie studio, and who inspired and stewarded its animation classics and later, Disneyland and Walt Disney World. **Disney** animation and comics had a significant impact upon **Tezuka** and other **mangakas**' early works and manga's "birth" and development into its modern form. **Disney**'s estate heavily funded the creation of the California Institute of the Arts, which would in turn graduate major Hollywood animators and animation directors, many of them manga/anime-influenced.

Donald Duck: This popular **Disney** character was an influence on **Tezuka**'s style.

Fleischer brothers: Dave and Max Fleischer were a New York filmmaking pair who created ***Betty Boop*** and produced the animated versions of *Superman* and *Popeye*. These were big influences on **Tezuka** and other **mangaka** and anime directors (**Miyazaki** mentions their works as influences).

Floating World culture: began in the red-light district of Edo (modern Tokyo). It was a celebration of the fleeting nature of life and youth before the onset of decay and death. Later it spread to other cities like Osaka. Geisha, Kabuki actors, samurai, and nature were often the subjects of the mass-produced woodblock prints about the "Floating World" culture called **Ukiyo-e**.

Kami-shibai (or **paper theaters**): a form of theater in which a performer would show ornately drawn picture boards inserted in sequence in a frame as he narrated. The performer traveled between performance locations on a bicycle, onto which he would attach the frame containing the picture boards. Another forerunner of manga. Once great in number, they largely disappeared with the advent of television and film, although a few remain.

Keiji Nakazawa: **mangaka** of ***Barefoot Gen***, the atomic bomb manga/anime and several other successful manga.

Opera Joe: According to manga scholar Ryan Holmburg, **Opera Joe** was the nickname of an unknown black American serviceman during the occupation who sang opera while **Tezuka** played piano while skipping his medical school classes. He gave **Tezuka** American comics as a gift, which were rare and invaluable for **Tezuka** in developing manga's style.

Pinocchio: Italian author Carlo Collodi's wooden puppet who grew a soul and conscience was animated by **Disney**'s team. Was a major influence on **Astro Boy**'s character. It also, along with ***Astro Boy***, probably influenced the Spielberg/Kubrick Hollywood film ***A.I. Artificial Intelligence***.

Scrooge McDuck: created by **Disney** animator Carl Barks, he was the rich uncle to hapless **Donald Duck**. Had a major impact on **Tezuka**'s style.

Shintakarajima (***New Treasure Island***): **Tezuka**'s break-out first manga hit, which sold over 400,000 copies in the devastated post-war economy of 1947. It had a massive impact on other fledgling **mangaka** and brought the highly cinematic modern "story manga" form into existence.

Snow White and the Seven Dwarfs: **Walt Disney**'s hit animated movie that, like other Disney classic animation from that period, had a major impact on **Keiji Nakazawa**, **Tezuka**, and other **mangaka**.

Ukiyo-e: manga's predecessor, the famous Japanese woodblock prints printed in many colors and mass-produced. **Ukiyo-e** depicted the "**Floating World**" culture. Included in its subject matter were the brothels, Kabuki theaters, and teahouses that were frequented by the expanding middle class.

Vaudeville: an American form of comedy that pre-dates motion pictures and died out not long after the advent of sound in film. Vaudevillian actors and performers would go on stage, "do their bits," and exit. Many early Hollywood stars came from a vaudeville background, and early American animation characters that influenced manga were often based upon Hollywood actors.

Charles Wirgman: an English cartoonist and illustrator (1832–91) who created *Japan Punch*, thus introducing Western cartooning style (consisting of single or paired satirical drawings) to Japan. He was a correspondent for the *Illustrated London News* in Yokohama, Japan. **Wirgman** also trained **Ukiyo-e** artists in Western-style drawing. And soon the Japanese acquired Western printing skills and technology, which made the expensive **Ukiyo-e** techniques outdated, and paved the way for manga's eventual rise and mass production.

Zen Pictures: the process of creating these pictures was supposed to allow the creator to reach a state of spiritual enlightenment.

Chapter 5

Deb Aoki: prominent anime/manga industry journalist and writer for *Publisher's Weekly* and other important periodicals.

Canning (kan-zume): the process by which **mangaka**, when they appear to be in danger of being late delivering their pages, are sequestered by their editors to finish their pages, often in a hotel room.

Dark Horse: prominent American graphic novel and manga publisher.

Seiji Horibuchi: founder of **VIZ Media**, the top North American publisher of manga.

Robert Kirkman: American creator of *The Walking Dead* graphic novel whose publisher (Image) allowed him to keep ancillary rights, and thus he benefitted tremendously when it became a hit American television show.

Salil Mehra: at the time of this book's interview with him, he was an international copyright law professor at Temple University's Beasley School of Law.

Moebius: a famous French artist, cartoonist, and writer, his real name was Jean Henri Gaston Giraud (1938–2012), who, incidentally, contributed storyboards and concept designs to landmark films such as *Alien* (director: Ridley Scott) as well as *The Abyss* (director: James Cameron). He was admired by **Miyazaki**.

A fed-up **mangaka** who is being "canned" tries to escape her editor out of a hotel window.

The Prince of Tennis: a popular manga/anime series by Takeshi Konomi that debuted in 1999. Published by **Shueisha**. Uses **deliberate decompression**, a hallmark of sports manga/anime.

Hikaru Sasahara: owner and President of Digital Manga Publishing (DMP), known in part for publishing mainstream titles like ***Berserk*** (with Dark Horse). *Vampire Hunter D* and also yaoi genre manga.

Felipe Smith: an Argentinian who created the manga ***Peepo Choo*** in Japan (which was serialized in Kodansha's *Morning* magazine, 2008–10).

Chapter 6

ADR (Automatic Dialogue Replacement): in live-action movies and television, the process where actors come into a recording studio to redub dialogue that wasn't recorded perfectly on the set, or to improve the previously recorded dialogue performance. They match the mouth movements as closely as possible.

Afureko[a]: stands for "after recording" and refers to the process of dubbing animation after production of visuals is complete, or as a process subordinate to the image production. The opposite of **puresuko**.

Batman: the iconic American DC comic about a caped avenger, which also was adapted into Japanese manga by early **mangaka** Jiro Kuwata. Became a multimedia Hollywood franchise. Batman's crime fighting sidekick Robin also appears in an American animated television show, *Teen Titans*, which has heavy anime styling.

Bewitched: a 1960s American television show comedy, starring Elizabeth Montgomery, about a female witch who is married to a normal human man (Japanese title, *My Wife is a Witch*). Said to have influenced **Magical Girl** anime/manga genre.

Broadcasting syndication: the sale of the right to broadcast radio and television shows by multiple radio and television stations. The American television syndication market is large and potentially very lucrative, and was the distribution model for *Astro Boy*, *Speed Racer*, and many other anime.

Hanna-Barbera: incredibly prolific low-cost animators of American limited-animation shows such as *The Flintstones* and *Wacky Racers* (which were also successful in Japan).

Hidden Fortress (literally, The Three Villains of the Hidden Fortress): a classic feature film by **Akira Kurosawa** that heavily influenced *Star Wars*.

I Dream of Jeannie: a 1960s American comedy/fantasy television show, starring Larry Hagman and Barbara Eden, about a magical female genie and a male astronaut with whom she is infatuated (in Japan, *Cute Witch Jeannie*). Said to have influenced **Magical Girl** anime/manga genre, including *Little Witch Sally*, **Tezuka**'s *Marvelous Melmo*, and the later superhit *Sailor Moon*.

Kimba the White Lion (*The Jungle Emperor*): the classic **Tezuka** manga about a young lion cub who is orphaned after his parents are killed by humans and grows up to be a great leader of animals towards peaceful co-existence. Was also adapted into the first color anime to be broadcast in the United States in close cooperation with NBC TV network—which was active from the story treatment stage (from when **Tezuka** proposed *Kimba* to them), onward. NBC co-financed the production.

Fred Ladd: a localizer who worked with NBC on the *Astro Boy* anime, successfully adapting it

---

[a] Definition provided by Michael Arias.

for American culture. He followed up with several other classic and major anime localization successes, including ***Gigantor*** and ***Kimba the White Lion*** for broadcast on American television in the first wave of anime to come to the US during the 1960s. Author of the book *Astro Boy Comes to the Americas* (written with Harvey Deneroff).

Localization: the process of dubbing and re-editing a show or movie to be understood and hopefully successful in the local culture where it is being broadcast/exhibited. Localizers can rewrite scripts, adjust the work to line up with local cultural norms, and supervise the local language voice actors' performances.

Mushi Productions: **Tezuka**'s first anime production company. Produced ***Astro Boy*** and many other anime, including *Ashita No Joe*, *1001 Nights*, and *Cleopatra* (the first X-rated animated film).

OAV: a type of anime, which is distributed in a similar way to "direct-to-video" film titles in America. These anime are often not broadast on TV and are often more edgy and adult.

Pinocchio in Outer Space: an animated project that Fred Ladd had previously worked on that, due to its success, made NBC executives think that ***Astro Boy*** might become successful in America.

Pokémon: a successful anime/merchandising hit in America that jump-started the beginning of the new millennium's cycle of manga/anime popularity in America.

Puresuko[b]: "pre-scoring," the technique common outside of East Asia wherein dialogue is recorded a priori. The opposite of **afureko**.

Don Rockwell: writer of the English lyrics of the ***Astro Boy*** theme song. It became a major hit record for American children, and **Tezuka** liked it so much that he commissioned a Japanese translation of the English words that then became part of the Japanese show's **Tatsuo Takai**-composed opening music.

Rocky Horror Picture Show: a bizarre rock opera and later highly successful cult film. ***The Rocky Horror Picture Show***'s intergalactic transvestite character Dr. Frank-N-Furter (played in that live-action movie by Tim Curry) was referenced in the naming of the character Franken Von Vogler of the anime *Giant Robo* **OAV** series according to *Giant Robo*'s director Yasuhiro Imagawa.

Tatsuo Takai: composer of the orchestral march opening music for ***Astro Boy***.

---

[b] Definition provided by Michael Arias.

Transformers: originally a 1986 animated movie and TV show produced at nearly the same time. It was adapted by Hollywood into a blockbuster live-action movie franchise (director: Michael Bay, Dreamworks, 2007, 2009, 2011, 2013, 2014), with its first three films grossing almost $3 billion worldwide. Featuring the Japanese giant robot aesthetic, ***Transformers***, although not directly derived from a manga or anime, is, according to **Robert Napton**, based on a Hasbro toy line that is itself based on the Diaclone and Microman toy lines originally created by Japanese toy manufacturer Takara.

Chapter 7

Arcs: in manga and anime, storylines that go on for several episodes. Frequently in anime adapted for TV, "**arcs**" last for a viewing season, making them a natural fit for television. Many arcs are defined by their own separate villains.

Battle manga: manga where fighting contests predominate and can involve major deliberate decompression.

Joseph Campbell (born 1904, died 1987): author of the classic book about comparative mythology *The Hero with A Thousand Faces*. Campbell was a specialist on myth studies, the knowledge of which can be applied to storytelling. George Lucas and **George Miller** are fans of Campbell's studies and his interview by Bill Moyers took place at Lucas's Skywalker Ranch.

Character herding: **mangaka** have developed ways to handle the massive number of characters often found in a long serialized manga, including by **sidelining** characters or grouping them into geometric and mathematical forms like "Love Dodecahedron" and "Unwanted Harem" (see TV.tropes.org for these and many more).

Character shot-gunning: a term invented by my student Andrew Cross for the frequent practice of some **mangaka** on long-running shōnen series of hurling large numbers of new characters into the plot hoping a few will grab the reader's interest. Allegedly ***Dragonball***'s **mangaka** Akira Toriyami had over 500 characters and did not remember some of their names.

Fighting arcs: a form of **filler arcs** and can sometime take **deliberate-decompression** to the extreme, with some fights lasting dozens of pages each.

Filler arcs: anime series often "get ahead" of the manga story on which they are based due to the faster rate anime is produced for TV. Scores of animators progress more quickly than the more artisan-like set-up of the **mangaka** and their smaller team of assistants who would have to rush to keep up with the anime team's faster production. To combat this, the anime producers may have to create their own **arcs** to stall for time while the **mangaka** and their team catches up.

Grand Fisher: a villain in ***Bleach***, who has his own small **arc**.

Tite Kubo: **mangaka** of the successful shōnen manga/anime franchise ***Bleach***.

Ryuk: ***Death Note***'s Shinigami death-god character, modeled partially on the Tim Burton film *Edward Scissorhands*' title character's appearance.

Sir Ridley Scott: Hollywood director (including of legendary science fiction movies *Blade Runner* and *Alien* as well as *Thelma and Louise* and *Gladiator*). *Blade Runner*'s look was influenced in part by Hong Kong's cityscapes as well as European comics like *Heavy Metal* and **Scott**'s own rainy North England upbringing, and in turn had an impact on several manga/anime.

Sidelining characters: the practice of **mangaka** taking characters out of the action or story for a while, and sometimes a very long time—usually for the purpose of making room to introduce other characters into the series. This is especially necessary when shot-gunning new characters into the story and because manga series running many years can accumulate so many characters.

Chapter 8

Geof Darrow: a prominent and highly imaginative artist/graphic novelist who worked with Frank Miller on various projects and who was also a lead conceptual designer on the **Wachowskis'** creative teams for *Speed Racer* and the *Matrix* trilogy.

Peter Fernandez: well-known localizer, first hired by *Astro Boy*'s American localizer **Fred Ladd** to write scripts and dub lines for *Astro Boy* and *Gigantor*. His most famous localization was for the *Speed Racer* anime. Appears in a cameo in the **Wachowskis'** *Speed Racer* adaptation.

John Gaeta: brilliant visual effects designer who pioneered with **Lana** and **Andy Wachowski** and the rest of their team the breakthrough techniques of the manga-and-anime-influenced *Matrix* trilogy and *Speed Racer* films.

Goldfinger: the classic James Bond movie (director: Guy Hamilton, United Artists, 1964) that was a huge hit in Japan and allegedly influenced the original *Speed Racer* manga and anime.

Grant Hill: Academy Award-winning Hollywood producer whose high-end adventurous and artistically ambitious films include the **Wachowskis'** *Speed Racer* adaptation and the *Matrix* sequels, both with principal producer **Joel Silver**. Hill was also a producer on *V For Vendetta*, *Tree of Life*, *The Thin Red Line*, *Jupiter Ascending*, *Titanic* and executive producer on the TV show *Sense8*.

Roy Lee: a successful Hollywood producer who has specialized in Asian remakes. Some of his commercially successful films include the 2007 Academy Award-winning *The Departed* (adapted from the Hong Kong movie *Infernal Affairs*) as well as horror films adapted from Japan (titled *The Ring and The Grudge* in Hollywood). He also produced *The Lego Movie* and is a principal producer on the *Death Note* Hollywood adaptation project along with Dan Lin, **Jason Hoffs** and Masi Oka.

Mahiro Maeda: director of the two *The Second Renaissance* segments of *The Animatrix*.

Speed Racer (in Japanese: ***MACH GO GO GO***): the original manga was adapted into the anime television show created by the three Tatsunoko brothers and became the biggest anime hit in America of the original wave of anime to be aired there. It has been syndicated worldwide and remains popular. It was remade into a Hollywood movie by the **Wachowskis** in 2008.

The Tatsunoko brothers: the creators of *Speed Racer*, consisting of Toyoharu Yoshida—a.k.a. Ippei Kuri (the youngest), Kenji Yoshida (anime producer and illustrator), and Tatsuo Yoshida.

Viva Las Vegas: an Elvis Presley movie (director: George Sidney, MGM, 1964) that was a big hit in Japan and apparently influenced the original *Speed Racer* manga and anime.

Lana and Andy Wachowski (a.k.a. **the Wachowskis**): inspired, innovative, and influential writers/directors of the anime/manga live-action adaptation *Speed Racer* and the anime-influenced *Matrix* trilogy, and producers of *The Animatrix* (and writers/directors of some segments). Like fellow A-list Hollywood director **Guillermo Del Toro**, the **Wachowski** siblings are, to all intents and purposes, scholars of manga/anime. Also directed the critically acclaimed, visually stunning movies *Cloud Atlas* and *Bound* as well as the wild and wacky *Jupiter Ascending*. These were followed by their television show *Sense8* (along with J. Michael Straczynski), which aired beginning in 2015–16.

Christine Yoo: co-writer on the anime television series *Afro Samurai* voiced by Hollywood actor Samuel Jackson, produced by GDH/Gonzo for America's Spike TV and Japan's Fuji TV, and a director.

Chapter 9

Aging up: the process of increasing a character's age, often to try to make him/her more relatable to the audience or readership; sometimes used in the American animation market.

David Bowers: director of the ***Astro Boy*** adaptation movie (previously directed *Flushed Away*).

Nicolas Cage: a Hollywood actor and comic-book collector who was the voice of **Astro**'s scientist/stepfather **Dr. Temna** in the David Bowers directed ***Astro Boy*** remake.

Chain of title: refers to the question of who owns the rights to anime, television shows, feature films, and so on. For various reasons examined in this book, **chain of title** can be complicated in Japan.

Dr. Temna: **Astro Boy**'s scientist/creator/father figure at the beginning of the original story, before rejecting **Astro**. **Temna** is the Director General of the Ministry of Science and Technology.

Errors and omissions insurance policy: used in part to protect the policy holder for inadvertent or unintentional errors in terms of ownership of title that may later cause problems. Additionally, it can protect writers who are added to the policy from having to pay to defend media lawsuits, which are very expensive even if they have no merit.

Joyce Jun: a Hollywood lawyer who partially specializes in Asian/Hollywood rights negotiations.

Mr. Mustachio: one of **Astro**'s two mentor figures and his teacher.

Studio rights form: A standardized document or set of criteria that the Hollywood studios try to adhere to when negotiating to obtain the rights to make movies and television shows from underlying works like books and comics.

Ken Tsumura: a producer of the ***Astro Boy*** Hollywood adaptation and an executive at Taiwan's Next Animation and previously at **Disney**.

Uran: **Astro**'s robot sister, built and given to him along with his robot parents by **Astro**'s other mentor, kindly Professor Ochanomizu, so that **Astro** can also have a normal family life.

Chapter 10

Green-light: a commitment to put the film or television show into active production.

Pitching: verbally presenting a story hoping to be hired to write/direct/produce it.

Production bonus: here defined as back-end money paid to credited screenwriters. Specifically, the bonus paid upon the actual production (shooting) of the film or television show to the credited writers. Which writers get credited is often decided by the **Writers Guild of America**.

Treatment: a story document that serves as the basis of a screenplay, TV series, etc. project.

WGA arbitration: the procedure in which credits are determined when at least one writer challenges the credits that were issued by the production company, studio, network, and so on.

Writer's Guild of America, West (or **WGA, West**): the Hollywood screen and TV writers' guild/ union with jurisdiction over all members who live west of the Mississippi River. The WGA, East covers those WGA members residing east of the river.

Chapter 11

Armored Troopers Votoms: A gritty **mecha** anime. Ryosuki Takahashi, another high-level **Sunrise** anime director, writer, and producer, said that anime's premise was partially inspired by an American rodeo movie, *Junior Bonner* (director: Sam Peckinpah, and starring Steve McQueen).

Avatar: The Last Airbender (Avatar: The Legend of Aang in some regions): an American hit animated television series that successfully incorporates elements of anime, American animation, and Chinese visual style and culture into its stories, characters, and visual design.

Ian Condry: MIT Associate Professor, cultural anthropologist, and author who specializes in media and popular culture including the Japanese anime industry. His book on the latter subject is *The Soul of Anime: Collaborative Creativity and Japan's Media Success Story* (Duke Press).

In-betweeners: before the advent of computer animation, the people who performed this job drew or painted the many animation cells "in between" the main key frames.

Jeffrey Katzenberg: successful Hollywood movie and Dreamworks studio animation executive known in part for his cultural sensitivity in developing the ***Kung Fu Panda*** movie series.

Key frame: the main reference frames often created in Japan or the United States. In the case of anime, they can be based upon images from the manga.

Kung Fu Panda: Dreamworks' blockbuster franchise that successfully incorporated Chinese culture into its storyline and visual style, helping making it a huge hit in the Peoples Republic of China as well and worldwide.

John Lasseter: CEO and a founder of Pixar and a big **Hayao Miyazaki** fan.

Sanford Panitch: President of International Film and Television at Sony Pictures.

Powerpuff Girls Z: the Japanese adaptation of ***Powerpuff Girls***. The original ***Powerpuff Girls*** was created by American Craig McCracken and has an anime style.

Samurai Jack: an example of a manga/anime-influenced American animation television show in a stylistic sense, but not based upon a pre-existing manga/anime's stories or characters.

Sym-Bionic Titan: like ***Powerpuff Girls***, ***Teen Titans***, and ***Samurai Jack***, this is an example of a manga/anime-influenced American animation television show in a stylistic sense, but is not based upon an existing manga/anime's stories or characters. Created by Genndy Tartakovsky, who also invented ***Samurai Jack*** and the anime-styled *Dexter's Laboratory* TV shows.

Teen Titans: teen spin-off American animation television show of the DC ***Batman*** property and with an anime style.

Yoshiyuki Tomino: has been called the "father of ***Gundam***," the hugely successful anime universe/franchise, as well as being noted for work on anime such as *Brave Radeen*. He is also a novelist and writer. Tomino cited the space-colony concept from *Star Wars* as being an influence upon ***Gundam***.

Endnotes

Preface

1   Jonathan Clements and Motoko Tamamuro, *The Dorama Encyclopedia: A Guide to Japanese TV Drama Since 1953* (Berkeley, CA: Stone Bridge Press, 2003), xvii.

2   Helen McCarthy, *The Art of Osamu Tezuka: God of Manga* (New York: Abrams ComicArts, 2009), 188.

3   Charles Solomon, "Ward Kimball, 88, Key Disney Animator," *Los Angeles Times*, July 9, 2002, http://articles.latimes.com/2002/jul/09/local/me-kimball9 (accessed May 23, 2014).

4   Ryan Wilson, "History of the Disneyland Railroad," Justdisney.com, http://www.justdisney.com/Features/disneyland_railroad/ (accessed October 16, 2014).

5   Marc Perez, "An Open Letter to the Attendees of Anime Expo," AnimeExpo.org, July 22, 2014, http://www.anime-expo.org/2014/07/an-open-letter-to-the-attendees-of-anime-expo/ (accessed July 29, 2014).

Chapter 1

1   "The Rise and Fall of *Weekly Shonen Jump*: A Look at the Circulation of *Weekly Jump*," ComiPress, May 6, 2007, http://comipress.com/article/2007/05/06/1923 (accessed April 3, 2015).

2   "The Rise and Fall of *Weekly Shonen Jump*," May 6, 2007, http://comipress.com/article/2007/05/06/1923 (accessed April 3, 2015).

3   "List of Best Selling Manga," Wikipedia, https://en.wikipedia.org/wiki/List_of_best-selling_manga (accessed October 16, 2014).

4   "*One Piece* Manga Has 345 Million Copies in Print Worldwide," Anime News Network, http://www.animenewsnetwork.com/news/2013-11-21/one-piece-manga-has-345-million-copies-in-print-worldwide (accessed November 22, 2013).

5   Harry Lodge, "Scholastic Celebrates 15 Years of *Harry Potter*," *Publishers Weekly*, June 11, 2013, http://www.publishersweekly.com/pw/by-topic/childrens/childrens-industry-news/article/57780-scholastic-celebrates-15-years-of-harry-potter.html (accessed June 14, 2014).

6   Albert Ching, "The 10 Bestselling Comic Book Issues of the Past Decade," Newsarama, September 12, 2011, http://www.newsarama.com/15422-the-10-bestselling-comic-book-issues-of-the-past-decade.html (accessed September 15, 2014).

7   Ibid.

8   Dawn Bryant, "Top Selling Manga in 2013," Saiyanisland, December 1, 2013, http://www.saiyanisland.com/2013/12/top-selling-manga-in-2013/ (accessed December 5, 2014).

9   "Top 10 *Shonen Jump* Manga by All-Time Volume Sales," Anime News Network,

October 23, 2012, http://www.animenewsnetwork.com/news/2012-10-23/top-10-shonen-jump-manga-by-all-time-volume-sales (accessed October 29, 2013).

10 *One Piece* Anime, Vizanime.com VIZ Website, http://www.vizanime.com/one-piece (accessed October 15, 2014).

11 Atsushi Ohara, "Manga *Golgo 13* Celebrates 45 Years of Continuous Publication," *The Asahi Shimbun*, December 2, 2013, http://ajw.asahi.com/article/cool_japan/style/AJ201312020004 (accessed February 3, 2014).

12 Ibid.

13 "*Golgo 13* Author Saito Discusses Manga's Hypothetical Ending," Anime News Network, November 16, 2013, http://www.animenewsnetwork.com/news/2013-11-16/golgo-13-author-saito-discusses-manga-hypothetical-ending (accessed December 15, 2014).

14 "List of Best Selling Manga," Wikipedia, https://en.wikipedia.org/wiki/List_of_best-selling_manga (accessed October 16, 2014).

15 Nobuo Masuda, "*Space Battleship Yamato*," email to author, July 11, 2014.

16 "Namco Bandai Holdings, Inc: Financial Highlights for the Fiscal Year Ended March 2014," Bandainamco.com, May 8, 2014, http://www.bandainamco.co.jp/files/E8A39CE8B 6B3E8B387E69699EFBC88E88BB1EFBC89.pdf (accessed December 10, 2014).

17 Rob Bricken, "*Gundam* Is Coming to America. All of It.," Io9, http://io9.com/gundam-is-coming-to-america-all-of-it-1647066568 (accessed October 15, 2014).

18 Tadashi Sudo, "Bandai Predicts More *Gundam* Sales, But Lower Toy/Model Sales," Anime News Network, May 5, 2012, http://www.animenewsnetwork.com/news/2012-05-12/bandai-predicts-more-gundam-sales-but-lower-toy/model-sales (accessed December 10, 2014).

19 David Kalat, *A Critical History and Filmography of Toho's Godzilla Series*, 2nd edn (Jefferson, NC: McFarland & Co, 2010), 85.

20 "*Ultraman*," Wikipedia, http://en.wikipedia.org/wiki/Ultraman (accessed October 18, 2014).

21 "Original *Godzilla* Reflects on Monster's Legacy," http://www.cbsnews.com/news/original-godzilla-actor-keeping-monstrous-legacy-alive/ (accessed November 1, 2014).

22 "Guinness Certifies *Sazae-San* as Longest Running Animated Show," *Mainichi Shimbun*, August 5, 2013, http://www.animenewsnetwork.com/news/2013-09-05/guinness-certifies-sazae-san-as-longest-running-animated-show (accessed August 8, 2013).

23 "Paper: Sazae-san's Father to Be Played by Staff After Voice Actor's Passing," *Daily Sports*, http://www.animenewsnetwork.com/news/2014-02-03/paper-sazae-san-father-to-be-played-by-staff-after-voice-actor-passing (accessed October 13, 2014).

24 Ian Condry, interview by author, January 24, 2012.

25 Scott McCloud, *Making Comics: Storytelling Secrets of Comics, Manga and Graphic Novels* (New York: Harper, 2006), 216.

26 Frederik L. Schodt, *The Astro Boy Essays: Osamu Tezuka*, Mighty Atom, *and the Manga/Anime Revolution* (Berkeley, CA: Stone Bridge Press, 2007), 77.

27 "Manga Sales Grew Over 6% in U.S. in 2013 So Far," Anime News Network, November 11, 2013, http://www.animenewsnetwork.com/news/2013-11-21/manga-sales-grew-over-6-percent-in-u.s-in-2013-so-far (accessed November 11, 2013).

28 Nobuo Masuda, "Fact Check *Captain Ultra* TV Series," email to author, August 26, 2014.

29 "*Ultraman*," Wikipedia, http://en.wikipedia.org/wiki/Ultramanhttp://en.wikipedia.org/wiki/Ultraman (accessed November 1, 2014).

30 Gerald Peary, "Missing Links: The Jungle Origins of *King Kong*," *Gerald Peary Film Reviews, Interviews, Essays & Sundry Miscellany*, http://www.geraldpeary.com/essays/jkl/kingkong-1.html (accessed October 13, 2014).

31 August Ragone, *Eiji Tsuburaya: Master of Monsters: Defending the Earth with Ultraman, Godzilla, and Friends in the Golden Age of Japanese Science Fiction Film* (San Francisco: Chronicle Books, 2007), 46.

32 Ibid., 47.

33 Ibid., 66.

34 Ibid.

35 Ibid., 46.

36 "Tokusatsu," Wikipedia, http://en.wikipedia.org/wiki/Tokusatsu (accessed May 11, 2014).

37 Ibid.

38 Nobuo Masuda, "Fact Check *Captain Ultra* TV Series," email to author, August 26, 2014.

39 John Gaeta, interview by author, July 25, 2014.

40 Roland Keltz and Peter Fernandez, "*Speed Racer* Film a Far Cry from Its Anime Roots (Interview with Roland Kelts and Peter Fernandez)," interview by Elizabeth Blair, *National Public Radio*, May 8, 2008, http://www.npr.org/templates/story/story.php?storyId=90268450 (accessed June 4, 2015).

41 Paul Lichter, *Elvis in Vegas* (New York: Overlook Duckworth, 2011), 64.

42 Eric Ditzian, "Fourth *Mad Max* In Development … As 3-D Anime Feature," MTV Movies Blog, March 5, 2009, http://moviesblog.mtv.com/2009/03/05/exclusive-fourth-mad-max-in-developmentas-3-d-anime-feature/(accessed June 29, 2014).

43 Yukito Kishiro, interview by Yoko Hayashi, March 9, 2012.

44 Susan Jolliffe Napier, *Anime from Akira to Howl's Moving Castle: Experiencing Contemporary Japanese Animation* (New York: Palgrave Macmillan, 2005), 22–3.

45 Hayao Miyazaki, *Starting Point 1979–1996*, trans. Beth Cary and Frederik L. Schodt (San Francisco: VIZ Media, 2008), 233.

46 Trish Ledoux, *Anime Interviews: The First Five Years of* Animerica, Anime & Manga Monthly *(1992–97)* (San Francisco: Cadence Books, 1997), 153.

47 Eugene Son, interview by author, July 5, 2010.

48 Gina McIntyre, "Guillermo Del Toro Shares His Aspirations for Urasawa's *Monster*," *Los Angeles Times*, http://herocomplex.latimes.com/movies/guillermo-del-toro-shares-his-aspirations-for-urasawas-monster/ (accessed November 1, 2014).

49 Ibid.

50 Ibid.

Chapter 2

1 Nobuo Masuda, interview by author, December 29, 2011.

2 Robert Napton, interview by author, July 15, 2011.

3 Schodt, *The Astro Boy Essays*, 20.

4 Ibid., 132.

5 A. Pablo Iannone, *Dictionary of World Philosophy* (New York: Taylor and Francis, 2001).

6 "List of Best-Selling Manga," Wikipedia, http://en.wikipedia.org/wiki/List_of_best-selling_manga (accessed October 16, 2014).

7 McIntyre, "Guillermo Del Toro Shares His Aspirations for Urasawa's *Monster*."

8   Frederik L. Schodt, *Dreamland Japan: Writings on Modern Manga* (Berkeley, CA: Stone Bridge Press, 1996), 28.

9   Ibid.

10   Jason Hoffs, interview by author, July 19, 2011.

11   Ibid.

12   Micheal Arias, interview by author, October 27, 2011.

13   Schodt, *Dreamland Japan*, 90.

14   Ibid., 55.

15   Ian Condry, interview by author, January 24, 2012.

16   Ken Tsumura, interview by author, July 11, 2012.

17   Napier, *Anime from Akira to Howl's Moving Castle*, 22–3.

18   Robert Napton, interview by author, July 15, 2011.

19   Miyazaki, *Starting Point 1979–1996*, 99.

20   Ibid., 99–100.

21   Ibid., 100.

22   John Gaeta, interview by author, October 9, 2014.

23   Ibid.

24   Robert Napton, interview by author, July 15, 2011.

25   Schodt, *Dreamland Japan*, 59.

26   Ibid., 61.

27   Ibid., 62.

28   Ibid., 60.

29   Schodt, *The Astro Boy Essays*, 51.

30   Ibid.

31   Gary P. Leupp, *Male Colors: The Construction of Homosexuality in Tokugawa Japan* (Berkeley, CA: University of California Press, 1997), 70–1.

32   H. Paul Varley, *Japanese Culture*, 4th edn (Honolulu: University of Hawaii Press, 2000), 186–7.

33   Schodt, *Dreamland Japan*, 61.

34   Tsugumi Ohba and Takeshi Obata, *Death Note*, Trans. Pookie Rolf (San Francisco: VIZ Media, 2005), 125.

35   Frederik L. Schodt and Osamu Tezuka, *Manga! Manga!: The World of Japanese Comics* (New York: Harper & Row, 1986), 142.

36   Schodt, *Dreamland Japan*, 237.

37   Schodt and Tezuka, *Manga! Manga!*, 142.

38   Ibid., 18, 22.

39   Schodt, *Dreamland Japan*, 24.

40   Ibid., 26.

41   Scott McCloud, *Making Comics: Storytelling Secrets of Comics, Manga and Graphic Novels* (New York: Harper, 2006), 216.

42   Ibid.

43   Ibid.

44   Ibid., 216.

45   Ibid., 16.

46   Ibid., 17.

47   Ibid., 15.

48   Ibid., 216.

49   Nobuo Masuda, email to author, September 1, 2014.

50   Schodt, *Dreamland Japan*, 29.

51   John Gaeta, interview by author, July 25, 2014.

Chapter 3

1   Schodt and Tezuka, *Manga! Manga!*, 28.

2   Ibid.

3   Ibid., 30.

4   hybridity, *Websters Online Dictionary*, http://www.merriam-webster.com/dictionary/%20 hybridity (accessed April 5, 2015).

5   Miyazaki, *Starting Point 1979–1996*, 96.

6   Schodt and Tezuka, *Manga! Manga!*, 30.

7   Ibid., 32.

8   Ibid.

9   Ibid.

10   "The Floating World of Ukiyo-E: Shadows, Dreams, and Substance," United States Library of Congress, http://www.loc.gov/exhibits/ukiyo-e/images.html (accessed May 1, 2015).

11   Schodt and Tezuka, *Manga! Manga!*, 34–5.

12   Ibid., 35.

13   Ibid., 41.

14   Keiji Nakazawa, *Hiroshima: The Autobiography of Barefoot Gen*, Trans. Richard H. Minear (Lanham, MD: Rowman & Littlefield, 2010), 107.

15   Schodt and Tezuka, *Manga! Manga!*, 62.

16   Steve Shibuya, interview by author, July 19, 2011.

17   "Interview: Fred Schodt," Anime News Network, October 27, 2009, http://www.animenewsnetwork.com/interview/2009-10-27/interview-fred-schodt (accessed October 1, 2012).

18   Schodt, *The Astro Boy Essays*, 28–9.

19   Ibid.

20   Gene Dannen, "Minutes of the Second Meeting of the Target Committee Los Alamos, May 10–11, 1945" (Los Alamos, NM: US National Archives, 1945), http://www.dannen.com/decision/targets.html (accessed December 06, 2014).

21   Schodt, *The Astro Boy Essays*, 29.

22   Helen McCarthy, *The Art of Osamu Tezuka: God of Manga* (New York: Abrams ComicArts, 2009), 24.

23   Schodt, *The Astro Boy Essays*, 30.

24   Ibid.

25   McCarthy, *The Art of Osamu Tezuka*, 24.

26   *Scrolls to Screen: A Brief History of Anime*, documentary, directed by Josh Oreck (Warner Brothers, 2003).

27   Schodt and Tezuka, *Manga! Manga!*, 62.

Chapter 4

1   McCarthy, *The Art of Osamu Tezuka*, 15.

2   Ibid.

3   Fred Ladd and Harvey Deneroff, *Astro Boy and Anime Come to the Americas: An Insider's View of the Birth of a Pop Culture Phenomenon* (Jefferson, NC: McFarland, 2009), 33.

4   Paul Gravett, *Manga: Sixty Years of Japanese Comics* (New York: Laurence King, 2004), 26.

5   McCarthy, *The Art of Osamu Tezuka*, 104.

6   Schodt, *The Astro Boy Essays*, 43.

7   Ibid., 59.

8   McCarthy, *The Art of Osamu Tezuka*, 104.

9   Ryan Holmberg, "Tezuka Osamu and American Comics," *The Comics Journal*, http://www.tcj.com/tezuka-osamu-and-american-comics/ (accessed November 3, 2013).

10   "Pirate Bowarl," "Character Descriptions of Osamu Tezuka's Work," Tezukaosamu.net, http://tezukaosamu.net/en/character/157.html (accessed October 25, 2014).

11   Matt Thorn, "Keiji Nakazawa, 1939–2012," *The Comics Journal*, http://www.tcj.com/keiji-nakazawa-1939-2012/ (accessed April 26, 2013).

12   Holmberg, "Tezuka Osamu and American Comics."

13   Tiffany Martin, "How Walt Disney Created Manga," *The Escapist*, June 8, 2010, http://www.escapistmagazine.com/articles/view/issues/issue_257/7659-How-Walt-Disney-Created-Manga.3#YXzAq7XiDWqZDbzi.99 (accessed August 7, 2014).

14   Schodt, *The Astro Boy Essays*, 92.

15   Micheal Arias, interview by author, October 27, 2011.

16   "Tezuka in English," http://tezukainenglish.com/?q=node/17 (accessed October 3, 2012).

17   Schodt, *The Astro Boy Essays*, 45.

18   Ibid.

19   Holmberg, "Tezuka Osamu and American Comics."

20   Schodt, *The Astro Boy Essays*, 22.

21   Ibid., 78.

22   Holmberg, "Tezuka Osamu and American Comics."

23   McCarthy, *The Art of Osamu Tezuka*, 73.

24   Ibid., 66.

25   "*Don Dracula,*" *Tezuka in English*, http://tezukainenglish.com/wp/osamu-tezuka-manga/manga-a-h/don-dracula-manga/ (accessed November 18, 2014).

26   Ibid., 88.

27   Ibid.

28   Ibid., 103–4.

29   Ibid.

30   McCarthy, *The Art of Osamu Tezuka*, 94.

31   Schodt and Tezuka, *Manga! Manga!,* 63.

32   Ladd and Deneroff, *Astro Boy and Anime Come to the Americas*, 179.

33   Oreck, *Scrolls to Screen*.

34   Ryan Holmberg, "Tezuka Osamu Outwits the Phantom Blot: The Case of *New Treasure Island* Cont'd," *The Comics Journal,* February 22, 2013, http://www.tcj.com/

tezuka-osamu-outwits-the-phantom-blot-the-case-of-new-treasure-island-contd/
(accessed February 24, 2013).

35 Ibid.
36 Holmberg, "Tezuka Osamu and American Comics."
37 Ibid.
38 Ibid.
39 Peter Chung, interview by author, December 11, 2011.
40 Nakazawa, *Hiroshima: The Autobiography of Barefoot Gen*, 107–8.
41 Ibid., 108.
42 Ibid.
43 Ibid., 109–10.
44 McCarthy, *The Art of Osamu Tezuka*, 69.
45 Nakazawa, *Hiroshima: The Autobiography of Barefoot Gen*, 110.
46 Ibid., 110–11.
47 Ibid., 111.
48 Ibid., 134.
49 Ibid., 110.

Chapter 5

1 "Hakusensha," Wikipedia, http://en.wikipedia.org/wiki/Hakusensha (accessed October 25, 2014).
2 Tsugumi Ohba and Takeshi Obata, *Bakuman*, Vol. 2 (San Francisco: VIZ Media, 2008).
3 Schodt and Tezuka, *Manga! Manga!*, 145.
4 Ibid.
5 "*Manga Zombie*" ComiPress, http://comipress.com/special/manga-zombie/manga-zombie-preface (accessed June 6, 2014).
6 Schodt and Tezuka, *Manga! Manga!*, 144.
7 Geof Darrow, interview by author, May 13, 2012.
8 Schodt, *Dreamland Japan*, 241.
9 Ibid., 242.
10 "Making A Living in Manga in Japan," San Diego Comicon Panel, moderated by Deb Aoki, Anime News Network, July 28, 2014, http://www.animenewsnetwork.com/convention/2014/san-diego-comic-con/making-a-living-in-manga-in-japan/.77039 (accessed July 29, 2014).
11 Ibid.
12 Ibid.
13 Ibid.
14 Ibid.
15 Ohba and Obata, *Bakuman*, 2:33.
16 Hikaru Sasahara, interview by author, November 15, 2013.
17 Ian Condry, interview by author, January 24, 2012.
18 Ibid.
19 Robert Napton, interview by author, July 15, 2011.
20 Salil Mehra, interview by author, May 13, 2011.
21 Hikaru Sasahara, interview by author, November 15, 2013.
22 Salil Mehra, interview by author, May 13, 2011.
23 Ibid.

Chapter 6

1   Clements and Tamamuro, *The Dorama Encyclopedia*, xix.
2   Ibid., xv.
3   Ibid., xvii.
4   Ibid.
5   Ladd and Deneroff, *Astro Boy and Anime Come to the Americas*, 100.
6   Jiro Kuwata et al., *Bat-Manga!: The Secret History of Batman in Japan* (New York: Pantheon Books, 2008), 14.
7   Clements and Tamamuro, *The Dorama Encyclopedia*, xvi–xvii.
8   Ibid., xvi.
9   Ibid., xv–xvi.
10   Ibid., 26.
11   Ibid., xx–xxi.
12   Stephen Prince, *The Warrior's Camera: The Cinema of Akira Kurosawa* (Princeton, NJ: Princeton University Press, 1999), 5.
13   Clements and Tamamuro, *The Dorama Encyclopedia*, xxvi.
14   Ian Condry, interview by author, January 24, 2012.
15   Terrence Canote, "1961: The Year Anime Arrived in America," *A Shroud of Thoughts*, http://mercurie.blogspot.com/2010/07/1961-year-anime-arrived-in-america.html (accessed October 3, 2012).
16   Clements and Tamamuro, *The Dorama Encyclopedia*, 14.
17   Tezuka Osamu, *Boku wa manga ka* [*I am a Cartoonist*] (Tokyo: Kodansha, 1984), 202–4.
18   Schodt, *The Astro Boy Essays*, 92.
19   McCarthy, *The Art of Osamu Tezuka*, 160.
20   Ladd and Deneroff, *Astro Boy and Anime Come to the Americas*, 67.
21   Lesley Aeschliman, "Biography of Osamu Tezuka," BellaOnline, http://www.bellaonline.com/articles/art15676.asp (accessed October 3, 2012).
22   Schodt, *The Astro Boy Essays*, 75.
23   Ibid.
24   Ibid., 63.
25   Ibid., 64.
26   Ibid., 66.
27   "Discover Kami-shibai," Kami-shibai for Kids, http://www.kamishibai.com/index.html (accessed October 3, 2012).
28   Clements and Tamamuro, *The Dorama Encyclopedia*, 262.
29   Oreck, *Scrolls to Screen*.
30   "Japanese Animation Theory," AniPages Discussion Forum.
31   Schodt, *The Astro Boy Essays*, 68.
32   Oreck, *Scrolls to Screen*.
33   Edward Douglas, "Exclusive Interview: Guillermo Del Toro Shifts to Animation," ComingSoon.net, November 16, 2012, http://www.comingsoon.net/news/movienews.php?id=97020 (accessed July 23, 2014).
34   "Japanese Animation Theory," AniPages Discussion Forum.
35   Peter Chung, interview by author, December 11, 2011.
36   "Japanese Animation Theory," AniPages Discussion Forum.

37   Micheal Arias, interview by author, October 27, 2011.

38   Nobuo Masuda, interview by author, December 29, 2011.

39   "Japanese Animation Theory," AniPages Discussion Forum.

40   Peter Chung, interview by author, December 11, 2011.

41   Schodt, *The Astro Boy Essays*, 135.

42   Ibid., 154.

43   Norman M. Klein, *Seven Minutes: The Life and Death of the American Animated Cartoon* (London and New York: Verso, 1998), 244.

44   Ladd and Deneroff, *Astro Boy and Anime Come to the Americas*, 11.

45   Ibid.

46   Chad Gervich, *Small Screen, Big Picture: Inside-the-Business Guide to Writing and Producing TV* (New York: Three Rivers Press, 2008), 46–50.

47   Ibid.

48   Ibid., 52.

49   William Penn, *The Couch Potato's Guide to Japan: Inside the World of Japanese TV* (Sapporo, Japan: Forest River Press, 2003), 182.

50   Ladd and Deneroff, *Astro Boy and Anime Come to the Americas*, 44.

51   Gervich, *Small Screen, Big Picture*, 38.

52   Ibid., 35–8.

53   Schodt, *The Astro Boy Essays*, 80.

54   Ladd and Deneroff, *Astro Boy and Anime Come to the Americas*, 52.

55   Schodt, *The Astro Boy Essays*, 80.

56   Ladd and Deneroff, *Astro Boy and Anime Come to the Americas*, 16.

57   Ibid.

58   Robert Napton, interview by author, July 15, 2011.

59   Donald Richie, *The Films of Akira Kurosawa* (Berkeley, CA: University of California Press, 1998), 80.

60   Schodt, *The Astro Boy Essays*, 85.

61   Ibid.

62   Ibid., 86.

63   Ladd and Deneroff, *Astro Boy and Anime Come to the Americas*, 34.

64   Schodt, *The Astro Boy Essays*, 86.

65   Ibid.

66   Ibid., 85.

67   Ladd and Deneroff, *Astro Boy and Anime Come to the Americas*, 44.

68   Ibid., 16.

69   Schodt, *The Astro Boy Essays*, 81.

70   Ladd and Deneroff, *Astro Boy and Anime Come to the Americas*, 24.

71   Nobuo Masuda, interview by author, December 29, 2011.

72   Schodt, *The Astro Boy Essays*, 88.

73   Ibid.

74   Ladd and Deneroff, *Astro Boy and Anime Come to the Americas*, 39.

75   Ibid., 65.

76   Ibid.

77   Ibid., 69.

78   Ibid., 53.

79 Ibid., 52.
80 Tsugumi Ohba and Takeshi Obata, *Bakuman*, Vol. 12, Trans. Tetsuichiro Miyaki (San Francisco, CA: VIZ Media, 2010), 40.
81 Ibid., 12:71.
82 Ian Condry, interview by author, January 24, 2012.
83 Miyazaki, *Starting Point 1979–1996,* 127.
84 Bricken, Rob, "Tite Kubo Interviews," Bleachwiki.com, http://bleach.wikia.com/wiki/Forum:Tite_Kubo_Interviews (accessed November 18, 2014).
85 Nobuo Masuda, interview by author, December 29, 2011.
86 "*Transformers*," Wikipedia, http://en.wikipedia.org/wiki/Transformers (accessed October 3, 2012).
87 Robert Napton, "*Transformers* Origins," email to author, August 31, 2012.
88 McIntyre, "Guillermo Del Toro Shares His Aspirations for Urasawa's *Monster*."
89 Ian Condry, interview by author, January 24, 2012.
90 Prince, *The Warrior's Camera*, 353.
91 Ibid., 351–2.
92 "*A Fistful of Dollars* and *Yojimbo*," Side B Magazine.com, http://sidebmag.com/2011/04/14/1535/ (accessed October 3, 2012).

Chapter 7

1   Ian Condry, interview by author, January 24, 2012.
2   Ibid.
3   Jason Hoffs, interview by author, July 19, 2011.
4   "Grand Fisher—*Bleach* Wiki—Your Guide to the *Bleach* Manga and Anime Series," http://bleach.wikia.com/wiki/Grand_Fisher (accessed October 4, 2012).
5   Toni Johnson-Woods, ed., *Manga: An Anthology of Global and Cultural Perspectives* (New York: Bloomsbury Academic, 2010), 72.
6   Ibid., 73.
7   Ibid., 74.
8   "Interview: Tite Kubo," http://manga.about.com/od/mangaartistinterviews/a/TiteKubo_2.htm (accessed October 1, 2012).
9   "Producer: Cameron Wants to Do *Battle Angel's* Motorball," Anime News Network, http://www.animenewsnetwork.com/news/2010-03-01/producer/cameron-wants-to-do-battle-angel-motorball (accessed October 5, 2012).
10 Ibid.
11 "Jim Cameron Steps up His Plans for *Battle Angel Alita*," Syfy, http://www.syfy.co.uk/news/jim-cameron-steps-his-plans-battle-angel-alita (accessed October 5, 2012).
12 "James Cameron: *Avatar* Will Do 'More Good' Than *Battle Angel*," Anime News Network, http://splashpage.mtv.com/2012/04/17/james-cameron-avatar-will-do-more-good-than-battle-angel/ (accessed October 5, 2012).
13 Ibid.
14 Ted Greenwood "Read the Full Transcript of *Wired's* Interview with Ridley Scott," *Wired Magazine*, September 26, 2001, http://www.wired.com/entertainment/hollywood/magazine/15-10/ff_bladerunner_full?currentPage=all (accessed October 5, 2012).

15 Fred Kaplan, "25 Years Later, Ridley Scott's '*Blade Runner*' Redux," *New York Times*, October 2, 2007, http://www.nytimes.com/2007/10/02/arts/02iht-runner.1.7713075. html?_r=0 (accessed March 20, 2015).

16 Ibid.

17 Paul Choate and Andrew Cross, interview by author, July 25, 2011.

18 Penn, *The Couch Potato's Guide to Japan*, 32.

19 "A Kishiro Yukito interview," The Sunny Spot.Org, http://thesunnyspot.org/manga/ gunnm/kinterv.html (accessed November 18, 2014).

20 Jason Hoffs, interview by author, July 19, 2011.

21 Ohba and Obata, *Death Note*, 185.

22 Micheal Arias, interview by author, October 27, 2011.

23 Austa Joye, "Speed's transformation in the tunnel," email to author, November, 14, 2014.

Chapter 8

1 Patrick Macias, "*Speed Racer*: Drawing on an Anime Legend," *The Japan Times*, July 3, 2008, http://www.japantimes.co.jp/culture/2008/07/03/films/speed-racer-drawing-on-an-anime-legend/#.VE5nbhYmzKd (accessed April 18, 2015).

2 Patrick Drazen, *Anime Explosion!: The What? Why? & Wow! Of Japanese Animation* (Berkeley, CA: Stone Bridge Press, 2003), 25.

3 Gene Gustines, "Return Laps for Peter Fernandez, the First Voice of *Speed Racer*," *New York Times*, May 10, 2008, http://www.nytimes.com/2008/05/10/movies/10speed. html?scp=28&sq=astro%20boy&st=cse&_r=0 (accessed March 11, 2015).

4 Robert Napton, interview by author, July 15, 2011.

5 Macias, "*Speed Racer*: Drawing on an Anime Legend."

6 Ladd and Deneroff, *Astro Boy and Anime Come to the Americas*, 13.

7 Macias, "*Speed Racer*: Drawing on an Anime Legend."

8 Keltz and Fernandez, "*Speed Racer* Film a Far Cry from Its Anime Roots."

9 Ibid.

10 "*Speed Racer*," Wikipedia, http://en.wikipedia.org/wiki/Speed_Racer (accessed October 27, 2014).

11 Macias, "*Speed Racer*: Drawing on an Anime Legend."

12 Ibid.

13 Ibid.

14 Ibid.

15 Ibid.

16 Ibid.

17 Gustines, "Return Laps for Peter Fernandez."

18 Ladd and Deneroff, *Astro Boy and Anime Come to the Americas*, 77.

19 Patrick Macias, "'Americanizing' a Cartoon Classic."

20 Valerie Nelson, "Peter Fernandez Dies at 83; Helped Bring Japanese Animation to American Audiences," *Los Angeles Times*, July 25, 2010, http://articles.latimes.com/2010/ jul/25/local/la-me-peter-fernandez-20100726 (accessed October 29, 2014).

21 Patrick Macias, "'Americanizing' a Cartoon Classic."

22 Ibid.

23 Nelson, "Peter Fernandez Dies at 83; Helped Bring Japanese Animation to American Audiences."

24 Ibid.

25 Macias, "*Speed Racer*: Drawing on an Anime Legend."

26 Grant Hill, interview by author, January 16, 2012.

27 Nelson, "Peter Fernandez Dies at 83; Helped Bring Japanese Animation to American Audiences."

28 Gustines, "Return Laps for Peter Fernandez."

29 John Gaeta, interview by author, October 9, 2014.

30 "*Speed Racer* DVD Interview: The Voice of Speed Racer Himself Talks about the Series," IGN, May 22, 2008, http://www.ign.com/articles/2008/05/23/speed-racer-dvd-interview (accessed, May 30, 2014).

31 John Gaeta, interview by author, October 9, 2014.

32 "*Speed Racer* DVD Interview: The Voice of *Speed Racer* Himself Talks about the Series."

33 Macias, "*Speed Racer*: Drawing on an Anime Legend."

34 Nelson, "Peter Fernandez Dies at 83; Helped Bring Japanese Animation to American Audiences."

35 Annalee Newitz, "10 Reasons Why '*Speed Racer*' Is an Unsung Masterpiece," io9, October 24, 2012.

36 John Gaeta, interview by author, October 9, 2014.

37 Ibid.

38 Newitz, "10 Reasons Why '*Speed Racer*' Is an Unsung Masterpiece."

39 Ibid.

40 Scott Holleran, "*Speed Racer*," Box Office Mojo, May 9, 2008, http://www.boxofficemojo.com/reviews/?id=2494&p=.htm (accessed October 18, 2014).

41 Ibid.

42 Micheal Arias, interview by author, October 27, 2011.

43 Grant Hill, interview by author, January 16, 2012.

44 Antonia Levi, *Samurai from Outer Space: Understanding Japanese Animation* (Chicago: Open Court, 1996), 7.

45 Ibid.

46 Drazen, *Anime Explosion!*, 9.

47 Michael Watt, "'Do You Speak Christian?' Dubbing and the Manipulation of the Cinematic Experience," *Bright Lights Film Journal* 29 (July 2000), http://brightlightsfilm.com/29/dubbing1.php#.VFPMDhYmzKd (accessed February 28, 2015).

48 Salil Mehra, interview by author, May 13, 2011.

49 Michael Arias, interview by author, October 27, 2011.

50 Geof Darrow, interview by author, May 13, 2012.

51 Micheal Arias, interview by author, October 27, 2011.

52 Roy Lee, interview by author, May 10, 2012.

53 *Writing for Episodic TV: From Freelancer to Showrunner* (Los Angeles: Writers Guild of America West and East, 2004), 29.

54 William Goldman, *Adventures in the Screen Trade: A Personal View of Hollywood and Screenwriting* (New York: Warner Books, 1984), 39.

55 Roy Lee, interview by author, May 10, 2012.

56 Jason Hoffs, interview by author, July 19, 2011.

57 Micheal Arias, interview by author, October 27, 2011.

58 Ibid.

59 Ibid.

60 Nobuo Masuda, interview by author, December 29, 2011.

61 "Lamenting the Loss of Australian Identitiy and Culture," Kytheria-family.net, http://www.kythera-family.net/index.php?nav=117-121&cid=227-49&did=3707 (accessed February 2, 2013).

62 Christine Yoo, interview by author, December 23, 2011.

63 Nobuo Masuda, interview by author, December 29, 2011.

64 Ibid.

Chapter 9

1   Schodt, *The Astro Boy Essays*, 42.

2   Ibid., 89.

3   Ian Condry, interview by author, January 24, 2012.

4   Schodt, *The Astro Boy Essays*, 51.

5   Hikaru Sasahara, interview by author, November 15, 2013.

6   Joyce Jun, interview by author, December 9, 2011.

7   Ibid.

8   Ibid.

9   Hikaru Sasahara, interview by author, November 15, 2013.

10 Joshua Long, interview by author, May 10, 2012.

11 Hikaru Sasahara, interview by author, November 15, 2013.

12 Schodt, *The Astro Boy Essays*, 168.

13 Ken Tsumura, interview by author, July 11, 2012.

14 Ibid.

15 Ibid.

16 Nobuo Masuda, "main characters tend to be younger in Japanese manga than in American counterparts," email to author, December 30, 2011.

Chapter 10

1   McIntyre, "Guillermo Del Toro Shares His Aspirations for Urasawa's *Monster*."

2   *Writers Guild of America 2015 Minimum Basic Agreement* (Writers Guild of America West and East), http://www.wga.org/uploadedFiles/writers_resources/contracts/min2014.pdf (accessed October 31, 2014).

3   Nobuo Masuda, interview by author, December 29, 2011.

4   Ibid.

5   Roy Lee, interview by author, May 11, 2012.

6   Robert Napton, interview by author, July 15, 2011.

7   Nobuo Masuda, interview by author, December 29, 2011.

8   Roy Lee, interview by author, May 11, 2012.

Chapter 11

1   Micheal Arias, interview by author, October 27, 2011.
2   Patrick Brzeski, "John Lasseter Pays Emotional Tribute to Hayao Miyazaki at Tokyo Film Festival," *The Hollywood Reporter*, October 24, 2014, http://www.hollywoodreporter.com/ news/john-lasseter-pays-emotional-tribute-743635 (accessed October 28, 2014).
3   Ian Condry, interview by author, January 24, 2012.
4   John Gaeta, interview by author, October 9, 2014.
5   Ledoux, *Anime Interviews*, 10.
6   Shinichirō Watanabe, interview by Yoko Hayashi, March 8, 2012.
7   Ibid.
8   Sanford Panitch, email to author, September 29, 2014.
9   Steve Shibuya, interview by author, October 4, 2013.
10 Ibid.
11 Ken Tsumura, interview by author, July 11, 2012.

Works Cited

Aeschliman, Lesley. "Biography of Osamu Tezuka." BellaOnline.com. http://www.bellaonline.com/articles/art15676.asp (accessed October 3, 2012).

Anime News Network. http://www.animenewsnetwork.com/ (accessed various times).

"Animism." The Concise Encyclopedia. http://www.merriam-webster.com/dictionary/animism (accessed October 18, 2014).

Blair, Elizabeth. "*Speed Racer* Film a Far Cry from Its Anime Roots." *National Public Radio.* May 8, 2008. http://www.npr.org/templates/story/story.php?storyId=90268450 (accessed June 4, 2015).

Bleach Wiki. "Grand Fisher—Your Guide to the *Bleach* Manga and Anime Series." http://bleach.wikia.com/wiki/Grand_Fisher (accessed October 4, 2012).

Bricken, Rob. "Tite Kubo Interviews." *Bleach* Wiki.

Bryant, Dawn. "Top Selling Manga in 2013." Saiyanisland. December 1, 2013. http://www.saiyanisland.com/2013/12/top-selling-manga-in-2013/ (accessed December 5, 2014).

Brzeski, Patrick. "John Lasseter Pays Emotional Tribute to Hayao Miyazaki at Tokyo Film Festival." *The Hollywood Reporter*, October 24, 2014. http://www.hollywoodreporter.com/news/john-lasseter-pays-emotional-tribute-743635 (accessed October 28, 2014).

Canote, Terrence. 1961: The Year Anime Arrived in America." A Shroud of Thoughts.com. http://mercurie.blogspot.com/2010/07/1961-year-anime-arrived-in-america.html (accessed October 3, 2012).

Ching, Albert. "The 10 Bestselling Comic Book Issues of the Past Decade." Newsarama. September 12, 2011. http://www.newsarama.com/15422-the-10-bestselling-comic-book-issues-of-the-past-decade.html (accessed September 15, 2014).

Clements, Jonathan, and Helen, McCarthy. *The Anime Encyclopedia: A Guide to Japanese Animation since 1917*. Berkeley, CA: Stone Bridge Press, 2001.

Clements, Jonathan, and Motoko, Tamamuro. *The Dorama Encyclopedia: A Guide to Japanese TV Drama since 1953*. Berkeley, CA: Stone Bridge Press, 2003.

Dannen, Gene. "Minutes of the Second Meeting of the Target Committee Los Almos, May 10–11, 1945." http://www.dannen.com/decision/targets.html (accessed December 6, 2014).

Ditzian, Eric. "Fourth *Mad Max* In Development ... As 3-D Anime Feature." MTV Movies Blog. March 5, 2009. http://moviesblog.mtv.com/2009/03/05/exclusive-fourth-mad-max-in-developmentas-3-d-anime-feature/ (accessed June 29, 2014).

Douglas, Edward. "Exclusive Interview: Guillermo Del Toro Shifts to Animation." ComingSoon.net. November 16, 2012. http://www.comingsoon.net/news/movienews.php?id=97020 (accessed July 23, 2014).

Drazen, Patrick. *Anime Explosion!: The What? Why? & Wow! Of Japanese Animation*. Berkeley, CA: Stone Bridge Press, 2003.

"*A Fistful of Dollars* and *Yojimbo*," Side B Magazine.com. http://sidebmag. com/2011/04/14/1535/ (accessed October 3, 2012).

"The Floating World of Ukiyo-E: Shadows, Dreams, and Substance," United States Library of Congress. http://www.loc.gov/exhibits/ukiyo-e/images.html (accessed May 1, 2015).

Gervich, Chad. *Small Screen, Big Picture: Inside-the-Business Guide to Writing and Producing TV*. New York: Three Rivers Press, 2008.

Goldman, William. *Adventures in the Screen Trade: A Personal View of Hollywood and Screenwriting*. New York: Warner Books, 1984.

"*Golgo 13* Author Saito Discusses Manga's Hypothetical Ending." Anime News Network. November 16, 2013. http://www.animenewsnetwork.com/news/2013-11-16/golgo-13-author-saito-discusses-manga-hypothetical-ending (accessed December 15, 2014).

"Grand Fisher." "Your Guide to the *Bleach* Managa and Anime Series." Bleachwiki. http.//bleach.wikia.com/wiki/Grand_Fisher (accessed October 4, 2012).

Gravett, Paul. *Manga: Sixty Years of Japanese Comics*. New York: Laurence King, 2004.

Green, Scott. "Guillermo Del Toro Mentions *Monster* Adaptation in Sugoi Japan Endorsement." Crunchyroll.com. August 14, 2014. http://www.crunchyroll.com/anime-news/2014/08/14/guillermo-del-toro-mentions-monster-adaptation-in-sugoi-japan-endorsement (accessed June 22, 2015).

Greenwald, Ted "Read the Full Transcript of *Wired*'s Interview with Ridley Scott." *Wired Magazine*, September 26, 2001. http://www.wired.com/entertainment/hollywood/magazine/15-10/ff_bladerunner_full?currentPage=all (accessed October 5, 2012).

"Guinness Certifies *Sazae-san* as Longest Running Animated Show." *Mainichi Shimbun*, August 5, 2013. http://www.animenewsnetwork.com/news/2013-09-05/guinness-certifies-sazae-san-as-longest-running-animated-show (accessed August 8, 2013).

"*Gundam* Is Coming to America. All of It." Io9.com. http://io9.com/gundam-is-coming-to-america-all-of-it-1647066568 (accessed October 15, 2014).

Gustines, Gene. "Return Laps for Peter Fernandez, the First Voice of *Speed Racer*." *New York Times*, May 10, 2008. http://www.nytimes.com/2008/05/10/movies/10speed.html?scp=28&sq=astro%20boy&st=cse&_r=0 (accessed March 11, 2015).

"Hakusensha." Wikipedia. http://en.wikipedia.org/wiki/Hakusensha (accessed October 25, 2014).

Holleran, Scott. "*Speed Racer*." Box Office Mojo. May 9, 2008. http://www.boxofficemojo.com/reviews/?id=2494&p=.htm (accessed October 18, 2014).

Holmberg, Ryan. "Tezuka Osamu and American Comics." *The Comics Journal*, July 16, 2012. http://www.tcj.com/tezuka-osamu-and-american-comics/ (accessed November 3, 2013).

Holmberg, Ryan. "Tezuka Osamu Outwits the Phantom Blot: The Case of *New Treasure Island* Cont'd." *The Comics Journal*, February 22, 2013. http://www.tcj.com/tezuka-osamu-outwits-the-phantom-blot-the-case-of-new-treasure-island-contd/ (accessed February 24, 2013).

Iannone, Pablo A. *Dictionary of World Philosophy*. New York: Taylor and Francis, 2001.

"Interview: Fred Schodt." Anime News Network. October 27, 2009." http://www.animenewsnetwork.com/interview/2009-10-27/interview-fred-schodt (accessed October 1, 2012).

"Interview: Tite Kubo." Mangaabout.com. http://manga.about.com/od/mangaartistinterviews/a/TiteKubo_2.htm (accessed October 1, 2012).

"James Cameron: *Avatar* Will Do 'More Good' than *Battle Angel*." MTV.com. http://splashpage.mtv.com/2012/04/17/james-cameron-avatar-will-do-more-good-than-battle-angel/ (accessed October 5, 2012).

"Japanese Animation Theory." AniPages Discussion Forum. http://www.pelleas.net/forum/viewtopic.php?f=1&t=238&start=15 (accessed June 4, 2015).

"Jim Cameron Steps up His Plans for *Battle Angel Alita*." Syfy.co.uk. http://www.syfy.co.uk/news/jim-cameron-steps-his-plans-battle-angel-alita (accessed October 5, 2012).

Johnson-Woods, Toni, ed. *Manga: An Anthology of Global and Cultural Perspectives*. New York: Bloomsbury Academic, 2010.

Kalat, David. *A Critical History and Filmography of Toho's Godzilla Series*. 2nd edn. Jefferson, NC: McFarland & Co, 2010.

"Kami-shibai for Kids: Homepage." Kami-shibai.com. http://www.kamishibai.com/index.html (accessed October 3, 2012).

Kaplan, Fred. "25 Years Later, Ridley Scott's *Blade Runner* Redux." *New York Times*, October 2, 2007. http://www.nytimes.com/2007/10/02/arts/02iht-runner.1.7713075.html?_r=0 (accessed March 20, 2015).

Keegan, Rebecca. "Muscle Summer-the Men of *Captain America*, *Thor* and *Conan*." *Los Angeles Times*, May 28, 2011. http://herocomplex.latimes.com/movies/muscle-summer-the-men-of-captain-america-thor-and-conan/ (accessed May 29, 2011).

Keltz, Roland and, Peter, Fernandez. "*Speed Racer* Film a Far Cry from Its Anime Roots (Interview with Roland Kelts and Peter Fernandez)," interview by Elizabeth Blair National Public Radio, May 8, 2008. http://www.npr.org/templates/story/story.php?storyId=90268450 (accessed June 4, 2015).

Klein, Norman M. *Seven Minutes: The Life and Death of the American Animated Cartoons*. London and New York: Verso, 1998.

Koppel, Niko. "Peter Keefe, Creator of Cartoon *Voltron* Dies at 57." *New York Times*, June 11, 2010. http://www.nytimes.com/2010/06/11/arts/design/11keefe.html?ref=obituaries&_r=0 (accessed March 20, 2015).

Kuwata, Jiro. *Bat-Manga!: The Secret History of Batman in Japan*. New York: Pantheon Books, 2008.

Ladd, Fred, and Harvey Deneroff. *Astro Boy and Anime Come to the Americas: An Insider's View of the Birth of a Pop Culture Phenomenon*. Jefferson, NC: McFarland & Co., 2009.

"Lamenting the Loss of Australian Identity and Culture." Kytheria-family.net. http://www.kythera-family.net/index.php?nav=117-121&cid=227-49&did=3707 (accessed February 2, 2013).

Ledoux, Trish. *Anime Interviews: The First Five Years of* Animerica, Anime & Manga Monthly *(1992–97)*. San Francisco: Cadence Books, 1997.

Leupp, Gary P. *Male Colors: The Construction of Homosexuality in Tokugawa Japan*. Berkeley, CA: University of California Press, 1997.

Levi, Antonia. *Samurai from Outer Space: Understanding Japanese Animation*. Chicago: Open Court, 1996.

Lichter, Paul. *Elvis in Vegas*. New York: Overlook Duckworth, 2011.

"List of Best-Selling Manga." Wikipedia. https://en.wikipedia.org/wiki/List_of_best-selling_manga (accessed October 16, 2014).

Lodge, Harry. "Scholastic Celebrates 15 Years of *Harry Potter*." *Publishers Weekly*, June 11,

2013. http://www.publishersweekly.com/pw/by-topic/childrens/childrens-industry-news/article/57780-scholastic-celebrates-15-years-of-harry-potter.html (accessed June 14, 2014).

Macias, Patrick. "'Americanizing' a Cartoon Classic." *The Japan Times*, July 3, 2008. http://www.japantimes.co.jp/culture/2008/07/03/films/americanizing-a-cartoon-classic/#.VFGNZBYmzKc (accessed April 18, 2015).

Macias, Patrick. "*Speed Racer*: Drawing on an Anime Legend." *The Japan Times*, July 3, 2008. http://www.japantimes.co.jp/culture/2008/07/03/films/speed-racer-drawing-on-an-anime-legend/#.VE5nbhYmzKd (accessed April 18, 2015).

"Manga Sales Grew Over 6% in U.S. in 2013 So Far." Anime News Network. November 11, 2013. http://www.animenewsnetwork.com/news/2013-11-21/manga-sales-grew-over-6-percent-in-u.s-in-2013-so-far (accessed November 11, 2013).

"*Manga Zombie*." Comipress. http://comipress.com/special/manga-zombie/manga-zombie-preface (accessed June 6, 2014).

"Making A Living in Manga in Japan." San Diego Comicon Panel, moderated by Deb Aoki, July 28, 2014. http://www.animenewsnetwork.com/convention/2014/san-diego-comic-con/making-a-living-in-manga-in-japan/.77039 (accessed July 29, 2014).

Martin, Tiffany. "How Walt Disney Created Manga." *The Escapist*, June 8, 2010. http://www.escapistmagazine.com/articles/view/issues/issue_257/7659-How-Walt-Disney-Created-Manga.3#YXzAq7XiDWqZDbzi.99 (accessed August 7, 2014).

McCarthy, Helen. *The Art of Osamu Tezuka: God of Manga*. New York: Abrams ComicArts, 2009.

McCloud, Scott. *Making Comics: Storytelling Secrets of Comics, Manga and Graphic Novels*. New York: Harper, 2006.

McCracken, Craig. "Q and A with Craig McCracken." In Joe Murray, *Creating Animated Cartoons with Characters*. New York: Watson-Guptill, 2010.

McIntyre, Gina. "Guillermo Del Toro Shares His Aspirations for Urasawa's *Monster*." *Los Angeles Times*, http://herocomplex.latimes.com/movies/guillermo-del-toro-shares-his-aspirations-for-urasawas-monster/ (accessed November 1, 2014).

Minto, Evan. "Otakon 2013: Fifty Minutes with Shinichiro Watanabe *Space Dandy*, *Cowboy Bebop*, and More at the Exclusive Press Event." Ani-Gamers. August 26, 2014. http://www.anigamers.com/posts/shinichiro-watanabe-space-dandy-otakon-2013-press-conference/ (August 8, 2013).

Miyazaki, Hayao. *Starting Point 1979–1996*. Translated by Beth Cary and Frederik L Schodt. San Francisco: VIZ Media, 2014.

Miyazaki, Hayao. *Turning Point: 1997–2008*. Translated by Beth Cary and Frederik L Schodt. San Francisco, CA: VIZ Media, 2014.

Nakazawa, Keiji. *Hiroshima: The Autobiography of Barefoot Gen*. Trans. Richard H. Minear. Lanham, MD: Rowman & Littlefield, 2010.

"Namco Bandai Holdings, Inc: Financial Highlights for the Fiscal Year Ended March 2014," Bandainamco.com. May 8, 2014, http://www.bandainamco.co.jp/files/E8A39CE8B6B3E8B387E69699EFBC88E88BB1EFBC89.pdf (accessed December 10, 2014).

Napier, Susan Jolliffe. *Anime from Akira to Howl's Moving Castle: Experiencing Contemporary Japanese Animation*. New York: Palgrave Macmillan, 2005.

Nelson, Valerie. "Peter Fernandez Dies at 83; Helped Bring Japanese Animation to American

Audiences." *Los Angeles Times*, July 25, 2010. http://articles.latimes.com/2010/jul/25/local/la-me-peter-fernandez-20100726 (accessed October 29, 2014).

Newitz, Annalee. "10 Reasons Why *Speed Racer* Is an Unsung Masterpiece." io9. October 24, 2012.

Ohba, Tsugumi and Takeshi Obata. *Death Note*. Trans. Pookie Rolf. San Francisco: VIZ Media, 2005.

Ohba, Tsugumi and Takeshi Obata. *Bakuman*. Trans. Tetsuichiro Miyaki. San Francisco: VIZ Media, 2008.

Ohara, Atsushi. "Manga *Golgo 13* Celebrates 45 Years of Continuous Publication." *The Asahi Shimbun*, December 2, 2013. http://ajw.asahi.com/article/cool_japan/style/AJ201312020004 (accessed February 3, 2014).

"*One Piece* Anime". vizanime.com. http://www.vizanime.com/one-piece (accessed October 15, 2014).

"*One Piece* Manga Has 345 Million Copies in Print Worldwide." Anime News Network. http://www.animenewsnetwork.com/news/2013-11-21/one-piece-manga-has-345-million-copies-in-print-worldwide (accessed November 22, 2013).

"Original *Godzilla* Reflects on Monster's Legacy." Cbsnews.com. http://www.cbsnews.com/news/original-godzilla-actor-keeping-monstrous-legacy-alive/ (accessed November 1, 2014).

Osamu, Tezuka. *Boku wa manga ka* [*I am a Cartoonist*]. Tokyo: Kodansha, 1984.

"Paper: Sazae-san's Father to Be Played by Staff After Voice Actor's Passing." *Daily Sports*, http://www.animenewsnetwork.com/news/2014-02-03/paper/sazae-san-father-to-be-played-by-staff-after-voice-actor-passing (accessed October 13, 2014).

Peary, Gerald. "Missing Links: The Jungle Origins of *King Kong*." *Gerald Peary Film Reviews, Interviews, Essays & Sundry Miscellany*. http://www.geraldpeary.com/essays/jkl/kingkong-1.html (accessed October 13, 2014).

Penn, William. *The Couch Potato's Guide to Japan: Inside the World of Japanese TV*. Hokkaido, Japan: Forest River Press, 2003.

Perez, Marc. "An Open Letter to the Attendees of Anime Expo." AnimeExpo.org. July 22, 2014. http://www.anime-expo.org/2014/07/an-open-letter-to-the-attendees-of-anime-expo/ (accessed July 29, 2014).

Prince, Stephen. *The Warrior's Camera : The Cinema of Akira Kurosawa*. Princeton, NJ: Princeton University Press, 1999.

"Producer: Cameron Wants to Do *Battle Angel*'s Motorball." Anime News Network. http://www.animenewsnetwork.com/news/2010-03-01/producer/cameron-wants-to-do-battle-angel-motorball (accessed October 5, 2012).

Ragone, August. *Eiji Tsuburaya: Master of Monsters: Defending the Earth with* Ultraman, Godzilla, *and Friends in the Golden Age of Japanese Science Fiction Film*. San Francisco: Chronicle Books, 2007.

Richie, Donald. *The Films of Akira Kurosawa*. Berkeley, CA: University of California Press, 1998.

"The Rise and Fall of *Weekly Shonen Jump*: A Look at the Circulation of *Weekly Jump*." ComiPress.com. May 6, 2007. http://comipress.com/article/2007/05/06/1923 (accessed April 3, 2015).

Schodt, Frederik L. *The Astro Boy Essays: Osamu Tezuka, Mighty Atom, and the Manga/anime Revolution*. Berkeley, CA: Stone Bridge Press, 2007.

Schodt, Frederik L. *Dreamland Japan: Writings on Modern Manga*. Berkeley, CA: Stone Bridge Press, 1996.

Schodt, Frederik L., and Osamu Tezuka. *Manga! Manga!: The World of Japanese Comics*. New York: Harper & Row, 1986.

Scrolls to Screen: A Brief History of Anime, documentary, directed by Josh Oreck (Warner Brothers, 2003).

Solomon, Charles. "Ward Kimball, 88, Key Disney Animator." *Los Angeles Times*, July 9, 2002. http://articles.latimes.com/2002/jul/09/local/me-kimball9 (accessed May 23, 2014).

"Speed Racer." Wikipedia. http://en.wikipedia.org/wiki/Speed_Racer (accessed October 27, 2014).

"*Speed Racer* DVD Interview: The Voice of *Speed Racer* Himself Talks about the Series." IGN. May 22, 2008. http://www.ign.com/articles/2008/05/23/speed-racer-dvd-interview (accessed Mary 30, 2014).

Tadashi, Sudo. "Bandai Predicts More *Gundam* Sales, But Lower Toy/Model Sales." Anime News Network. May 5, 2012. http://www.animenewsnetwork.com/news/2012-05-12/bandai-predicts-more-gundam-sales-but-lower-toy/model-sales (accessed December 10, 2014).

"Tezuka in English." http://tezukainenglish.com/?q=node/17 (accessed October 3, 2012).

Thorn, Matt. "Keiji Nakazawa, 1939–2012." *The Comics Journal*, http://www.tcj.com/keiji-nakazawa-1939-2012/ (accessed April 26, 2013).

"Three Steps over Japan: The Machiko Hasegawa Memorial Museum of Art." Threestepsoverjapan.blogspot.com. http://threestepsoverjapan.blogspot.com/2009/06/machiko-hasegawa-memorial-museum-of-art.html (accessed October 4, 2012).

"Tite Kubo." http://manga.about.com/od/mangaartistinterviews/a/TiteKubo_2.htm (accessed October 1, 2012).

"Tokusatsu." Wikipedia. http://en.wikipedia.org/wiki/Tokusatsu (accessed May 11, 2014).

"Top 10 *Shonen Jump* Manga by All-Time Volume Sales." Anime News Network. October 23, 2012. http://www.animenewsnetwork.com/news/2012-10-23/top-10-shonen-jump-manga-by-all-time-volume-sales.

"Transformers." Wikipedia. http://en.wikipedia.org/wiki/Transformers (accessed October 3, 2012).

"Ultraman." Wikipedia. http://en.wikipedia.org/wiki/Ultramanhttp://en.wikipedia.org/wiki/Ultraman (accessed November 1, 2014).

Varley, H. Paul. *Japanese Culture*. 4th edn. Honolulu: University of Hawaii Press, 2000.

"Wacky Races." http://wackyraces.wikia.com/wiki/Wacky_Races (accessed October 3, 2012).

Watt, Michael. "'Do You Speak Christian?' Dubbing and the Manipulation of the Cinematic Experience." *Bright Lights Film Journal* 29 (July 2000). http://brightlightsfilm.com/29/dubbing1.php#.VFPMDhYmzKd (accessed February 28, 2015).

Wilson, Ryan. "History of the Disneyland Railroad." Justdisney.com. http://www.justdisney.com/Features/disneyland_railroad/ (accessed October 16, 2014).

Writing for Episodic TV: From Freelancer to Showrunner. Los Angeles: Writers Guild of America West and East, 2004.

"Writers Guild of America 2015 Minimum Basic Agreement." Writers Guild of America West and East. http://www.wga.org/uploadedFiles/writers_resources/contracts/min2014.pdf (accessed October 31, 2014).

"A Yukito Kishiro interview." ASunnySpot.org. http://the.sunnyspot.org/manga/gunnm/kinterv.html (accessed November 18, 2014).

Index

Entries in *italics* indicate figures